Kenneth Clark defines civilization by citing Rus[kin: "Great] nations," Ruskin said, "write their autobiographie[s in three books,] the book of their deeds, the books of their words, [and the book of their] art... But of the three, the only trustworthy one is th[e last."]

The present book sheds light on the mutual insights (and the tools) of both psychoanalysis and literature, in order to explore, in an unprecedented manner, our daily modes of practicing civilization through the activity of reading. What happens when we read? We are introduced into this mystery in cumulative ways, by looking closely – through the author's psychoanalytic eyes – at a whole mosaic of exemplary reading experiences, as depicted by a great diversity of literary writers who originate from different cultures and who write in different languages. We are presented with a sort of world-wide encyclopedia of (literary) reading experiences, as illuminated by the author's psychoanalytic observations.

Psychoanalysts as well as literary scholars, students of humanities as well as teachers, and anyone who loves to read, can gain a deeper understanding of themselves and others, and a subtler grasp of the meaning and the use of literature for life, by engaging with the insights of this book.

– Shoshana Felman, author of *Testimony: Crises of Witnessing in Literature, Psychoanalysis and History*

'Merav Roth's book makes an important and unique contribution to the burgeoning study of reciprocal relations between literature and psychoanalysis. It will enrich true readers and writers alike with better understanding of the deep psychic processes involved in reading. As an author with a wealth of experience in both writing and teaching literature, as well as someone for whom – thanks to my late wife, the psychoanalyst Rivka Yehoshua – psychoanalysis was "family", I was astonished to discover through this book intriguing ideas of which I was previously unaware. At a time when writing workshops are flourishing and people write more than they read, Merav Roth's book is particularly important in challenging both readers and writers to delve ever more deeply into the hidden layers of the process of writing and reading.'

– A.B. Yehoshua, writer and Professor of Literature, Haifa University, Israel

'This book represents the confluence and mutual enrichment of two centrally important explorations of the human mind: literature and psychoanalysis. Its originality and uniqueness lie in the fascinating way in which they are brought together as equal partners in this dialogue. While well versed in the breadth and depth of psychoanalytic thought, both classical and contemporary, it is not a psychoanalytic attempt to explain literature. Rather, using a range of literary works, it takes the reader-within-literature as the subject who articulates that which psychoanalysis reads in our minds. Thus, it brilliantly and simultaneously recreates the immediacy of the experience of reading and the experience of being read and understood in terms of psyche and mind. For this enrichment it is warmly recommended for all readers, both literary and psychoanalytic.'

– Shmuel Erlich, Sigmund Freud Professor of Psychoanalysis (Emeritus), The Hebrew University of Jerusalem; past president, Israel Psychoanalytic Society

A Psychoanalytic Perspective on Reading Literature

What are the unconscious processes involved in reading literature? How does literature influence our psychological development and existential challenges? *A Psychoanalytic Perspective on Reading Literature* offers a unique glimpse into the unconscious psychic processes and development involved in reading. The author listens to the 'free associations' of various literary characters, in numerous scenarios where the characters are themselves reading literature, thus revealing the mysterious ways in which reading literature helps us and contributes to our development.

The book offers an introduction both to classic literature (Poe, Proust, Sartre, Semprún, Pessoa, Agnon and more) and to the major psychoanalytic concepts that can be used in reading it – all described and widely explained before being used as tools for interpreting the literary illustrations. The book thus offers a rich lexical psychoanalytic source, alongside its main aim in analysing the reader's psychological mechanisms and development. Psychoanalytic interpretation of those literary readers opens three main avenues to the reader's experience:

- the transference relations toward the literary characters;
- the literary work as means to transcend beyond the reader's self-identity and existential boundaries; and
- mobilization of internal dialectic tensions towards new integration and psychic equilibrium.

An Epilogue concludes by emphasizing the transformational power embedded in reading literature.

The fascinating dialogue between literature and psychoanalysis illuminates hitherto concealed aspects of each discipline and contributes to new insights in both fields. *A Psychoanalytic Perspective on Reading Literature* will be of great interest not only to psychoanalytic-psychotherapists and literature scholars, but also to a wider readership beyond these areas of study.

Merav Roth, PhD is a training analyst and cultural researcher. She is former chair of the postgraduate Klein studies programme and of the doctoral unit for the interdisciplinary psychoanalytic PhD and is currently chair of the psychotherapy programme at the Sackler School of Medicine, Tel-Aviv University, Israel. She co-edited *Melanie Klein: Essential Writings Volume II* with J. Durban (2013).

Art, Creativity and Psychonalysis Book Series

Series editor
George Hagman, LSCW

The *Art, Creativity and Psychoanalysis* book series seeks to highlight original, cutting-edge studies of the relationship between psychoanalysis and the world of art and the psychology of artists, with subject matter including the psychobiography of artists, the creative process, the psychology of aesthetic experience, as well as the aesthetic, creative and artistic aspects of psychoanalysis and psychoanalytic psychotherapy. *Art, Creativity and Psychoanalysis* promotes a vision of psychoanalysis as a creative art, the clinical effectiveness of which can be enhanced when we better understand and utilize artistic and creative processes at its core.

The series welcomes proposals from psychoanalytic therapists from all professional groups and theoretical models, as well as artists, art historians and art critics informed by a psychoanalytic perspective. For a full list of all titles in the series, please visit the Routledge website at: https://www.routledge.com/Art-Creativity-and-Psychoanalysis-Book-Series/book-series/ACAPBS.

A Psychoanalytic Perspective on Reading Literature

Reading the Reader

Merav Roth

Routledge
Taylor & Francis Group
LONDON AND NEW YORK

First published in the English language by Routledge 2020
2 Park Square, Milton Park, Abingdon, Oxon OX14 4RN

and by Routledge
52 Vanderbilt Avenue, New York, NY 10017

Routledge is an imprint of the Taylor & Francis Group, an informa business

© 2020 Merav Roth

The right of Merav Roth to be identified as author of this work has been asserted by her in accordance with sections 77 and 78 of the Copyright, Designs and Patents Act 1988.

All rights reserved. No part of this book may be reprinted or reproduced or utilised in any form or by any electronic, mechanical, or other means, now known or hereafter invented, including photocopying and recording, or in any information storage or retrieval system, without permission in writing from the publishers.

This book is a translation of a work first published in Hebrew as *Reading the Reader: A Psychoanalytic Perspective on Reading Literature* as part of the Psychoanalysis, Hermeneutics and Culture book series, Carmel, Jerusalem, 2017.
English language translation © Dan Gillon, 2020.

Trademark notice: Product or corporate names may be trademarks or registered trademarks, and are used only for identification and explanation without intent to infringe.

British Library Cataloguing-in-Publication Data
A catalogue record for this book is available from the British Library

Library of Congress Cataloging-in-Publication Data
A catalog record has been requested for this book

ISBN: 978-1-138-39130-7 (hbk)
ISBN: 978-1-138-39131-4 (pbk)
ISBN: 978-0-429-42278-2 (ebk)

Typeset in Times New Roman
by Swales & Willis, Exeter, Devon, UK

The cover for this book was created by Tsibi Geva, 2019.

To my beloved parents

'Books act as introductions to dreams.'
— Fernando Pessoa

Contents

Preface	xiii
Acknowledgements	xiv
Permissions acknowledgements	xv
Introduction: reading the reader	1

PART I
Transference relations of the literary reader 23

1	The distancing paradox	33
2	The bestowal of meaning	40
3	Seven types of identification	55
4	Resistance to reading	80
5	The idealization of the author	91
6	Mutual witnessing	104
7	Reparation of the ethical position	108

PART II
Reading literature as a means of transcendence 115

8	Transcendence beyond self-identity	121
9	Transcendence beyond the boundaries of human vulnerability and mortality	155

PART III
From psychic equilibrium to psychic change: the dialectic forces of literature 183

10 The dialectic between the present and the absent 187

11 The dialectic between the familiar and the uncanny 219

12 The dialectic between the symbolic order and disorder 236

13 The dialectic between 'continuous doing' and 'emergent being' 251

    13a First illustration: Aharon Appelfeld's book *The Man Who Never Stopped Sleeping* 260

    13b Second illustration: Søren Kierkegaard's book *Fear and Trembling: Dialectical Lyric* 268

    13c Third illustration: Otto Dov Kulka's book *Landscapes of the Metropolis of Death* 279

14 Epilogue: the transformative power of reading literature 296

Index 310

Preface

My maternal grandfather died at the age of 101. He spent the last two weeks of his life lying still, stunned by finality, his withered hands clutching a book.

I am descended from a family of writers stretching over generations. The sound I grew up with was not the ticking of a clock but the tapping of a typewriter. The morning began with the clicking of its keys; their silence announced that it was time for lunch. The intervals between my mother's bursts of writing left us all in suspense. When the writing resumed we sighed with relief.

My mother's silences were rarely spoken; they were translated into written words. Her writing was testimony to a fact that every child wants to deny; that most of her inner being was inaccessible and that within her were worlds I would never reach. 'Reading the writer' was to remain an enigma.

Throughout my life whenever someone in my family completed a book they would circulate the manuscript between us to read and respond. By doing so I found myself 'reading the reader' from an early age. I was invited to read in the name of all readers and try to fathom what the text would arouse in them.

In this book I look at 'our side' – the readers' side – from a psychoanalytic viewpoint: I will be reading the reader.

Acknowledgements

This book is based on my PhD thesis, which was supervised by Professor Avi Sagi – whom I thank deeply – at the Culture and Hermeneutics Department in Bar Ilan University, and it is an edited translation of a Hebrew version of the book, which was published in 2017 by Carmel publishing house.

I deeply thank my mother, the author Shulamit Lapid, for translating three poems in this book, and for her illuminating readings of the book along the way.

I warmly thank Dani Roth, Yair Lapid, Joshua (Shuki) Durban, Dr Ruth Calderon, Dr Dana Amir, Dr Michal Ben Naftali, Dr Rina Lazar, Dr Aner Govrin, Dorit Rabinian, Dr Roni Alfandary, Professor Erlich, Professor A.B. Yehoshua and Professor Shoshana Felman for their wisdom and generosity along this challenging journey.

I wish to also thank my translator, Dan Gillon, for his devoted work and great contribution to the final version of the book.

I am profoundly grateful to Tsibi Geva for creating the most beautiful image I could dream of for the book's cover.

Permissions acknowledgements

Every effort has been made to contact the copyright holders for their permission to reprint selections of this book. The publishers would be grateful to hear from any copyright holder who is not here acknowledged and we will undertake to rectify any errors or omissions in future editions of this book.

Excerpts throughout the book taken from *The Book of Disquiet*, by Fernando Pessoa, edited by Jeronimo Pizarro, translated by Margaret Jull Costa, © 2017 by Margaret Jull Costa, © 2013 by Jeronimo Pizarro. Reprinted by permission of New Directions Publishing.

Excerpts throughout the book taken from *Literature or Life* by Jorge Semprún, translated by Linda Coverdale, translation © 1997 by Penguin Books USA. Original text © 1994 by Editions Gallimard. Used by permission of Viking Books, an imprint of Penguin Publishing Group, a division of Penguin Random House LLC. All rights reserved.

Excerpts throughout the book taken from *The Words* by Jean-Paul Sartre. English translation © 1964 by George Braziller. Originally published in France as *Les Mots* © 1964 by Editions Gallimard. Reprinted by permission of Georges Borchardt, Inc., for Editions Gallimard.

Excerpts throughout the book taken from *'What Is Literature?' And Other Essays* by Jean-Paul Sartre, Cambridge, MA: Harvard University Press, © 1988 by the president and fellows of Harvard College. Reprinted by kind permission.

Excerpts from *Lost in Translation: A Life in a New Language* by Eva Hoffman, © 1989 by Eva Hoffman. Used by permission of Dutton, an imprint of Penguin Publishing Group, a division of Penguin Random House LLC. All rights reserved.

Excerpts from 'Eating Poetry' appearing in Chapter 3 are taken from *Selected Poems* by Mark Strand, © 1979, 1980 by Mark Strand. Used by permission of Alfred A. Knopf, an imprint of the Knopf Doubleday Publishing Group, a division of Penguin Random House LLC. All rights reserved.

The lyrics to Nathan Zak's 'How to Sweeten the Days' featured in Chapter 3 are reprinted by kind permission of ACUM Music Publishing, © Nathan Zach and ACUM.

Excerpts from *Landscapes of the Metropolis of Death* by Otto Duv Kulka, Penguin Books, 2013. Text © Otto Dov Kulka, 1984, 2006, 2013. Reprinted by kind permission of Penguin Random House, LLC.

Excerpts from 'In Memoriam of Paul Éluard' by Paul Celan, Von Schwelle zu Schwelle © 1982, Deustche Verlags-Anstalt, München, in der Verlagsgruppe Random House GmbH. Reprinted by kind permission of Penguin Random House, LLC.

Excerpt from *Caged Bird* by Y. Horowitz, Tel Aviv: HaKibbutz HaMeuchad, © 1987. Reprinted by permission of Hakibbutz Hameuhad/Yair Horowit heirs.

Excerpts throughout the book taken from *The Man Who Never Stopped Sleeping: A Novel* by Aharon Appelfeld, © 2009, Aharon Appelfeld, used by permission of the Wylie Agency (UK) Ltd. Also © 2017 by Penguin Random House LLC. Used by permission of Schocken Books, an imprint of the Knopf Doubleday Publishing Group, a division of Penguin Random House LLC. All rights reserved.

Introduction
Reading the reader

This book explores both the conscious and unconscious mental processes involved in reading literature. It describes and illustrates the ways in which the reading experience helps the reader in both his psychological coping and his existential development.

In my search for accounts that accessed the unconscious facets of the reading experience I came up with an idea that led to several years of study. I obtained 'testimonies' about the reading experience from 18 works of literature that differ in genre, style and contents (nine books, two short stories, a play and six poems). In each of these works the reading experiences of their literary heroes appear directly and indirectly, openly and covertly. It has to be emphasized that I will be exploring *the reading experiences of the various characters in these literary works* rather than analysing *my* reading experience as the reader, though that aspect is not, of course, entirely absent.[1]

In the course of the book I invite readers to join me in leafing through the pages of these literary works and in reading the quotations that I have selected. Wherever in the text there is a description of the reading experiences of its heroes I analyse their responses from a psychoanalytic perspective, concentrating on the unconscious processes experienced by the reader and the ways in which reading literature helps him to cope with his inner world and the reality of his life.

Sister disciplines: literature and psychoanalysis

The affinity between psychoanalysis and literature dates back to their founding as academic disciplines at the turn of the twentieth century. It was not until the middle of the twentieth century that 'reader research' came to occupy centre stage (Iser, W., 1978, pp. 15–21). From then on, researchers in the fields of literary criticism and psychoanalysis became increasingly interested in the rich and complex experience of the reader of literature.

Towards the end of the nineteenth century and the early years of the twentieth century major technological and commercial advances in the printing and publishing industries, together with the spread of secular education, greatly accelerated the general public's interest in reading literature. This mounting curiosity was manifested in the establishment of more and more public libraries, an increase in the number of private subscription libraries and a significant upsurge in the teaching of reading. Reading soon became a widespread pastime across wider segments of the population who had learned to read and write (Proust, M., 1905, p. 24)

As the achievements of the era of Enlightenment were undermined so the importance of literature rose (Iser, W., 1978, p. 6). This field was increasingly perceived as one that could reveal *the* 'meaning' or *the* 'truth'. Literature was thus viewed as a domain encompassing 'an apocalypse of nature, a revealing of the open secret' (ibid., p. 7).

The boom in the field of general literature was accompanied by a pivotal change of direction in various fields of academic enquiry within the disciplines of literary criticism and psychoanalysis, which shifted the scientific and cultural focus from 'scientific facts' to 'the subject'. This stemmed from a number of factors: the publication of Freud's method of psychoanalysis in his book *The Interpretation of Dreams* (1900); the reinforcement of the link between the subject and the object in Edmund Husserl's philosophy of phenomenology (Husserl, [1931] 2012); and the discovery of the structure of language as a system of signs in the linguistic theory of Ferdinand de Saussure (1916). Following these theoretical turns, a number of canonical writers stressed the significant role of the reader. Thus, for example, Franz Kafka, in his famous 1904 letter to his friend Oscar Pollak noted that,

> I think we ought to read only books that bite and sting us. If the book we are reading doesn't shake us awake like a blow to the skull, why bother reading it in the first place? ... A book must be the axe from the frozen sea within us. That is what I believe. (Kafka, F., [1904] 2003, p. 25).

A year later, Marcel Proust wrote an essay about reading as a preface to his translation of John Ruskin's book *Sesame and Lilies*. This essay, published under the title *On Reading* (Proust, M., 1905), preceded the emergence of contemporary literary theory as a separate discipline. In the essay Proust presents a kind of literary theory of relativity, which deals with the relations between a trio composed of the author, the book and the reader. As is the case in the initial meeting between analyst and analysand at the beginning of the therapeutic process with its clues as to the continuation of the therapy, so too one can find in Proust's essay clues foreshadowing key ideas that would, in due course, be part and parcel of research dealing with the literary reader. For example, among such clues, Proust points to the powerful somatic and mental experience that accompanies the act of reading; to the power of the reading experience in detaching us from reality; to the sense of time while reading as opposed to 'real' time; and to the identification and powerful emotions that the characters arouse in the reader (ibid., pp. 29–30). Proust alludes to relations crammed with the reader's expectations of the imagined author in a way that resembles the phenomenon that Freud subsequently termed 'transference relations':

> We feel very clearly that our own wisdom begins where that of the author leaves off, and would like him to provide us with answers, when all he can do is provide us with desires ... 'Lead us' we would like to say.
> (ibid., pp. 30–31)

Proust even points to the desire of the reader to read literature in order to advance his personal life, or in Proust's own words 'To learn other facts about all these characters, to learn something about their lives now, to employ our own life on things not altogether alien to the love they had inspired in us' (ibid., p. 22). Proust concludes that, 'For as long as reading is for us the instigator whose magic keys open deep within us the door to those dwelling places into which we would have been unable to penetrate, its role in our lives is salutary' (ibid., p. 36). Some 15 years after this essay was written a new discipline was founded and literary theory was born.

Traditionally, literature was perceived as imitating and reflecting reality (mimesis), a classical idea that first appeared in Aristotle's *Poetics*, the earliest known treatise dealing with literature scientifically (Aristotle, [1447–1462] 1895). Already in Aristotle's writing descriptions of the creative work are accompanied by references to the passions and the activation of the mind that it arouses: pity, fear and catharsis (ibid.). Nevertheless, more than half a century was to pass between the establishment of the school of literary theory in the 1920s and the positioning of the reader at the centre of literary study.

Prior to the focus on the reader as being at the very heart of literary theory, literary science's most important schools of thought during that period (Russian formalism, New Criticism and structuralism) concentrated on interpreting literature through two key prisms; the contextual interpretation of the literary text on the one hand, and its interpretation as a 'closed unit' on the other. The contextual interpretation may focus on revealing the author's intentions or, alternatively, concentrate on the epochal, psychological, societal or historical contexts as a means of understanding the literary text. In contrast to these approaches, the second prism of literary interpretation views the text as a 'closed' structure, advocating a closed reading of the text as standing in and of itself. This approach focuses on the reciprocal relations between the text's components. The text as a unit thus encompasses both the meaning and the text's 'instructions' to the reader. Despite researching the text 'in and of itself', the New Criticism school of thought and the structuralist approach did not turn a blind eye to the concept of 'the reader'. However, these approaches only viewed the reader as being self-evidently 'the other side' of their central interest – the text itself. An additional meaning related to the reader is subsumed here; namely that these two schools of thought deal with what is common to all literary work – the poetic, linguistic and structural rules and the way in which they influence the reader. The reference to a general reader implies a universal reading experience (Lodge, D., 1988, pp. xi–xiv). These were the perspectives and practices of both these schools prior to approaching the reader's experience as a unique and particular event.

From the death of the author to the birth of the reader

'Reader-response' theories began to be published in the 1960s and 1970s. During this period the theory of 'reception aesthetics' in Germany (*rezeptionsästhetik*) and the 'reader-response' school in North America, began to consider the reader's active response to the literary text. The act of reading was then still perceived as a function of the text's stratagems but had, in addition, become recognized as a pivotal partner in determining the text's meaning. The focal point shifted from the mutuality of relations between the text's components to the reciprocal relations between the text and the reader. The tendency in literary study turned the emphasis from the message and meaning of the text to the influence on and receptivity by the reader as a partner who endows the literary text it's meaning (Iser, W., [1972] 1988).

The philosopher of hermeneutics Hans-Georg Gadamer, significantly influenced researchers by urging them to turn their attention to the interpreter of the text, any text, i.e. to the role of the reader (Gadamer, H, 1976, pp. 3–17). Gadamer stressed the importance of the reader being acquainted with the 'critical method' he brings with him to the reading of a text. He shed light on the 'fusion of horizons' embedded in every reading (ibid., pp. 273, 337–341). Gadamer saw the encounter between the reader and the text as a dialogue to which the reader brings his inevitable prejudices. In his view, the reader couldn't possibly avoid reading from a particular perspective rooted in the horizon of his culture, tradition and era – asking the text a question answered from the viewpoint of another time, place and tradition.

Two other key influences on reader research theories were those of the linguistic turn (Rorty, R., 1967) and the shift to 'post-structuralism', foreshadowed by Roland Barthes' essay *Death of the Author* (Barthes, R., 1967). Barthes' essay and the philosophical thinking that followed indicated that the text's borders had dissolved and were being endlessly recreated in each reading. Moreover, the meaning of the text was no longer viewed as solely dependent on the author or the body of the text but rather as being reconstructed *de novo* by the reader in each reading. The structuralists had regarded every text as a closed structure whereas now it was perceived as a dynamic event. The attitude towards the reader also changed. In the past he was viewed as the obvious complementing side of the author and the text. Now, however, the reader had moved to centre stage. In his essay *Death of the Author* (which may also be thought of as the 'birth of the reader') Roland Barthes notes:

> There is one place where this multiplicity is collected, united, and this place is not the author, as we have hitherto said it was, but the reader: the reader is the very space in which are inscribed, without any being lost, all the citations a writing consists of (ibid., pp. 5–6).

Barthes goes on to explain that historically the text's meaning had been perceived as inherent, to be deduced from an analysis of its linguistic tropes. Now it was viewed as a dormant entity to be awakened and brought back to life by the reader who would recreate it and establish its meaning (ibid.). Thus, the reader was henceforth perceived as a partner in the process of the literary creation.

In the course of those same years Jean Paul Sartre described reading as 'the synthesis of perception and creation ... the reader is conscious of disclosing in creating, of creating by disclosing' (Sartre, J., [1948] 1988, p. 43). The encounter between the reader and the text is from then on described as a meeting point that establishes a mutually shared meaning. The process of ascribing meaning to the text by the reader is never ending, as ceaseless as the attempt we make from birth till death to find meaning in human existence (Bachmann, I., 1978, p. 83; Iser, W., 1978; Geldman, M., 1998, p. 119; Sagi, A., 2009, pp. 79–81, 193).

The reader as an active partner in establishing meaning

Defining 'text' as a communicative event provides us with a platform for exploring how readers create meaning. Since meaning has ceased to be seen solely as the property of the text but instead a product of the reader's participation, the key questions are no longer 'What does the text mean?' or even 'What is it that the text does?' Rather, the question to be answered becomes 'How do readers create meaning?' In other words, the research examines the relations between the reader and the text as intersubjective (Berman, E., 2003, pp. 119–129). The text is viewed in relation to the mode of communication it forms with the reader. Thus, for example, relations between closed and open aspects of the text and the way in which they stimulate the reader are investigated. So too is the aesthetic effect and the way it mobilizes personal experiences in the reader.

The more vivid and open the text is to interpretation and playfulness the more it can be expected to create a different meaning for every reader. Thus, for the same 'Hamlet' there will be different interpretations in line with the different projections of the various readers on to the text depicting 'their' Hamlet (Holland, N., 1993, pp. 5–21).

Reading as an encounter

Henceforth reading literature was perceived as an encounter between the text and the reader.

According to Gadamer, who portrayed the reading experience as a hermeneutical encounter, the reading is likely to facilitate an open and vivid dialogue between the text and the reader, irrespective of the fact that the text was written sometime in the past and met by the reader in the moment of reading. In Gadamer's view, the reader reaches the peak of this hermeneutic experience when faced with the question being asked of him by the text; thus, the reader enables the text to 'tell him' a truth. As long as the reader recognizes the text's 'otherness' and suspends his dogmas and prejudices, he can open himself up to the questions posed by the text and through it acquire a new horizon of possibilities (Gadamer, H., 1960, p. 267). The philosopher Paul Ricoeur described the inherent otherness essential to every work of understanding between two subjects in general and between every reader and text in particular. According to Ricoeur, reading contains this otherness as well as the task of translation that is needed in order to bridge the gap between the text and the reader (Ricoeur, P., [2004] 2006). The philosopher of hermeneutics Wilhelm Dilthey goes even further claiming that the reader can get to know the author better than the author knows himself by projecting experiences of his life into the written work (Dilthey, E., [1900] 1996, pp. 235–251).

The perception comparing the reading experience to an encounter also appears as a leitmotif in literary theory. The literary researcher Poulet notes that

> a work of literature becomes (at the expense of the reader whose own life it suspends) a sort of human being, that is a mind conscious of itself and constituting itself in me as the subject of its own objects. (Poulet, G. in Iser, W., 1978, p. 105)

Sartre relates to the literary text as a 'clarion call' beseeching the reader to show 'generosity and choose to act accordingly. In the moment of the meeting between them the text also comes up against the reader's 'demands' (Sartre, P., [1948] 1988, p. 56). Every such meeting is dependent on the respective characteristics of the two participants. The matrix of phantasies, fears, defence mechanisms and all the other components that constitute the identity of the reader, affect the manner in which he will meet the text (Holland, N., 1993). The bibliotherapy researcher Rachel Zoran argues that the fact that the literary text is an undefined world within a defined model makes it possible to relate to it as an 'actual fellow being' with whom 'human relations' can be conducted (Zoran, R., 2009, p. 37). In each part of the reading experience, the reader might focus on his encounter with the text's narrator, with its main character, with one of the secondary characters or with the author of his imagination. Even Barthes, herald of *The Death of the Author*, declares that as 'institution the author is dead ... but in the text, in a certain way, *I desire* the author' (Barthes, R., 1967, pp. 45–46).

In the dialogue between reader and text the reader's decision to participate is a mark of his freedom (Sartre, J.P., [1948] 1988, pp. 46–53; Zoran, R., 2009, p. 52). The reader projects into the text central questions of his life such as the search for meaning; coping with existential fears (above all the fear of death); and the enigma of 'the other'. At the same time, the text is frequently perceived as representing a mentor, who, in Proust's words, the reader expects to be 'the one wise custodian of the truth' (Proust, M., 1905, p. 29). This description resembles Lacan's idea that perceives the analyst as a 'subject who is supposed to know' (Felman, S., 1977, p. 7).

The reading experience doesn't begin and end in the actual moment of reading. Rather, it is a protracted event beginning with the reading itself and, influenced by that reading, continues its course in the reader's mind after the reading has ended. Thus the encounter with the text is divided into two main stages. In the first stage, the actual reading stage, the reader's involvement with the text is immediate and contemporaneous. This phase of involvement by the reader doesn't yet enable him to fully process the text or reflect upon it in detail. In the second stage, once the actual reading is completed, there is a continuation by way of an internalized processing of the text; this processing is largely accomplished internally and unconsciously. The working through remains concealed until a stimulus of one kind or another brings it into conscious awareness as in Virginia Woolf's poetic description:

> Then suddenly without our willing it, for it is thus that Nature undertakes these transitions, the book will return, but differently. It will float to the top of the mind as a whole. And the book as a whole is different from the book received currently in separate phrases. (Woolf, V., 1932, p. 50)

However romantic Woolf's view may seem, it does reflect the two stages of the encounter that involve two kinds of processes in each phase of the reading experience; the creative involvement of the reader (the reader who 'writes the text' in the course of his reading) along with the protracted processing of the text and the reader's continuing reflection about what he has read. These two processes are interwoven into both phases of the encounter and beyond, because the voyage towards establishing meaning 'begins with the personal and private, transcends the general and returns to the personal and private', a circuitousness that may continue throughout the reader's life (Sagi, A., 2011, p. 37).

The therapeutic aspects of reading

The extent of literature's actual power to assist the reader is the subject of profound debate among scholars who question whether that is literature's mission and if so whether it does, in fact, help the reader to look into his life in a pragmatic way and invest it with meaning. There are those who suggest that one has to be careful about this aspiration. As noted by Proust 'To make [reading] into a discipline is to give too large a role to what is only an incitement. Reading is on the threshold of the spiritual life; it can introduce us to it: it does not constitute it' (Proust, M., 1905, p. 72). Iser warns that 'the very idea of literary texts changing the psyche of readers, in a therapeutic sense, by virtue of their true meaning being uncovered, is, to say the least, rather far-fetched' (Iser, W., 1978, p. 29).

Nevertheless, the most commonly accepted view on this subject posits the very opposite, perceiving reading as a formative act, shaping identity and creating change (Zoran, R., 2009, p. 27) According to the philosopher Søren Kierkegaard, the singularity of literature facilitates a dialectical movement between the unique private self and the external, general and universal. This movement enables the individual to transcend his subjectivity by objectifying the self and reflecting about it. Both processes carry a developmental value (Sagi, A., 1991, pp. 69–109). Kierkegaard was mostly interested in the value to him of the literary work as its creator. The act of writing for him was a way of taking care of his subsistence, of his existence, a means of moulding or educating himself. But from what he wrote one can deduce that for Kierkegaard reading was also perceived as an opportunity to engage in the same 'open and tense dialectical movement – never fully realized – between the particular and concrete personal experience and reflexivity which is accomplished with universal tools' (ibid., p. 78). As noted by Milan Kundera 'A novel examines not reality but existence' (Kundera, M., [1986] 1988, p. 23). Kundera finds an example of this in Kafka's novels, 'because they grasp one possibility of existence (a possibility for man and for his world) and thereby make us see what we are, what we are capable of' (ibid. p. 23). The researcher Orly Lubin explains how reading changes the reader:

> The act of reading is also an act of self-formation (temporary, momentary – but cumulative). Every text causes the readers to question themselves; and every response is within the ambit of formation; in effect the reader is engaged in an act of writing of their own ... so that this process also contains the option for change. (Lubin, O., 2003, p. 69)

The reader's couch and the analyst's couch

In many respects psychoanalysis and literature are 'sister disciplines' and the reading experience has much in common with the therapeutic experience. For example, the two events are concerned with stories about life, and the basic component parts of both are text, narrator, addressee, experience and meaning. Scholars who research literature from a psychoanalytic perspective investigate the psychological aspects of the literary text, whereas researchers of psychoanalytic texts investigate the ways in which the 'reading' and 'writing' of the therapeutic dialogue creates a pseudo literary text (Stein, R., 1993, pp. 233–239). In both situations communication is achieved through stories and metaphors (Schafer, R., 1976 pp. 345–351; Spence, D.P., 1982, pp. 163–170, 102–113). In this sense, literary and psychoanalytic texts are endowed with common aesthetic features (Berman, E., 1993, pp. 374–402).

In both literature and psychoanalysis it is taken for granted that the text influences the reader's emotions and in each field this 'obviousness' is, at the same time, highly enigmatic. How does a text become an emotion? How is one to explain the mysterious process by which words influence? Why does a story told by one person influence another? How does the establishment of meaning and identity lead to processes of transformation and development? These questions arise in both psychoanalysis and literature. Psychoanalytic 'reader research', the bridge between these two disciplines, attempts to provide answers to these questions.

In the introduction to her book *Women Reading*, Gail Hareven describes the reader in a way that, to a great extent, is reminiscent of the patient's situation:

> [He] determines the pace, chooses which paragraph he wants to return to or which to skip and, while still reading, links one thing to another and fills in the blanks … and we also read so as to bring about some kind of order in the midst of chaos; to search for cause and effect and calm ourselves in the form of the story. We read to be bothered and to be read. We also read in order to refine our observations both of ourselves and of others. (Hareven, G., [2005] 2009, pp. 14–15)

The patient in analysis, like the reader of literature, is invited to drop everything else and raise, without any form of censorship, every topic that appears 'in the pages' of his awareness, so as to give the analyst the opportunity to read his mind through the text he narrates and via what is hidden between the words. In both cases it is assumed that this situation will create the optimum conditions both for regression and for 'transference' relations towards the analyst and towards the characters in the reading. This will awaken the internalized memories that form the internal and external relations from their slumber. The patient, like the reader of literature, is, paradoxically, at one and the same time invited to be fully involved in the situation but to also be aware of the context within which it is taking place. The patient 'writes' a text that the analyst is invited to read. But he also 'reads' his written story as well as the analyst's 'stories' (i.e. the analyst's interpretations) of his narrative. Together the two weave 'the psychoanalytic dialogue as a written and read text' (Stein, R., 1993).

The advantages of the reader being 'alone in the presence of his book' overlap the advantages of talking 'alone in the presence of someone' during analysis. (Winnicott, D.W., 1958, p. 418). Both situations require relative quiet and an enabling atmosphere. In each, the individual plummets psychic depths that were not necessarily active in the moment prior to the reading or the analytic session and that will also mostly fade away between sessions. The tears will be wiped away and the daily routine will once again demand to be accompanied by the reality principle. It is only natural that since Freud and subsequently, various experiments using psychoanalytic techniques were devised in an attempt to decipher the discipline of literature in general and the reader of literature in particular. These experiments are described in what follows.

The Freudian approach to literary research

Reading literature involves the engagement of a number of complex psychic mechanisms, mostly unconscious and inaccessible to the self in daily life (Geldman, M., 1998). Not by chance have psychoanalytic researchers tried and continue to try to shed light on the role of the reader in actualizing literature and literature's role vis-à-vis the reader. The fields of literary and psychoanalytic research have been linked since they were first established as academic disciplines and the exploration of the relations between them has undergone significant change since the beginning of the twentieth century and continue to this day. Shoshana Felman, a researcher of literature and psychoanalysis, has described these changes as a transition from Hegelian master and slave dialectic relations to relations of equal power and status (Felman, S., 1977, pp. 5–10). Freud regarded artistry as one of man's most prominent capacities for sublimation, that is to say for the refinement of sexual drives and channelling them into acts of creativity (Freud, S., 1910b, pp. 111–166). Though infrequently, Freud did take an interest in the literary reader. He addressed such matters as the link between the reader's experiences in life and his reading experiences; his yearning for the story to the extent that he loses his sense of judgment; the empathic process involved in reading; and the reader's echoing of the emotion from which the writing originally stemmed (Geldman, M., 1998, pp. 18–27). In his essay on Wilhelm Jensen's Gradiva Freud writes: 'During the treatment of this genuinely poetic material the reader had been stirred by all kinds of thoughts akin to it and in harmony with it' (Freud, S., 1907, p. 10). Freud is impressed by the story's impact on the reader. What excited Freud more than anything else was the exactitude with which literature captures the complex and tortuous ways of the psyche and therefore he found it fruitful to exemplify his psychoanalytic insights via that medium. So, somewhat modestly, he continues to note in the same article:

> In short, let us ask whether this imaginative representation of the genesis of a delusion can hold its own before the judgement of science. And here we must give what will perhaps be an unexpected answer. In fact the situation is quite the reverse: it is science that cannot hold its own before the achievement of the author. Science allows a gulf to yawn between the hereditary and constitutional preconditions of a delusion and its creations, which seem to emerge ready-made – a gulf which we find that our author has filled. Science does not as yet suspect the importance of repression. (ibid., p. 53)

Freud saw another advantage in reading literature. By identifying with the heroes of the story the reader is given an opportunity to deal with experiences that in his actual life would have aroused intolerable fears whereas in the framework of literary fiction they can be processed in secure conditions (Freud, S., 1915, pp. 289–290).

For Freud literature was also a beacon in the search for cultural codes to psychic phenomena. Thus, for example, the myths of Oedipus (1910a) and Narcissus (1914) became the metaphorical names of key psychic phenomena.

However, alongside the respectful use Freud made of culture and literature as part of his psychoanalytic thinking, when he turned to analysing literary texts he assumed the role of the authoritative psychoanalytic interpreter who, for example, on occasion placed the author on the analyst's couch while at other times has characters in the story laying there. This approach is also prevalent in the psychoanalytic writings of Freud's colleagues and his followers until the middle of the twentieth century.

Two parallel phenomena contributed to this. First, during this period the three mainstream literary theories focused on the text itself either in the contexts in which it was written, which included the author, the history and the language, or else viewed the text as a subject of research viewed 'in and of itself'. Second, and in line with the above, at that time psychoanalysis under the decisive influence of Freud, related to the patient's text – the succession of free associations – as also being a text in and of itself which, like a dream, paved the way to the unconscious. In other words, the patient's text was understood to contain all the allusions required to decipher the hidden meaning concealed within it. Its interpretation was bound up with deciphering the biographical and historical contexts that could be reconstructed through the transference relations to the analyst. Shoshana Felman maintains that the psychoanalytic analysis of literature influenced by this environment of interpretation suggests that it is as if the literary analyst of that period came to find what he was looking for and that the story was 'once again' interpreted as the embodiment of the Oedipal complex and its derivatives, as if 'the question is itself but an answer in disguise; the question is the answer's hiding place' (Felman, S., 1977, pp. 5–10).

With the benefit of hindsight it is evident that this kind of analysis did indeed often lead to interpretations that missed an important part of what was concealed in the literary as well as in the analytic space – that part which cannot be captured in schematic interpretations.

Psychoanalytic research discovers the literary reader

The change was gradual. In the middle of the twentieth century the theories of literature and psychoanalysis changed in step with one another and even influenced each other in their perception of meaning as an occurrence in constant movement and shaped within an encounter. This was in contrast to the idea that meaning was concealed underneath the text as in the Freudian metaphor of an archaeological treasure that the analyst has to expose to the light of day. In the course of developing his thinking, Freud himself changed his mind about the locus of meaning from the sexual seduction that was experienced by the patient externally, to the portrayal of the unconscious fantasy that had been aroused within them.

Just as at first Freud understood sexual seduction as an actual event, so in reader research the reader is first understood as emanating from the 'body of the text'. The later understanding of the patients' narratives as the realization of fantasy, parallels reader research focusing on the 'reading experience' itself. Moreover, Freud recognized the phenomenon of transference from the patient to the analyst in which the patient, in relating to the analyst, reconstructs his early relations, for example, with his father or mother. The relevance of this concept in understanding the reader's relations to the book's characters and its author becomes readily apparent.

Freud also recognized the phenomenon of 'countertransference'. This phenomenon relates to the '[w]hole of the analyst's unconscious reactions to the individual analysand – especially to the analysand's own transference' (Laplanche, J. and Pontalis, J.B., 1973, loc. 2554). These views adopted by the analyst vis-à-vis the patient emanate from the analyst's inner unconscious world. Essentially, Freud regarded this phenomenon as a dangerous encroachment on the therapist's psychic responses, which are irrelevant to the understanding of the patient and thus interfere with the analyst's ability to maintain an unprejudiced 'analytic stance' (Freud, S., 1915, p. 124). However, with the continued development of psychoanalytic thinking dating back to the 1950s and onward, psychoanalysts began to understand that this phenomenon was an essential and significant part of the analytic meeting and an important key to an understanding of the patient. A decisive development in the discovery of countertransference that greatly influenced reader research was that the patient actively, though unconsciously, influences the inner world of the analyst. Fundamental to this understanding is the concept of 'projective identification', a term coined by the psychoanalyst Melanie Klein, (Klein, M., 1946, p. 11) and developed by Wilfred Bion (Bion, W., [1967] 2018). 'Projective identification' implies that the patient projects internal experiences that he is unable to bear and psychologically digest by himself into the analyst's psychic container. The therapist experiences the patient's raw psychic material and by containing and processing this 'information' endows it with meaning. The analyst interprets and the patient internalizes both the analyst's interpretations and his way of mental metabolization. In the wake of such a protracted process the patient is himself able to gradually contain and metabolize the emotional elements that were previously felt to be malignant. In the light of this conceptualization an emphasis was placed on observing the analyst's psychic processing as a key to understanding the deeper layers of the patient's mind. Additional psychoanalytic conceptualizations were delineated to express what was happening within the analyst's mind, such as 'role responsiveness' (Sandler, J., 1976, pp. 43–47); 'countertransference neurosis' (Racker, H., 1953, pp. 312–313); and 'projective transidentification' (Grotstein, J., 2005, pp. 1051–1069). All these concepts are part of the development that perceives the analytic meeting as a mutual event in which the analyst is a partner in the writing and reading of the therapeutic situation.

Subsequent to the emphasis on 'transference relations', 'countertransference' and the discovery of the communicational aspect of the patient while projecting experiences into the analyst, psychoanalytic literary study accordingly redirected its own emphasis from the text to the reader. Current research focuses on the reader's transference relations towards the characters in the story as well as the author. This is based on the assumption that the reader projects his inner world into the text and its characters and colours its meaning in line with his internalized object relations and the psychic dynamic – be it conscious or unconscious – with which he approaches the reading.

Among the prominent researchers who investigated the reader's transference relations to the literary work, the psychoanalysts Norman N. Holland and Simon O. Lesser are especially noteworthy. Each one of them underwent self-analysis of their own reading experience. Holland viewed literature first and foremost as an experience ahead of it being an artistic creation, a means of communication or a mode of expression (Holland, N., 1993, pp. 323–340). In the self-analysis of his reading experience he examined how literature had influenced him. Holland identified literature's liberating influence and concluded that it was linked to the organizing form of the text enabling the reader to set himself free of the need to control his drives and thus endow him with a sense of freedom. Lesser's self-analysis of his literary reading found reading to be a process that involves unconscious phantasies and at the same time satisfies the demands of the mind's various agencies – the id, the ego the superego – leading to a more balanced ego. Lesser suggested that the reader meets his anxieties and forbidden desires through identification with the unconscious encoded in the literary work, giving him an opportunity for movement and development (Lesser, S.O., 1957). The work of both Holland and Lesser reinforce Freud's saying that

> many things which, if they were real, could give no enjoyment, can do so in the play of phantasy, and many excitements which, in themselves, are actually distressing, can become a source of pleasure for the hearers and spectators at the performance of a writer's work. (Freud, S., 1908, p. 144)

The psychoanalyst Rivka Eifermann has also engaged in this kind of observation by an in-depth self-analysis of her reading of the fairy tale *Little Red Riding Hood*. This enabled her to show very clearly that each reading is a distinct and independent event that creates new psychological outcomes (Eifermann, R.R., 1993, pp. 439–455).

However, these are among the few attempts at self-analysis undertaken with a view to gaining a profound understanding of the ways in which a text influences the reader. Most psychoanalytic reader study continues to use psychoanalytic descriptive tools for literary research. In what follows I present the main concepts used in psychoanalytic 'reader research' theory.

The psychoanalyst Donald Winnicott formulated the concepts of 'transitional phenomena' and 'potential space' (Winnicott, D.W., 1971), referring to an idea that rapidly became a central tool in the study of the reading experience as an event with a potential for transformation (Zoran, R., 2009, pp. 44–45). Winnicott's concept describes a psychic space that has the quality of enabling 'dreaming' and playfulness similar to the moments in which a child is immersed in a game and has the simultaneously paradoxical experience of internal and external realities; of me and not me; of illusion and real. This, by its very nature, is a transformative space. According to Winnicott's follower the psychoanalyst Christopher Bollas, a person transfers his yearning for transformation – which in infancy was linked to his relations with the mother figure – to the aesthetic dimension of art (Bollas, C., 1987). In the same vein Geldman (1998, pp. 76–77) and Zoran (2009, pp. 47–55) describe the reading experience as a meeting with the potentially transformative quality of the literary text.

An additional concept formulated by Winnicott – 'the use of an object' – also contributed to the understanding of the reading experience

(Winnicott, D.W., 1969, pp. 711–716). This idea relates to the way in which the infant 'uses' his mother and accordingly to the way the patient 'uses' his analyst. Winnicott argued that the possibility of 'using' another object in relations is a developmental achievement involving an attempt to destroy the object and the painful and yet reassuring awareness that the object survived the onslaughts. This experience gives birth in the infant to the profound and important understanding that the object is separate and beyond his omnipotent control. Inspired by this concept, we can describe the reader as 'using' the literary text, meaning that the text in its entirety is unreservedly open to the reader's projections – both benign and destructive. The text remains whole during and after the reading, notwithstanding its absorption of the reader's projections thus fulfilling the role of the object that survives the projections. This process aids the reader in developing his ability to see in the other 'an objective object' – the separateness and otherness of which is recognized – as opposed to a 'subjective object' that is given to relations of objectification and omnipotence. A literary illustration of such an early attempt to use a literary object 'awakened' by 'the book's survival' appears in Jean Paul Sartre's book *The Words* ([1964] 1981). Sartre describes his first experience with a book before he was even able to read:

> I took the two little volumes, sniffed at them, felt them, and opened them casually 'to the right page', making them creak. In vain: I did not have the feeling of ownership. I tried, with no greater success, to treat them like dolls, to rock them, to kiss them, to beat them. On the verge of tears, I finally put them on my mother's lap. (Sartre, J.P., [1964] 1981, p. 45)

In the view of researchers, all the above processes – the reader's transference relations vis-à-vis the text, his positioning in the potential space of the text, the reader's projective identification towards the text and its usage – turn reading into a transformative event.[2]

The influence of postmodernism on psychoanalytic literary study

Another aspect of psychoanalytic literary study was influenced by the contribution of postmodernist ideas, which discussed the centrality of language in intertextual processes and the mutual reflections between the self, the other and texts. This viewpoint seeped into psychoanalytic literary theory as it was gradually formulating the perception of analyst/patient and reader/text relations as being intersubjective, influencing and shaping each other's text. Within the framework of these changes, not only can psychoanalysis read the literary text using its interpretative tools, but literature too can read and analyse psychoanalytic writings as literature. Furthermore, henceforth every reading gained the standing of a subjective and particular event, the meaning of which is not settled and known, but rather comes into being and changes in step with the unique meeting between reader and text at any given moment. The psychoanalyst Donald Spence went further still and argued that psychoanalysts cannot deal with historical truth but only with the narrative truth because we are constantly shaping history through our use of language (Spence, D., 1982). Accordingly, psychoanalysis is viewed by Spence as a practice that structures and shapes identity whose transformation doesn't stem from the revelations of the unconscious but rather emerges from an intertextual discourse between two unconscious systems or between two readings. In the same vein, the psychoanalyst Roy Schafer sought to describe a new psychoanalytic language that he termed 'action language', arguing that language's hegemony in general had been undermined and that this was particularly true of the language of psychoanalytic interpretation, in its expression of an 'inner truth' (Schafer, R., 1976). The understanding is of the 'other' as being shaped by a sequence of narratives, i.e. a text formed by actions, has also permeated the study of literature.

In the wake of these developments, most postmodern psychoanalytic literary study has been split between two main groups: One group studies the intertextual contexts and the influences of reading within the framework of a comprehensive set of social practices. This group focuses on the reader and sees in him a subject participating in the maintenance, establishment and shaping of gender relations, ethnicity, nationalism and class. A further focal point of research by this group examines the way in which the reader's identity and personality are shaped by the texts he reads (Felman, S., 1977, pp. 133–134; Green, A., 1978, pp. 271–292; Jameson, F., 1988, pp. 349–359).

A second group focuses on other aspects of the reading of literature, challenging both the concept of the centrality of knowledge and the authoritativeness of an idea. In this group the impact of the French philosophers Lacan and Derrida is unmistakable. Their influence led to the investigation of as yet unexplored aspects of the reading experience such as the reader's encounter with absence (Green, A., 1978), with madness, with chaos and with the elusive in the unconscious, in existence and in meaning (Felman, S., 1977). The psychoanalyst Andre Green suggests that just as the patient 'invents' the analyst in sync with the transference relations to him, so too the reader can 'invent' a literary text in line with his projections on to the text. Green's view of the reader's projective and transference relations to the text is radical. According to this conceptualization the analyst and literary writing constitute a presence that, at the same time, is characterized by absence. The patient and the reader fill this absence with their unconscious phantasies (Green, A., 1978, pp. 271–292).

The American school of intersubjective and relational psychoanalysis nowadays conducts a fertile discourse with postmodernist thinking and describes the psychoanalytic encounter as one between two subjects combining to create a third composition that is always new and unique (Berman, E., 2003). This school in psychoanalysis considers the subjective reading by the analyst of the therapeutic situation as well as the patient's reading of his therapist as a crucial part of the analytic process that influences, shapes and constitutes a significant component in the establishment of meaning (Aron, L., 1996). Correspondingly, research in the field of inter-subjective psychoanalytic literature searches for ways to describe the 'subjective' and the novel in each reading. It follows that this research is also preoccupied with descriptions of the 'subjective' and the new in the text that is moulded following each reading (Eifermann, R., 1993). According to this view the reader has two roles: on the one hand, he assumes the same position as does the analyst vis-à-vis the patient's text; he reads it, deciphers it and, by dint of his subjectivity, even enriches it. On the other hand, the reader takes on the role of the patient, relating to the text and the author as he would to an analyst who has the power to provide him with answers to the riddles of his existence (Berman, E., 1993, pp. 6–12). These ideas led the encounter between the reader and the text to being perceived as an intersubjective event in which meaning is established and even interpreted mutually rather than unilaterally (Berman, E., 2003, p. 122).

Acceptable methodologies in reader study: an inherent 'catch'

Despite the significant understanding that the key to all these puzzling questions is to be found in the reader's mind, there is a glaring and continuing difficulty in psychoanalytic reader study – in extracting and generalizing the unconscious aspects of the literary reading experience (Holland, N., 1998, p. 1205). One methodology focuses on the text itself and attempts from that to reach conclusions about the reader without involving actual readers. This approach distances us from the reader's unconscious voice. A second methodology does indeed involve actual readers who report on their reading experiences. However, because this is a 'report', it places us in the field of the conscious, which again means missing out the perspective to be gained from the rich unconscious processes involved in the reading of literature. A third methodology attempts to reach the unconscious perceptions through the self-analysis of a particular reader (as in Holland, Lesser or Eifermann cited above). However, because this approach is limited to a single reader the results of such study cannot be generalized, as Holland himself has noted (Holland, N., 1982).

It is these methodological limitations that gave birth to this book, which aims to pave the way *to the unconscious* of readers of literature.

The reading experiences of the literary characters

We cannot report directly about our unconscious, which is, by definition, unknown to us. In looking for a way out of the restrictions I have described, I was forced to cling to a paradox and find a way of extracting the unconscious perceptions linked to the reading experience from the conscious reports of the readers. In psychoanalysis we are aided by the patient's free associations and dreams as the pathway to the unconscious. From this I conceived an idea that was aimed at circumventing the obstacles and capturing the unconscious twists and turns of reading literature. As a psychoanalyst, I have decided to delve deeply into the descriptions *by the characters in literary works of their reading experiences*. These texts were not written as responses to an enquiry that intentionally asked the author about the reading experiences of the character. Descriptions of such reading experiences are interwoven into the stories themselves, usually in the form of incidental tales, and in this sense written without deliberate intent. Their writing is therefore more the outcome of the author's creative associations and intuitions about the reading experiences. These literary descriptions were for me the highway to the unconscious of the reader. I assembled numerous reading experiences of figures in literary texts and the psychoanalytic analysis of *their* experiences revealed a rich variety of psychological processes and ways in which the human unconscious responds to reading a book.

In choosing to use the literary texts, I join an accepted approach in literary and philosophical research that uses literary writings as evidence and recognizes literature's power 'to capture the "blink of an eye" in which one can grasp life ... to suggest a complex phenomenology of life and the contingencies and possibilities it embodies' (Sagi, A., 2011, p. 44). In this spirit I too found in the texts 'a kind of profound witnessing about a reality that suddenly surges towards the language of literature and becomes embodied within it' (Sagi, A., 2011, p. 12). This is the 'phenomenological given' (ibid., p. 13) against which the reading experience is examined. The literary researcher Wolfgang Iser defined the relevance of the phenomenological tool for the analysis of literature thus:

> The phenomenological theory of art lays full stress on the idea that, in considering a literary work, one must take into account not only the actual text but also, and in equal measure, the action involved in responding to that text ... The question now arises as to how far such a process can be adequately described. For this purpose a phenomenological analysis recommends itself. (Iser, W., [1972] 1988, p. 189).

In other words, I am about to read the phenomena handed to me by literature, while I sustain, as much as I can, my personal taste, judgment and prejudices, and let the text and its heroes tell me their stories as openly as possible. Only later in the process will I turn to interpret the material – just as I would listen to a patient's free associations during an analytic hour – in 'evenly suspended attention' (Freud, S., 1912), before I turn to interpret the unconscious aspects in the patient's associations.

Now all that is left for us to do is to delve into our store of books, begin to leaf through their pages, study the reading experiences described in them and reflect on them from a psychoanalytic perspective.

Notes

1 The book includes a study of the reading experiences of the heroes in the works of Aharon Appelfeld, Maya Bejerano, Hayim Nahman Bialik, Henry James, Eva Hoffman, Yair Horvitz, Nathan Zach, Jean Paul Sartre, Mark Strand, Jorge Semprún, Samuel Yossef Agnon, Edgar Allan Poe, Luigi Pirandello, Fernando Pessoa, Marcel Proust, Paul Celan, Otto Dov Kulka and Søren Kierkegaard.
2 Bibliotherapy is a school in literary research that has become a therapeutic practice employing the 'therapeutic qualities of literature' (Zoran, R., 2009, p. 12).

References

Aristotle. ([1447–1462] 1895). *Poetics*. S.H. Butcher (Ed. and trans.). London and New York: Macmillan & Co.
Aron, L. (1996). *A Meeting of Minds: Mutuality in Psychoanalysis*. Hillsdale, NJ: Analytic Press.
Bachmann, I. (1978). *Lectures on Problems of Contemporary Literature*. Munich: Piper Verlag GmbH.
Barthes, R. (1967). The Death of the Author. In: D. Lodge (Ed.) *Modern Criticism and Theory: A Reader*. New York: Pearson Education, pp. 145–150.
Berman, E. (Ed.) (1993). *Essential Papers on Literature and Psychoanalysis*. New York and London: New York University Press.
Berman, E. (2003). Reader and Story, Viewer and Film: On Transference and Interpretation. *International Journal of Psychoanalysis*, 84, pp. 119–129.
Bion, W.R. ([1967] 2018). *Second Thoughts*. London and New York: Routledge.
Bollas, C. (1987). *The Shadow of the Object: Psychoanalysis of the Unthought Known*. New York: Columbia University Press.
de Saussure, F. (1916). *Course in General Linguistics*. Roy Harris (trans.). La Salle, IL: Open Court Classics.
Dilthey, E. ([1900] 1996). The Rise of Hermeneutics. In: R.A. Makkreel and R. Frithjof (Eds.) Fredrick R. Jameson and Rudolf A. Makkreel (trans.) *Hermeneutics and the Study of History: Selected Works, Vol. IV*. Princeton, NJ: Princeton University Press, pp. 235–251.
Eifermann, R.R. (1993). Interactions Between Textual Analysis and Related Self-Analysis. In: E. Berman (Ed.) *Essential Papers on Literature and Psychoanalysis*. New York and London: New York University Press, pp. 439–455.
Felman, S. (Ed.) (1977). *Literature and Psychoanalysis: The Question of Reading, Otherwise*. Baltimore, MD and London: John Hopkins University Press.

Freud, S. (1900). The Interpretation of Dreams. In: J. Strachey (Ed.) *The Standard Edition of the Complete Psychological Works of Sigmund Freud, Vol. IV*. London: Hogarth Press, pp. 1–338.

Freud, S. (1907). Delusions and Dreams in Jensen's Gradiva. In: J. Strachey (Ed.) *The Standard Edition of the Complete Psychological Works of Sigmund Freud, Vol. IX*. London: Hogarth Press, pp. 3–95.

Freud, S. (1908). Creative Writers and Daydreaming. In: J. Strachey (Ed.) *The Standard Edition of the Complete Psychological Works of Sigmund Freud, Vol. IX*. London: Hogarth Press, pp. 141–153.

Freud, S. (1910a). Leonardo Da Vinchi and a Memory of His Childhood. In: J. Strachey (Ed.) *The Standard Edition of the Complete Psychological Works of Sigmund Freud, Vol. XI*. London: Hogarth Press, pp. 57–137.

Freud, S. (1910b). A Special Type of Choice of Object Made by Men (Contributions to the Psychology of Love I). In: J. Strachey (Ed.) *The Standard Edition of the Complete Psychological Works of Sigmund Freud, Vol. XI*. London: Hogarth Press, pp. 163–175.

Freud, S. (1912). Recommendations to Physicians Practising Psycho-Analysis. In: J. Strachey (Ed.) *The Standard Edition of the Complete Psychological Works of Sigmund Freud, Vol. XII*. London: Hogarth Press, pp. 109–120.

Freud, S. (1914). On Narcissism: An Introduction. In: J. Strachey (Ed.) *The Standard Edition of the Complete Psychological Works of Sigmund Freud, Vol. XIV*. London: Hogarth Press, pp. 67–102.

Freud, S. (1915). Thoughts for the Times of War and Death. In: J. Strachey (Ed.) *The Standard Edition of the Complete Psychological Works of Sigmund Freud, Vol. XIV*. London: Hogarth Press, pp. 273–302.

Gadamer, H.G. (1960). *Truth and Method*. Joel Weinsheimer and Donald G. Marshall (trans.). London and New York: Continuum.

Gadamer, H.G. (1976). The Universality of the Hermeneutical Problem. In: D. E. Linge (Ed. and trans.) *Philosophical Hermeneutics*. Berkeley: University of California Press, pp. 3–17.

Geldman, M. (1998). *Psychoanalytic Literary Criticism*. Tel Aviv: Hakibutz Hameuchad.

Green, A. (1978). The Double and the Absent. In: A. Roland (Ed.) *Psychoanalysis, Creativity and Literature: A French–American Inquiry*. New York: Columbia University Press, pp. 271–292.

Grotstein, J. (2005). 'Projective Transidentification': An Extension of the Concept of Projective Identification. *International Journal of Psychoanalysis*, 86(4), pp. 1051–1069.

Hareven, G. ([2005] 2009). Forward: On Women Books and Hunger. In: S. Bollmann, (Ed.) *Reading Women*. London: Merrell; Hebrew Edition: Kineret, Zmora-Bitan, Dvir, pp. 13–19.

Holland, N.N. (1982). Unity Identity Text Self. In: E. Berman (Ed.) *Essential Papers on Literature and Psychoanalysis*. New York and London: New York University Press, pp. 323–340.

Holland, N. (1993). Psychoanalysis and Literature: Past and Present. *Contemporary Psychoanalysis*, 29(1), pp. 5–21.

Holland, N. (1998). Reader-Response Criticism. *International Journal of Psychoanalysis*, 79, pp. 1203–1211.
Husserl, E. ([1931] 2012). *Ideas: General Introduction to Pure Phenomenology*. London and New York: Routledge.
Iser, W. ([1972] 1988). The Reading Process: A Phenomenological Approach. In: D. Lodge (Ed.) *Modern Criticism and Theory: A Reader*. New York: Pearson Education, pp. 188–205.
Iser, W. (1978). *The Act of Reading: A Theory of Aesthetic Response*. Baltimore, MD and London: John Hopkins University Press.
Jameson, F. (1988). The Politics of Theory: Ideological Positions in the Postmodernism Debate. In: D. Lodge (Ed.) *Modern Criticism and Theory: A Reader*. New York: Pearson Education, pp. 348–359.
Kafka, F. ([1904] 2003). A Letter to Oscar Polak. In: K. Brophy (Ed.) *Explorations in Creative Writing*. Melbourne: Melbourne University Press, p. 25.
Klein, M. (1946). Notes on Some Schizoid Mechanisms. In: *Envy and Gratitude and Other Works 1946–1963*. London: Vintage, pp. 25–42.
Kundera, M. ([1986] 1988). *The Art of the Novel*. New York: Grove Press.
Laplanche, J. and Pontalis, J.B. (1973). *The Language of Psychoanalysis*. London: Hogarth Press [Kindle edition].
Lesser, S.O. (1957). *Fiction and the Unconscious*. Boston, MA: Beacon Hill Press.
Lodge, D. (Ed.) (1988). *Modern Criticism and Theory: A Reader*. New York: Pearson Education.
Lubin, O. (2003). *A Woman Reading A Woman*. Haifa: Haifa University Press.
Proust, M. (1905). *On Reading*. New York: Three Syrens Press.
Racker, H. (1953). A Contribution to the Problem of Counter-Transference. *International Journal of Psychoanalysis*, 34, pp. 313–324.
Ricoeur, P. ([2004] 2006). *On Translation: Thinking in Action*. London and New York: Routledge.
Rorty, R. (Ed.) (1967). *The Linguistic Turn: Essays in Phillosophical Method*. Chicago, IL and London: University of Chicago Press.
Sagi, A. (1991). *Kierkegaard: Religion and Existence: The Voyage of the Self*. Jerusalem: Bialik Institute.
Sagi, A. (2009). *The Human Voyage to Meaning: A Philosophical-Hermeneutical Study of Literary Works*. Ramat Gan: Bar Ilan University Press.
Sagi, A. (2011). *To Be a Jew: Brener – An Existentialist Jew*. Tel Aviv: Hakibbutz Hameuchad.
Sandler, J. (1976). Countertransference and Role-Responsiveness. *International Journal of Psychoanalysis* II, 3, pp. 43–47.
Sartre, J. ([1948] 1988). *What Is Literature?* Cambridge, MA: Harvard University Press.
Sartre, J. ([1964] 1981). *The Words*. New York: Vintage Books.
Schafer, R. (1976). *A New Language for Psychoanalysis*. New Haven, CT and London: Yale University Press.
Spence, D.P. (1982). *Narrative Truth and Historical Truth*. New York: Norton.
Stein, R. (1993). What Is the Story? The Literary Signifiers of the Psychoanalytic Process. *Sihot: Israeli Journal of Psychotherapy*, 5(1), pp. 45–52.

Winnicott, D.W. (1958). The Capacity to Be Alone. *International Journal of Psychoanalysis*, 39, pp. 416–420.
Winnicott, D.W. (1969). The Use of an Object. *International Journal of Psychoanalysis*, 50, pp. 711–716.
Winnicott, D.W. (1971). *Playing and Reality*. London: Tavistock Publications.
Woolf, V. (1932). How Should One Read a Book. In: *The Second Common Reader*. London: Hogarth Press.
Zoran, R. (2009). *The Letter's Imprint: Reading and Identity within the Bibliotherapeutic Dialogue*. Jerusalem: Carmel.

Further reading

Poulet, G. (1969). Phenomenology of Reading. *New Literary History*, 1(1), pp. 53–68.

Part I

Transference relations of the literary reader

Introduction

Part I explores the nature of the transference relations of the reader towards characters in a literary text, including the narrator and author. Before discussing the texts themselves I wish to clarify the main psychoanalytic concepts discussed in this section and their relevance to the transference relations triggered by the reading experience.

Object relations: a psychoanalytic perspective

The form of relations portrayed in a literary text parallels actual relations in our lives in both the external world as well as in our internal world. In an individual's internal world there are numerous unconscious representations of the 'self' and of 'objects' (the meaningful others internalized in his mind). From a psychoanalytic point of view we continuously conduct – partly in awareness but mostly unconsciously – relations in the internal world between representations of self (the 'romantic self', the 'persecuted self', etc.) and representations of objects (the 'sadistic father' the 'seductive mother' and so on). These relations are termed 'object relations'. According to the psychoanalyst Melanie Klein 'There is no instinctual urge, no anxiety situation, no mental process that does not involve objects, external or internal; in other words, object relations are at the centre of emotional life' (Klein, M., 1952, p. 53). These relations shape our mental health, influence our encounters with others and the way we conduct ourselves in the world.

Internal objects

'Internal objects' are not solely the outcome of an internalization of the actual figures in our lives. They are derived from the sum total of all phantasized and real experiences, which combine to form an array of inner objects. In her article 'What Are Internal Objects?' the psychoanalyst Catalina Bronstein points out that 'internal objects underlie a multiplicity of phenomena and affective states which are conditioned by them. Consciously, they appear to us through images, memories, dreams, of an infinite variety' (Bronstein, C., 2009, p. 117). Thus, for example, we don't have just one memory of *the* mother within us but rather a reservoir of 'mother objects'. For instance, the 'depressed internal mother' is a representation expressing a collection of phantasized and real experiences with the mother figure in her moments of depression. On the other hand, moments of contentment with the mother create the internal 'good mother', etc.

In *The Book of Disquiet* ([1982] 2017) the Portuguese writer Fernando Pessoa describes this poetically, in a way that can be applied to both the internal world as well as to the characters in the literary text. Analogously to the multiplicity of internal objects there are within us also 'multiple selves'. These develop from the diverse modes of existence of our 'self' in the course of a lifetime, which have created multiple representations of our selves. Fernando Pessoa offers an insightful description of these representations:

> Each of us is more than one person, many people, a proliferation of our one self ... Today, as I note down these few impressions in a legitimate break brought about by a shortage of work, I am the person carefully transcribing them, the person who is pleased not to have to work just now, the person who looks at the sky even though he can't actually see it from here, the person who is thinking all this, and the person feeling physically at ease and noticing that his hands are still slightly cold. And, like a diverse but compact multitude, this whole world of mine, composed as it is of different people, projects but a single shadow, that of this calm figure writing on Borges's high desk, where I have come to find the blotter he borrowed from me (Pessoa, F., [1982] 2017, p. 363).

Elsewhere, Pessoa briefly notes that 'I only know myself as the symphony'. He sums up the existence of the internal objects and multiple selves within him thus:

> Is it that my habit of placing myself in the souls of other people makes me see myself as others see or would see me if they noticed my presence there? It is. And once I've perceived what they would feel about me if they knew me, it is as if they were feeling and expressing it at that very moment. It is a torture to me to live with other people. Then there are those who live inside me. Even when removed from life, I'm forced to live with them. Alone, I am hemmed in by multitudes. I have nowhere to flee to, unless I were to flee myself (ibid., p. 71).

Transference relations

In psychoanalysis transference is a term indicative of:

> A process of actualisation of unconscious wishes. Transference uses specific objects and operates in the framework of a specific relationship established with these objects. Its context par excellence is the analytic situation. In the transference, infantile prototypes re-emerge and are experienced with a strong sensation of immediacy (Laplanche, J., and Pontalis J.B., 1973, loc. 12083).

The patient 'transfers' his internalized relations with the significant others in his life (from early childhood and onward) to the analyst. This revival in the transference relations enables the patient to become reacquainted with and work through these early relations and their impact on shaping his psyche and ways of coping with his past and present.

A person enters every relationship in his life with a store of memories. This reservoir is loaded with drives, anxieties, wishes and defences that he directs at people with whom he makes contact, not only because he fears recalling painful aspects of his past but also out of a wish for reparation. The deeper the relationship so the individual will direct the more significant and complex aspects of his internalized relations towards the person with whom he is in a relationship. These aspects include: anxieties that stem from the past (abandonment, rejection, aggression, loss of love etc.); unrequited yearnings (the fulfilment of wishes coming to terms with deprivations, recalling the good and repairing the bad); reconstructed conflicts looking for resolutions in the newly formed relationship (such as the conflict between the wish for merger and the fear of being swallowed up); or, for example, between the desire for supremacy and the sense of guilt for the defeat of the object; and typical defences (such as schizoid or manic defences). In the course of the psychoanalytic process the transference relates most profoundly to the figure of the analyst.

It is important to note transference's live and dynamic characteristics. Betty Joseph (1985) highlights the idea that transference is not a static replica of one of the figures from the patient's internal world and his past projected on to the analyst. Rather, it is a live happening subjecting the analyst to various pressures stemming from drives, feelings, anxieties and defences awakened in the here-and-now relations of the patient towards the analyst as a transference figure. This is what turns transference relations into a catalyst for movement and change. In what follows we will discover that in literature there are powerful transference relations towards the work's fictional characters. The vivid characteristics of transference relations in analysis are also highly relevant to the nature of the reader's transference towards the literary characters and to his ability to use them for psychic development (Joseph, B., 1985, pp. 447–454).

Transference relations towards literary characters

In his essay *On Reading* (1905), Marcel Proust describes the reader's powerful psychic responses to the fictional characters and takes the argument to an extreme in claiming that this response is sometimes even more intense than anything we allow ourselves to feel towards the real people in our lives:

> These beings to whom one had given more of one's attention and affection than to those in real life, not always daring to admit to what extent one loved them (and even when our parents found us busy reading and seemed to be smiling at our emotion, closing the book with a studied indifference or pretence of boredom); one would never again see … these people for whom one had yearned and sobbed, would never again hear of them (Proust, M., 1905, p. 21).

In the same vein, Fernando Pessoa writes: 'I've often noticed that certain characters in novels take on for us an importance that our acquaintances and friends, who talk and listen to us in the real and visible world, could never have' (Pessoa, F., [1982] 2017, p. 313).

There are significant areas of similarity between the framework of the psychoanalytic and the reading structures that contribute to the awakening of transference relations in both. Thus, for example, the nature of the setting for these two kinds of encounter reinforces the capacity of both to set internal processes in motion. Freud observed that in the therapeutic space transference relations are also facilitated by a certain vagueness on the part of the analyst, enabling the patient to project on to him in accordance with his internal and historical relations (Freud, S., 1915). The literary textual space is similarly characterized by ambiguity, (Kris, E., 1993), indeterminacy (Iser, W., 1972) and poetic expressiveness (Iser, W., 1978). All the above encourage active and projective communication with the literary text and its characters on the part of the reader (Zoran, R., 2009). Moreover, 'the fact that the literary text is an undefined world in a defined format (aesthetic structure) opens up the possibility of relating to it as one would to "another person"' (ibid., p. 93). The textual space is rich in possibilities but definitionally ambiguous, thus inviting the reader to lend meaning to the disposition of the characters involved and the nature of the relationships described in the story in accordance with his evolved transference relations. In other words, he identifies with the characters and also projects his internal objects and relations on to the fictional characters described in the text.

Jean Paul Sartre describes such identification and a strong transference reaction to the literary character thus: 'Raskolnikov's waiting is my waiting which I lend him … His hatred of the police magistrate who questions him is my hatred' (Sartre, J.P., [1948] 1988, p. 45). The characters are experienced as real fellow beings to whom we 'lend' our feelings. In the playwright Pirandello's ironic tongue:

> A character may always ask a man who he is. Because a character has really a life of his own, marked with his especial characteristics; for which reason he is always 'somebody'. But a man – I'm not speaking of you now – may very well be 'nobody' (Pirandello, L., 1921, p. 60).

The literary characters both mirror the reader's experiences of his own self as well as echoing the significant others in his life – both the internal and external objects – and so awaken in the reader communication with his internal objects. The more intense the involvement the bolder the reader's transference relations become, and what Shoshana Felman (2003) has termed the 'reading effect' will also be reinforced.

The reader's transference relations towards the text's characters are bidirectional. He sometimes experiences the characters as 'taking care' of *his* existential issues, at other times he experiences himself as 'taking on' *their* existential challenges. As the psychoanalyst Emmanuel Berman has noted:

> The experience of the reader, viewer or listener, whether a layman or a professional critic, is conceived in this perspective as combining an attempt to uncover and spell out the work's meanings, with unavoidably personal identifications and emotional reactions – positive, negative and ambivalent. It therefore necessarily combines transference (to the work of art as a source of insight and growth), countertransference (the fantasy of artist and figures as patients – maybe sick patients – to be analysed) and interpretation (the striving to understand more deeply) (Berman, E., 2003, p. 122).

The reader of literature alternately takes on the perspectives of the analyst and of the patient (Berman, E., 1993). On the one hand, he turns to the characters, the narrator and the writer just as a patient turns to the analyst, a figure capable of helping him cope with his world and lending meaning to his life. In doing so the reader places himself in a position similar to the transference position of the patient. On the other hand, he takes on the role of the text's interpreter who endows it with meaning. In his sense he listens to the character's text as an analyst would listen to a patient's text and attempts to lend it new meaning. The text 'needs' the reader to breathe life into it and lend it meaning (Sartre, J.P., [1948] 1988). Relational psychoanalysis emphasizes the fact that there is no 'pure' interpretation of the patient's free associations because every such interpretation also includes the analyst's inner world as a crucial part of forming the interpretation. In the same way, the reader of literature is involved in the interpretation that he lends to the text and its heroes. Every bestowal of meaning in the course of reading – be it conscious or unconscious – is an act that opens up the reader's horizon of possibilities.

Novelists, we are told by Milan Kundera, 'grasp one possibility of existence (a possibility for man and for his world) and thereby make us see what we are, what we are capable of' (Kundera, M., [1986] 1988, p. 44) The more dynamic the transference relations towards the characters is, the more interested and involved we become in their lives; our curiosity as to how the story will unfold now heightened by our own needs, desires and fears. At times the sense of anticipation is so intense that we can't put the book down or, alternatively, feel compelled to stop reading at least for a while. As Sartre noted:

> In reading, one foresees; one waits. He foresees the end of the sentence, the following sentence, the next page ... The reading is composed of a host of hypotheses, of dreams followed by awakenings, of hopes and deceptions. Readers are always ahead of the sentence they are reading in a merely probable future which partly collapses and partly comes together in proportion as they progress, which withdraws from one page to the next and forms the moving horizon of the literary object (Sartre, J.P., [1948] 1988, p. 41).

From a psychoanalytic perspective every expectation we have of our fellowman and of the future stems from our past experience and its internal representations in the present. It is therefore inevitably suffused with both anxiety and hope. Accordingly, the particular encounter between every reader and every literary text at any given moment in time is shaped by this past as represented in the present and determines the transference relations that the reader conducts with the text's literary characters. Therefore, with the exception of certain situations that at a later stage in the book will be analysed as 'resistance to reading', the process of transference towards the literary text is not predominantly intellectual but rather experiential and emotional. In Sartre's words 'One certainly creates the aesthetic object with feelings. If it is touching it appears through tears; if it is comic it will be recognized by laughter' (Sartre, J.P., [1948] 1988, pp. 49–50). Furthermore, the reader's encounter with the text's inhabitants (characters, narrator and writer) is intensified and constitutes a unique space in which internal events can be revived. In contrast with human encounters in daily life that have to take the reality principle into account, the aesthetic space is characterized by a certain degree of illusion, playfulness and potentiality (Winnicott, D.W., 1971). Moreover, in reading a book we dare to allow ourselves to experience all those feelings aroused by our most profound anxieties, which in real life we do our utmost to avoid. We yearn for stories about unrequited love, betrayal, disgrace and death. No less alarming, we indulge in fantasies about omnipotent conquests, impossible love stories and eternal lives. This explains why the usage of literary texts in bibliotherapy and sometimes even in psychoanalysis, can open up 'a potential space ... which is developmental, creative and intersubjective' (Eshel, O., 1996, p. 182). The accumulation of these kinds of reading experiences can lead the reader to work through his internal object relations to the benefit of a reflective view that may result in psychological growth and the sprouting of new coping capacities.

The psychoanalyst Norman Holland, who studied the reading experience through self-analysis, explains this phenomenon in the following way:

> All of us, as we read, use the literary work to symbolize and finally to replicate ourselves. We work out through the text our own characteristic patterns of desire and adaptation. We interact with the work, making it part of our own psychic economy and making ourselves part of the literary text – as we interpret it ... we interpret the new experience ... in the terms of our characteristic ways of coping with the world. That is, each of us will find in the literary work the kind of thing we characteristically wish or fear the most (Holland, N., 1982, p. 330).

This description is consistent with Zoran's assumption that 'the literary text has inherent therapeutic qualities' (Zoran, R., 2009, p. 81). Given that the reading experience is an encounter between the reader's inner world and the text, it follows that each reader's experience will be different. Moreover, because the mind is not static, even when the same text is read at different times by the same reader the feelings aroused will differ as will the nature of the encounter.

Using Franz Kafka's *Metamorphosis* (Kafka, F., [1915] 1996) the psychoanalyst Emanuel Berman (2003) describes the range of options for transference towards the literary text by comparing the responses of four readers of Kafka's work. As Berman shows, each reader interprets the text differently in light of his differing transference relations, which derive from the individual's inner position as reader. The writer A.B. Yehoshua points to Gregor Samsa's incestuous lust for his sister and the displacement of his oedipal desires, involving sexual drive and a sense of guilt. Contrastingly, the psychoanalyst Heinz Kohut, as reader, emphasizes the position of the child whose presence in the world was not blessed by an empathic welcome. The psychoanalyst Roy Schafer highlights the family's rejection of Gregor, which arouses in him feelings of depersonalization (a warped perception of his body) and derealisation (a distorted view of reality). Finally, the English theatrical director Steven Berkoff's staged production of Kafka's work seeks to shed light on Gregor as an innocent and helpless victim pitted against his psychologically disturbed family. Berman writes:

> Identifications are prominent in all versions. Schaefer and Berkoff identify with Gregor, and are enraged with his selfish, uncaring family. Yehoshua

is contemptuous of Gregor, and identifies with the suffering of the family which has to live with its unbearable regressed member (Berman, E., 2003, p. 124).

Through these different reading responses Berman shows that every reading is a standalone event and derives from the transference relations aroused towards the text and its characters in a particular reader at a given moment in time. Berman's exemplification is consistent with the idea that the work of art is not concealed in the written words but rather in their encounter with the reader. In his transference relations towards the characters and the story's plot, the reader revives the written situation accordingly. This is a particular and unique outcome of an encounter between the reader's inner world and his internalized object relations on the one hand, and the literary creation and its heroes, on the other. As a consequence of this encounter the aesthetic literary object gains its meaning. For its part, the new meaning breathes life into the reader's internal object relations – now open to being newly worked through via the transference relations he has developed towards the characters in the text. In this way the act of reading becomes a catalyst for change.

I will now turn to the central psychic mechanisms involved in the reader's transference relations. From the literary examples I have assembled, seven psychic mechanisms were the most prominent: the distancing paradox; providing meaning and significance; seven forms of identification; resistance to reading; idealization of the writer; mutual witnessing; and reparation of the ethical position. These mechanisms will now be explored along with an explanation as to how each of them serves the processes of psychic and existential development in the reader.

References

Berman, E. (Ed.) (1993). *Essential Papers on Literature and Psychoanalysis*. New York and London: New York University Press.
Berman, E. (2003). Reader and Story, Viewer and Film: On Transference and Interpretation. *International Journal of Psychoanalysis*, 84, pp. 119–129.
Bronstein, C. (Ed.) (2009). *Kleinian Theory: A Contemporary Perspective*. London and Philadelphia: Whurr.
Eshel, O. (1996). Therapeutic Stories. *Sihot: Israeli Journal of Psychotherapy*, 10(3), pp. 182–193.
Felman, S. (2003). *Writing and Madness*. Stanford, CA: Stanford University Press.
Freud, S. (1915). Thoughts for the Times of War and Death. In: J. Strachey (Ed.) *The Standard Edition of the Complete Psychological Works of Sigmund Freud, Vol. XIV*. London: Hogarth Press, pp. 273–302.
Holland, N. (1982). Unity Identity Text Self. In: E. Berman (Ed.) *Essential Papers on Literature and Psychoanalysis*. New York and London: New York University Press, pp. 323–340.

Iser, W. (1972). The Reading Process: A Phenomenological Approach. *New Literary History*, 3(2), pp. 279–299.
Iser, W. (1978). *The Act of Reading: A Theory of Aesthetic Response*. Baltimore, MD and London: John Hopkins University Press.
Joseph, B. (1985). Transference: The Total Situation. *International Journal of Psychoanalysis*, 66, pp. 447–454.
Kafka, F. [1915] (1996). *The Metamorphosis and Other Stories*. New York: Barnes & Noble.
Klein, M. (1952). Some Theoretical Conclusions regarding the Emotional Life of the Infant. In: *Envy and Gratitude and Other Works 1946–1963*. London: Vintage, pp. 48–56.
Kris, E. (1993). Prince Hal's Conflict. In: E. Berman (Ed.) *Essential Papers on Literature and Psychoanalysis*. New York and London: New York University Press, pp. 150–166.
Kundera, M. [1986] (1988). *The Art of the Novel*. New York: Grove Press.
Laplanche, J. and Pontalis, J.B. (1973). *The Language of Psychoanalysis*. London: Hogarth Press [Kindle edition].
Pessoa, F. [1982] (2017). *The Book of Disquiet*. London and New York: Penguin Books.
Pirandello, L. (1921). *Six Characters in Search of an Author*. Mineola, NY: Dover Books.
Proust, M. (1905). *On Reading*. New York: Three Syrens Press.
Sartre, J. [1948] (1988). *What Is Literature?* Cambridge, MA: Harvard University Press.
Winnicott, D.W. (1971). *Playing and Reality*. London: Tavistock.
Zoran, R. (2009). *The Letter's Imprint: Reading and Identity within the Bibliotherapeutic Dialogue*. Jerusalem: Carmel.

Chapter 1

The distancing paradox

The first imperative for activating all other psychic processes during reading is the 'distancing paradox'.[1] This process is set in motion by the reader's illusion that he is distancing himself from the realms of his inner and actual life to a faraway imaginary literary world. Paradoxically it is precisely this illusion that brings him closer to his internal world. This phenomenon is illustrated in Jorge Semprún's book *Literature or Life* (1994).

A brief introduction to Jorge Semprún's *Literature or Life*

The reading of every book is accomplished in two phases. The first involves the actual physical act of reading. The second, which carries the reader beyond the confines of time and awareness, involves an ongoing reading of the book long after the first phase has ended. In other words, the book continues to be read from its traces stored in memory (Woolf, V., 1925, p. 5). The book *Literature or life* (1994) describes Semprún's memories of the Buchenwald concentration camp and the way he has had to cope with these memories after his release and forever thereafter. His book is loaded with 'readings' of books etched in his memory that aided him in his psychological survival.

Literature or life is an autobiographical novel. Therefore, my analysis does not differentiate between Semprún the writer and Semprún the character and narrator, because they are intertwined. Throughout the book, Semprún recalls numerous texts he has read in the past that aided him while coping in the camp and once again as he tried to retrospectively recollect and write his experiences. As a writer, Semprún describes the entrapment of someone who had crossed the line between life and death. In order to stay emotionally alive he is compelled in his writing to describe 'the death he faced'. But at the very same time, accessing the experience of death through writing would mean being once more ensnared in its web. In his own words:

> I possess nothing more than my death, my experience of death, to recount my life, to express it, to carry it on. I must make life with all

that death. And the best way to do this is through writing. Yet that brings me back to death, to the suffocating embrace of death. That's where I am: I can live only by assuming that death through writing, but writing literally prohibits me from living (Semprún, J., 1994, p. 189).

Despite Semprún's quest for liberation through writing, his book is filled with faithful companions from his reading, literary and philosophical characters and writers who accompanied his coping throughout his life and especially in his incarceration in Buchenwald during World War II. Semprún describes the way in which his reading experiences influenced him at different moments in the course of his actual and inner voyage. Even the comment cited above conceals a reference to reading, as it paraphrases lines from a poem by the Peruvian poet Cesar Vallejo whom he loved and also quotes directly in another context in the book: 'In sum, I possess nothing to express my life, except my death' (ibid., p. 144).

The range of writers mentioned in his book – philosophers, novelists, playwrights and poets – attests to the significance for Semprún of being able to turn to the figures of writers and characters (of whom he generally speaks as if they are one and the same) in order to cope and even to survive. When Semprún 'reads' from memory extracts from Hegel, Goethe, Marx, Kafka, Keats and dozens more that closely echo his experiences and lend meaning to those episodes, the 'reading' serves both as a container and as a reparative interpretation, reconciling his inner and actual reality as one. Time and again he turns to the authors of the books he has read and to their characters as if they were fellow voyagers helping him survive the almost unendurable:

> I've always been lucky with poets. I mean that my encounters with their creations have always been well timed: at the opportune moment, I inevitably find a poetic work that can help me to live, to sharpen my consciousness of the world (ibid., p. 166).

Exploring Semprún's reading experiences reveals the way in which he uses the text to create the 'distancing paradox'. It shows how, in the context of the transference relations towards a literary character, the reader distances himself from an immediate psychic experience that he finds hard to contain, and sometimes, as in Semprún's example, the experience is traumatic. The fascinating fact is that he is distancing himself from the immediate traumatic situation towards a literary scene that is also traumatic. Paradoxically this enables the reader to reapproach his hitherto unbearable anxiety and allow for the beginning of some psychological metabolization and working through. Such an achievement would have been well-nigh impossible given the reality of the reader's proximity to the trauma that made any working through unendurably painful.

For example, Semprún recounts a situation in which he sat and listened to an Auschwitz survivor describing his experiences as a member of the Sonderkommando[2] clearing the dead from the gas chambers and transferring bodies to the crematorium. Semprún already had a vague idea about the gas chambers, having heard about them from his friend Diego Morales who had been transported to Buchenwald from Auschwitz. But this was the first time that he had received a detailed report about what was happening there. As seen in the following quote, that testimony triggered a welter of physical and mental responses; his mind froze, his body felt emptied and stressed and his sense of time and place were blurred:

> He spoke for a long while; we listened to him in silence, frozen in the pallid anguish of his story. Suddenly ... we realized that wintry night had fallen, that we had been shrouded in darkness for some time already. We had sunk body and soul into the night of that story, suffocating, without any sense of time (ibid., pp. 50–51).

While listening, Semprún describes how his thoughts spontaneously wondered to a book he had once read. His reading experience of a novel by Andre Malraux surfaces:

> The survivor of Auschwitz remained motionless, his hands spread out flat on his knees: a pillar of salt and despairing memory. We remained motionless, too. I'd been thinking for long minutes, about Andre Malraux's last novel, *La lutte avec l'ange* ... At the heart of Malraux's *oeuvre* is a meditation on death, and consequently a series of reflections and dialogues on the meaning of life ... This meditation reaches one of its most extreme and significant formulations in the description of the gas attack unleashed in 1916 by the Germans on the Russian front of the Vistula River (ibid., p. 51).

The associations racing through Semprún's mind are self-evident. The description of the gas chambers drove the reader inside him to leaf through the pages of a novel etched in his memory dealing with the gas attack launched by the Germans in World War I. I shall try and shed light on the psychic processes enfolded here.

Fear of disintegration and the transitional phenomena

The evidence delivered in the first person about the gas chambers and transferring the bodies for cremation shattered those listening, threatening to destroy the human ability to absorb and understand. Semprún's spontaneous transition from 'far beyond our ability to listen to them' to 'I've been thinking, for long minutes, about Andre Malraux's last novel', is evidence first of the human mind's ability to distance his testimony from the immediate situation to a literary situation and from the immediate witness to the literary witness. Malraux's testimony is also about a gas attack but unlike the Jewish survivor sitting in the room with Semprún and talking to him, and unlike Semprún himself who has also just endured the concentration camp, Malraux is an 'other' who Semprún meets in the 'transitional phenomena' of literature. Malraux the narrator is a more remote witness who enables the reader to cope with the immediate threat to his psychic integration and to create a space in which he can reflect upon the situation in which he finds himself.

I shall clarify this process from a psychoanalytic perspective. The concept of 'transitional phenomena' was coined by the psychoanalyst Donald Winnicott to depict a psychological space that evolves early in the child's development where coexistence and transitionality occur simultaneously between 'me' and 'not me'; between an inner and outer world; and between reality and illusion. Subsequently in life this psychological state, also termed 'potential space', enables a person to enjoy the playful and illusory in life in general and, in particular, to gain pleasure from the unique presence of illusion in art. A 'transitional object' is also created within this space. This object, such as a pacifier, a blanket or a doll, becomes extremely special to the infant and toddler, being infused with 'me' and mother, felt as truth and illusion and simultaneously experienced as internal and external. In the course of the child's development this type of relation is broadened to objects in the world in general, including aesthetic objects such as literary creations (Winnicott, D.W., 1953). The transitional phenomenon is related to the 'The infant's capacity to create, think up, devise, originate, produce an object' (ibid., p. 2).

In a way that somewhat resembles the infant experiencing his transitional object, the reader experiences a book as if he had both created and found it. Winnicott suggested that once it has been enabled by the transitional phenomena, the psyche's optimal situation would be not to have to decide whether the object had been found or created. Both the creators and the consumers of art use art's transitional quality as a way of coping with their inner world through the artistic space. The creative space touches upon the psyche's most daunting questions while at the same time distances them to that twilight zone in which the self can play more securely with representations of his inner world. The inner world as it appears on canvas, on the theatrical stage or in the pages of a literary novel, is an illusion located between 'me' and 'not me', between phantasy and reality and between the internal and the external world. In fact, the transitional phenomena of the potential space are spread out 'over the whole cultural field' (ibid., p. 7).

Extreme situations threatening the physical and/or the mental integrity lead to a collapse of the transitional phenomena. The psyche experiences a fear of disintegration and is prone to disintegrate when it cannot endure all the anxiety and pain overwhelming it. When the psyche fragments itself, the feeling of terror is replaced by a feeling of psychic deadness (Eigen, M., 1996). Apparently, the threat in experiencing psychic deadness is not as menacing as the pain and dread felt as long as the mind is still integrated. At the very same time, psychic deadness is intolerable to the individual who feels lost both mentally and emotionally. As Klein noted:

> This lack of anxiety in schizoid patients is only apparent. Though the schizoid mechanisms imply a dispersal of emotions including anxiety, these dispersed elements persist in the patient's mind. Such patients have a certain form of latent anxiety; it is kept latent by the particular method of dispersal. The feeling of being disintegrated, of being unable to experience emotions, of losing one's objects, is in fact the equivalent of anxiety. This becomes clearer when advance in synthesis has been made. The great relief a patient then experiences derives from a feeling that his inner and outer worlds are not only more united but have returned to life. At such moments it appears in retrospect that when emotions were lacking, relations were vague and uncertain and parts of the personality were felt to be lost, everything was felt to be dead. All this is the equivalent of anxiety of a very serious nature. This anxiety, kept latent by dispersal, is to some extent experienced all along, but its form differs from the latent anxiety which we can recognize in other types of case (Klein, M., 1948, p. 10).

Semprún's description of his experience listening to the Auschwitz survivor in eerie silence and the sense of body and mind disintegrating is a chilling literary portrayal of the psyche's inability to remain whole in the presence of such terrifying anxiety. He describes how momentarily everything collapses; the transitional phenomena crumbles, as does the ability to play, to dream, to create or be nourished by creation. Semprún's psychic ability to see the other, his capacity to understand complexity and to come to terms with the painful decrees of fate out of a sense of responsibility and maturity, are lost. Moreover, the feeling that it will be possible to create and repair reality in the future is also impaired. All these capacities are seriously damaged by trauma. Extreme anxieties had penetrated the mental envelope in a destructive way. Fragmentary corporeal feelings and a halt to the capacity to think took their place, thus defending the psychic system from an emotional link to a source of unbearable pain.

Semprún's encounter with the Auschwitz survivor illustrates the impressive tendency of the human mind to search for an 'other' that is able to serve as a helpful object in overcoming distress, however radical it may be. As Semprún listens to the survivor, he describes fragmentation of the psyche and soma, characterized by physical numbness, lungs devoid of air, utter silence, loss of communication with reality and a detachment from a sense of time and place. Nevertheless, his psyche employs his love of literature and through it his inner belief in the internalized good objects that help him time and again to find his way in the dark.[3] Semprún's transference relations towards Malraux's narrator come to life spontaneously because Malraux had dealt with a situation similar enough to the one in which Semprún finds himself.

An additional therapeutic aspect is hidden in this unique self-displacement from the live to the literary testimony: The ability of an author to write testifies to internal strength, creativity and reparatory potential. The reader unconsciously realizes that the writer succeeded in mobilizing fossilized features within him and in transforming the failure to think into creativity. In other words, the literary work attests to the preliminary process that enabled it, i.e. using the transitional phenomena in order to turn personal pain and anxiety into a story. In Sartre's words:

> Certainly I do not deny when I am reading that the author may be impassioned, nor even that he might have conceived the first plan of his work under the sway of passion. But his decision to write supposes that he withdraws somewhat from his feelings, in short, that he has transformed his emotions into free emotions as I do mine while reading him (Sartre, J.P., [1948] 1988, p. 55).

Through identification with the internal strengths possessed by the literary author to create the story, Semprún regains his ability to think, to feel and to reflect. His belief in the human freedom to bestow meaning, or at least to create a new meaning, even in the face of the worst of horrors, is restored. The disintegrated self found a way to begin to reintegrate. We can see that in this act of distancing there is something of a paradox in that the proximity to the testimony of the survivor is so traumatic that it doesn't enable Semprún to be present. Thus, against his will, he in fact finds himself distanced and estranged from both the external and the internal witness who is overpowered by defences of detachment and splitting.

This understanding allows us to see the distancing to the literary in a new light. After the initial distancing via the psychic defence of inner splitting and disintegration, the mind makes an effort to reapproach the situation safely. This approach is enabled via the presence of an additional witness to listen to – the literary character. Thus a chain of testimonies and witnesses is created; the testimony of the survivor from Auschwitz to whom Semprún becomes a disabled witness; the testimony of the literary character whose ability to reflect and give words and symbolic meaning endows it with a therapeutic quality; Semprún's literary testimony; and the internal witnessing of Semprún's reader, revived through the distancing paradox.

Notes

1 'The distancing paradox' is linked to the concept of 'defamiliarization' coined by Victor Shklovsky in his article 'Art as a Device' (Shklovsky, [1917] 2015). However, whereas 'defamiliarization' emphasizes 'the estrangement of things', the 'distancing paradox' actually creates the contrary: The distant story enables the reader to become more familiarized with parts in his internal world through identification with the literary characters. In other words, the literary text enables the reader to come closer to himself from a safe distance.
2 The Sonderkommando was a small unit of Jews who worked in the crematoria during World War II.
3 On recovering from a traumatic loss by relying on the good internal objects, see Klein, M. (1940).

References

Eigen, M. (1996). *Psychic Deadness*. London and New York: Routledge.
Klein, M. (1940). Mourning and Its Relation to Manic-Depressive States. In: *Love, Guilt and Reparation and Other Works 1921–1945*. London: Vintage, pp. 344–369.
Klein, M. (1948). On the Theory of Anxiety and Guilt. In: *Envy and Gratitude and Other Works 1946–1963*. London: Vintage, pp. 25–42.
Sartre, J. [1948] (1988). *What Is Literature?* Cambridge, MA: Harvard University Press.
Semprún, J. (1994). *Literature or Life*. London and New York: Penguin Books.
Shklovsky, V. [1917] (2015). Art as Device. *Poetics Today: International Journal of Theory and Analysis of Literature and Communication*, 36(3), pp. 151–174.
Winnicott, D.W. (1953). Transitional Objects and Transitional Phenomena: A Study of the First Not-Me Possession. *International Journal of Psychoanalysis*, 34, pp. 89–97.
Woolf, V. (1925). *The Common Reader*. New York: Harcourt.

Further reading

Amir, D. (2018). *Bearing Witness to the Witness: A Psychoanalytic Perspective on Four Modes of Traumatic Testimony*. London and New York: Routledge.

Chapter 2

The bestowal of meaning

At the beginning of his book *The Human Voyage to Meaning, A Philosophical-Hermeneutical Study of Literary Works* (2009) Avi Sagi notes that:

> Human existence confronts every person with numerous complex issues arising in the course of his life. The most difficult of these revolves around an individual's attempt to understand his place in the world and the meaning of his life. At the root of these questions is an existential distress whose origin is ontological. Man is not only an 'entity' existing in the world but rather as Heidegger phrased it he is an entity whose existence is his interest; a 'being' inquiring about his existence (Sagi, A., 2009, p. 9).

The examples from Semprún's *Literature or Life* present a literary example of the coping of a subject who has reached the very edge of human capacity. Semprún's recurrent turn to the books he has read sheds light on one of the roles of reading as a therapeutic means, helping to repair the reader's fundamental ability to establish meaning.

Aharon Appelfeld was one of Israel's foremost novelists who devoted his life after World War II to writing about his memories and impressions rooted in his experiences during and following the Holocaust. In his book *Essays in the First Person* he wrote that 'every forced suffering is devoid of meaning' (Appelfeld, A., 1979, p. 88). All the more so when the suffering is bound up with a deliberate effort to erase the meaning of what is human in a person:

> What was revealed to the Jew in those years surpassed the scope of his reason and the scope of his soul. He was, in fact, the casualty of the atrocity and having escaped it, all he wished for was to regard it as a horror, a rift in life which must be mended quickly, an atrocity that cannot serve but as a byword for mockery. As the survivor tells his story, revealing, he is at the same time concealing. For it is, after all, impossible not to tell, but no less impossible to live in this void. This

revelation and concealment continues to this very day and is the creator of the almost unbridgeable divide between an apocalyptical world and the world of the living (ibid., p. 19).

In his book *Literature or Life* Semprún's attentiveness to the survivor's description of the gas chambers being cleared transcends the human capacity to understand. The Jewish survivor, as well as Semprún the political prisoner, were the 'casualties' of the atrocity in the face of which all grasp of meaning collapsed. Winnicott termed this kind of inner terror as 'unthinkable anxieties' – fears the mind does not permit itself to dwell upon, think about or understand (Winnicott, D.W., 1974).

In a later segment of his book Semprún uses words to describe the essential features of situations in which meaning collapses, situations that do not allow for transcendence beyond the facts towards the 'essence' of the subject.

> The essential part? I think I know, yes. I think I'm beginning to understand. The essential thing is to go beyond the clear facts of this horror to get at the root of radical evil, das radikal Bose ... Besides, the essential thing about this experience of Evil is that it will turn out to have been lived as the experience of death ... And I do not mean 'experience' ... Because death is not something that we brushed up against, came close to, only just escaped, as though it were an accident we survived unscathed. We lived it ... We are not survivors, but ghosts, revenants ... One can only express this abstractly, of course ... Because it's not believable, it can't be shared, it's barely comprehensible – since death is, for rational thought, the only event that we can never experience individually ... That cannot be grasped except in the form of anguish, of foreboding or fatal longing (Semprún, J., 1994, pp. 87–89).

Semprún experienced the 'unbelievable death', and all that is unimaginable about it and is searching for a literary character for transference, somewhat like the search by a patient for an analyst. He turns to Malraux and his book 'to ask him' how he had coped with death and what kind of meaning he had succeeded in establishing in the wake of his encounter with the gas chambers and the hellish inferno. This is how Semprún the reader revives meaning in the face of the trauma that threatens to destroy every remnant of meaning.

Four prominent aspects of the establishment of meaning

Four prominent aspects of the establishment of meaning are to be found in the reading experience: a view of the world through the eyes of the literary character; the reparation of the capacity to symbolize; active reading; and twinship as a transformational interpretation. The reader withdraws to the literary space, repairs his thinking processes and reorientates himself in both the real world and his inner world. He establishes new meanings in his existence and re-establishes himself as a sentient, thinking, reflective subject.

1. A view of the world through the eyes of the literary character

At times due to curiosity and the desire to know the world as a natural part of the life drive, and on other occasions due to a loss of direction, the reader turns to literature not only in order to find an explanation for his situation but also to 'hear truths' about the world from literary characters. As Sartre writes in his book *The Words* (Sartre, J.P., [1964] 1981): 'It was in books that I encountered the universe: assimilated, classified, labelled, pondered, still formidable' (Sartre, J.P., [1964] 1981, p. 51).

As Lubin writes,

> a text is not merely a narrow opening to see through. It is fitted with a filtering prism which magnifies and minimizes, signifies the important and unimportant, indicates the vital and the true: a prism which deciphers the multitude of objects on the other side of the opening and lends them meaning, turns them into a 'world'. Thus the act of reading is analogous to that glimpse beyond the narrow opening, a glimpse which reveals to the inquiring eye the world as well as the meaning of that world (Lubin, O., 2003, p. 97).

Semprún's description of Malraux's novel as 'a meditation on death, and consequently a series of reflections' makes it clear that the establishment of meaning does not come about as a result of a view of the world from afar, but rather as a consequence of a view that internalizes the world into the thinking subject. Such a view integrates reality with the inner world, an integration that includes facts and experience. But this process is far from being simple. It involves a mental struggle. Semprún as a writer has reservations and doubts about the power of his words to serve as an aid in explaining the meaning of the world and in shedding light on events within it. He wishes for but also doubts the possibility of conveying the meaning of what was experienced in the concentration camp – an experience that even those who were there found virtually impossible to grasp. He struggles with the question of whether, through his book, he can create symbols that will convey meaning in relation to situations that the human mind cannot decipher. His dual attitude of hope and doubt towards the power of words to convey deep meaning is evident in the following lines:

> In short, you can always say everything. The 'ineffable' you hear so much about is only an alibi. Or a sign of laziness. You can always say everything: language contains everything. You can speak of the most desperate love, the most terrible cruelty. You can speak of evil, its

poisonous pleasures, its poppy flavour. You can speak of God, and that's saying a lot. You can speak of the rose, the dewdrop, the span of a morning. You can speak of tenderness, and the infinite succour of goodness. You can speak of the future, where poets venture with closed eyes and wagging tongues ... But can people hear everything, imagine everything? (Semprún, J., 1994, pp. 13–14).

I shall now try to clarify the psychological process of turning words into meaning.

2. Reparation of the capacity for symbol formation

Reparation of the capacity for symbol formation is imperative for the establishment of meaning. Conscious human thought differs from unconscious thought (which Freud termed 'thing presentation') in that it uses linguistic signs (termed by Freud 'word representation') (Freud, S., 1915, p. 201). The capacity to symbolize is the ability to think about the external and internal world through language. Language can function as a system of 'live' signs that lends meaning to the encounter between the inner world and reality. However, it can also serve as a fossilized system of 'dead' signs that 'points to' but does not create a true 'connection to' its signified. In such a case the sign functions without its symbolic quality. As described by the psychoanalyst Dana Amir, a living language has the capacity 'of transcending itself as well as observing itself, one that enacts truth rather than just describing it' (Amir, D., 2014, p. 3). In contrast, the words of a dead language do not transfer and communicate genuine experience.

According to Klein (1930) and Segal (1950, 1957), the process of symbol formation is linked to the transition from the paranoid-schizoid position to the depressive position.[1] The latter recognizes loss and deprivation and frees the subject from the need to omnipotently control both life and death. This process also requires recognition that we designate by name something over which we have no direct control. Naming it is our compromise. As noted by Amir, 'Letting things be is in effect letting ourselves mourn over them and part from them' (Amir, D., 2014, p. 25).

The psychoanalyst Hanna Segal in working on the link between thinking and art further developed the idea of symbolization and found that the need for symbolic expression was at the heart of all artistic creativity: 'Art is essentially a search for a symbolic expression' (Segal, H., 1991, p. 87). Segal shows how the movement of the psyche towards the depressive position unravels the severe repression or the collapse of the capacity for symbol formation, thus rescuing awareness from the limitation and paucity imposed by acute anxiety. Segal points to the essential paradox latent in artistic work that functions to protect what already exists, while at the same time giving birth to a new world. Precisely for this reason the reader can turn to literature in safety with the feeling that he can momentarily rest from his conflicted inner world as he sets out to travel and explore a new world whose heroes are strangers to him. However, in effect, reading's power stems from the same paradox in which 'the new' in the reading experience is bound up with the 'old' in the reader's life and the fictitious echoes of his reality. The process of symbol formation enables the reader to begin to re-examine the old and move between the spaces of the imaginary world, his inner world and the real world, as in a room of mirrors where the various reflected images become the source of new meanings.

Thus the symbol conveys what already exists yet at the same time also creates from it something new that casts a light on the old so that the two are no longer one and the same. It is in the gap created between them that the reader is able to reflect on his own life.

In a traumatic situation the symbol fragments into its component parts. The traumatic situation violates the inter-dialectic structure between the two triangles from which the symbol is formed (anxiety, sadism and thought; anxiety, self and object) (Durban, J. and Roth, M., 2013, p. 87). It is the inter-dialectic structure that enables a language to function as endowed with meaning and facilitates the establishment of new meaning. If the structure fragments we shall find that either a 'symbolic equation' is created, in which the signifier and the signified are not separated from each other in terms of quality or meaning; or, alternatively, that meaning has been voided, so that the word functions as a meaningless phonetic unit.

The terrifying human moment when Semprún the survivor sits and listens to the testimony of the Polish Jewish survivor from Auschwitz involves the collapse of the distinction between the symbolizer and the symbolized. This is an instinctive defensive act of the mind, collapsing the ability to think in the same way as a deliberate interruption in the supply of electricity acts as a protection against electrocution. 'The story' transcends the ontological uncertainty and contingency of human existence that we constantly confront. Instead of arousing thought it appears to the tortured psyche as a single prosaic, hazy and dangerous object. As noted by the psychoanalyst Wilfred Bion, 'What should be a thought ... becomes a bad object, indistinguishable from a thing-in-itself, fit only for evacuation' (Bion, W.R., 1962a, p. 307). Failure to think resembles a defence against unbearable anxiety and debilitating pain, whereas the collapse of the ability to think means the breakdown of the individual as a thinking, observing 'being'.

The researcher of trauma Werner Bohleber has written that trauma bursts through a protective shell. It is indelibly imprinted on the body and has a direct impact on the organic foundation of psychic functioning. The unique nature of the trauma lies in experience because the psychic space has been breached and the capacity of symbolization has been destroyed. Bohleber argues that the traumatic experience is in essence a case of 'too much' (Bohleber, W., 2007, pp. 329–352). Klein has pointed out that an encounter with either extreme sadism, be it from within or without, the inability to tolerate anxiety and exaggerated identification with an attacked object all lead to the blocking of curiosity, a retreat from reality and a halt to the capacity for symbol formation. According to Kline, in order to revive the system from its paralysis, the anxiety has to be worked through by searching for an access to the unconscious that will reactivate the instinct to be inquisitive (epistemophilia) and the capacity to symbolize (Klein, M., 1930). But the willingness to learn about the world also opens up the possibility of defending oneself against a real connection to meaning.

Wilfred Bion (1962b), distinguished between two forms of learning that differ in their contribution to psychic coping: 'learning about the world' as opposed to 'learning from experience'. In learning about the world the learner is facing the world from the outside. This is likely to serve the interests of practical or scientific learning but it could also be defensive learning, which is designed to avoid a connection with knowledge in its psychic sense. Contrastingly, 'learning from experience' internalizes what has been learned and integrates the 'data' with the psyche and soma and thus enables psychological development.

In Bion's terms, Semprún's traumatic experience was an attack on his capacity for mental linking (Bion, W., 1959, pp. 308–315). Because he had been unable to continue to 'learn about the world' and become 'curious' about the survivor's experience in the given reality, Semprún withdrew into reading experiences he had internalized as a way of recovering spontaneously. In another segment of his book he also tries to explain the different ways inmates of the concentration camps were able to survive psychically by quoting from a radio interview conducted by the writer Philip Roth with yet another survivor and witness, Primo Levi:

'As far as survival is concerned,' Primo Levi once said during an interview with Philip Roth, 'I often wonder about it, and many people have asked me that question. I maintain that there was no general rule, except perhaps arriving at the camp in good health and speaking German. I saw cunning people and idiots survive, brave souls and cowards, "thinkers" and madmen' (Semprún, J., 1994, p. 300).

Semprún expands on Levi's thoughts by saying the following about himself:

To these objective elements, I would add – as Primo Levi also does, in his remarkable interview with Roth – a subjective factor: curiosity. It helps you to hang on in a way that is impossible to evaluate, of course, but is surely decisive' (ibid.).

Semprún points to the presence of curiosity in Primo Levi's story as well, when he said this about his experience in the camp thus:

I never stopped observing the world and the people around me so intensely that these images still remain clear in my mind, I felt a deep desire to understand, I was constantly filled with a curiosity that someone later described, in fact, as nothing less than cynical (ibid., pp. 300–301).

And Semprún concludes: 'To be healthy, curious about the world, and know German. The rest is down to luck' (ibid.).

Clearly Semprún is discussing 'curiosity' in its most profound sense – the desire to be alert, to be present, an attentive witness to everything happening both internally and externally. A curious individual investigates the world, endows it with a dictionary of terms (linguistic symbols), narrative contexts (consciously or through unconscious phantasies) and lends it meaning. Intuitively, Semprún identifies the crucial importance of curiosity to psychic as well as to physical survival. As survivors, Semprún and Primo Levi use their curiosity in differing ways and as a result are possibly assisted by it differently. Conceivably, Primo Levi's descriptions of survival, as understood by Semprún, and his sense of curiosity in the camp, were an attempt to learn about the world from the perspective of a participant. Primo Levi poured himself into learning about the world of atrocity. Semprún, on the other hand, provides the reader with a description of his desperate attempt to integrate his curiosity vis-à-vis external and internal reality – his understanding of the external atrocity, with an understanding of the human mind including his own subjective state of mind.

These descriptions shed light on Semprún crediting his reading of Malraux with the reparation of his capacity for symbol formation. Semprún's ability to think about the horror through the insights borrowed from Malraux restored his ability to rethink matters in terms of their psychic meaning. This involved the activation of unconscious phantasies, internal and historical links, as well as the personal and the collective meaning. It is only then that he regains his status as a subject possessing inner space and the capacity for reflection and existential independence. According to the psychoanalyst Thomas Ogden:

> The establishment of the distinction between the symbol and the symbolized is inseparable from the establishment of subjectivity ... To distinguish symbol from symbolized is to distinguish one's thought from that which one is thinking about one's feeling from that which one is responding to ... The achievement of the capacity to distinguish symbol and symbolized is the achievement of subjectivity. From this point on, symbolic function always involves the threeness of the interrelationship of three distinct entities: (1) the symbol (the thought); (2) the symbolized (that which is being thought about); and (3) the thinker (the interpreting self), who is creating his thoughts and who stands

apart from both the thought and the thing being thought about (Ogden, T., 1986, p. 229).

When Semprún 'the thinker' felt that he was 'lost', he had the literary transference object, Malraux, to turn to remind him of his subjectivity, his thinking and symbolizing capacities, even when facing the far edge of existence.

Repairing the capacity for symbol formation in Eva Hoffman's *Lost in Translation*

Eva Hoffman's book *Lost in Translation* (1989) is an illuminating example of an additional aspect of the way literature helps in repairing the capacity for symbol formation by the transference relations of the reader *towards the language itself*.

Hoffman's autobiographical novel revolves around a crisis of migration. The book is an account of her own emigration from Poland, the country of her birth, to Canada and then to the United States. No less importantly, it describes the passage from Polish, her mother tongue, to English. Hoffman describes the relations between the individual and language through her own particular experience of acquiring a new language at an age when she was already self-aware and could explore and reflect upon the process of language acquisition. This significantly differs from the experience of an infant who acquires a language in tandem with his developing awareness. Hoffman depicts the path to language acquisition as if moving across an entire range of experiences, representing the gradual development of the capacity for symbol formation. Its progression begins at the lowest level as an empty or dead symbol – words that do not represent but rather function as some kind of phonetic gibberish or just slightly more than that. At the next level the symbol does not acquire subjective emotional reference but nonetheless communicates meaning. Once it reaches the middle of the range the symbol becomes meaningful and can serve as a medium of communication and of a pragmatic understanding of the world. Finally, at the top of the range, the symbol becomes enriched by experience, emotion and meaning, enabling the subject to transcend the familiar in language as well as in awareness.

3. Transference towards the language as object

At times a literary text serves as 'an additional other' towards whom transference relations are developed.[2] In Hoffman's descriptions it is evident that the integration between the linguistic symbol and the body, psyche and awareness of the symbol's user, is a gradual process. Particularly noticeable is the link between the sensory-somatic dimension of the language experience and the capacity to 'dream' in that language (Ogden, T., 2003). In other words, to experience the language in a vivid and playful way, open to all kinds of possibilities rather than being inescapably trapped in its functional role. For example, at one point Hoffman writes about her reading experience as if it were an infantile and passionate transferential eruption towards the words she was reading.

> I've become obsessed with words. I gather them, put them away like a squirrel saving nuts for winter, swallow them and hunger for more. If I take in enough, then maybe I can incorporate the language, make it part of my psyche and my body (Hoffman, E., 1989, p. 216).

Elsewhere, Hoffman describes the way in which English words appear in her dreams where the transference relations towards the words expresses identification with them. In her dreams English words seem to be going through a process of reorganization in a new form, just as she, an exile in a foreign land, had been required to discard one form and assume a new one: 'I've had English words in my dreams for a long time. But now they break up, de-form, and re-form as if they were bits of chromosomal substance trying to rearrange itself' (ibid., p. 243). This description influences her reading experience in English, which is now also accompanied by a sensual and playful quality of transference relations towards the words themselves: 'When I study the poetry of Dryden, I have a dream about a town called "Dry Den," which, of course, suffers from a shortage of water. Sometimes, my unconscious does me proud by coming up with bilingual puns' (ibid.). In her account of the gradual process of acquiring the English language, Hoffman shows how the language becomes a 'live' medium of meaning vis-á-vis both herself and her world:

> Perhaps I've read written, eaten enough words so that English now flows in my bloodstream. But once this mutation takes place, once the language starts speaking itself to me from my cells, I stop being so stuck on it. Words are no longer spiky bits of hard matter, which refer only to themselves. They become, more and more, a transparent medium in which I live and which lives in me – a medium through which I can once again get to myself and to the world (ibid.).

In one of the most moving moments in her book Hoffman's descriptive skills distil in a remarkable way the transformation that occurs in the midst of the reading experience during which the symbol expands to its full capacity and meaning. This transformation occurs while Hoffman reads a poem by T.S. Eliot:

> But it's not until many years later, not until I've finished graduate school successfully, and have begun to teach literature to others, that I crack the last barrier between myself and the language – the barrier

The bestowal of meaning 49

> I sensed but couldn't get through, as I read 'Among School Children'. It happens as I read 'The Love Song of J. Alfred Prufrock', which I'm to explicate to a class of freshmen at the University of New Hampshire the next morning. 'Let us go then, you and I,' I read, 'When the evening is spread out against the sky/Like a patient etherised upon a table;/ Let us go, through certain half-deserted streets,/The muttering retreats ...' My eye moves over these lines in its accustomed dry silence; and then – as if an aural door had opened of its own accord – I hear their modulations and their quiet undertones. Over the years, I've read so many explications of these stanzas that I can analyze them in half a dozen ingenious ways. But now, suddenly I'm attuned, through some mysterious faculty of the mental ear, to their inner sense; I hear the understated melancholy of that refrain, the civilized restraint of the rhythms reining back the more hilly swells of emotion, the self-reflective, moody resignation of the melody. 'And I have known the eyes already, known them all – The eyes that fix you in a formulated phrase ...' I read, tasting the sounds on the tongue, hearing the phrases somewhere between tongue and mind. Bingo, I think, this is it, the extra, the attribute of language over and above function and criticism. I'm back within the music of the language, and Eliot's words descend on me with a sort of grace. Words become, as they were in childhood, beautiful things – except this is better, because they're now crosshatched with a complexity of meaning, with the sonorities of felt, sensuous thought (ibid., pp. 185–186).

In Hoffman's illustration one can easily detect the transition from the usage of the language's symbols for the purposes of 'function and criticism' as she puts it, towards the additional transcendent dimension that she terms 'the music of the language', apparently also inspired by her musical talent, a gift she had to neglect in the course of her migration. Eliot's words 'descend on me with a sort of grace' Hoffman notes, suggesting a drop from the heavens above, thus linking language to the transcendent and the sublime, enabling her to breach the boundaries of common usage towards and beyond the limits of being. The ear hearing all of this is not the physical, practical ear, but rather the 'mental ear', an inner rather than a pragmatic facility. It is apparent from Hoffman's narrative that the new dimension of the linguistic symbols is not entirely novel but rather an addition to the already familiar. This is in line with the view that the linguistic symbol acquired in early childhood is forever the bearer of primary object relations, so that exile from the language was, in Hoffman's experience, accompanied by a sort of exile from childhood. It was only in the moment of reading Eliot's poem that Hoffman experienced the powerful, and at the same time ever so gentle, transformation that had occurred. The moment at which the words assume their full meaning, and 'words become, as they were in childhood, beautiful things – except this is better'. Better because the early days and symbols of childhood are enriched by those that follow.

4. Active reading

The reading experience stimulates an individual to regain his ability to interpret and bestow meaning to his life in an active way. This offers him the opportunity of emerging from his slumber as a passive or helpless spectator of his own existence. To be a person who establishes meaning in his life is one of the psyche's most vital and imperative qualities, in the absence of which the individual lives as a 'false self'. Extreme situations are liable to temporarily block a person's ability to establish meaning in a vital and active way. At times it is only within the framework of the reading experience – in the playful intermediary space of the text – that the reader will dare to attempt once more to set it in motion.

In his book *What Is Literature?* Sartre illustrates the idea of active reading of a book by likening it to having been recreated by the reader and the instilment of meaning through the act of his reading: 'The operation of writing implies that of reading as its dialectical correlative' (Sartre, J.P., [1948] 1988, p. 43). Virginia Woolf has also argued that a 'good' reading experience involves the reader to such an extent that he becomes the writer. She writes: 'Do not dictate to your author; try to become him, be his fellow-worker and accomplice. If you hang back, and reserve and criticise at first, you are preventing yourself from getting the fullest possible value from what you read' (Woolf, V., 1925, loc. 23).

The early approach to literary criticism viewed the text as a unit in and of itself while the reader was seen as merely discovering its structure and components. It was not before the second half of the twentieth century that the reader was seen as the powerhouse of the creative work. His activity was now being viewed as lending life and meaning to the text and so were considered to have created the work anew. In Sartre's words:

> The reader must invent them all in a continual exceeding of the written thing. To be sure, the author guides him, but all he does is guide him. The landmarks he sets up are separated by the void. The reader must unite them; he must go beyond them. In short, reading is directed creation (Sartre, J.P., [1948] 1988, p. 45).

The researcher Orly Lubin explains that the reader's 'writing' results from the fact that reading is accompanied by questions readers ask about themselves: 'Every text prompts its reader to question themselves; and every answer falls within the realm of subject formation. In effect, the reader is engaged in personal writing ... so that this activity also includes the option for change' (Lubin, O., 2003, p. 69). The process of bestowing meaning is reciprocal and bidirectional. Viewing the reader as an active partner in establishing meaning also alters the locus of the meaning itself from the core of the written creation to other possible locations – in the middle ground between the written and the reader or in the consciousness of the reader himself. In the context of his transference relations towards the literary characters the reader finds meaning for his life and actively lends meaning to both the text and its hero.

The literary 'transference twin'

Reading literature often leads the reader to an encounter with 'twin heroes' who formulate for him what needs to be contained, worked through and articulated. The reader is searching for meaning, an aspiration that Victor Frankel described as the primary, most profound human motivation and driving force (Frankl, V., [1946] 2006). Situations arise in the course of reading in which a process worked through by the reader's literary twin promotes the resolution of internal uncertainty and anxiety. As we shall see, this experience of twinship, of the mirror image, enables the reader to use his literary twin as an interpreter of his inner world.

A LITERARY TWIN IN EVA HOFFMAN'S *LOST IN TRANSLATION*

Hoffman's experience as an émigré from her country and language is for the most part dominated by a feeling of loneliness. She discovers an echo of that experience in her reading of Peter Schneider's novel *The Wall Jumper* (1983) and in particular in the story of its heroine Lena: 'In Schneider's novel the West German narrator has an East German girlfriend named Lena. Lena has chosen to live on the Western side of the Berlin Wall, but she's severe about what she sees there' (Hoffman, E., 1989, p. 204).

The lonely Hoffman develops strong transference relations towards Lena, her 'transference twin'.[3] Hoffman identifies with the character of the 'foreigner' and her outsider attitude. From this position Lena is able to hone her thoughts about the place and society in which she finds herself, at times deploring its decadence, frivolity and vapid pleasures. Hoffman views Lena as being overly emotional and this is also the reason why the heroine distances her beloved from her: 'I know what I'm supposed to think of Lena, but I identify with her. I think she's in the right. I want more severe standards of seriousness to obtain. In other words, I'm a scourge' (ibid.).

The power of a 'transference twin' in literature stems from a combination of powerful feelings of identification and the distancing paradox; that thinly veiled distance that enables the reader to be enriched by her literary twin. It is kind of 'non-identical twin' resembling a good interpretation in therapy echoing the patient's inner world but at the same time adding a further layer of some sort in terms of content or in the way in which matters are worked through. Wilfred Bion termed the unconscious raw material 'beta elements', which need to be mentally digested and mentalized (in infancy by the mother and in therapy by the analyst) in order to become 'alpha elements' (Bion, W., 1962b). When, in the course of analysis, unconscious 'beta elements' are processed into symbolic 'alpha elements' by the analyst and returned to the patient in their contained and processed form, they remain based on the patient's psychic material and yet at the same time they are transformed into a new and different piece of psychic information.

Throughout Hoffman's book the confusion between the two women is evident. Lena, the literary character, talks in Berlin, and Hoffman, the reader, becomes the prophetess of rage in Boston. Hoffman projects her inner world on to Lena. Through her transference twin's conduct she has come to understand her own views. Thus Hoffman's reading was sufficiently mobilizing to turn it into an active reading and Hoffman the reader completes the picture of the psychic motivations of Lena the character. She alternately refers to the unconscious motives for Lena's and her own stormy behaviour, thus psychologically learning about herself. This is the interpretive power of reading in its purest form. The interpretation is not provided by the 'text alone' but rather is formed by relations woven between the reader and the characters, including the surfacing and working through of unconscious motives.

> I think I also know the cause of Lena's defensiveness and seeming arrogance: it's that her version of things is automatically under suspicion and at a discount. That's the real subtext of my fights ... My sense of reality, powerful and vulnerable, is in danger of coming under native domination (Hoffman, E., 1989, p. 204).

Here too there is the same transition of overlapping shadows out of a feeling of identification with her transference twin expressed in moving from third to first person. Which one of them was in danger? Whose freedom was under threat? Whose unconscious is Hoffman writing about? Undoubtedly the supposed syntactical and linguistic confusion testifies to a temporary confusion of identity between reader and character. The linguistic confusion, the tracking of Lena's actions and attitudes, and the activation of an inner interpretive process as to the literary character's psychic motivations, provides Hoffman with a 'literary interpretation' of her own psychic state. Like the title of the book she had been reading, she becomes a 'wall jumper' – hurdling over the barriers of place and language, fiction and reality. The similarity and difference between the reader and her heroine are a basis for reflection and mobilize a process of transforming the experience of the reader. In viewing her surroundings the reader is condescending and combative. The encounter with her literary twin makes her realize that such views are nothing other than defensive mechanisms against her vulnerability and fear of 'native domination'. From Hoffman's description it is apparent that a space is also created that is intended to avoid total identification with the heroine's stance – and therefore her own – as being aloof and quarrelsome. Lena, her non-identical twin, enabled her to transcend for a time toward the 'third subject' as Thomas Ogden has termed it in the psychoanalytic context (Ogden, T., 2004). Here we see how the third subject is also created through the encounter between the reader and her twin in the literary text. This transcendence facilitates a new interpretation of the situation, of her experience and behaviour, and leads to a psychic transformation that has the power, in the wake of her reading, to lead to a real transformation in her construction as subject and her relations with her surroundings.

Finally it is important to point out again that the four processes cited above are linked to the establishment of meaning in the context of transference relations in reading: viewing the world through the eyes of the literary character; reparation of the capacity to symbolize; active reading; and transference twins as a transformative interpretation. These processes do not all occur separately but rather are intertwined with one another in a continuum of mutual movement and sustenance. The literary examples show that when the reader delves deeply into the textual space he gains an opportunity to get in touch with his anxieties and psychic pains, repair his thinking processes, renew his orientation in the real world, and establish new meanings in his existence, thus re-establishing himself as a sensitive, thoughtful and observing subject.

Notes

1 The terms 'paranoid-schizoid position' and 'depressive position' are confusing because of their pathological connotation; one can think of the first as tending to refuse reality, leading to primitive defences and disturbances in reality testing, while the second promotes perceiving, integrating and accepting reality to be what it is. Klein is describing to and fro movements between these two psychic developmental positions throughout life. The paranoid-schizoid position is characterized by annihilation anxiety and is accompanied by the tyranny of primitive defence mechanisms that seek to falsely control reality. The depressive position is characterized by anxiety of losing the loved object. This position, if not defended against by manic defences, enables the development of a mature understanding of the complexity of existence via working through and mourning. Thus this position offers an opportunity for reparation as well as existence that is more honest, responsible, compassionate and creative.
2 For more on 'transference to the text' see Zoran, R., (2000), pp. 35–118.
3 For more on 'transference twins' in reading see Zoran, R., (2000), p. 90.

Bibliography

Amir, D. (2014). *Cleft Tongue: The Language of Psychic Structures.* London: Karnac Books.
Applefeld, A. (1979). *Essays in the First Person.* Jerusalem: Bialik Publishing.

Bion, W.R. (1959). Attacks on Linking. *International Journal of Psychoanalysis*, 40, pp. 308–315.
Bion, W.R. (1962a). The Psycho-Analytic Study of Thinking. *International Journal of Psychoanalysis*, 43, pp. 306–310.
Bion, W.R. (1962b). *Learning from Experience*. London: Tavistock.
Bohleber, W. (2007). Remembrance, Trauma and Collective Memory: The Battle for Memory in Psychoanalysis. *International Journal of Psychoanalysis*, 88, pp. 329–352.
Durban, J. and Roth, M. (Eds). (2013). *Melanie Klein: Essential Papers*. Tel Aviv: Bookworm.
Frankl, V. [1946] (2006). *Man's Search for Meaning*. Cambridge, MA: Beacon Press.
Freud, S. (1915). The Unconscious. In: J. Strachey (Ed.) *The Standard Edition of the Complete Psychological Works of Sigmund Freud, Vol. XIV*. London: Hogarth Press, pp. 159–215.
Hoffman, E. (1989). *Lost in Translation*. New York: Penguin Books.
Klein, M. (1930). The Importance of Symbol Formation in the Development of the Ego. In: *Love, Guilt and Reparation and Other Works 1921–1945*. London: Vintage, pp. 219–232.
Lubin, O. (2003). *A Woman Reading A Woman*. Haifa: Haifa University Press.
Ogden, T. (1986). *The Matrix of the Mind: Object Relations and the Psychoanalytic Dialogue*. London: Karnac.
Ogden, T. (2003). On Not Being Able to Dream. *International Journal of Psychoanalysis*, 84(1), pp. 17–30.
Ogden, T. (2004). The Analytic Third: Implications for Psychoanalytic Theory and Technique. *Psychoanalytical Quarterly*, 73(1), pp. 167–195.
Sagi, A. (2009). *The Human Voyage to Meaning: A Philosophical-Hermeneutical Study of Literary Works*. Ramat Gan: Bar Ilan University Press.
Sartre, J. [1948] (1988). *What Is Literature?* Cambridge, MA: Harvard University Press.
Sartre, J. [1964] (1981). *The Words*. New York: Vintage Books.
Schneider, P. (1983). *The Wall Jumper*. Chicago, IL: University of Chicago Press.
Segal, H. (1950). Some Aspects of the Analysis of a Schizophrenic. *International Journal of Psychoanalysis*, 31, pp. 268–278.
Segal, H. (1957). Notes on Symbol Formation. *International Journal of Psychoanalysis*, 38, pp. 391–397.
Segal, H. (1991). *Dream Phantasy and Art*. Hove, UK and New York: Routledge.
Semprún, J. (1994). *Literature or Life*. London and New York: Penguin Books.
Winnicott, D.W. (1974). Fear of Breakdown. *International Review of Psychoanalysis*, 1, pp. 103–107.
Woolf, V. (1925). *The Common Reader*. New York: Harcourt [Kindle edition].
Zoran, R. (2000). *The Third Voice: The Therapeutic Qualities of Literature and Their Applications in Bibliotherapy*. Jerusalem: Carmel.

Further reading

Amir, D. (2012). The Inner Witness. *International Journal of Psychoanalysis*, 93, pp. 879–896.

Chapter 3

Seven types of identification

One of the psychic mechanisms most active while reading is that of identification. Psychoanalytic literature describes various ways in which the individual identifies with the other. Literary characters are likely to arouse various types of identification in the reader. In the literary works that I have explored, I found seven central types of identification triggered by reading. In this chapter I shall describe them and explain the significance of using all these types of identification when considering the reader's experience and development.

The involvement of the mechanism of identification in the reading of literature can be intuitively assumed with relative ease. Different reading experiences are characterized by differing kinds and levels of identification ranging from 'normal' to 'pathological'. As will be shown, a single reading can combine various types of identification that serve the reader's diverse psychic objectives. The movement between differing types of identification has a decisive role in the psychic working through that occurs while reading.

The quotation below from Sartre's *The Words* exemplifies movement between varying types of identification that take place in the course of a single reading. At first the narrator experiences a breakdown of boundaries and an extreme outpouring of emotion stemming from the split between a Garden of Eden like 'goodness' and pure evil, between wonderment and terror and between life and beauty as against death and danger. This loss of boundaries involves 'projective identification' that, from a psychoanalytic perspective, combines mechanisms of splitting and projection, characterizing the paranoid-schizoid position. As the reading continues, Sartre withdraws from the intensity of this identification and attains a different position that affords him an overarching reflective position and an ironic view of life as well as a sense of calming orderliness and of being at a safe distance from anxiety. These are the experiences encountered by Sartre in the orderly and playful 'sterile' terms of literature.

> I adored the works in the Hetzel series … I owe to those magic boxes … my first encounters with Beauty. When I opened them,

I forgot about everything. Was that reading? No, but it was death by ecstasy. From my annihilation there immediately sprang up natives armed with spears, the bush, an explorer with a white helmet. I was vision, I poured forth light on the beautiful dark cheeks of Aouda, on Phineas Fogg's sideburns. Freed from himself at last, the little wonder became pure wonderment ... Twenty inches from the floor, an unfettered, a perfect happiness was born. The New World seemed at first more disturbing than the Old; there were murder and pillage; blood flowed in torrents ... It was pure Evil ... Everything would be set to rights in the next chapter. Brave Whites would come and slaughter the savages ... Only the wicked died ... Moreover, death itself was asepticized. One fell to the ground, arms outstretched, with a little round hole under the left breast ... I would imagine that straight white flash, the blade; it sank into the body as into butter and came out at the back; the villain would collapse without losing a drop of blood ... How funny it was! The two halves of the body began to fall, describing a semi-circle around each stirrup; ... I noted that the return to order was always accompanied by progress; ... From these magazines and books I derived my most deep seated phantasmagoria: optimism (Sartre, J.P., [1964] 1981, pp. 73–74).

In Proust's *In search of Lost Time* (1927), the narrator offers various explanations of the advantages of reading over relations between people. The reader's identification with what is being narrated is more profound than his feelings towards reality or the people in his life and enables him to undergo a wider range of experience and change. Thus, for example, this is what the hero says in the first part of his voyage, comparing his relations to 'real' people and the literary ones:

Next to this central belief, which, while I was reading, would be constantly a motion from my inner self to the outer world, towards the discovery of Truth ... These were the events which took place in the book I was reading. It is true that the people concerned in them were not what Françoise would have called 'real people'. But none of the feelings which the joys or misfortunes of a 'real' person awaken in us can be awakened except through a mental picture of those joys or misfortunes; and the ingenuity of the first novelist lay in his understanding that, as the picture was the one essential element in the complicated structure of our emotions, so that simplification of it which consisted in the suppression, pure and simple, of 'real' people would be a decided improvement. A 'real' person, profoundly as we may sympathise with him, is in a great measure perceptible only through our senses, that is to say, he remains opaque, offers a dead weight which our sensibilities have not the strength to lift. If some misfortune comes to him, it is only in one small section of the complete idea we have of him that we are capable of feeling any emotion ... The novelist's happy discovery was to think of substituting for those opaque sections, impenetrable by the human spirit, their equivalent in immaterial sections, things, that is, which the spirit can assimilate to itself ... since we have made them our own, since it is in ourselves that they are happening, that they are holding in thrall, while we turn over, feverishly, the pages of the book, our quickened breath and staring eyes. And once the novelist has brought us to that state, in which, as in all purely mental states, every emotion is multiplied ten-fold, into which his book comes to disturb us as might a dream, but a dream more lucid, and of a more lasting impression than those which come to us in sleep; why, then, for the space of an hour he sets free within us all the joys and sorrows in the world, a few of which, only, we should have to spend years of our actual life in getting to know, and the keenest, the most intense of which would never have been revealed to us because the slow course of their development stops our perception of them. It is the same in life; the heart changes, and that is our worst misfortune; but we learn of it only from reading or by imagination; for in reality its alteration, like that of certain natural phenomena, is so gradual that, even if we are able to distinguish, successively, each of its different states, we are still spared the actual sensation of change. (Proust, M., 1927, loc. 44381–44393).

In both Proust's and Sartre's descriptions there is a discernible movement between various forms of the reader's identification with the characters, and even the narrator, which involves a search for truth. This effort facilitates a dreamlike approach to the entire array of joyful and calamitous occasions in life and to every emotional and experiential experiment that can lead to change which, in his real life, the reader doesn't dare experience. The narrator distinguishes between these and experiences of identification with a 'real other', which can only be perceived by our limited senses. In real life the other remains for ever different and an outsider. We do not allow him into our midst in such a powerful and experiential way. Thus we learn less about him and so also learn less about ourselves through him. Reading a book, on the other hand, incorporates within what is happening to and in the other, as told in a much deeper and complex manner than that which is perceived through our senses in real life, enabling us to also feel ourselves and the complex processes of change we are undergoing through identifying with the literary character.

In what follows I shall cite a number of excerpts from books that provide clear evidence of the reader's unique types of identification with the characters of literary texts. Seven types of identification involved in the reading experience have been prominently expressed in literary creations:

internalized identification; projective identification; distractive identification; adhesive identification and objectifying identification; intrusive identification; raw identification and chimeric identification. Every type of identification and the movement between them will be henceforth defined from a psychoanalytic perspective and illustrated by the literary excerpts.

I shall begin with presenting a general description of the concept of identification from a psychoanalytic perspective.

Identification: a psychoanalytic perspective

In psychoanalysis 'identification' is described as

> a psychological process whereby the subject assimilates an aspect, property or attribute of the other and is transformed, wholly or partially, after the model the other provides. It is by means of a series of identifications that the personality is constituted and specified' (Laplanche, J. and Pontalis, J.B., 1973, loc. 5518–5520).

Freud noted that an individual uses the mechanism of identification when he finds it difficult to part from the object and thus introjects him as part of his 'ego' by identifying with him (Freud, S., 1917). In his subsequent writing Freud showed how identification helped in resolving the Oedipus complex through identification with the father/mother – an identification that leads to the development of the superego. This process is quite similar to the process of internalizing the codes of dos and don'ts gained from parents and turned into internal object representations that serve as an internal compass and conscience. The process of transference is closely connected to the processes of identification. As the psychoanalyst Betty Josephs has noted,

> Freud's ideas developed from seeing transference as an obstacle, to seeing it as an essential tool of the analytic process, observing how the patient's relationships to their original objects were transferred, with all their richness, to the person of the analyst. Strachey (1934), using Melanie Klein's discoveries on the way in which projection and introjection color and build up the individual's inner objects, showed that what is being transferred is not primarily the external objects of the child's past, but the internal objects, and that the way that these objects are constructed help us to understand how the analytic process can produce change.
>
> Melanie Klein, through her continued work on early object relationships and early mental mechanisms, perhaps particularly projective identification, extended our understanding of the nature of transference and the process of transferring. In her (1952) paper 'The Origins of Transference'

she wrote: 'It is my experience that in unravelling the details of the transference it is essential to think in terms of total situations transferred from the past into the present as well as emotion defenses and object relations' (Joseph, B., 1985, p. 447).

Let us now turn to explore the seven types of identification that come to life while we read literature.

1. Internalized identification

'Internalized identification' is the type of identification involved in internalizing the object or a part of its features. This means that the object or its characteristics become part of the representations of the self.

Internalized identification with the 'good object' was seen by Melanie Klein as the key imperative for mental health. The reading experience resembles the portrayal of an individual who internalizes a good object. Unconsciously, the reader attempts to use the internalizing identification with the literary characters in order to repair the internal good object that he needs as a stable anchor strengthening him from within and helping him to cope with his life and fate. The internalization of the good object is also essential for thinking, learning about the world and lending meaning to it.

We need to distinguish between two phases of internalized identification: first in the context of the paranoid-schizoid position (which refuses reality through primitive defences); and second in the context of the depressive position (which integrates, mourns and accepts reality). Each one of them arouses an entirely different reading experience. The following literary examples demonstrate this very well.

Internalized identification in the context of the paranoid-schizoid position

According to Melanie Klein internalized identification occurring within the context of the paranoid-schizoid position is characteristic of the first few months of life. This identification takes place in line with this position characterized by splitting of the self and the 'object' into 'total good' and 'total bad'. The central anxiety in this position revolves around the annihilation of the self. Moreover, this position is characterized by the dominance of the oral drive and unconscious phantasies, which are linked by a desire to control the mother and penetrate her body or introject her by devouring her in a predatory and greedy manner. Every perception of the mother as separate and as having sovereign control over the good (milk and breast) is liable to arouse envy towards her and a desire to rob her of her treasures. In contrast, the feelings of satisfaction from the mother are accompanied by pleasure, by phantasy that the mother is 'total good' that floods the individual with feelings of love, gratitude and security.[1]

Mark Strand's poem 'Eating Poetry'

The poem 'Eating Poetry' by the Jewish American poet Mark Strand illustrates the link between reading and the experience of infant oral internalization in a straightforward and amusing way.

Eating Poetry

Ink runs from the corners of my mouth.
There is no happiness like mine.
I have been eating poetry.
The librarian does not believe what she sees.
Her eyes are sad
and she walks with her hands in her dress.
The poems are gone.
The light is dim.
The dogs are on the basement stairs and coming up.
Their eyeballs roll,
their blond legs burn like brush.
The poor librarian begins to stamp her feet and weep.
She does not understand.
When I get on my knees and lick her hand,
she screams.
I am a new man.
I snarl at her and bark.
I romp with joy in the bookish dark
                    (Strand, M., [1979] 2014).[2]

In Strand's poem one can evidently discern an experience of oral pleasure based on reading poetry that leads to animalistic dog-like happiness, lacking wisdom but filled with romping joy. If the poem is on the top floor, its 'eating' brings the dogs up from the basement similarly to the way the unconscious drive is raised to consciousness on the upper floor. The reader/suckling infant/puppy feels full and satisfied with the good inky milk of poetry. The librarian/mother's breasts are emptied ('The poems are gone'). She is worried about the uncontrolled and senseless behaviour embodied in the metaphor of 'the bookish dark', which is contrary to the more common metaphor of light to signify wisdom and knowledge. In the metaphor of the hand-licking dog there is a hint of the dog eating from his master's hand. Yet at the same time this is a concealed threat to oral gluttony intimidating the 'poor librarian' as the dog's eyeballs roll in the dark.

Such a reading of Strand's poem represents one view of oral internalization. This internalization does not lead to the enrichment of personality or wisdom but rather anticipates it. Here reading creates a Garden of Eden-like sense of satisfaction – the reader being described as filled with absolute goodness. Yet there is possibly here also a kind of ironic view of the excessive craving for poetry as an act of incorporation – a psychic mechanism designed to 'swallow the object' as a defensive internalization instead of internalizing it in an integrative way as a good object. This ironic view echoes Proust's thoughts in his essay *On Reading*, which also include an oral metaphor on reading:

> For as long as reading is for us the instigator whose magic keys open deep within us the door to those dwelling-places into which we would have been unable to penetrate, its role in our lives is salutary! It becomes dangerous on the other hand when, instead of awakening us to the personal life of the mind, reading tends to take its place, when truth no longer appears to us as an ideal we can only realize through the intimate progress of our own thought and through the strivings of our own heart, but as something material, deposited between the leaves of books like a honey ready-made by others and which we need only take the trouble to reach down from the shelves of libraries and then sample passively in a perfect repose of mind and body (Proust, M., 1905, pp. 77–78).

It should be remembered that the to-and-fro movement between the paranoid-schizoid and the depressive positions continues throughout an individual's life. However, people tend to experience life more in line with one or other position as an outcome of the processes of psychological adaptation and development that they have experienced in the course of their lives. It is therefore not surprising that other literary examples present another phase of internalizing identification, which stems from and promotes integration of the self. This identification occurs when it is bound up with the more advanced psychic developmental position – namely the depressive position.

Internalizing identification in the context of the depressive position

Internalizing identification in the framework of the depressive position leads to the assimilation of parts of the object in the 'self' in an integrative way. In the depressive position the 'self' becomes aware of both its complexity and that of the other, recognizing that each of them is both good and bad, aggressive as well as benign. This recognition is accompanied by psychic achievements such as the development of a mature sense of guilt, which leads to a search for ways of reparation and sublimation; to feel remorse on the one hand and gratitude on the other, followed by a developing sense of responsibility. In the course of the depressive position we don't find predatory incorporation but rather an internalization that enables a psychic metabolization that is likely to lead to significant psychic change. Instead of the primitive splitting of the self and the object to ideal versus total bad parts, in the depressive position bad and good come closer together. The good object is internalized into the inner world in proximity to the bad parts, and is in dialogue with them. The inner presence of the good object is pivotal. It strengthens the 'self' and enriches it, assisting the self in re-enforcing the benign components of the psyche: compassion, empathy, gratitude and creativity.

One of the previous literary examples from Semprún's book revealed how 'reading' Malraux's novel (stored in his psyche) enabled him to internalize a good object when faced by a traumatic situation. By internalizing Malraux's psychic position, Semprún the reader is aided in coping with the acute distress overwhelming him. A prerequisite of establishing meaning that will be of value to the reader is therefore his ability to identify with the literary hero. It is for good reason that Semprún turns to read a novel describing a similar situation to his own – the German gas attack on Russia during World War I. Had this been a description of an act of coping with a very different set of circumstances, Semprún would have been less identified with it and it would have been of no help to him. But the fact that he regards the situation faced by Malraux as resembling his own enables Semprún to feed on Malraux's words as a way of recovering, like a baby suckling milk when distressed. He identifies with him, internalizes his words so that Malraux can become the 'good mother' or the 'defending father' inside him, the intermediary and guide.

Moreover, reading Malraux also enabled Semprún to internalization him as a good object that had found the strength to mourn real and symbolic loss and work it through in a creative way. Since the loss that the literary hero mourned and recovered from involved a situation comparable to Semprún's, the literary object 'shows him' how to find anchors of meaning in the midst of hell. Moreover, the literary good objects breathe life into the internal good objects in his psyche. In Klein's view,

> While it is true that the characteristic feature of normal mourning is the individual's setting up the lost loved object inside himself, he is not doing so for the first time but, through the work of mourning, is reinstating that object as well as all his loved internal objects which he feels he has lost. He is therefore recovering what he had already attained in childhood (Klein, M., 1940, p. 143).

In a clinical example during a time of terrible crisis when a patient had lost her son (which was later revealed to have been her own loss) Klein noted that:

Ultimately this stood for re-creating her good parents, internally and externally, unifying them and making them happy and creative. In her mind she made reparation to her parents ... In the mourner's situation, the feelings of his internalized objects are also sorrowful. In his mind, they share his grief, in the same way as actual kind parents would (ibid., p. 142).

The reader's identification is not merely a matter of the 'reading self' identifying with the literary character. Such identification involves the internalization of certain aspects that characterize the literary figure and are relevant to the psychic state of the reader at that time. Through the process of internalizing identification with the good object, the reader no longer feels alone in the situation. The psychological and existential processes that the literary character copes with can help the reader in working through his own struggles.

Nathan Zach's poem 'How to Sweeten the Days'

How to Sweeten the Days

How else to sweeten days, if not with poetry.
Sweeten with what? Young lads will hear
Will dance dreaming, maidens will wipe a tear. Elders,
Enjoying the poems, will forget
Their bad heart, they too will wipe a tear. How to sweeten?
Children
Torn away from their far home
Or indeed their bad home
Let the poems of this poet be their solace
He too yearns for solace
Let them know they were written in dusk
Let them know they were written with love
Let them stand before them like floods
And many waters will not quench the family pictures
And when they will drink from them – sounds will rise
Joyful, joined by barefoot dance
On all mountains
Where forever joyful is children's sadness,
The dark memory of their youth.
(Zach, N., 1966)[3]

Zach is considered one of the most prominent innovators in Hebrew poetry since the 1950s. He has had a great influence on the development of modern Hebrew poetry as editor and critic, as well as translator and poet. Zach contended that the poet should represent the 'I' rather than the 'we'; an 'I' that would create and express individual subjectivity. He was born Harry Seitelbach to an Italian mother and German father.

Their families remained in Europe and didn't survive and they never successfully found their place in Israeli society. Zach himself, as an act of individuation and probably out of the need to differentiate himself from the identity and pains of 'the immigrant', changed his name and detached himself from his life's history till then. The researcher Glusman contends that because Zach was unable or unwilling to know himself and his particular historicity, his ability to portray subjecthood in its full sense was impaired and left his poetry suffused with melancholy and fragmented selfhood (Gluzman, M., 2018).

The poem cited above is the first in Nathan Zach's anthology titled *All the Milk and Honey* (1966), a biblical metaphor for Israel as a land of abundance. This *airs-poetic* poem includes poetry in the metaphor of oral desires. 'The poems of this poet' sweeten the days of the readers, 'And when they will drink from them – sounds will rise / Joyful', joined by dancing. The oral image that repeats itself and accompanies the internalization of the poem as nourishing and gratifying, testifies to the associative analogy between reading and nourishment. But unlike the case in Strand's poem, the internalizing identification with the poems is not here the source of that all-encompassing, impulsive, sensual and enjoyable gratification – devoid of wisdom and lacking constraint. Zach's poem brings the reader closer to internalizing identification with a good object who understands the complexity of life and doesn't deny it. Maidens wipe away their tears along with their elders, children and the poet himself. In accordance with Gluzman's view, they all have experienced their 'bad home' and yearn for sweet solace. Nevertheless, the possibility of being comforted in this way is closer to the use of the good object that characterizes the depressive position, that recognizes the limitations and unavoidable pains of human existence. The solace to be found in 'drinking the poems' does not lead to a detachment from human suffering but rather brings good closer to bad; it is aided by the warm milk of the poems that balance the suffering, lending an ameliorating touch to soothe it. The poetic solace does not extinguish the memories. Rather it feeds them with the love of the poet and the memory of the loved objects from home and from within. When Zach writes 'forever joyful is children's sadness', the sadness does not fade away, nor does 'the dark memory of their youth' vanish. Rather they are consoled by the joy of internalizing the songs despite their sadness and while recognizing it. In this, the poem does not fit in with Gluzman's description of an alienated poetic self, but rather carries a depressive wish to be soothed by the sweet milk and honey of creativity and poetry.

2. Projective identification

The concept of 'projective identification' (Klein, M., 1946, pp. 99–110), describes the way in which an individual projects an aspect of his inner world on to and into the object (Klein saw it as merely an internal process, while her followers saw it as an interpersonal phenomena). In general the projected aspect is connected to anxiety, aggression or a sense of persecution, although in special circumstances good aspects are also projected. The projected aspect is assigned to the other. For example, an angry person projects his anger into the other and is then convinced that it is the other who is angry with him; he is now in the firm grip of the other, the unconscious bearer of his anger. In daily life behaviour reflecting projective identification is discernible when a person succeeds in ridding himself of a powerful emotion – such as anger, resentment, his fear of abandonment – and arousing that emotion in the other while he himself remains apparently 'indifferent'.

Bion discovered that projective identification has two major functions: to be rid of the source of psychic anxiety and suffering and to entrust the projected psychic material so that it can be worked through in and by the object's internal container. Its second function is therefore communicative, because it facilitates the metabolization of the projected material in the other's mind, after which it can be re-introjected back to the projector's mind in a transformed shape, which now becomes tolerable and meaningful (Bion, W. R., 1962).

Bion distinguished between pathological projective identification and normal projective identification. Pathological projective identification mainly serves evacuation; the removal and parting from feelings of tension, anxiety and pain, and is bound up with the avoidance of thinking or learning from experience. By contrast, normal projective identification is mainly used for communication, namely for containment and transformation (ibid.). Normal projective identification is considered to be one of the most important psychic mechanisms in assisting an individual through the containment of another person when he senses that his own self-containment cannot tolerate the magnitude of the threat or the extent of anxiety and pain with which he is attempting to cope.

In his book *What Is Literature?* Sartre ([1948] 1988) writes about the influential power of reading and his words exemplify the way in which projective identification functions in the reading of literature.

> On the one hand, the literary object has no other substance than the reader's subjectivity; Raskolnikov's waiting is my waiting which I lend him. Without this impatience of the reader he would remain only a collection of signs. His hatred of the police magistrate who questions him is my hatred which has been solicited and wheedled out of me by

signs and the police magistrate himself would not exist without the hatred I have for him via Raskolnikov. That is what animates him, it is his very flesh (ibid., p. 45).

The reader's projection of his expectation into Raskolnikov; and his projection of his hatred into the police magistrate – enables him to read into and learn about his emotions and fears through the course of action adopted by his literary hero to whom the reader attributes internal motives, anxieties and hopes. He now explores these as if they were at one and same time his own and not his own, inside him as well as belonging to the other. For a while he thus achieves one of the central advantages of using the defence of projective identification, i.e. the evacuation of unbearable feelings. Earlier his mind had experienced excessive expectation or excessive hatred that threatened his inner psychic equilibrium. But now the literary hero's psyche serves as the phantasized container of his internal burden. Nor is that all: if the hero reflects or acts upon certain emotional difficulties in the reader's mind, the literary character would be fulfilling a similar function to that which the mother and therapist fulfill vis-à-vis her infant and the analyst's patient – containing the most fragile experiences, metabolizing them inside the mother/therapist/character's mind, thus lending new meaning and a better way of coping with those psychological elements. The reader enjoyed the opportunity to follow, work through and learn his emotions and anxieties through his literary character, now to be reintrojected in a meaningful and less anxiety-provoking shape.

The non-identical twin

Freud emphasized the sense of similarity between the reader and the literary character as being central to the reading experience. In his article about the story *Gradiva* Freud writes:

> The author, who has called his story a 'phantasy', has found no occasion so far for informing us whether he intends to leave us in our world, decried for being prosaic and governed by the laws of science, or whether he wishes to transport us into another and imaginary world. As we know ... we are prepared to follow him there without hesitation (Freud, S., 1907, p. 17).

The bibliotherapist and researcher Rachel Zoran writing about the transference twins notes that it is the most accessible of all the forms of transference of the reader of literature (Zoran, R., 2009, p. 91) As we saw earlier when reading into Semprún's transference relations with the literary narrator and characters, it is of vital importance that the character is placed in a very similar position, but at the very same time, that there is this slight difference, a gap, which enables the reader to use the distancing paradox in order to encounter himself in the image of his non-identical literary twin. This duality is also expressed in reality or during therapy; we can be helped by someone who can understand our experiences due to a capacity to internally and empathetically recognize our inner feelings, but that person has to possess additional tools that help him to help us. As in reality, so too in literature. On the one hand, the literary object has to face sufficiently similar emotional challenges so that the reader can attribute and project into him his own internal hopes and dreads. On the other hand, the object must be sufficiently different to offer new horizons and enable new processes to take place during the reader's meeting with his imaginary literary twin (Bion, W.R., 1967). According to Bion, the 'imaginary twin' is a fantasized twin who omnipotently assists in the denial of reality, which leads to neither change nor development. Thus for Bion an imagined twin is an identical twin. But as we saw earlier, for Semprún Malraux is a non-identical twin. Like Semprún, Malraux's hero had to cope with a gas attack, which threatened to annihilate him and everyone around him. But in Malraux's book he is depicted in a more integrated state of mind than in Semprún's account when facing annihilation. Moreover, Malraux offers the possibility of processing his history through recounting it in literary creative work. While Semprún is still wrestling with his traumatic response Malraux's hero enables him to recreate meaning and survive mentally, and he also 'shows him the way' towards creative recovery. We see how projective identification of Semprún's deep anxiety and temporal loss of orientation into Malraux's hero as his non-identical twin-object helped him in remobilizing internal capacities and psychic strengths.

Container-contained relations

The literary character is often assigned to the role of containing the reader's inner struggle. We saw for instance how Semprún's transference relations towards Malraux leads him to choose the latter as a containing object. He quotes Malraux saying that,

> Few 'topics' withstand the threat of death. This one [i.e. the gas attacks to which both Malraux and Semprún 30 years later were exposed to] brings into confrontation fraternity, death, and that part of mankind which is today seeking to define itself as something far beyond the individual ... If I return to this event, it's because I seek the crucial region of the soul where absolute Evil and fraternity hang in balance (Semprún, J., 1994, pp. 52–53).

It is this internal working through by Malraux – while he is lending meaning to his situation and actively searching for a better balance between the life and death inside him – which, for Semprún the reader, functions as a container. He moves in step with his literary hero combating the dominance of the death drive and moving towards the struggle between the life drive and death drive, in the hope that the life drive will, eventually, moderate the death drive and govern the psychic kingdom.

3. Extractive identification

'Extractive identification' applies to situations in which the ability to identify has been 'extracted' from an individual's mind in extremely traumatic and injurious circumstances. This term derives from Christopher Bollas' concept of 'extractive introjection' (Bollas, C., 1987) 'A procedure in which one person invades another person's mind and appropriates certain elements of mental life. The victim of extractive introjection will feel denuded of parts of the self' (ibid., p. 163). Bollas describes situations in which the self has been robbed by the object of his ability to respond in an authentic and spontaneous way. Bollas gives the example of a child who drops a glass of milk. Before he has the chance of expressing regret and self-criticism (or accepting blame), the child is confronted by his father's rage leaving him shocked – as if the father had extracted his ability to respond spontaneously for ever. If such an event is limited to a single occasion a spontaneous recovery can be expected. But an ongoing dialogue of this kind may fundamentally extract certain mental abilities. Bollas suggests that, 'A child who is the victim of consistent extractive introjection may choose to identify with the aggressive parent and install in his personality this identification, which then functions as a false self' (ibid, p. 164).

In a traumatic situation, the self is also robbed of its most fundamental internal qualities and capacities. When Semprún describes listening to the Auschwitz survivor, his ability to identify with him clearly collapses. The psychic and somatic detachment experienced by Semprún in the face of the survivor's testimony drives him to search for a literary situation sufficiently similar and yet sufficiently different so as to enable him to identify with the literary character and thereby to regain his lost capacity to identify, to care, to feel, to think – in the traumatic here and now. Klein links the capacity for identification to the ability to sacrifice immediate needs for the benefit of the other.

> To be genuinely considerate implies that we can put ourselves in the place of other people: we 'identify' ourselves with them. Now this capacity for identification with another person is a most important element in human relationships in general, and is also a condition for real and strong feelings of love. We are only able to disregard or to some extent sacrifice our own feelings and desires, and thus for a time to put the other person's interests and emotions first, if we have the capacity to identify ourselves with the loved person (Klein, M., 1937, p. 311).

The torment suffered by Semprún listening to the survivor's story extracted his ability to respond spontaneously to the fate of another, the way a concerned and involved person such as him would be expected to respond. What is highlighted here is the way Semprún, while suffering a momentary disintegration, turns to Malraux in search of the lost functions of his psyche, looking for a way of re-introjecting them through his identification with Malraux as an integrated and whole object.

It is interesting to note that this turn to Malraux is bidirectional. On the one hand, Semprún had lost something and was looking for a way to re-introject it. On the other hand, he also looks at Malraux and feels his literary hero's distress, reads about his traumatic experiences, so that it is Semprún who offers the hero his identification, his attentiveness and his compassion. While living out these vital internal possibilities while in the company of the literary character, the same capacities shattered in the here and now of his traumatic situation are revived within the literary space. Encountering the ferocity of the Auschwitz survivor's story extracted these capacities from Semprún, so that he unconsciously seeks to revive them through his reading and perhaps even find a way of returning to the immediate situation and succeed, as Klein phrased it, to 'for a time ... put the other person's interests and emotions first' (ibid.). He may only then become a witness to the Auschwitz survivor in a broader sense, being there as a live presence, fully attentive, thus not only being caring and supportive but also becoming a human antidote in combating the erasure of the injustice.

4. Identifications belonging to the primitive edge of experience: adhesive and objectifying identifications

The psychoanalyst Thomas Ogden (Ogden, T., 1989) formulated a psychic position that precedes Klein's paranoid-schizoid position in psychic development. This position is termed 'the autistic-contiguous position'. Even though its most dominant phenomena characterize the autistic range, moments and aspects of experiences connected to it are also to be found in the 'normal' mind (ibid.). In this position two modes of identification are involved: 'adhesive identification'[4] and a mechanism that I suggest be termed 'objectifying identification'.

Adhesive identification

The mechanism of 'adhesive identification' (termed by Bick, E., 1968 and later developed by Meltzer, D., 1975) serves as a defence in the face of very primitive anxieties that are accompanied by feelings of being torn, leaking or having no 'psychic skin' to feel protected by (Bick, E., 1968, pp. 484–486). The subject attaches himself to the object in an adhesive manner, as in adhesion to an area of skin or a magnet that attracts and unifies the dispersed and disintegrated body-mind. This identification thus protects the self against the threat of annihilation and disintegration. Adhesive identification does not involve a meeting between the self's inner world and the inner world of the other. Instead, it involves a surface-to-surface contact, like that of an anxious infant attaching himself closely to his mother so as to feel protected and enveloped by the surface of her skin and body.

Literary evidence shows that among the types of identification that occur in the course of reading, adhesive identification is certainly one of them. This type of identification is evident when the reader attaches himself to the book or the text without really internalizing what is written. Instead, the book's body, or that of the words, serves defensively as a psychic envelope.

In his book *The Words*, Sartre describes his flowering in the shadow and light of reading and, subsequently, also in the shadow and light of writing. He describes situations in which the narrator uses books as a defence against his solitude and detachment from the adult world that at times is accompanied by profound anxiety. There are occasions when Sartre describes an adhesive identification with the characters, which gives him a sense of security and protection. An example of this can be found in his description of how he lies down to read, but in fact, he attaches himself to the book's concrete physical form as if it was the body of a transferential motherly figure. Since he perceives the book as representing the omniscient and all-powerful adult, he phantasizes that by gluing himself to the book his adhesive identification with it would protect him.

> How could I determine – especially after so many years – the imperceptible and shifting frontier that separates possession from hamming? I would lie on my stomach, facing the windows, with an open book in front of me, a glass of wine-tinted water at my right, and a slice of bread and jam on a plate at my left. Even in solitude I was putting on an act. Karlemamie and Anne Marie had turned those pages long before I was born; it was their knowledge that lay open before my eyes. In the evening, they would question me: 'What did you read? What have you understood?' I knew it, I was pregnant, I would give birth to a child's comment. To escape from the grown-ups into reading was the best way of communing with them (Sartre, J.P., [1964] 1981, p. 70).

And so:

> I liked to please and wanted to steep myself in culture. I would recharge myself with the sacred every day, at times absentmindedly. It was enough to prostrate myself and turn the pages. My friends' works frequently served as prayer mills (ibid., p. 71)

Sartre the child, relieves his loneliness and acquires phantasized worth and a sense of exhilaration through his physical attachment to the book. Through adhesive identification with it he feels a physical and psychic closeness to the world of the great and the sublime. Subsequently, the adhesive identification leaves him ashamed for having simulated an act of assimilation that was in fact nothing other than an act of deception, because it had not involved the bidirectional reading process of projection and internalization. The inner world remained anxious and empty after he had lain on the 'prayer mills'. This way of seeking protection through concrete attachment is uncharacteristic of Sartre, who most of the time reflects introspectively both as a reader and as a writer. Even the remark 'I would give birth to a child's comment' testifies to his profound feeling that he has a mental interior analogous to a womb that contains ideas and gives birth to them. This example shows that one cannot infer the psychic structure and personality from observing a given example. Even if we observe the usage of such primitive defence mechanism as adhesive identification, it very well may be (and almost always is) that at other times the psyche will exhibit a broader range of adaptive forms of identification and defensive mechanisms.

Objectifying identification

Normal infants and autistic and psychotic children and adults defend themselves against primitive anxieties of disintegration by, among other methods, using autistic objects[5] These objects lend themselves to absolute control, thus pacifying the anxiety of separation and dependence on an other. Denial of separation is bound up with an incapacity to mourn and use symbolic language.

We can assume that at the unconscious level the authors who Sartre imagines as being actually and physically trapped in his books are also giving voice to Sartre's father who died when Jean-Paul was an infant and the longing for whom is actively denied by him. At certain moments Sartre feels that the writers live in the actual body of the books they have written, or in other words, that the books – as objects – are the physical personification of their authors. Sartre plays with the books as if they were the authors themselves and in doing so he humanizes them and erases their humanity at one and the same time. As Frances Tustin noted, '"Hardness" is a characteristic feature of most autistic objects. This gives the child the feeling that they keep him safe' (Tustin, F., 1980, p. 29).

> I subjected them to my whims. I would take them in my arms, carry them, put them on the floor, open them, shut them, draw them from nothingness, and thrust them back into it. Those garbled figures were my dolls, and I pitied that wretched, paralyzed survival which was called immortality (Sartre, J.P., [1964] 1981, p. 67).

Instead of feeling a longing for his father, the pain of his loss, as well as perhaps the pain of losing his mother whom he'd experienced more as a sister than a strong and protective mother, and instead of feeling anxious or pained by his own helplessness, Sartre chooses to attach himself to the physical and immortal body of the books. He attributes to them features of live authors given to his whims and thus is able to totally deny feelings of longing and neediness. Sartre's descriptions are positioned along the seam line between objectification and personification. It would seem that this is exactly the juncture he is confronting during those moments; between the desire to connect to the literary characters and the books' authors and the desire to turn them into objects with which he can do with as he pleases, omnipotently in control and free of anxiety.

A further example of this is to be found in the way that Sartre's alienation is turned into persecutory anxiety, as he feels the authors are watching him. In this instance the book is experienced as a physical space on the other side of which is an observing (father) figure.

> The pages were windows; outside, a face was pressed against the pane, someone was watching me. I pretended not to notice and would continue reading, with my eyes glued to the words beneath the fixed stare of the late Chateaubriand (ibid., p. 67).

The psychoanalyst Emanuel Berman cites a passage by the American art critic Lionel Trilling, expressing a similar idea:

> A real book reads us. I have been read by Eliot's poems and by *Ulysses* and by *Remembrance of Things Past* and by *The Castle* for a good many years now, since early youth. Some of these books at first rejected me; I bored them. But as I grew older and they knew me better, they came to have more sympathy with me and to understand my hidden meanings (Berman, E., 1993, p. 17).

The young Sartre, and Trilling too, sense that the writers are looking at them through the eyes of the pages or through the outward facing window panes. The writers are peeping at the reader and following him as he is reading. This coupling of gazes in the confusion between object and self and between watching and being watched, combines the primitive objectification of the book with the paranoid attitude in the transference relations towards the imagined authors and characters. This bidirectional look is of a primitive nature in contrast to the mutual ability to see each other in more developed states of mind. Nonetheless, it is also a representation to the denied longing for a caring gaze from a significant other.

The adhesive and objectifying identification experienced momentarily frees the reader from feelings of separation and loss, and this advantage is apparent in the joyful and somewhat manic way Sartre describes these two states of identification. And yet beneath the descriptions of adhesion and objectification by Sartre as reader, there is also a flicker of deep anxiety because the primitive defence mechanisms are always extremely fragile and unreliable.

5. Raw identification

'Raw identification' is a term I suggest to describe a particular defence against traumatic experiences. It is characterized by identification with an object with which traumatic relations were conducted and that on the one hand the mind attempts 'to hold on to' via a physical representation of the object, and on the other hand tries to leave the relations with him repressed. The reason for holding on is that in addition to causing great pain, this object is also a very significant object that the self finds hard to detach from completely. Since these relations were traumatic, full internalization was prevented. Instead of it being internalized, the object was introjected in a raw form through identification with a feature or a trait it possessed that is often accompanied by a prominent bodily imprint. The subject – identified with the object in this raw form – does not realize that this trait of his is, in fact, a remnant and a permanent reminder of his traumatic relations with that object. Thus a patient of mine whose mother suffered from bowel cancer during the patient's early childhood developed symptoms of an ulcer syndrome and of compulsive obsessive disorder characterized by excessive preoccupation with her failing body. She was unconsciously carrying her mother's physical and emotional collapse in her own body and mind. My patient felt anxious of losing her mother, wanted to repair her illness and felt intolerable guilt for wishing to be rid of her and with that to be freed from the pain and anxiety she was causing. Thus, through her raw identification with her mother, she was unconsciously trying to take care of her mother inside her, while at the same time she was still unable to separate herself from the 'object' and get on with her life.

Lending the raw identification mechanism to reading results in applying a process that takes place over a period of years to one that occurs in an instant. These are moments during which the reader experiences identification with physical traits described in the story, and these echo old identifications permeated with fears and pain that had not been worked through in any significant sense and remained only in the form of their raw representation.

An example of this is to be found in Sartre's description of his experience while reading a story titled *Wind in the Trees* published in the daily newspaper *Le Matin*. Sartre confesses that as he opened the paper he was 'frozen with fear'. The story was about a sick woman alone on the first floor of a country house who suddenly sees the leaves of a chestnut tree shaking even though outside there was no sign of 'a breath of air'.

At that moment, a cry! The sick woman's husband rushes upstairs and finds his young wife sitting up in bed. She points to the tree and falls over dead. What did she see?' The writer starts a new paragraph and concludes casually: 'According to the people of the village, it was Death that shook the branches of the chestnut tree.' I threw the paper aside, stamped my foot, and cried aloud: 'No! No!' My heart was bursting in my chest (Sartre, J.P., [1964] 1981, p. 150).

And Sartre concludes the description of this reading experience thus: 'I was afraid of the water, afraid of crabs and trees. Afraid of books in particular. I cursed the fiends who filled their stories with such atrocious figures. Yet I imitated them' (ibid., pp. 150–151). Sartre's identification with the woman looking at the tree and dying or with her husband as he watches her, is amazingly profound, though it is evident that he is unable to assimilate the event and so identifies himself with the character via his own body ('My heart was bursting in my chest'). Nearly 40 pages earlier Sartre recalls a childhood memory that can be seen as an allusion to the possibility that the literary personification of death aroused early unconscious phantasies experienced by Sartre the child. At the beginning of his book the infant Sartre is described imagining his dead father embodied in the wind whistling through the trees alongside other images perceived as the mysterious shadow of the missing father. One autobiographical memory described earlier in the book clearly brings to mind Sartre's later description of the *Le Matin* story and his identification with the characters of the woman and her husband;

> I saw death. When I was five, it lay in wait for me. In the evening, it would prowl on the balcony, press its nose against the window. I saw it, but I dared not say anything … In that period, I had an appointment with it every night in bed (ibid., p. 94).

It seems that as a child Sartre felt anxious about death's visitations but within the anxiety was probably enfolded its opposite – a yearning to meet his father. The textual resemblance between his descriptions from childhood and the portrayal of the later reading experience offers a hint that the fantasized meetings with the father or with death that Sartre experienced as a child at night, return to life in his raw identification with the characters in the story the *Wind in the Trees*. Reading about death playing out among the leaves of the chestnut tree, his identification sends a terrifying signal to his body. The silenced heroine's heart, her husband's heart that is about to burst, the reader's heart identifying with both – all echoes of an old raw unconscious identification with his father's corpse and stilled heart. Behind this raw identification was a child's repressed and wounded heart longing for his missing father.

6. Intrusive identification

The concept of 'intrusive identification', developed by Donald Meltzer (1990, pp. 66–68), originates at the very beginning of life in the infant's unconscious phantasy of forcibly invading the mother's body so as to violently and lustfully control her and rob her of her internal possessions. This phantasy can also take a complementary form, where the intrusive part is projected on the object, now felt as intruding the self violently and greedily.

In the complementary phantasy the character penetrates the reader's psyche and forcefully controls it. In such reading experiences the reader finds himself momentarily in the tight grip of a powerful and overwhelming emotional experience.

> I let venomous words enter my head, words infinitely richer than I realized; a foreign force recomposed within me, by means of discourse, stories about madmen that didn't concern me, a dreadful sorrow, the ruin of a life: wasn't I going to be infected, to die poisoned? Absorbing the Word, absorbed by the picture. With what cowardly relief, with what disappointment I returned to the family small talk when my mother entered and put on the light, crying: 'My poor darling, you're straining your eyes (Sartre, J.P., [1964] 1981, pp. 56–57).

In this fantastic description we can see intrusive identification's bidirectionality as experienced by Sartre the reader. He penetrates the characters and becomes them or they penetrate and invade him and occupy him both at a somatic level (through the head and eyes he is filled with venomous words) and the psychic level (he is filled with dreadful sorrow and the ruin of a life). The force of these intrusive identifications momentarily fills Sartre with mortal fear. It is interesting to note that the exit from this extreme state yields no relief but rather disappoints ('with what disappointment I returned to the family small talk'). It reveals that hidden deep pleasure that every bookworm can easily connect to – of penetrating the literary characters and being invaded by them.

7. Chimeric identification

An especially early type of identification in the development of the psyche and the most pathological of all has been described by the psychoanalyst Joshua Durban as 'chimeric identification' (Durban, J., 2011, pp. 903–924). This type of identification prevents the dread of separateness through the phantasized mixture of self and object, forming a single chimeric object. Chimeric identification thus involves a severe loss of the connection to reality. Among reading experiences described in literature one can find examples of momentary chimeric identification of the reader with a literary character. There is also rare literary evidence presenting massive chimeric identification with the literary text to the extent that reality testing gives way to a momentary delusion of actually living in the alternative reality of the story. This is so, for example, in the case of Don Quixote, the paradigmatic hero whose identification with chivalrous noblemen instilled in him the identity of a wandering nobleman, thus eliminating the divide between him as the reader and the characters he was reading about.

Sartre describes his anxiety of falling into a chimeric identification with the literary characters and text thus: 'I was afraid of falling head first into a fabulous universe and of wandering about in it in the company of Horace and Charbovary without hope of getting back to the Rue le Goff, Karlemami, and my mother' (Sartre, [1964] 1981, p. 56).

One of the most horrifying yet amazing examples of chimeric identification with literary characters in circumstances of extreme stress is to be found in Margarete Buber-Neumann's book *Milena* ([1976] 1997). Buber-Neumann was married to Martin Buber's son and when she divorced him married a Jew by the name of Neumann. In the concentration camp she became friendly with Milena Jesenská, known mainly for her fascinating correspondence with the writer Franz Kafka. Milena didn't survive and Buber-Neumann wrote a book chronicling her story. Buber-Neumann recounts how, while she spent about 40 days in solitary confinement in a cell in the Ravensbrück concentration camp in Germany, she was so totally absorbed in a literary text, that it led to a complete collapse of the boundaries between the reader and her heroes. Buber-Neumann describes the chimeric process she experienced thus:

> Even under normal conditions nothing is more dangerous to a concentration camp inmate than self-pity, than constant worry about his own personal fate. This is especially true in a dark cell. Terror gives way to apathy. I knew that if I was to survive I had to pull myself together and keep busy ... In telling stories I took great pains not to leave anything out ... But my storytelling was to take a dangerous turn.
>
> I started retelling Maxim Gorki's story 'Birth of Man'. In retelling this story, a strange transformation occurred in me. I couldn't drop it. A daydream took over, and the story went on. I slipped into the skins of the protagonists. I myself became the boy and the peasant woman, walking along the Black Sea shore that I knew so well. From that point on I was two people, two fugitives from reality. We found a hut on the edge of a dense forest. A friendly place, though not much larger than my cell; it, too, had no window, but it had a door that could be opened. Now that there were two of me, I took twofold pleasure in our refuge. My days now had a bright morning. I went to the open door, looked out over the glittering sea, and breathed the salt air. A happy ending in every respect ... There was nothing vague about the paradise I dreamed

up; I relished every detail, every hour, every minute of the day. I lost all sense of time and reality ... One Sunday the cell door opened and I was released from the Bunker. I hated the daylight and the ghastly reality. I wanted to shut my eyes again and go back to my fantasies.

I would have been lost without Milena's help. She understood the danger I was in, because mentally deranged inmates were put to death. She got me into the annex of the infirmary with a Czech *Block-älteste*. Whenever she could get away from her work, she came to see me. Over and over again I would tell her about the life of my heroes by the seashore, and she would listen with infinite patience. In this way she enabled me to return slowly to the reality of concentration camp life (Buber-Neumann, M., [1976] 1997, pp. 191–192)

In her book *The Third Voice*, Rachel Zoran describes this text as depicting an 'alternative world, meeting all her needs, which she sorely missed during her solitary confinement' (Zoran, R., 2000, p. 147). Zoran explains the way in which Maxim Gorky's story offers a textual space enabling the reader to be 'reborn'. Buber-Neumann's encounter with the heroes in a hut in the midst of nature helped her overcome her solitude even though in reality she was confined to a cell. Her sense of relief was made all the more palpable as she imagines being 'two people' – both hero and heroine. Her identification with the book's make believe heroes who eat and drink, sleep, get up and love, is so total that she no longer feels anxious or deprived when her hell becomes a hallucinatory Garden of Eden. As Zoran argues, Buber-Neumann's identification with the text's heroes was designed to protect her from feeling helpless and shield her from the fear of death and loss of orientation and faith in the intolerable conditions inside her prison cell.

In addition to these insights, Buber-Neumann's reading experience in captivity illustrates the way her transference relations towards the story's characters and their situation had been magnified by the stressful circumstances she'd found herself in and turned into chimeric identification. She'd found a defensive shelter within the characters with whom she'd become fused in her unconscious phantasy, where all sign of solitude, separation or even distinction between the self and the other(s); between here and there, now and then; between snippets of reality in the hell of her confinement and the mythical literary 'reality' that had overtaken her is negated. This chimeric unification is dramatically expressed in that the reader becomes both the hero and the heroine as well as the protective hunter – which can be defined in Kleinian terms as a 'combined object'.

This 'pathological' reading of Buber-Neumann exemplifies a poignant fact: every defence mechanism, as pathological as it may appear to be to the external observer, is the mind's best strategy; the last line of defence against unendurable psychic torment.

Notes

1 See for example in Melanie Klein 'Our Adult World and Its Roots in Infancy' (1959).
2 Translated from Hebrew by Shulamit Lapid.
3 Translated by Shulamit Lapid. © Nathan Zach and ACUM.
4 The concept of 'adhesive identification' was coined by Donald Meltzer (1975).
5 A child attaches himself to an autistic object as a defence against contact with the world around him, and as a defence against catastrophic primary anxieties within him.

References

Berman, E. (Ed.) (1993). *Essential Papers on Literature and Psychoanalysis*. New York and London: New York University Press.
Bick, E. (1968). The Experience of the Skin in Early Object-Relations. *International Journal of Psychoanalysis*, 49, pp. 484–486.
Bion, W.R. (1962). *Learning from Experience*. London: Tavistock.
Bion, W.R. (1967). *Second Thoughts*. London and New York: Routledge.
Bollas, C. (1987). *The Shadow of the Object: Psychoanalysis of the Unthought Known*. New York: Columbia University Press.
Buber-Neumann, M. [1976] (1997). *Milena: The Tragic Story of Kafka's Great Love*. New York: Arcade Publishing.
Durban, J. (2011). Shadows, Ghosts and Chimeras: On Some Early Modes of Handling Psycho-Genetic Heritage. *International Journal of Psychoanalysis*, 92, pp. 903–924.
Freud, S. (1907). Delusion and Dreams in Jensen's Gradive. In: J. Strachey (Ed.) *The Standard Edition of the Complete Psychological Works of Sigmund Freud, Vol. IX*. London: Hogarth Press, pp. 1–95.
Freud, S. (1917). Mourning and Melancholia. In: J. Strachey (Ed.) *The Standard Edition of the Complete Psychological Works of Sigmund Freud, Vol. XIV*. London: Hogarth Press, pp. 237–258.
Gluzman, M. (2018). *The Poetry of the Drowned: Sovereignty and Melancholia in Hebrew Poetry after 1948*. Rishon LeZion: University of Haifa Press and Miskal– Yediot Ahronot Books and Chemed Books.
Joseph, B. (1985). Transference: The Total Situation. *International Journal of Psychoanalysis*, 66, pp. 447–454.
Klein, M. (1937). Love, Guilt and Reparation. In: *Love, Guilt and Reparation and Other Works 1921–1945*. London: Vintage, pp. 306–343.
Klein, M. (1940). Mourning and It's Relation to Manic-Depressive States. In: *Love, Guilt and Reparation and Other Works 1921–1945*. London: Vintage, pp. 344–369.
Klein, M. (1946). Notes on Some Schizoid Mechanisms. In: *Envy and Gratitude and Other Works 1946–1963*. London: Vintage, pp. 25–42.
Klein, M. (1959). Our Adult World and its Roots in Infancy. In: *Envy and Gratitude and Other Works 1946–1963*. London: Vintage, pp. 247–263.
Laplanche, J. and Pontalis, J.B. (1973). *The Language of Psychoanalysis*. London: Hogarth Press [Kindle Edition].
Meltzer, D. (1975). Adhesive Identification. *Contemporary Journal of Psychoanalysis*, 11, pp. 289–310.

Ogden, T. (1989). *The Primitive Edge of Experience*. Lanham, MD: Jason Aronson.
Proust, M. (1905). *On Reading*. New York: Three Syrens Press.
Proust, M. (1927). *In Search of Lost Time: Complete Edition*. New York: The Modern Library [Kindle Edition].
Sartre, J. [1948] (1988). *What Is Literature?* Cambridge, MA: Harvard University Press.
Sartre, J. [1964] (1981). *The Words*. New York: Vintage Books.
Semprún, J. (1994). *Literature or Life*. London and New York: Penguin Books.
Strand, M. [1979] (2014). Eating Poetry. In: *Collected Poems*. New York: Penguin Random House.
Tustin, F. (1980). Autistic Objects. *International Review of Psychoanalysis*, 7, pp. 27–39.
Zach, N. (1966). *All the Milk and Honey*. Tel Aviv: Am-Oved.
Zoran, R. (2000). *The Third Voice: The Therapeutic Qualities of Literature and Their Applications in Bibliotherapy*. Jerusalem: Carmel.
Zoran, R. (2009). *The Letter's Imprint: Reading and Identity within the Bibliotherapeutic Dialogue*. Jerusalem: Carmel.

Further reading

Davidson, D. (1984). What Metaphors Mean. In: *Inquiries into Truth and Interpretation*. Oxford: Clarendon.
Freud, S. (1915). Thoughts for the Times of War and Death. In: J. Strachey (Ed.) *The Standard Edition of the Complete Psychological Works of Sigmund Freud, Vol. XIV*. London: Hogarth Press, pp. 273–302.
Freud, S. (1923). The Ego and the Id. In: J. Strachey (Ed.) *The Standard Edition of the Complete Psychological Works of Sigmund Freud, Vol. XIX*. London: Hogarth Press, pp. 3–66.
Klein, M. (1955). On Identification. In: *Envy and Gratitude and Other Works 1946–1963*. London: Vintage, pp. 141–175.
Klein, M. (1963). On the Sense of Lonliness. In: *Envy and Gratitude and Other Works 1946–1963*. London: Vintage, pp. 300–313.
Lubin, O. (2003). *A Woman Reading A Woman*. Haifa: Haifa University Press.
Meltzer, D. (1990). *The Claustrum: An Investigation of Claustrophobic Phenomena*. London: Karnac.
Ogden, T. (1986). *The Matrix of the Mind: Object Relations and the Psychoanalytic Dialogue*. London: Karnac.
Ogden, T. (1994). The Analytic Third: Working with Intersubjective Clinical Facts. *International Journal of Psychoanalysis*, 75, pp. 3–19.

Chapter 4
Resistance to reading

The French philosopher Maurice Blanchot noted that:

> Were someone to confide in us: 'Always anxious when I got to read', or were a person unable to read except at rare privileged moments, or were he to overturn his whole life, renounce the world with its activities and all its happiness just to make his way towards a few minutes of reading – doubtless we would assign him a spot beside that patient of Pierre Janet's who did not like to read because, she said, 'a book one reads becomes dirty' (Blanchot, M., [1955] 1982, p. 171).

This raises an intriguing question. Why is it that certain people or people in certain periods of their lives do not want or feel unable to read? There are also readers who feel indifferent or distanced by the act of reading. Before opening up this discussion I'll briefly explain three concepts relevant to this phenomenon: 'resistance ', 'surrender' and the 'false self'.

Resistance

In Laplanche and Pontalis' dictionary of psychoanalytic terms, resistance is defined thus: 'In psycho-analytic treatment the name "resistance" is given to everything in the words and actions of the analysand that obstructs his gaining access to his unconscious' (Laplanche, J. and Pontalis, J., 1973, loc. 10485–10487). The forces at work in resistance are the same as those at play in repression. For Freud the interpretation of resistance was one of the crucial aspects of the analytic technique. Freud also saw resistance as an integral aspect of transference relations. However, in Freud's view, though resistance may make use of transference, it did not constitute it. Resistance is, in fact, an expression of the force that activates a defence against representations that arouse anxiety since they are connected to the repressed. At the same time it also expresses the force of repetition compulsion, i.e. the compulsive tendency to repeat time and time again some form of internal and or external activity as a resistance to change. In the development of psychoanalytic thought various attempts were made to deal with the term 'resistance' because psychoanalysts felt that this term implied an accusation against the analysand. There were significant efforts to cease using the concept of resistance in order to instead investigate the hidden motivations aimed specifically at communication and development.

Surrender

The relational psychoanalyst Emmanuel Ghent (1990) wrote about a position antithetical to resistance that he termed 'surrender':

> Resistance is the name given to motivational forces operating against growth or change and in the direction of maintenance of the status quo. Surrender might be thought of as reflective of some 'force' towards growth ... Submission, on the other hand ... operates in the service of resistance ... The superstructure of defensiveness, the protections against anxiety, shame, guilt, anger are, in a way, all deceptions, whether they take the form of denial, splitting, repression, rationalizations, evasions. Is it possible that deep down we long to give this up, to 'come clean' as part of an even more general longing to be known, recognized? Might this longing also be joined by a corresponding wish to know and recognize the other? As to the developmental origins of such longings I would locate them as being rooted in the primacy of object-seeking as a central motivational thrust in humans (Ghent, M., 1990, pp. 108–136).

In other words, Ghent raises the possibility that our yearning for an object is of such significance to us that we are eager to surrender to it, to let it know us undefended and mounting no resistance. Ghent's thinking seeks to view the phenomenon of resistance as a consequence of the absence of an object prepared to meet the self's yearning to be known by another.

The false self

The psychoanalyst Donald Winnicott described a psychic structure that he termed the 'false self' (Winnicott, D.W., 1960, 1965). Winnicott compares the role of the 'false self' to that of the 'true self'. The 'false self's' role is to protect the 'true self' from harm. The 'false self' has its origin in early development when the 'true self's' expressions were experienced as dangerous in light of the mother's responses.

> Periodically the infant's gesture gives expression to a spontaneous impulse; the source of the gesture is the True Self and the gesture indicates the existence of a potential True Self. We need to examine the way

the mother meets this infantile omnipotence revealed in a gesture ... In the first case the mother's adaptation is good enough and in consequence the infant begins to believe in external reality which appears and behaves as by magic ... and which acts in a way that does not clash with the infant's omnipotence. On this basis the infant can gradually abrogate omnipotence. The True Self has a spontaneity, and this has been joined up with the world's events. The infant can now begin to enjoy the illusion of omnipotent creating and controlling ... In the second case ... the mother's adaptation to the infant's hallucinations and spontaneous impulses is deficient, not good enough. The process that leads to the capacity for symbol-usage does not get started (or else it becomes broken up) ... The infant remains isolated. But in practice the infant lives, but lives falsely (Winnicott, D.W., 1965, pp. 146–147).

Summing up Winnicott writes that:

The False Self has one positive and very important function: to hide the True Self, which it does by compliance with environmental demands ... [to the extent] that spontaneity is not a feature in the infant's living experiences. Compliance is then the main feature, with imitation as a speciality (ibid.).

Returning to the various reasons preventing an individual from reading we must first say that there are of course reasons unconnected to resistance, such as cognitive difficulties, periods of overload and more. On the other hand, the refusal to read originated by resistance is likely to be expressed in a variety of ways, such as ignoring books or quickly falling asleep when starting to read; easily losing concentration and a critical and sceptical view of the text being read. Such tendencies are often evidence of the difficulty involved in 'surrendering' to the yearning to be known to the other and to know him. The elusive and misleading ways of resistance to reading are also to be found among those readers who appropriate the text as if they are collectors of precious artefacts. Alternatively it is to be found among readers who attach themselves to the text adhesively, when in fact they do not introject it in a way that would enable them to reflect about themselves, to feel themselves and to grow as subjects in their world. An additional form of resistance to reading is one that opposes the active psychological participation of the reader who limits his reading experience to a purely intellectual or detached participation and therefore won't profit from the use of literature as a means of transformation and psychic development.

I shall now explore resistance to reading, expressed mostly by a *false attachment to the text* and also by a detached reading – both involve an unconscious refusal to respond emotionally to the reading.

False reading in Marcel Proust's writings

Proust discusses resistance to reading in two written works published more than two decades apart; in his short essay *On Reading* published in 1905 and in *Time Regained*, the final volume of *In Search of Lost Time* published in 1927.

On Reading (1905) is in part a theoretical essay, in part a literary creation. The essay includes memories and portrayals of childhood alongside meta-literary thoughts similar to those that he wrote about later on in *In Search of Lost Time* (1927). Already in his early essay Proust writes in a passage quoted in full earlier in the previous chapter, about readers' attempts to appropriate both the books and the wisdom of their authors as their own without being required to experience a real internal transformation.

> It becomes dangerous ... when, instead of awakening us to the personal life of the mind, reading tends to take its place ... like a honey ready-made by others and which we need only take the trouble to reach down from the shelves of libraries and then sample passively in a perfect repose of mind and body (Proust, M., 1905, p. 36).

Nor does Proust spare intellectuals from his wrath:

> It is not at all the same for the literary man. For him, the book is not the angel who takes wing the moment he has opened the gates into the celestial garden, but a motionless idol, which he worships for its own sake and which, instead of receiving a true dignity from the thoughts it awakens, communicates a factitious dignity to everything around it (ibid., pp. 39–40).

In 'Time Regained', 2,800 pages into *In Search of Lost Time*, the hero who became an author recounts his own experience when he was engaged in reading children's books. This evokes lost memories but is also accompanied by pain due to the realization that what is read in adulthood lacks the vitality of childhood reading. Its full influence in later stages of life is somewhat resisted. The worst resistance to literature is expressed in its appropriation for the purpose of 'salon conversations', described by Proust as a 'pseudo' cultural experience, behind which there is neither live penetrative reading – setting in motion a process of change – nor an internalization of the text being read or of the artistic creation to which the individual has been exposed. Proust devotes a number of pages to this topic in gushing prose and descriptions parodying the gesticulations and rolling eyes of these philistines supposedly enjoying a bit of culture. Here the narrator's voice is mingled with the voice of the character who became an author and with the voice of the author himself. The narrator discusses two literary genres that invite transference relations from such an appropriation: The theoretical genre, on the one hand, and the genre that imitates life instead of creating it, on the other.

The number of pages that Proust devotes to the subject testifies to the importance that he attributed to it. Let us read two profound examples:

> Even when we seek artistic delights for the sake of the impression they make on us, we manage quickly to dispense with the impression itself and to fix our attention on that element in it which enables us to experience pleasure without penetrating to its depth, and thinking we can communicate it to others in conversation because we shall be talking to them about something common to them and to us, the personal root impression is eliminated ... which, being unfathomable because it is exterior to ourselves, causes us no fatigue; ... in that flight far away from our own life which we have not the courage to face called erudition ... And how many stop at that point, get nothing from their impression, and ageing useless and unsatisfied, remain sterile celibates of art! To them come the same discontents as to virgins and idlers whom the fecundity of labour would cure. They are more exalted when they talk about works of art than real artists, for their enthusiasm, not being an incentive to the hard task of penetrating to the depths, expands outwards, heats their conversation and empurples their faces; they think they are doing something by shrieking at the tops of their voices: 'Bravo! Bravo!' (Proust, M., 1927, loc. 2937–2949).

Later in this volume Proust also points an accusing finger at artistic creation collaborating with or even inviting this kind of resistance, placing reading at the top of the list, grumbling in particular about its emptiness.

> [A]rt as crude as life, without beauty, a reproduction so wearisome and futile of what our eyes have seen and our intelligence has observed, that one asks oneself how he who makes that his aim can find in it the exultant stimulus which gives zest to work. The grandeur of veritable art [...] is to recapture, to lay hold of, to make one with ourselves that reality far removed from the one we live in, from which we separate ourselves more and more as the knowledge which we substitute for it acquires a greater solidity and impermeability, a reality we run the risk of never knowing before we die but which is our real, our true life at last revealed and illumined, the only life which is really lived and which in one sense lives at every moment in all men as well as in the artist (ibid., loc. 2998–3001).

These two excerpts express Proust's incisive views on appropriate and inappropriate reading. He regards what I have termed here the 'reader's resistance' as a refusal by the reader to open himself up to the literary work and a refusal to enable it to shed light and meaning on the reality of the his internal and external life which may lead to reflection and development. But letting literature influence you and even transform you requires mental courage.

The sophisticated expression 'celibates of art', which Proust attributes to a false connection with art and literature, expresses his view in two ways. It conveys a societal image of a man of leisure, probably bored, boastful of his knowledge of art. But the expression also hints at a failure to establish a genuine link to art, a devoted connection, and so remain 'celibates of art' throughout their lives. Proust suggests that their familiarity with art is actually hollow and their false connection to it only exacerbates their obtuseness. This approach blocks the opportunity to be nurtured by art, enriching one's mind and knowledge of the world. But at times, Proust argues, the 'guilty party' is art itself with its superficiality and falsehood. Readers who are 'celibates of art' will not sense this, resulting in a twofold falsehood: that of art itself, and that of its false consumers.

Detached reading in Proust and Agnon

Proust writes:

> As to the verities which the intellect – even of highly endowed minds – gathers in the open road, in full daylight their value can be very great; but those verities have rigid outlines and are flat, they have no depth because no depths have been sounded to reach them – they have not been recreated (ibid., loc. 3043–3045).

In an article about reading, the psychoanalyst James Strachey cited clinical descriptions of patients on the basis of which he suggests that every patient who reads in a compulsive and sterile way does so in an attempt to control deep-seated fears of disintegration (Strachey, J., 1930, pp. 322–331). Winnicott, who saw in the 'false self' a structure protecting the psyche from fears of destruction and disintegration, also posits a link between the 'false self' and intellectual functioning:

> A particular danger arises out of the not infrequent tie-up between the intellectual approach and the False Self. When a False Self becomes organized in an individual who has a high intellectual potential there is a very strong tendency for the mind to become the location of the False Self ... an attempt on the part of the individual to solve the personal problem by the use of a fine intellect (Winnicott, D.W., 1965, p. 143).

The researcher Rachel Zoran described two avenues of escape in relation to reading; escape from reading and escape into reading (Zoran, R., 2000, pp. 119–121). The following excerpt from Agnon's *A Simple Story* (1935) presents a dialogue between a father and his daughter that, in Zoran's view, sees the father, Hayyim Nacht, escaping into reading while his daughter, Blume, is escaping from it:

> Blume was a quick learner. Almost before she knew all the letters of the alphabet she was reading fairy tales and legends. Yet it astounded her father, who shed so many tears when he read that they all but rotted the pages, how little feeling she showed. None of the passages over which he was used to weeping or heaving a sigh, no one's sufferings or sorrows, seemed to move her in the least. A tragic tale that made him break down in sobs left her totally dry-eyed.
>
> 'But Papa,' she might say when he tried explaining the full poignancy of some character's predicament, 'it's his own fault. If he hadn't done what he did, it would never have happened to him.'
>
> 'Blume, my Blume,' replied Hayyim Nacht. 'How can any daughter of mine talk like that?' (Agnon, S., 1935, p. 22)

Zoran regards Hayyim Nacht's approach to literature as a search for an alternative, a substitute reality and, as such, sees it as a mirror image of the daughter's approach. Nacht wants to escape into the sanctuary of literature as an alternative reality, whereas Blume denudes literature from its richness in favour of the realms of plain reality. Another perspective would suggest that the father's disappointment testifies to him being a 'true reader'. His genuine openness to reading causes him to be astonished by his daughter's detachment and indifference to what she reads. Nor does he understand how this is consistent with her sharp intellect. Agnon describes Nacht's process of identification with the characters, the compassion he feels towards them when he introjects their suffering into his internal world, and so cannot understand how his daughter can remain detached. In my own view, Nacht's reading experience expresses a profound existential pain and a capacity for identification that would not have been possible for a false reader or someone escaping into literature so as not to experience the sorrows of life. The intellectual who, like Blume, resists 'real reading', is immune to such pains because he derives from literature what is already known, reinforces the ordinary that is his lot in life in any event.

The transformative reading described by Proust as 'recapturing' cannot be actualized while the false self or the detached self are in control of and defending the hidden true self. The false reader actively blocks dynamic, participatory, reading. Only the true self can enable the mind to play and to experiment within the transitional space. 'Only the True Self can be creative and only the True Self can feel real' (Winnicott, D.W., 1965, p. 143). Transformative reading is open to the reader who is willing to transcend the narrow confines of the already known and who dares to play in the transitional space of the text in which the true self is the central participant. In Proust's words:

> It is, of course, a great temptation to recreate true life, to renew impressions. But courage of all kinds is required, even sentimental courage. For it means above all, abrogating our most cherished illusions, ceasing to believe in the objectivity of our own elaborations
> (Proust, M., 1927, loc. 3016–3017).

In the dialogue between Hayyim Nacht and his daughter Blume in Agnon's story, there is a comment by Agnon on a failure of the parental role. Hayyim the parent fails to enable his daughter to transcend the preset parameters of her life and find a space in which to observe and develop in the midst of reading. One can see this as a comment about a parental role in the lives of his children in general and with respect to reading and the horizons it opens up in particular – to teach his children to sail beyond the obvious to areas of the world and of the self not yet revealed and towards the opportunity of seeing the other.

There is still more that we can learn from the mirror images posited by Proust between the false reader/the false writer and the true reader/true writer. Both couples collaborate with one another; the one in fear, avoidance, imitation and detachment; the other by a mutual desire to create a connection and open themselves up to a new and creative space. Proust likens the true dialogue between author and reader to an encounter between an optician and an individual whose eyesight the optician wishes to improve.

> In reality, every reader, as he reads, is the reader of himself. The work of the writer is only a sort of optic instrument which he offers to the reader so that he may discern in the book what he would probably not have seen in himself. The recognition of himself in the book by the reader is the proof of its truth and vice-versa ... the difference between the two texts being often less attributable to the author than to the reader ... the author must not take offence at that but must, on the contrary, leave the reader the greatest liberty and say to him: 'Try whether you see better with this, with that, or with another glass.' (ibid., loc. 3239–3240).

It is evident that Proust doesn't ascribe the capacity to write or read to any transcendent force. He regards these capacities as a means of gaining access to the inner self and encountering forgotten experiences of the distant past, experiences that had had a primal life that had been lost, a life that can be reawakened through reading like that which Proust himself experienced when he tasted the famous madeleine cake: 'that made me perceive that a work of art is the only means of returning and finding lost time ... I understood that all the material of a literary work was in my past life' (ibid., loc, 3056). As with the author, so the reader is also invited to meet up with his past life.

> That life which cannot observe itself, the outer forms of which, when observed, need to be interpreted and often read upside down, in order to be laboriously deciphered. The work of our pride, our passion, our spirit of imitation, our abstract intelligence, our habits must be undone by art which takes the opposite course and returning to the depths where the real has its unknown being, makes us pursue it (ibid., loc. 3013–3016).

Such a beautiful description by Proust to what is imminently to be found in us but with which we have lost contact. He does not relate to the work of art as introducing the transcendent unconscious as do, for example, Heidegger and Blanchot, as will be detailed in what follows. But the inner being with which contact is re-established must consent to the process. Were a gatekeeper in the form of the false self to be posted in front of it, he wouldn't enable the journey into time and memory, the encounter with the unknown from the past and from within, which returns to life through reading and creates a new experience.

The psychoanalyst Wilfred Bion wrote an article titled 'Notes on Memory and Desire' (Bion, W., [1967] 1988, pp. 17–21), in which he discusses the difficulties faced by the analyst when meeting a patient afresh, as if not remembering anything about the patient's history or about their last session, about the analyst's theoretical approach, not being led even by his desire to cure. Bion, and in his footsteps other writers such as Ogden and Bollas, challenge the tendency to become attached to the known in favour of an openness to a live and true meeting for which one has to be in a kind of active dreamlike state, which Bion termed 'reverie'. The origin of his idea is to be found in Freud's notion that the analyst must be openly attentive to the free associations of the patient.

The technique, however, is a very elementary. It consists of simply not directing one's notice to anything in particular and in maintaining the same 'evenly suspended attention'.

> We avoid a danger which is inseparable from the exercise of deliberate attention ... In making this selection he [the analyst] will be following his expectations and inclinations. This, however, is precisely what must not be done. In making the selection, if he follows his expectations he is in danger of never finding anything but what he already knows; and if he follows his inclinations he will certainly falsify what he may perceive (Freud, S., 1912, pp. 111–112).

Freud presents the analyst's hovering attentiveness as complementary to the free associations of the patient who, to the extent that it is possible, is required to follow the basic rule in psychoanalysis, to talk without censorship and without deliberately directing his speech. This complementary relationship between patient and analyst is akin to the relations between writer and reader. The notion of the false reader on the one hand, and the false writer on the other. A false reading and writing encounter would leave the repressed and the unknown in place and continue to exist in relative poverty. Such a reading conceals a missed opportunity. A live and transformative communication requires both the reader and the writer to discard previous prejudices and the false appearances of the self by surrendering to a live, contemporary encounter that is open to the new and the unknown that exists in the inner world, in the other, as well as in what is formed between them.

Bearing all of this in mind, it is important to point out that Winnicott's account does not posit a binary choice between the true and false self but rather a continuum between a true self with minimal activity by the false self and a false self with a minimal presence of the true self. In this sense it has to be remembered that reading is also neither 'true' or 'false' but rather characterized by an increased dominance of one or other tendency that can change between one reading and another or between different periods of the reader's life. The process of reading reaches its height when it discards its false shell in favour of a genuine meeting with the literary text and through it with oneself.

References

Agnon, S. (1935). *A Simple Story*. Jerusalem and Tel Aviv: Shocken.
Bion, W. [1967] (1988). Notes on Memory and Desire. In: E.B. Spillius (Ed.) *Melanie Klein Today: Developments in Theory and Practice, Vol 2: Mainly Practice*. London and New York: Routledge, pp. 17–21.
Blanchot, M. [1955] (1982). *The Space of Literature*. London: University of Nebraska Press.
Freud, S. (1912). Recommendations to Physicians Practicing Psycho-Analysis. In: J. Strachey (Ed.) *The Standard Edition of the Complete Psychological Works of Sigmund Freud, Vol. XII*. London: Hogarth Press, pp. 109–120.
Ghent, M. (1990). Masochism, Submission, Surrender: Masochism as a Perversion of Surrender. *Contemporary Psychoanalysis*, 26, pp. 108–136.
Laplanche, J. and Pontalis, J.B. (1973). *The Language of Psychoanalysis*. London: Hogarth Press [Kindle Edition].
Proust, M. (1905). *On Reading*. New York: Three Syrens Press.
Proust, M. (1927). *In Search of Lost Time: Complete Edition*. New York: The Modern Library [Kindle Edition].
Strachey, J. (1930). Some Unconscious Factors in Reading. *International Journal of Psychoanalysis*, 11, pp. 322–331.

Winnicott, D.W. (1960). The Theory of the Parent–Infant Relationship. *International Journal of Psychoanalysis*, 41, pp. 585–595.
Winnicott, D.W. (1965). *The Maturational Processes and the Facilitating Environment*. London: Hogarth Press and the Institute of Psychoanalysis.
Zoran, R. (2000). *The Third Voice: The Therapeutic Qualities of Literature and Their Applications in Bibliotherapy*. Jerusalem: Carmel.

Further reading

Freud, S. (1920). Beyond the Pleasure Principle. In: J. Strachey (Ed.) *The Standard Edition of the Complete Psychological Works of Sigmund Freud, Vol. XVIII*. London: Hogarth Press, pp. 1–64.
Zoran, R. (2009). *The Letter's Imprint: Reading and Identity within the Bibliotherapeutic Dialogue*. Jerusalem: Carmel.

Chapter 5
The idealization of the author

The psychoanalyst Heinz Kohut (1984) suggested a special affinity between the infant and his caretaker and termed it the 'self-object'. The 'self-object' (the parent during infancy or the analyst in psychoanalysis) has to be fully prepared to devote himself to the developmental needs of his ward – the developing infant or the patient.

Kohut identified three key forms of relations with the self-object: relations of mirroring, idealization and twinship. Transference based on these forms of relations occur in the framework of psychoanalysis and, as Rachel Zoran has noted, all three forms of transference appear in the reader's transference relations with the literary heroes, the most accessible form of transference being twinship transference (Zoran, R., 2000, p. 91).

In this chapter I shall focus mainly on the idealizing transference, which is directed most prominently towards the author of the literary text. Let's begin by briefly describing the phenomena of idealization.

Melanie Klein believed that the origin of the 'idealizing transference' is in infancy, in the experiences that occur within the framework of the paranoid-schizoid position. In this position the infant copes with his anxieties by splitting the 'self' and the object into absolute good and absolute bad. Thus the breast/mother who is 'total good,' and who inspires confidence in the infant, is split from the complementing part-object – the breast/mother who is total bad, and who, in the infant's phantasy, threatens his survival. According to this view, in later life states of idealization always involve an ambivalent or even a concealed negative attitude. Only if maturity is achieved (in and thanks to the depressive position) does one recognize the complexity of the 'self' and the object as being both good and bad. It is expected that this maturation will also lead to a less radical and more stable perception of good and bad. Unlike Kohut, Klein suggested that every expression of idealizing transference in therapy is undermined by anxiety and negative transference. For example, when a patient tells the analyst in tones of excitement and admiration that the analyst is 'omniscient', there is an expectation that the patient will at the same time be anxious about a number of things: the possibility that the analyst is not 'omniscient';

the sense that he himself feels inferior to this ideal object; the uncomfortable feeling of utter dependence on the analyst; resentment of being left alone between sessions by this ideal object that the patient is dependent on, etc. In addition, the idealizing transference is unconsciously accompanied by anxiety and envy related to the disparity of qualities between the idealizer and the idolized as well as the fear of being disappointed by or failing to gain the favour of the idealized person. As we shall see in what follows, the evidence gleaned from literature will include examples of both 'Kohutian' and 'Kleinian' idealizing transference – some that are more harmonious and others that are more ambivalent.

As will be exemplified in this chapter, the idealizing transference towards the author has a crucial influence on the reader's experience. According to Lacan, the patient relates to the analyst as a 'subject who supposedly knows'. Inspired by this, Shoshana Felman realized that this is also the way in which the reader relates to the author (Felman, S., 1977, p. 7). The reader projects his existential puzzles on to the author and attributes to him a superior wisdom. The reader hopes that if he were to possess this ideal wisdom, it would open up the pathway to a rich, stable, and tranquil existence.

Relations of idealization vis-à-vis the author assume three key forms: paranoid-schizoid idealization, depressive idealization and the idealization of the author as sublime.

Paranoid-schizoid idealization

First of all a reminder. The term paranoid-schizoid position does not suggest that someone in this position suffers from paranoia or a schizoid disorder. Rather, it describes an individual who is dominated by his more primitive anxieties. This position is characterized by a tendency to deny reality through excessive use of primitive defensive mechanisms such as splitting, projection and an omnipotent denial of the sense of dependency and danger. Splitting the object into 'total bad' and 'total good' is formed so as to be protected by the good internal object from the bad object and from the bad parts of the 'self', and enjoy its goodness to the full. Another very important mechanism – internalizing identification – enables the internalization of the good object, which helps to reinforce the 'self' and its development.

The idealization of the author, linked by Klein to the paranoid-schizoid position, is accompanied by anxiety because it is undermined by its complementary facet – the envy and hostility towards the object whose power and importance are a threat to the 'self'. Therefore, this idealization is expected to quickly turn into a negative transference. Nonetheless, in reading we shall see that even during bursts of negative transference, there is a connection to the idea that the author possess an abundance of virtues. As will be illustrated in what follows, the kind of idealization characteristic of the paranoid-schizoid position is also associated with an archaic rigid 'superego'. Often it will also be characterized by the attribution to the author of heightened moral and ethical capacities. The reader will accordingly face him with tough and exacting demands and severely judge his every misstep. This sort of idealization also attributes to the author the power of an internal compass or beacon that in certain cases the reader may attribute to one of the characters in the story. The reader expects the author or the hero to function as a superior being who knows the answers to all questions and the right way to think and act. In the reader's phantasy the author or the hero apply value judgments in a tyrannical and uncompromising way as a means of repairing injustices and irregularities that preoccupy the reader. If so the paranoid-schizoid idealization carries with it a yearning and dependency that are powerful and yet at the same time fragile and vulnerable, hanging by a thread. Explosive forces thus smoulder beneath the paranoid-schizoid idealization, seeking to smash it to pieces, violently destroying the object, hoping with his destruction to obliterate the feelings of dependency, envy and anxiety.

Paranoid-schizoid idealization in Paul Celan's poem 'In Memoriam Paul Éluard'

In Memoriam Paul Éluard

Lay those words into the dead man's grave
which he spoke in order to live.
Pillow his head amid them,
let him feel
the tongues of longing,
the tongs.
Lay that word on the dead man's eyelids
which he refused to him
who addressed him as thou,
the word
his leaping heart-blood passed by
when a hand as bare as his own
knotted him who addressed him as thou
into the trees of the future.
Lay this word on his eyelids:
perhaps
his eye, still blue, will assume
a second, more alien blueness,
and he who addressed him as thou
will dream with him: We
               (Celan, P., [1955] 1972).

Paul Celan's elegy was written in memory of the French poet Paul Éluard, one of the pillars of the communist world's intelligentsia. The poem addresses an immoral side of Éluard's, fidelity to the communist party. It was written as a disappointed response to the poet's refusal in 1950 to intervene in favour of the Czech poet Zavis Kalandra who'd been sentenced to death. Kalandra was executed and Éluard himself died two years later.

Celan turns to the poet in the name of Zavis Kalandra and asks that he view him as 'thou'. But Éluard turned his back on him as 'thou' and so 'knotted him who addressed him as thou into the trees of the future' – the gallows.

The poet's unique role in Celan's poem is stressed by the inclusion of his name in its title. In Celan's view Éluard had been handed a divine mission – to condemn a man to death or let him live. Celan eulogizes the poet but it is a eulogy crammed with expressions of Celan's deep pain due to Éluard's abdication of responsibility not only in the practical sense but also by his failure to adopt an ethical stand and act in a moral way. Celan writes about the poet for turning a blind eye, 'him who addressed him as thou', words that appear to relate to the poet Kalandra. Conceivably Celan is alluding to Martin Buber's essay *I and Thou*, which ascribes ontological importance and ethical meaning to the way in which humans position themselves vis-à-vis one another (internally and externally). A relation of I/thou places the other in a dialogue that fully recognizes him and is why he is addressed in the second-person singular as 'thou', engaging on equal terms with the 'I'. Such a position does not create an estrangement from the other as would be the case were he to be addressed in the third-person singular as the 'he' who is talked about but is not met nor recognized as the divine 'thou'.

Celan's relation of idealization towards the poet hints to his assumption that Éluard as a poet, is supposed to see the face of the other as obligating (Levinas, E., [1961] 1991). 'Lay that word on the dead man's eyelids', Celan writes. Éluard 's eyes are mentioned several times in the poem. His eyes were turned away and now Celan demands that the word, the missing word, the unspoken word should be put on the poet's closed eyes, speaking both concretely (as he is a dead poet) and metaphorically (blind to the 'thou'). The poetic word is placed twice on Éluard's eyes – once, through Celan's words and twice in the narrative of the poem. The word will be repositioned, perhaps as a sign of redemption, to the idealized poet's eye that is obligated to see the other.

It would seem that it was not only the physical death to which Éluard condemned Kalandra that preoccupied Celan. More than anything else he was concerned at the way in which Éluard had betrayed the Czech poet. The idealization turned into negative transference. The poet was expected to perform as an idealized parent with whom the infant feels safe and protected, as the parent's most fundamental obligation is to keep him alive physically and psychologically. The milk in the poet's breast is the 'word', used here by one poet to lambast the other: 'Lay that word on the dead man's eyelids / which he refused to him ... / the word / his leaping heart-blood passed by'. The particular situation in which the word of the poet is requested in the political reality to save Kalandra's life is intertwined with the poetic situation where the poet's role is not to allow his 'heart-blood pass by' the word. He is accused of refusing to acknowledge another whose hand is as 'bare as his own'; and who addresses him as 'thou'. Celan ends with the words 'will dream with him: We'. Perhaps the dream is a state of openness and reverie, as opposed to the internal deadness of the one who turns his back to the other. 'We' is the very last word in the poem, the missing word. The idealized poetic parent had left the hand of the dependent reader, forgetting its loyalty and devotion. The idealized poet is expected to never betray the big ethical demand to see us all as 'we', never to turn a blind eye. And in these last words 'will dream with him: We' is hidden again the idealizing transference of Celan who dreams to repair history and reunite, become 'we' again, with the idealized poet.

Depressive idealization

Again a reminder. The term 'depressive position' does not mean that the individual suffers from depression. Rather it is a position of mourning that recognizes an individual's transience, partialness, vulnerability and dependency in the face of the vastness of existence and the finality of death. One of the crucial achievements of the depressive position is the acquisition of language. The psychoanalyst Dana Amir explains:

> Language is first and foremost a depressive achievement involving both the concession of what cannot be articulated – and the giving up of the symbiosis with the other by acknowledging him or her as a distinct subject. Indeed, acknowledging separation is simultaneously the driving motivation to speak as well as an essential condition for establishing language (Amir, D., 2014, p. 1).

Amir also notes that one can use language in an alienated or false manner, and that a live use of a language requires that a particular set of conditions be in place. Amir Asks:

> What are the conditions necessary for the creation of a living language? A language which gives the interior a sense of measure but also maintains its quest after immortality; its transcendental, godlike features; its prayer, its cry? A language that is capable of transcending itself as well as of observing itself, one that enacts truth rather than just describing it? (ibid., p. 3).

Maya Bejerano's poem 'The Face and the Voice' (2001) dedicated to the poet Yehuda Amichai describes a unique psychological state that I suggest be termed 'depressive idealization'. It has to be said that Kleinian psychoanalysis would view the expression 'depressive idealization' as an oxymoron. It does not relate to the possibility of idealization in the framework of the depressive position but rather regards it as an outcome of a split that is characteristic of the paranoid-schizoid position. However, literary evidence shows that while reading such a split can be triggered. We must therefore explore, and maybe learn anew from literature, a special kind of idealization, which is characterized by a true and modest recognition of the artist's unique qualities for which he is indeed idealized. This kind of idealization does not assume an omnipotent denial of the poet's limitations in other areas and in his existence as a human being. We might even be able to say that the evidence to be found in literature requires the field of psychoanalysis to think again about the possible linkage between idealization and the depressive position beyond the realms of literature.

Reading from a position of depressive idealization elevates the author to a level of excellence but not one that is beyond human achievement. It does not erase the complexity of existence nor does it catapult the author into the realm of the transcendent. On the contrary, his greatness lies in the ability to be a container who, through a living language, transmits the diverse and the complex, the cantankerous and the quiescent, the eternal and the finite, without all of these becoming his ornaments or palaces. He serves as a conduit capable of transmitting all of these through language. The author is a unique object in that he is both a transformative container and also one who teaches the craft of containment and transformation. In the course of reading, those matters that in daily life arouse anxiety turn into hoped-for destinations. Depressive idealizing-transference uses the poet as an inspiration to reach the depths of the riddle of human existence.

In accordance with the depressive position's integrative quality, the depressive image of the idealized poet contains the entire gamut of brightness and darkness, squalor and purity. Moreover, the poet is idealized for his sweat; for his readiness to touch upon all that comes with life courageously, with open eyes and with talent beyond the horizons of most of us.

'The face and the voice', by Maya Bejerano (dedicated to Yehuda Amichai)

The Face and the Voice

Amichai's face arises from the abyss,
covering and uncovering the suffering of the whole body
one glance from both eyes strengthening and hidden
through the veil dividing between here and there

between life and what's beyond
and a poet is always at a double foothold,
for a moment he is allowed to go on wondering
and the reverberating voice arises while multiplying
a voice that touches everybody and includes him in the convoy
a voice identified- the same voice I heard 30 years ago
Amichai's voice in the old city of Jerusalem, a poetry workshop.
And if he likened his life experiences to chalices, arising from the abyss
Full of grass and shell-sand and see-weed
Still, their form remained that of chalices
The voice is the holy grail
And the face is the experiencing

(Bejerano, M., 2001).[1]

The face of Yehuda Amichai, the poet to whom Bejerano dedicates her poem, rises from the abyss, revealing suffering. The poet is flesh and blood, bringing up from the abyss (contrary to bringing from above, from the divine – as in the third form of idealization described below), all that is to be found: 'grass and shell-sand and see-weed'. The image of the poet as lifting the earth's materials from the abyss is reminiscent of the idea proffered by the philosopher Martin Heidegger in relation to the work of art: 'The work lets the earth be an earth' (Heidegger, M., [1950] 1993, p. 78). Heidegger describes the creative movement from the common to the unique and from understanding to pre-understanding.

> This setting forth of the earth is what the work [work of art] achieves by setting itself back into the earth ... To be sure, the poet, too, uses words, not, however, like ordinary speakers and writers who must use them up, but rather in such a way that only now does the word become and remain truly a word (ibid, p. 27).

Heidegger's approach distinguishes between the 'known', the already thought, the 'as-if' understanding based upon what is already commonly known about the world on the one hand, and the 'unthought', something that has not yet been considered, on the other. That the uniqueness of a work of art lies in its capacity to develop into the unthought is an idea reminiscent of the term 'unthought-known', coined by the psychoanalyst Christopher Bollas (Bollas, C., 1987, pp. 287–293). Bollas alludes to states of mind in which things that were known to us become thought by us, recognized. When we are faced with the 'unthought-known' we feel a mixture of utter surprise and at the same time deep familiarity. We might suggest that the poet's words reveal the 'unthought-known' of his and of his readers. In his book *The Space of Literature* the French philosopher Maurice Blanchot, influenced by Heidegger, wrote:

> Thus the work points us toward the deep of obscurity ... Hölderlin [a poet admired and researched by Heidegger] calls it Mother Earth, the earth closed upon its silence, the subterranean earth that withdraws into its shadow. Rilke speaks to it thus: 'Earth, is this not what you want, to be reborn invisible in us?' ... Here, however, where we seek only to take cognizance of the principal features of the work, let us remember that it is turned toward the elemental deep, toward that element which would seem to be the depth and shadow of the elemental ... For when the work takes place, certainly the elemental is illuminated and the deep is as if present, as if attracted toward the daylight (even though the work also pushes this deep down deeper by resting its full weight there (Blanchot, M., [1955] 1982, p. 204).

Heidegger, and in his footsteps Blanchot, thus distinguish between the artist and the work of art in a way that is similar to the theme of Bejerano's poem. The poet brings up from the earth its treasures as an emissary, as a workman who has the quality or the ability to step back from the known and familiar and pave the way into being. This is the unique attribute of the depressively idealized poet. He is not divine but rather a man who is endowed with the ability to find an opening to the divine and the primeval and in Blanchot's words, 'the work, finally, knows him not. It closes in around his absence as the impersonal, anonymous affirmation that it is – and nothing more' (ibid., p. 3).

According to Heidegger, the opportunity of 'being-in-the-world' ('*Dasein*') is to open up to the truth of 'what is'.

> It is not only the creation of the work [the work of art] that is poetic; equally poetic, though in its own way, is the preservation of the work. For a work only actually is as a work when we transport ourselves out of the habitual and into what is opened up by the work so as to bring our essence itself to take a stand within the truth of beings (Heidegger, M., Heidegger, [1950] 1993, p. 45)

The poet is idealized for his ability to place himself, in Bejerano's words, 'through the veil' dividing between here and there, between life and what's beyond. The reader turns his gaze towards the poet because the poet's sight that is 'always at a double foothold' opens the reader's eyes towards what is beyond. The poet's voice 'arises while multiplying'. His voice rises above the conventional possibilities and simultaneously holds on to the possibilities of 'here' and 'there', of 'life' and 'what's beyond' – hence the multiplicity. Usually the reader only holds on to what is known to him and understood by him. However, the poet's voice 'touches everybody and includes him'; For a moment the poet's voice enables the reader to open up, to join and become part of a greater being, of the multiplicity, not only here but at the same time, for a moment, also 'there', beyond.

The depressively idealized poet as a container

Transference relations dominated by the depressive position facilitate the patient's use of the analyst, and the reader of the author, as containers into which they can project anxieties, drives, tensions, longings, etc. and enable the containing object to metabolize and transform these explosive psychic materials into benign and meaningful psychological experiences. Bejerano's poet 'liken[s] his life experiences to chalices, arising from the abyss / Full of grass and shell-sand and see-weed / Still, their form remained that of chalises'. The poet doesn't lose the form of the container in which he carries the world's materials from the abyss and hands them to the reader, enables him to open himself up to them and transcend the boundaries of his vision and being. A further characteristic of the depressive position that is evident in Bejerano's description of the poet is an all embracing view of reality – both good and bad, life and death, ability and helplessness, unity and separateness. In Bejerano's poem the poet's unique ability stems from his willingness to experience variety and his tendency to do so. In this sense too, his experience is always one of a double foothold.

Maya Bejerano concludes her poem with the voice and face of the poet. Heidegger spoke of the poet's voice as the conveyor of a tone that was not his, but that listens and intones.

> The poet speaks by virtue of a tone (*Stimmung*) which sets (*Bestimmt*) the ground and base and stakes out (*Durchstimmt*) the space from and in which the poetic saying establishes a mode of being. This tone we name the fundamental tone of the poetry (cited in Clark, T., 2002, loc. 2127–2129).

Similarly, in Bejerano's poetry the voice of the poet doesn't express his inner feelings but rather what he pulled up from the depths of the sea, resonating the tone of being. He is idealized for his capacity to hear the fundamental tone of being (*Grundstimmun*). In his inspiration he is essentially passive but in an attentive way – listening to the fundamental tone of earth, of the depths of life. 'As in classical theories of inspiration, as an apprehension of the world under a deeper and defamiliarizing sense. In that revelation the poet responds to something that comes from the outside' (ibid., loc. 2111–2112).

The notion of the face as 'covering' and 'uncovering' is also addressed in Nahman Bialik's essay 'Language: Closing and Disclosing' ([1915] 2002) in which he distinguishes between the prose spoken in the 'marketplace' and the language of poets. According to Bialik, poets are

> [m]asters of the hidden and secret meaning, are all their lives obsessed by the singularity of things, by that unique something, by that one

point which binds into a coherent unit all phenomena and the language forms that denote them, by the ephemeral moment which can never return, by the particular soul and immanent nature of things as grasped in a certain moment by the mind of the observer. (Bialik, H. N., [1915] 2002, pp. 5–11)

Thus, in a vein similar to that of Heidegger and Blanchot, Bialik suggests that in this way

> the language is revitalized and transformed; a minute change can put a new gleam on an old word ... meanwhile betwixt and between closing the chasm glimmers. And that is the secret of the tremendous influence of the language of poetry (ibid.).

The idealizing transference conveyed in Bejerano's poem and dedicated to the poet Yehuda Amichai is depressive in that it simultaneously captures the essence of the poet's suffering, the modesty in him as a listener of the creation as opposed to the creator himself, and at the same time of the divine in him. The idealizing transference is directed at the experienced face that can voice what is contained, is exchanged for words and joins each one to the convoy.

As Bejerano – a poet herself – is telling us something about her transference relations with the poet Amichai, she also conveys her burden and duty as a poet, and while doing that she also evokes in us an idealizing transference for her and for her ability to join us on this poetic convoy.

Idealization of the writer as sublime

A third kind of idealizing transference endows the author with the quality of 'total good' as is the case in paranoid-schizoid idealization. However, in this form of idealization there is no evidence for the counterpart, of the negative transference seeking to undermine it. In certain situations the reader's experience is accompanied by a feeling of supreme joy when he feels he has succeeded in touching the divine. In such situations, an unqualified idealized transference towards the author is aroused in the reader that is characterized by a quality of transcendence, a religious dimension and a relation to the divine. This form of idealization is more akin to the description by the psychoanalyst Kohut of the transference towards the idealized self-object, where the subject admires and feels happy and safe in his strong and idealized embrace.

The reader, who feels such idealizing transference towards the writer, surrenders himself to him without any reservations or distortions. This stems from the unique experience of an encounter with a person and his creation, which inspires the reader and reveals to him something that is beyond his usual scope of experience. Conceivably idealization of this kind belongs to moments of spiritual sublimation or even to a connection to an existential option of reparation. The author is perceived as touching transcendence and will often attain epithets that indeed will link him to the divine.

Idealizing the author as divine in Bialik's poem 'To the Poet'

To the Poet

Head full of thought
Heart carving flame ...
The almighty's voice is heard in the voice ...
A thousand eyes he has,
A myriad ears he has,
He foresees, He listens everywhere
To him opens the window
To the purity in the sky
In him chants a song of holiness and glory ...
The divine itself
Listens to the joyous song,
Angels take sweet counsel with him ...
And looking from above
To north, to south,
Deep deep is the abyss ...
In it he sees all filth,
And knows, and understands all ...
           (Bialik, H.N., 1891)[2]

Bialik's poem was apparently written in October or November 1891 in Odessa, inspired by the poetry of the Jewish/Russian poet Shimon Shmuel Frug about whom Bialik wrote in a letter to his friend Eliyahu Friedman:

> Just moments before writing this letter I finished reading Frug's poems, Oh, Friedman, How fortunate for Frug to have been endowed from heaven with such a pure and lofty soul ... Such a man will be called a poet! He who is loved by the muse! He who is the child of God! One of the small, tiny angels ... I cannot describe the powerful impression Frug's poems have had on me. (ibid., p. 493)

The idealizing transference evident in his letter is no less conspicuous in his poem anonymously dedicated 'To the Poet', and is in this way directed at whoever is able to speak in a divine, Godly voice, in the language of poetry. Bialik's idealizing transference is absolute. The poet is endowed with Godly features: 'A thousand eyes he has, / A myriad ears he has, / He foresees, He listens everywhere'. Alternatively, at one level below this, 'To him opens the window / To the purity in the sky / In him chants a song of holiness and glory'. Which is to say that the poet is a person who is a conduit or a container in which the holy song is sung. If so, he is either divine or divinity has come to dwell in him and reveal his secret to him. 'The divine itself / Listens to the joyous song, / Angels take sweet counsel with him'. Interestingly, Bialik's idealization of the poet does not insulate him from the dark side of existence. One could even say that the very opposite is true. In one of the Talmudic images of the angel of death he is all eyes (*Babylonian Talmud*, Idolatory, 22, in Epstein, I., 1948). Perhaps in that way too the poem depicts the poet's power as identical to the most powerful forces in existence. He is able to see into the depths of the abyss and observe the outcasts of society. But he turns away from them and is endowed with an understanding of everything with great knowledge and the ability to observe from above, which is a hint at a transcendent, divine, God-like perspective.

In contrast to the two previous forms of idealizing transference, the reader's experience here is completely surrendered and devoted to the poet as an object of idealization possessed of divine capabilities and omniscience, which transcends that of the reader. The reader who spends time in the embrace of this object is happy and rejoices at having had the opportunity of hearing the voice of the son of god and the muse. Bialik's voice, also the voice of a poet, seems to be devoid of any sign of envy. He too has experienced the sublimation that belongs to the reader's and worshipper's encounter with the spiritual; the transcendence beyond the common, a sublimation that arouses a profound sense of happiness and gratitude

It is also possible to read Bialik's letter and his poem as written with tongue in cheek, in irony. Even if so, through his alleged use of irony Bialik would still point to the representation in him of the idealized author as touching upon the divine, perhaps denied through irony to alleviate his envy or to avoid the sin of arrogance as a poet himself.

Notes

1 Translated from Hebrew by Shulamit Lapid.
2 Translated from Hebrew by Shulamit Lapid.

References

Amir, D. (2014). *Cleft Tongue: The Language of Psychic Structures*. London: Karnac Books.
Bejerano, M. (2001). *Beauty Is Rage*. Tel Aviv: HaKibbutz HaMeuchad.

Bialik, H.N. (1891). To the Poet. In: A. Holzman (Ed.) *Hayim Nachman Bialik: The Poems*. Or Yehuda: Dvir, pp. 493–494.

Bialik, H.N. [1915] (2002). Language Closing and Disclosing. In: D. Joseph (Ed.) *The Heart and the Fountain*. Oxford and New York: Oxford University Press, pp. 255–261.

Blanchot, M. [1955] (1982). *The Space of Literature*. Lincoln: University of Nebraska Press.

Bollas, C. (1987). *The Shadow of the Object: Psychoanalysis of the Unthought Known*. New York: Columbia University Press.

Celan, P. [1955] (1972). In Memoriam Paul Éluard. In: *Paul Celan: Selected Poems*. London and Australia: Penguin Books, p. 40.

Clark, T. (2002). *Martin Heidegger*. New York: Routledge.

Epstein, I. (1948). *The Babylonian Talmud*. London: Soncino Press.

Felman, S. (Ed.) (1977). *Literature and Psychoanalysis: The Question of Reading, Otherwise*. Baltimore, MD: John Hopkins University Press.

Heidegger, M. [1950] (1993). The Origin of the Work of Art. In: *Martin Heidegger: The Basic Writings*. London: Routledge, pp. 143–212.

Klein, M. (1946). Notes on Some Schizoid Mechanisms. In: *Envy and Gratitude and Other Works 1946–1963*. London: Vintage, pp. 25–42.

Kohut, H. (1984). *How Does Analysis Cure?* Chicago, IL: University of Chicago Press.

Levinas, E. [1961] (1991). *Totality and Infinity*. Dortrecht: Kluwer Academic.

Zoran, R. (2000). *The Third Voice: The Therapeutic Qualities of Literature and Their Applications in Bibliotherapy*. Jerusalem: Carmel.

Chapter 6

Mutual witnessing

A return to Semprún's book *Literature or Life*

Yet another psychic process experienced by the reader in the framework of his transference relations towards literary characters is linked to his ability to bear witness to himself and to others.

In the book *Witnessing* by Dori Laub and Shoshana Felman (1992), Philip Müller – one of the witnesses in Claude Lanzmann's film *Shoah* is quoted. Like the survivor witnessing in Semprún's book, Müller was also forced to deal with the corpses in the Auschwitz crematorium. He testifies:

> I couldn't understand any of it. It was like a blow on the head, as if I'd been stunned. I didn't even know where I was ... I was in shock, as if I'd been hypnotized, ready to do whatever I was told. I was so mindless, so horrified (Felman, S. and Laub, D., 1992, p. 231).

The question is raised by Dori Laub:

> How to attest to the way things were from within the very situation of delusion and illusion – from inside the utter blindness to what in reality things were? How to bear witness to historic truth from inside the radical deception (amplified by self – deception) by which one was separated from historic truth at the very moment one was most involved in it? ... It is impossible to testify from the inside because the inside has no voice ... Who would be in a position, then, to tell? The truth of the inside is even less accessible to the outsider. If it is indeed impossible to bear witness to the Holocaust from inside, it is even more impossible to testify to it from the outside (ibid., pp. 231–232).

The psychoanalyst Michael Balint compared the psychological reaction to traumatic situations to examples in geology and crystallography in which 'the word fault is used to describe a sudden irregularity in the overall structure, an irregularity which in normal circumstances might lie hidden but, if strains and stresses occur, may lead to a break, profoundly disrupting the overall structure' (Balint, M., 1968, p. 21). Melanie Klein showed how dissociation between the different functions of the mind, which can reach psychic death, serves as a defence against the experience of an existential threat (Klein, M., 1946).

This unique mental state lead to Semprún's preoccupation throughout his book with the challenge of bearing 'impossible witnessing' (Felman, S. and Laub, D., 1992, p. 58). This quandary is already represented in the title of Semprún's book: *Literature or Life* (1994). Semprún claims that as someone who crossed death he is unable to write about his witnessing but at the same time is also unable not to write about it. It is evident that when he is already in Buchenwald concentration camp he is repeatedly coping with the tension between the mind's tendency to split and be absent from the inferno and the search for ways to survive mentally by a desperate search for structure and meaning. It seems that the recurring solution adopted by Semprún is to turn to the literary space both as reader and writer.

Listening to the survivor from the Sonderkommando, Semprún is in the same situation as the survivor testifying in the film *Shoah* – his functioning as a witness collapses when he recalls Malraux's novel. There are three witnesses here: the surviving witness from Auschwitz who bears witness in words; Semprún who listens to him; and Malraux, the witness to whom Semprún turns to read his testimony about his coping in another war.

Dori Laub distinguishes between three levels of witnessing inferred from Holocaust witnessing but that can also be applied to other traumatic situations: 'The level of being a witness to oneself within the experience; the level of being a witness to the testimonies of others; and the level of being a witness to the process of witnessing itself' (Felman, S. and Laub, D., 1992, p. 75). In listening to the witness from Auschwitz Semprún is witnessing the other and at the same time witnessing himself, because he too is a survivor. Though he is not a survivor of the hell of transferring corpses from the gas chambers to the crematoria, he nonetheless endured a harsh enough hell for him to repeatedly declare in his book that he had crossed death. In a certain sense, the affinity of the two survivors turns them into too similar witnesses for the one to bear the witnessing of the other.

The literature dealing with trauma refers extensively to the essential role of the 'other' in bearing witness to a trauma the victim could not have witnessed himself as a live experience. The mind's ability to experience is a psychological precondition to every course of psychic development. If the 'self' is not psychologically present in his experience, as is the case in the face of trauma for example, he will be unable to learn, think, reflect upon and grow from his experience. Nor will he be able to feel, contain or cope with the profound emotional harm inflicted. Bion termed this state 'minus K' (knowledge), in which meaning is dismissed and presents a naked representation. Thus the witness might be able to describe the chain of verbal representations of events, but without a link to its meaning, because such a link would lead to a psychological catastrophe.

The psychoanalyst Dana Amir describes mental states characterized by an absence of the psychic functioning of the internal witness. In the course of development, the mother witnesses her child's experiences and he internalizes her witnessing eyes and heart, gradually becoming a crucial internal function of the mind – and inner witness to our own experiences. Amir's concept, shared with Shoshana Felman, is that witnessing is the moment at which the story and the personal history meet (Amir, D., 2014, p. 97).

When Semprún ceases to be present as a witness to the Auschwitz survivor and of his own experience, he feels paralyzed and lost. And then and there literature arrives as a last resort. Semprún, intuitively led by his strong life instinct and his great faith in the curative power of literature, resorted to a meeting with a third literary witness.

Through the encounter with Malraux a highly effective experience of mutual witnessing that has a healing function was formed: Malraux is experienced as a witness to Semprún's story and lends a voice to his screaming muteness. At the very same time Semprún the reader experiences himself as a present and attentive witness to Malraux's painful story. This simultaneous happening revives Semprún's lost inner-witness functioning.

It is no wonder, that when Semprún is troubled by the possibility that the written examples will fail to convey the nature of the experiences in the concentration camp to the readers, afraid that '[t]he other kind of understanding, the essential truth of the experience, cannot be imparted' (Semprún, J., 1994, p. 127), he once again puts his faith in the power of literature.

So he writes anxiously:

> I imagine there'll be a flood of accounts ... And there will be documents ... Everything will be said, put in record ... . Everything in these books will be true ... except that they won't contain the essential truth, which no historical reconstruction will ever be able to grasp, no matter how thorough and all-inclusive it may be (ibid., pp. 124–125).

Semprún realizes that documented accounts cannot communicate the essence of the experience when they are limited to providing 'objective'descriptions of what took place.

Only fiction, he says, not facts, could offer 'live' evidence and bring into being the conditions that will allow the reader's mind to form a connection with the essence of the intolerable human experiences. Semprún believes that only the reader's encounter with the literary story will enable him to imagine and come closer to the evidence about the traumatic reality. All other straightforward documentation or testimonies given in the first person would arouse detachment and unconscious resistance. In Semprún's words:

Literary narratives, at least, that will go beyond simple eyewitness accounts, that will let you imagine, even if they can't let you see ... Perhaps there will be a literature of the camps ... . And I do mean literature, not just reportage ... What's problematical is not the description of this horror. Not just that, anyway – not even mostly that. What's at stake here is the exploration of the human soul in the horror of Evil ... We'll need a Dostoyevsky! (ibid., p. 127)

This is also the opportunity created by Semprún for us, his readers: he enables his readers who encounter his testimony as a narrator to connect to his experience in a profound way. His witnessing being both autobiographical and literary grants us the opportunity to repair our inner witness and helps us to reflect on moments in our (and our loved ones') lives in which our inner witness ceased to function.

References

Amir, D. (2014). *Cleft Tongue: The Language of Psychic Structures*. London: Karnac Books.
Balint, M. (1968). *The Basic Fault*. London: Tavistock.
Felman, S. and Laub, D. (1992). *Testimony: Crises of Witnessing in Literature, Psychoanalysis and History*. New York and London: Routledge.
Klein, M. (1946). Notes on Some Schizoid Mechanisms. In: *Envy and Gratitude and Other Works 1946–1963*. London: Vintage, pp. 25–42.
Semprún, J. (1994). *Literature or Life*. London and New York: Penguin Books.

Chapter 7

Reparation of the ethical position

The ethical covenant

From the moment we are born we belong to an unspoken, self-evident covenant that is nonetheless always overshadowed by the fear that it will be violated. It is a covenant that binds us to protect each other's wholeness. If, in light of this covenant we return to Martin Buber's phrasing, it can be said that as the mother (at least supposedly) views her baby everyone should see the other as 'thou' and not 'he' (Buber, M., [1923] 2010). The baby being cared for by his mother is the beneficiary of her protecting his health and the integrity of his body and soul. However, according to the psychoanalytic view, every pain experienced by the infant arouses in him unconscious phantasies that the mother has violated the fundamental covenant to protect the baby's integrity or might violate it in the future and harm him. According to Melanie Klein, this is the origin of the primary splitting between the 'good mother' and the 'bad mother' to occur in the infant's psyche in a defensive way. This splitting also stems from the inborn dialectic of the life and death drives and feelings of love and hate that are projected on to the mother and, in a split way, shape her imagined character and the infant's inner world. In the process of normal development the ability to view the other as whole and separate is acquired gradually. From that develops the ability to sufficiently respect his freedom, separateness and his needs. In addition, there is a development of the recognition that there won't always be congruity between my needs and those of the object and yet it is up to me to accept a certain responsibility for the fate of the other. These are the achievements of the depressive position that, according to Klein, integrate the image of the 'other' and of the 'self' and thus promote the realization that in me as well as in the other there is good and bad and that one has to deal with their constant inner struggles gently and wisely. Moreover, because this position acknowledges the separateness of the other it achieves a range of recognitions that constitute lofty human and psychic achievements, including consideration, empathy, gratitude, compassion, creativity, capacity for reparation and openness to inspiration.

This covenant is silent and, like the air we breathe, isn't noticed. It is concerned with ensuring that the I/thou relations are honoured and maintained, that the 'I' is remembered by the 'other' as the 'I who is other', and that through the identification with the 'I in the other' the most basic rights of a person will be protected.

In traumatic situations one of the most fundamental components of a person's life that is damaged is the structure of the 'I/thou' relation. Not only does the individual reveal that his own integrity is in danger or has been desecrated, he has also to face the fact that he has been damaged by one of the most profound covenants – the covenant to ensure mutual integrity.

In traumatic situations that are caused by people, beginning with personal incidents such as rape and murder and ending with genocide, the 'other' is set apart from the human race and dispossessed of the recognition that he is in fact a part of the 'I and thou community'. The traumatised 'other' is erased as 'an-other I' and his subjectivity is brutally attacked by the party that is being violent towards him. These occur along a continuum from the victims of 'stubborn trauma' (Ziv, E., 2012, pp. 55–73), which is the result of persistent social depression and up to extreme cases of collective trauma such as the Armenian or Jewish Holocaust that comprehensively excludes whole populations in an attempt to annihilate them.

Traumatic situations undermine and attack the recognition of the victim's legitimate right to exist as a human being whose wholeness, rights and freedom must be protected by the other, recognizing me as his 'thou' and also being seen by me as 'thou'.

As Dori Laub has noted:

> To understand it one has to conceive of the world of the Holocaust as a world in which the very imagination of the Other was no longer possible. There was no longer an other to which one could say 'Thou' in the hope of being heard, of being recognized as a subject, of being answered. The historical reality of the Holocaust became, thus, a reality which extinguished philosophically the very possibility of address, the possibility of appealing, or of turning to, an-other. But when one cannot turn to a 'you' one cannot say 'thou' even to oneself (Felman, S. and Laub, D., 1992, pp. 81–82).

In one of the examples Semprún holds the hand of Diego Morales who arrived to Buchenwald during the summer of 1944 after a brief stay in Auschwitz. He immediately captured Semprún's heart because like him Morales was a lover of books and had a superb talent of his own for storytelling. Morales said that the reading of a book had had a revolutionary impact on his life. He used to say that a book was responsible for the adventurous nature of his life, '"A fucking little book", he'd say, laughing.

Un jodido librito ... Reading this book had turned his life upside down' (Semprún, J., 1994, p. 189).

Semprún further says of Morales that he 'credited Stendhal's book with effects ... albeit in a different domain ... (The Red and the Black) had initiated him into the mysteries of the human soul' (ibid., p. 190).

It seems as if Semprún turns to Morales' reading experiences as he is confronted by his near death, so as to endow the collapsing body with a human and spiritual dimension by an allusion to him as a bibliophile. Subsequently he writes:

> 'It's not fair', Morales has just murmured to me, moments after I've sat down next to his cot, moments after I've taken his hand in mine.
> He's right, it's not fair that he should die now ... It's not fair to die idiotically of the runs after so many chances to die weapons in hand ... I don't tell him that death is stupid, by definition. As stupid as birth, at least. And just as stupefying. This would not be any consolation (ibid., pp. 190–191).

Semprún faces the loss of meaning. He holds his friend's hand, a friend who so clearly understands that his humanity has been crushed, emptied and that he is about to end his life in a most humiliating and ignoble way from diarrhoea. Semprún describes his death as 'stupid' and 'stupefying', insufferably ridiculous that his friend is going to die from diarrhoea in Buchenwald concentration camp. In times of need he turns to literary segments etched in his memory, and takes down the poems of Baudelaire from his 'inner' bookshelf to read to Morales a poem he had previously read to his mentor Halbwachs at the moment of his death. But he feels that this is not the appropriate poem, and instead turns to Cesar Vallejo's poems. Then, in reading a poem from Vallejo, Semprún with chilling delicacy revokes the violent erasure of his friend's humanity a moment before his death.

From an ethical point of view, reading the poem repairs the sacred covenant according to which 'the other is a free being of self-worth, not dependent on me' (Sagi, A., 2012, p. 98). Morales had been subdued by these measures; he was in captivity and his value had been erased. Semprún symbolically liberates him through poetry. In his book *Facing Others and Otherness* Sagi describes four ethical stands of facing the other. In the first, the subject is passive in the presence of the other while 'the presence of the other is compelling and obliging ... the other's face obliges the subject' (ibid., p. 95). This approach is based on the suggestion of the philosopher Emmanuel Levinas, who regarded the affinity between the 'self' and the other as being bound up with responsibility whether or not it is actualized: 'The tie with the Other is knotted only as responsibility, this moreover, whether accepted or refused, whether knowing or not knowing how to assume it, whether able or unable to do something concrete for the sake of the Other' (Levinas, E., 1985, p. 3). The second stand is based on the suggestion by the philosopher Husserl, which offers the very opposite picture to that presented by Levinas. It claims that the 'transcendental self' has to be active in order to establish the other as a subject. A third ethical stand suggests 'an intermediate attitude which intercedes between the subject and his preparatory role ... and the primacy and lack of dependency of what is seen and appears in the subject himself' (Sagi, A., 2012). The main thinkers maintaining this approach are Heidegger, Merlo Ponti and Jean-Luc Marion. The fourth and last stand is offered by Avi Sagi and has been termed by him 'ethics of loyalty to the visible'. Sagi argues that:

> Interpersonal relations are shaped by the continuous tension between two actions: The objectification which turns the other into an object and the uncompromising presence of the other ... two different and contradictory perspectives in our lives – the sovereignty of the subject and turning the other into an object which is for the benefit of the self on the one hand, and the other's refusal to become a mere object on the other hand. Unlike other objects in the world 'the human 'object' frequently refuses to his existence as an absolute object (ibid., p. 96).

Sagi suggests that the 'ethics of loyalty to the visible' seeks to restrain the subject's tendency to objectify the other. This ethics requires seeing of the other in his totality and does not allow for the negation of his visibility as a whole 'being'.

The ethics of loyalty to the visible 'not only lessens the alienation from the other. It lessens people's alienation from themselves' (ibid., p. 105). There is an affinity between this idea and Klein's theory of the depressive position. The recognition of a person as a lacking 'being', separate from the other, in need of the other and not his master, is what leads to that individual's psychic development and enables him to attempt to accept himself and the other as a whole and complex person who establishes truth and value both vis-à-vis his own life and the life of another. This is an aspired achievement that is never fully gained. This too is part of being a whole and at the same time an incomplete being. Klein also links this to the inherent capacity to bestow love and consideration. This capacity, if not overly assailed by reality or by destructive drives, will contribute to the willingness of the 'self' to see the 'other' and to exist for his sake (Klein, M., 1940).

Klein's views make it clear that the ethical stand offered by Sagi is not in any way easy to follow and maintain. It depends on crucial human achievements that are the fruits of psychological development and maturity.

I suggest applying the fourth ethical stand suggested by Sagi to the use of literature by the reader in the service of reparation of the ethical dimension in his life and in his mind.

The violation of an individual's freedom and his most basic rights in the concentration camp turns him into an 'absolute object'. The traits defining him as a free being in his own right and worth are erased. Even Semprún is confused by Morales' immediately visible state. His birth like his death are viewed by him as stupid and stupefying. Over a lengthy period of time and across so many plains of life the sight of the camp's inhabitants offers a confirmation of them being objects devoid of a past, value and essence. Even in their own eyes their existence gradually becomes a matter of doubt. Acts of dehumanization gradually become convincing to all sides that this is not a humanitarian failure but rather versions of subhumans towards whom there is no need to adopt any ethical stance. Moreover, the state of the unique individual is denied. He becomes part of a mass that blurs his face and erases his unique identity. Semprún's turn to literature derives from its healing power, of its loyalty to the individual, as sketched by Aharon Appelfeld in his essay 'The Remedy and the Meaning' (1979):

> Literature certainly asks, and also answers in its own way ... constructing is not only its labor, but also its moral ... and its great precept: the individual. That individual whose father and mother gave him his name, taught him their language, gave him their love, inherited him their faith. This individual, who's particular face was erased in the crowd, and therefore became one of many, this individual is the core and essence of every literary vision. And once you are faced again with that simple truth ... you learn to humbly ask who is this individual that his sole you wish to touch, his roots you pretend to delve into. This individual is a Jew. Willing or forced – he is a Jew. Knowingly and unknowingly he bears inside his ancestors' heritage, and a language he bears, and existential being, facial lines and laughter and cry (Appelfeld, A., 1979, pp. 90–91).

Here Appelfeld is writing about the Jew but it is in the power of literature to call upon us to scrutinize the language and existence and facial lines and laughter and the weeping of every human being and so repair the right of every individual for recognition.

Semprún looks for a way to counter his friend, the bibliophile Morales' scathing words: 'It's not fair'. He is broken hearted in the face of the outrageous victory of the obliteration of man's worth. He is looking for a way of escaping the reduction of Morales to a defeated body and soul, so detached from the rich and worthy subject he once was. He is searching for a remedy in literature. 'But what can I say to Diego Morales? What words can I murmur in consolation? Can I console him at all?' (ibid., p.192) Finally he turns to a poet he particularly loves and refers to many times throughout the book. Again we can see how particular his choice is.

Only one text comes to mind, A poem by Cesar Vallejo. One of the most beautiful in the Spanish language ...

When the battle was over,
And the soldier was dead, a man came to him
And said, 'Do not die, I love you so!'
But the corpse, alas! Continued dying.

Before I can murmur the beginning of this heart-breaking poem, a convulsion runs through Morales, a kind of pestilential explosion ... His eyes roll back: he is dead.

I feel like crying, No mueras, te amo tanto, like the man in Vallejo's poem. 'Do not die, I love you so!' But the corpse, alas! Continued dying (ibid.).

On the other side of the scale of the lousy diarrhoea, the hero of the poem placed an expression of love, a scream of mourning and a cry of pain because that death does not return to our pleas. The poem's hero extracts Semprún from his silence and through the poetic character's expression of love and pain enables him to lend value and meaning to his parting from Morales.

How amazing and powerful is Semprún's referral to a poem in those moments. There are some other friends of theirs in the room but Semprún doesn't turn to them. He needs a literary image that will regain for him what he and his friends had lost: their faith in the 'ethics of loyalty to the visible'. The shadow of the poem's hero – which contains his past, his values, his humane positions, spiritual and mental – is laid upon Morales and becomes a reminder of his full and whole visibility from the past and from the depths. From the literary mirror his full image is reflected, flickers beyond the thin and inhuman peel of the defeated body and the present moment. Conceivably it is no accident that Semprún looked to poetry, which has the capacity to contain a broad body of meaning in a few short lines.

From one perspective, the 'man' in Vallejo's poem, looking at the dying soldier, is the literary twin of Semprún gazing at dying.

From a different and yet complementary perspective, one can see how Semprún's encounter with the 'Man' in Vallejo's poem expands his vision not only of Morales but also of himself. Semprún too is a soldier overwhelmed by the hobnailed Nazi soldiers who aim to crush his value as a subject of the human race. In this sense also, his use of Vallejo's words is heart-rending in its fragile forcefulness and its therapeutic role. As he is lost for words the literary hero becomes his voice, the voice that lets Semprún shout: 'Don't die, I love you so much!' And in doing so he manages to restore both Morales' position as a subject of worth and also to conduct himself as such a subject by finding appropriate words of parting from a person he loves. Semprún's reading of Vallejo provides him with a transitional space in which he allows himself to experience, to feel, to mourn, thus rescuing both of them from the ethical violation each of them had suffered.

We see how just as the erasure of the actual presence of the other or of the self constitutes an act of ethical harm, reparation is enabled through the reader's referral to literature and his identification with the hero from whose eyes the full visibility of the other is reflected:

> As a whole 'being' whose existence stretches between his visibility in the past to the visibility in the present ... this is a continuous and full revelation which expresses the fullness of what there is and what appears before me in a complete and holistic form. It rejects the tendency to erase the actual presence of the other by labelling it and including it in the familiar schema which negates its completeness, such as 'Jew' 'Arab', 'Man', 'Woman', etc., which limits the sight. (Sagi, A., 2012, p. 101)

A man comes to life into the loving gaze in his mother's eyes, and has the right to leave life followed by a loving look of an (m)other's eyes.

It is no accident that the hero of the poem is named in the most general and open manner: Man.

References

Appelfeld, A. (1979). *Essays in the First Person*. Jerusalem: Bialik Publishing.
Buber, M. [1923] (2010). *I and Thou*. Eastford, CT: Martino Publishing.
Felman, S. and Laub, D. (1992). *Testimony: Crises of Witnessing in Literature, Psychoanalysis and History*. New York and London: Routledge.
Klein, M. (1940). Mourning and Its Relation to Manic-Depressive States. In: *Love, Guilt and Reparation and Other Works 1921–1945*. London: Vintage, pp. 344–369.
Levinas, E. (1985). *Ethics and Infinity: Conversations with Philippe Nemo*. Pittsburgh, PA: Duquesne University Press.
Sagi, A. (2012). *Facing Others and Otherness: The Ethics of Inner Retreat*. Tel Aviv: HaKibbutz HaMeuchad.
Semprún, J. (1994). *Literature or Life*. London and New York: Penguin Books.
Ziv, E. (2012). Stubborn Trauma. *A Lexical Journal of Political Thinking*, 5, pp. 55–73.

Part II

Reading literature as a means of transcendence

Introduction

Part II describes a phenomenon that I have termed 'the human longing for transcendence'. The reader uses literature as a way of transcending the circumstances of his existence. The reader ascends on the wings of the text to reach beyond his boundaries and then 'returns' to himself the same and yet altered. The transcendence occurs in two central planes of the reader's existence: transcendence beyond the boundaries of self-identity and transcendence beyond the boundaries of the human body (and death). Readers long to transcend the circumstances of their lives in many senses: they seek to transcend their fate; their flaws, the boundaries of their awareness, the boundaries of their lives, including the knowledge of their inevitable death. These transcendences are partly and temporarily gained through processes of identification by readers with literary heroes whose identity and fate differ from theirs. In addition, the transcendences derive from the psychic processes aroused in the course of reading, which transport the reader to a dreamlike, playful experience that itself constitutes transcendence beyond the confines of mental realty. Readers are also transported into a spiritual space of existence that is accompanied by the fantasy of 'symbolic immortality' (Lifton, J.R., 1973, pp. 3–15), and even transcend beyond the constraints of actual time and space, through what I have termed 'symbolic timelessness' and 'symbolic spacelessness', which are characteristic of literature. Literature as 'omniscient' gives the reader an illusion of transcendence beyond his limited knowledge, as if potentially able to encompass all.

It is important to point out that the central phenomenon in the movement of transcendence is the movement 'to and beyond' rather than that of 'reaching the destination'. This movement liberates the 'self ' ensnared in the shackles of his real present, facilitating a departure from actual barriers towards the space of possibilities.[1]

Existential philosophy assumes that man is anchored in the circumstances of his life and the tradition in which he has grown up (Gadamer, H., 1975). He faces a continuous existential struggle to carve out for himself a space for reflection and choice within the framework of these givens (Sagi, A., 1991). The 'self ' is anchored in his existence. Sagi points to the tension between the given, the possible and the potential movement between them.

The literary text activates the imagination, enabling readers to transcend their given circumstances towards their possibilities and potentiality. It may be that this transcendence is merely temporary. Nonetheless it has a developmental value because of the opportunity it lends to the reader to reflect upon the tension in him between the given and the potential and between the finite and the possible. As Sagi argues, there is special meaning that reflection evokes from the literary text, given that it is always dynamic, as is our personal growth (ibid., p. 82).

One of the major ways of attaining self-reflection through literature is bound up with an opportunity explored in this section: a creative process of letting our unconscious soar on the wings of the written word, offering a bird's-eye view both of the reader's life and of the different paths taken by others (real and imagined). Back on earth that inner being is richer than it was when it leapt from the realistic ground to the literary sky.

The longing for transcendence: a psychoanalytic perspective

The psychoanalyst Hannah Segal draws attention to an analogy between Freud's structural model and Melanie Klein's distinction between the paranoid schizoid and the depressive positions (Segal, H., 1991).

Freud's structural model (1923) distinguishes between three major structures of the mind: the 'id' the 'ego' and the 'superego'. The model is based on a change in Freud's thinking expressed in his article 'Beyond the Pleasure Principle' (1920), which presents the conflict between the life drive and death drives. Subsequently in his article 'The Ego and the Id' (1923), Freud described the mind as engaged in a continuous struggle between three forces: 'the pleasure principle', which urges to minimise tension and maximise gratification (the 'id'); 'the reality principle', which follows the requirement to adapt and comply to the demands of reality (the 'ego'); and the call of conscience, derived from internalized demands of parents and society (the 'superego'). Freud's interest in the struggle between the death drive and the life drive was prompted by the events of World War I and his observation of humanity's acts of murder and destruction that he linked to the struggle between the psychic principles: between the pleasure drive, the perception of reality and 'conscientious' behaviour. In effect, these two theories describe the human existential difficulty in enduring life's burdens in harmony. Unconsciously, the individual rebels against the limitations to his desire for unceasing pleasure. He is fearful of the potential destruction that might befall him from within and from without. He either develops adaptive defensive mechanisms such as suppression so as to cope with the immanent existential tensions, or suffers from symptoms related to them.

Melanie Klein continued to develop these Freudian ideas. She stressed the tension between the destructiveness that exists within us as result of the inborn death instinct and the need to assume responsibility for one's own life and that of the other. Klein, following Freud, argued that this drive is, from the outset, projected on to the object that in unconscious phantasy thus becomes the object endangering the life of the infant (Klein, M., 1958).

As mentioned in Part I, according to Klein these internal threats are experienced in two major types of anxiety. The first is annihilation anxiety of the self and is experienced in the framework of the paranoid-schizoid position. The second type of anxiety is of harming and losing our loved object. This type of anxiety is experienced within the framework of the depressive position. In a continuous process of mourning and working through these two types of anxiety, the individual gradually accepts reality and learns to endow it with meaning. However, in order for this opportunity to open up one has to recognize existence's terms for what they are: I am born into a life that will end, my power is limited, I am dependent on the (m)other who, at the same time, I am separate from, and I cannot allow my drives unrestrained freedom as I must assume responsibility for the life I lead and for my influence on my own fate and that of the other.[2] In both Freud and Klein's ideas the existential difficulty of enduring life's tidings features prominently. One can borrow from the Portuguese writer Fernando Pessoa the notion of 'Disquiet' (Pessoa, F., [1982] 2017) to articulate in one word the human stand in the face of these existential challenges.

Freud, Klein and their followers describe, each in their own way, three forms of efforts to transcendence, activated to escape from his existential distress:

1. Manoeuvres of psychological organization that are within the normal scope of coping, such as, for example, using mechanisms of defence, dreaming, daydreaming, humour and intellectualization.
2. Excessive use of such exercises leading to pathology. For example, manic states, obsessive-compulsive behaviour, delusional thinking and paranoia.
3. Searching for self-fulfilment and endowment of meaning along paths that transcend beyond the immediate limitations and the fetters of daily existence, such as creativity, art and spiritual practice.

Thus, the longing for transcendence takes place along a continuum that moves from transcendence through distortions in the perception of reality (either normative or pathological) to transcendence through creativity and finding meaning, even in the face of radical strains. Viktor Frankl argued that the longing for transcendence beyond fear and death and, in effect, beyond the terms and conditions of human existence, is permanent and that each individual is free to transcend his life's terms at any given moment by his immanent capacity for self-definition (Frankl, V., [1946] 2006).

One of the ways available to fulfil this longing – even if only partially and temporarily – is in the fertile realm of artistic creation in general, and literary creation in particular. The creative space affords us the opportunity for a non-pathological transcendence. Freud himself, and in his footsteps Klein and her followers too, wrote about the creative process as a unique means of coping with the terms of our existence. Freud maintained that this way of coping resembled the opportunity to fantasize and 'dream' (Freud, S., 1908). Klein and Winnicott saw in creativity an opportunity similar to that afforded by phantasizing instead of being 'trapped' in concrete reality playing (Klein, M., 1929, 1930; Winnicott, D.W., 1953). Dreaming, playing and unconscious phantasy are linked, each in their own way, to the unconscious processes aroused by the encounter with an artistic creation.

As we shall see in what follows, through transcendences that occur mostly unconsciously, reading helps the subject to cope with being trapped by the terms and conditions of human existence, be they the fairest among them or those that arouse 'disquiet'. Even though the 'visit' to the literary work is temporary, it contributes to the processes of transcendence and the formation of the 'self', which continue to take place in the reader's inner world long after the physical act of reading. Some of the different ways of transcending described in literature present views of psychic transcendence that psychoanalysis has not to date described directly and from which it can profit. The chapters in this section will explore the use of literature for the purpose of transcendence beyond the borders of 'self-' identity, and the use of literature as a means of transcending beyond the boundaries of the body and death.

Notes

1 In her book *Walking Through Trauma: Rituals of Movement in Jewish Myth, Mysticism and History*, Haviva Pedaya offers the idea that transcendence is thought of anchorage, a place that compensates for some other place that has been lost. It would be interesting to think of the variety of attempts at transcendence as unconscious phantasies of a faraway place that the 'self' intends to reach as if he were arriving or returning to the promised land (Pedaya, H., 2011, p. 92).
2 In this sense the Kleinian psychoanalytic school of thought is close to the existentialist philosophy outlined by Sartre in his article *Existentialism Is Humanism* (1945): 'One can find in Klein's ideas an echo of Sartre's thinking expressed in this article: If it is true that existence is prior to essence, man is responsible for what he is. Thus, the first effect of existentialism is that it puts every man in possession of himself as he is, and places the entire responsibility for his existence squarely upon his own shoulders' (Sartre, J., [1946] 2007, p. 3).

References

Frankl, V. [1946] (2006). *Man's Search for Meaning*. Boston, MA: Beacon Press.
Freud, S. (1908). Creative Writers and Daydreaming. In: J. Strachey (Ed.) *The Standard Edition of the Complete Psychological Works of Sigmund Freud, Vol. IX*. London: Hogarth Press, pp. 141–153.
Freud, S. (1920). Beyond the Pleasure Principle. In: J. Strachey (Ed.) *The Standard Edition of the Complete Psychological Works of Sigmund Freud, Vol. XVIII*. London: Hogarth Press, pp. 1–64.
Freud, S. (1923). The Ego and the Id. In: J. Strachey (Ed.) *The Standard Edition of the Complete Psychological Works of Sigmund Freud, Vol. XIX*. London: Hogarth Press, pp. 3–66.
Gadamer, H. (1975). *Truth and Method*. London and New York: Bloomsbury.
Klein, M. (1929). Infantile Anxiety Situations Reflected in a Work of Art and in the Creative Impulse. In: *Love, Guilt and Reparation and Other Works 1921–1945*. London: Vintage, pp. 210–218.
Klein, M. (1930). The Importance of Symbol Formation in the Development of the Ego. In: *Love, Guilt and Reparation and Other Works 1921–1945*. London: Vintage, pp. 219–232.
Klein, M. (1958). On the Development of Mental Functioning. In: *Envy and Gratitude and Other Works 1946–1963*. London: Vintage, pp. 236–246.
Lifton, J.R. (1973). The Sense of Immortality: On Death and the Continuity of Life. *American Journal of Psychoanalysis*, 33, pp. 3–15.
Pedaya, H. (2011). *Walking Through Trauma*. Tel Aviv: Resling.
Pessoa, F. [1982] (2017). *The Book of Disquiet*. London and New York: Penguin Books.
Sagi, A. (1991). *Kierkegaard: Religion and Existence – The Voyage of the Self*. Jerusalem: Bialik Institute.
Sartre, J. [1946] (2007). *Existentialism Is a Humanism*. London and New Haven, CT: Yale University Press.
Segal, H. (1991). *Dream Phantasy and Art*. Hove and New York: Routledge.
Winnicott, D.W. (1953). Transitional Objects and Transitional Phenomena: A Study of the First Not-Me Possession. *International Journal of Psychoanalysis*, 34, pp. 89–97.

Chapter 8

Transcendence beyond self-identity

Identity: a psychoanalytic perspective

We all exist within a self-identity that, on the one hand, is constantly being formed and changing. However, since the change occurs along a continuum the illusion created is of a homogeneous and constant identity. In the words of the Italian writer Pirandello:

> For the drama lies all in this – in the conscience that I have, that each one of us has. We believe this conscience to be a single thing, but it is many-sided. There is one for this person, and another for that. Diverse consciences. So we have this illusion of being one person for all, of having a personality that is unique in all our acts. But it isn't true (Pirandello, L., 1921, p. 23).

Melanie Klein describes the way in which the 'self' is formed in our inner world – rich and varied in experiences and characteristics:

> But what are our selves? Everything, good or bad, that we have gone through from our earliest days onwards; all that we have received from the external world and all that we have felt in our inner world, happy and unhappy experiences, relationships to people, activities, interests and thoughts of all kinds – that is to say, everything we have lived through – makes part of our selves and goes to build up our personalities. If some of our past relationships, with all the associated memories, with the wealth of feelings they called forth, could be suddenly wiped out of our lives, how impoverished and empty we should feel! How much love, trust, gratification, comfort and gratitude, which we experienced and returned, would be lost! Many of us would not even want to have missed some of our painful experiences, for they have also contributed to the enrichment of our personalities (Klein, M., 1937, p. 338).

And she later adds: 'I have used the rather odd phrase "the relation to ourselves". Now I should like to add that this is a relation to all that we cherish and love and to all that we hate in ourselves' (ibid., p. 340). There is tension between the defined and restricted experience of identity and the dimension of identity as a reservoir of continuous experiences. As Klein says, this reservoir continues to be formed and change throughout life. Moreover, the reservoir of experiences is also dependent on the interpretation that the mind lends to the events, an interpretation that in turn also changes according to the psychic position of the subject. In other words, there is tension between the subject's consolidated experience of his identity and the fact that the processes of constituting the subject are in the process of being constantly formed. A number of crucial aspects of our experience of identity constitute a limit beyond which we are unable to transcend. An individual's personal ID includes unalterable data such as his age, the place where he was born and grew up, his family and ancestors; to these are added less definitive pieces of information such as the profession he has chosen, his social affiliation and such like. All these are experienced as a wall separating an individual from many alternative identifications. As Sagi points out, what is vital here is the distinction between 'identification' and 'identity':

> The act of identification is achieved via tags such as names, descriptions, characteristics, etc. This enables a discourse about a certain subject by setting it apart from other issues ... as a certain fixed entity that it is possible to discuss. The act of identification in and of itself does not provide an answer to the question of identity. That is because it is mostly actualized in the discourse about the subject and does not describe the dynamic and complex process of generating identity. That is built up by a complex dialogue conducted by an individual with himself, his fellow man, his past, his possibilities and his hopes. It is formed in the course of the actual history of the individual's life and is not static (Sagi, A., 2009, p. 75).

Our identity changes from one moment to the next in light of our experiences and our formation as developing and changing human beings. This is also the reason why psychoanalysis leads to a profound change in a person's experience of his identity, as he moves from a sense of a stable self-identification to self-exploration as a means of enriching one's sense of identity. The working through of the experience of identity is partly connected to working through the aspects that are unalterable – such as country of birth, body build, etc. The recognition that certain major traits in the individual's identification cannot be otherwise, can easily be experienced as an insult, a defeat, a source of anxiety, of envy and pain, of hatred of the idea that not all possibilities open themselves up to us at any given moment. The process of acceptance and reconciliation with what is limited and fixed in our identity in effect transforms it; not because the fixed particulars change but because our subjective identity is then enriched by modesty, empathy, compassion, genuineness and the ability to create from what there is instead of wasting resources in trying to deny it.

In the course of psychoanalytic treatment the person does not of course acquire new firm facts about the basic terms of his existence (time and place of birth, who the parents are and so forth), but he can regain a rebirth of the 'self'. That is to say, he achieves a renewed view of the solid, as well as the flexible, particulars of his life; an attitude that lends a degree of freedom within the framework of what is enforced. He finds freedom to establish meaning in the context of the tension between the finite and the ever changing. This achievement, much of which is gained unconsciously, requires a lifetime's work. It constantly slips away and has to be achieved anew. Melanie Klein (1946) argued that the primary development involves phantasies of omnipotence in the framework of which the infant has to experience his limitations – fear of his smallness, his dependency and his fragility. In this sense phantasies of omnipotence constitute a defence mechanism against the anxiety and pain involved in the realistic recognition of the limitations of the 'self'. Therefore every feeling of grandiosity is always bound up with denial. Throughout life there continues to be a movement between the adult attitude that recognizes the limitations and the ambition to feel omnipotent in denying the limitations. In the context of the depressive position one mourns the 'contours' of his self-identity. Eventually we give up on manic grandiosity and cease to repudiate our realistic size and powers. At the very same time it is this process that is responsible for opening up the possibilities of transcendence for the 'self' that were not available to him for as long as he continued to invest his psychic energy in protecting himself from facing reality.

Other situations that lend themselves to transcendence from the boundaries of the 'self' are falling in love, dreaming, hallucination and play. These situations constitute a source of yearning and satisfaction (and at the same time anxiety) to that part of us that wants to unravel our borders. They restrict the functioning of the reality principle in favour of a heightened activity of unconscious drives and desires. The restricting consciousness vacates its place in favour of an unconscious flow that doesn't submit to the dictates of logic, rationality and the facts of reality. Temporary retreats of this kind can also serve the reflective processes of an individual and inspire his freedom to spread his wings and fly beyond what is perceived as the barriers of the self.

Literary transcendence beyond self-identity

The longing to transcend beyond one's self identity is at the core of our attachment to literature. The literary space grants the reader a rare opportunity to transcend his sober recognition of the limitations of his reality, without endangering it. Literature unravels the borders within the safe and ordered setting of a story (Zoran, R., 2000, p. 93; 2009, p. 53).

The safe literary setting and the opportunities offered by a story, allow the reader to 'play' with the possibilities (and impossibilities) open to him from within and according to his life journey. In this sense, reading allows one to transcend beyond one's established sense of identity, and no less importantly, it allows one to return from an experience and integrate it into the developing self.

Identity, Fernando Pessoa and *The Book of Disquiet*

One of the most astonishing exponents of the struggle against the imprisonment of the self's identity is the Portuguese author Fernando Pessoa. Pessoa wrote in numerous voices and in more than 70 'heteronyms' – fictitious characters for whom Pessoa created different biographies, physical features, personalities and even styles of writing. In this way and others Pessoa was one of the most parabolic, enigmatic and fascinating writers of the twentieth century.

The Book of Disquiet ([1982] 2017) was written by Pessoa over a period of nearly two decades. It is a kind of diary in which philosophically and artistically he lays bare his meditations about his existence. Pessoa's life story revolves around meticulously tracking the inner forms of his existence, trying to be an invisible observer of his innermost theatre and to report his findings without succumbing to any of humanity's natural self-deceptions. This while fully recognizing that he is bound to fail. Pessoa's story is not a chronology of his life. He simply listens deeply to whatever comes to mind and reports it, including the changing moods accompanying every association.

Pessoa's writing bears the imprint of his total devotion to his investigation. He offers a complex and to some extent paradoxical viewpoint, be it in terms of content or linguistic style. He assumes a view that could be labelled 'psychoanalytic', a view characterized by the ability to look deeply into the sequence of free associations unconditionally, uncensored, with total transparency and maximal honesty. He constantly strives for 'truth' while recognizing all its inner contradictions and ongoing transformations. In the context of this viewpoint Pessoa tenaciously conducts a realistic and uncompromising observation of his existence, an observation that is not satisfied with looking at the object of his gaze but also observes and constantly reflects upon his own reflection.

The more evident fountainheads of Pessoa's existential and personal disquiet derived from noticing that in every situation of awareness, including the simplest states of thinking about something, being alert to something, identifying with something – his identity alters accordingly, even if in the most subtle of ways. He is upset with the notion that both the subject of his thoughts and he, as the thinker, lose something of their authentic presence, which is not given to compartmentalization and being held on to anything. At the moment of becoming aware of something the experience inevitably collapses into some kind of order, becomes a sign, gains definition. In Pessoa's mind these are all strangers to the ongoing changing nature of things. For Pessoa every identification and feeling of identity, be it big or small, is personified by a particular 'disguise'. Every realization would lead to a form and consequently to the loss of all other forms: 'The moment I find myself, I am lost' (Pessoa, F., [1982] 2017, p. 301).

Pessoa feels a slave to his selfhood and so expresses a desperate longing to transcend beyond the self's boundaries of identity. He writes: 'Slavery is the law of life, and it is the only law ... [I myself] suffocating where I am and because I am' (ibid., p. 280). From Pessoa's point of view it is not simply slavery, but slavery in a prison of falsehood, because the 'self' is not 'somebody' but rather the centre of the movement of events in which he is a participant during the years of his existence:

> I am nobody, absolutely nobody ... My soul is a black maelstrom, a great madness spinning around a vacuum, the swirling of a vast ocean around a hole in the void ... and in the waters, more like whirlwinds than waters, float images of all I ever saw or heard in the world (ibid., p. 309).

He feels disquiet because of the self's constant tendency to identify itself *de novo* with things, while, in effect, 'I'm the nothing around which everything spins ... the centre of everything with nothing around it' (ibid.).

Throughout the book Pessoa moves between a psychic and existential exploration and description of the course of events and a search for a way out of his psychic torment, being trapped in humanity's fate to continuously evolve into a certain form of awareness, identity, identification, name. His deep longing is to transcend to a pre-form, characterized by all potentialities existing simultaneously.[3] He sets up an ideal of a liberated consciousness though he is realistic about the extent to which that is achievable: 'The consciousness of the unconsciousness of life is the greatest martyrdom imposed on the intelligence' (ibid., p. 150). *The Book of Disquiet* indeed does move with disquiet between the ideal of that consciousness denuded of identification, definition and demarcation, and of the human tendency to repeatedly retreat into the trap of the ordained form.

Identity, Pessoa and reading literature

Of all his attempts at transcendence from the confines of the 'self' there is no pursuit described by Pessoa in more emotionally powerful and glorifying terms than the reading of literature: He declares: 'I read and I am set free' (Pessoa, F., [1982] 2017, p. 204).

On the one hand his total devotion to writing and his search for its raw essence sometimes makes him a naïve, theatrical reader and, momentarily, even tending towards the bathetic. But on the other hand this paradox too suits his willingness to deal with paradoxes and his curiosity as to why explanations of 'the mystery of being' and of human existence are so persistently elusive. These aspects of Pessoa's perspective make him a twofold literary 'witness'. On the one hand he is a witness whose evidence is scathing and total, his senses sharp and his expression lucid, which makes him a highly effective guide to the understanding of the reading experience. On the other hand his inclusiveness and desire to microscopically investigate the smallest particles of internal existence occasionally lack distance.

Pessoa's writing about his reading experiences illustrates three of the most prominent ways whereby literature enables the reader to transcend beyond his identity of 'self': transmitted into a dreamlike state; liberation through the language of literature; and identification with the literary characters.

1. Transmitting the reader into a dreamlike state

Pessoa writes: 'I know no pleasure like that of books ... Books are introductions to dreams' (Pessoa, F., [1982] 2017, p. 235). It is precisely this dreamlike state brought about by reading that offers Pessoa the opportunity to transcend the boundaries of 'self'. The affinity between literature and dreaming is significant. Dreaming is an alternative to reality – it is a different space of consciousness, with different rules weakening the rigidity of reality's boundaries. Dreaming transcends the rational chains of cause and effect, of identities, of the linearity of time. As was discovered by Freud (1900), in the primary processes involved in a dream one can swap roles, different characters can be condensed into one, contradictions can live side by side, one can travel forward and backward on the axis of time and more. Similarly, as we read literature we are liberated from the chains of the logical order and the confines of the secondary processes of thinking that belong to conscious awareness by the experience of dreamlike reading, which creates a whole new world of possibilities.

Dreaming, creativity and language: a psychoanalytic perspective

One of the psychoanalysts who deepened the debate on the psyche's transitional states between dreaming and reality was D.W. Winnicott. As described briefly in the first chapter, Winnicott defined this psychic space as a 'potential space', also termed 'transitional space' (Winnicott, D.W., 1953). This space is characterized by an open imaginary transition between 'me' and 'not me', between 'internal 'and 'external', between imagination and reality. It is a psychological space that small children live in in the most natural way and its developmental objective is to enable the infant to survive the separation from his mother and the anxiety accompanying that separation. It enables the child to preserve the phantasy that he is omnipotent, controls the object and is its creator, thus lessening his anxiety that stems from him being fragile and dependent on the object. For Winnicott the potential space is a mental state that is also linked to processes of creativity – it is a space in which one can play, dream and imagine and still maintain a grip on reality. It is a positive withdrawal of the mind to a creative and open state.

According to Winnicott's follower Christopher Bollas, there is a link between the transitional object and the artistic object: 'With the infant's creation of the transitional object, the transformational process is displaced from the mother-environment (where it originated) into countless subjective-objects' (Bollas, C., 1987, p. 15). Bollas contends that an adult's search for objects identified with such metamorphosis in the self occurs

> usually on the occasion of the aesthetic moment ... that an individual feels a deep subjective rapport with an object (a painting, a poem, an aria or symphony, or a natural landscape) and experiences an uncanny fusion with the object, an event that revokes an ego state that prevailed during early psychic life ... the adult subject tends to nominate such objects as sacred (ibid., pp. 16–17).

According to Bollas this search stems from the knowledge that the object will indeed bring about a transformation in the individual searching for it; a reminder of the primary transformations in the 'self' in his early relationship with his mother. For this reason Bollas terms an object of this kind a 'transformational object' (Bollas, C., 1979, pp. 97–107). This transformation involves not only gratification but also frustration, just as aesthetic experiences are not necessarily 'beautiful', the principle being that they are 'profoundly moving because of the existential memory tapped' (ibid., p. 29).

Bollas connects the relationship with the mother and the development of language acquisition: 'The mother's facilitation of the word-forming experience, together with the infant's grasp of grammatical structure, is the most significant transformation of the infant's encoded utterance, until the grasp of a word' (ibid., p. 35).

Bollas points out that having found 'words' the infant has a new transformational object 'which facilitates the transition from deep enigmatic privacy towards the culture of the human village' (ibid.).

Pessoa's dreamlike reading

I read and I abandon myself, not to reading, but to myself. I read and fall asleep, and, as if among dreams, I follow Father Figueiredo's descriptions of rhetorical figures (Pessoa, F., [1982] 2017, p. 235). Here Pessoa is describing a connection between reading literature and the experience of the 'self on a number of levels: between reading and abandonment; between reading and falling asleep; between reading and the rhetorical form; and between reading and dreaming. When Pessoa writes 'I read and abandon myself' he adds that when reading he abandons the 'self' to himself and not to the reading. It is a crucial point, stressing the fact that reading actually distances him from his sense of self-identity, from what he 'knows' about his reality, from the limitations of wakefulness. Pessoa 'reads and falls asleep', i.e. retreating into figures of speech offered by the literary character (Father Figueiredo), freed to conduct a temporary alternative dreamt-like existence.

Remember that for Pessoa wakeful consciousness in daily life is constantly at the mercy of human traps and disguises such as presenting a persona, self-image, identity and even self-fulfilment – all experienced by him as traps and limitations. For example, if he publishes a book Pessoa mourns the fact that he is no longer the person who is yet to be published. Reading and the dreamlike state it involves facilitate an encounter with the main opportunities and potentialities before they become a fixed shape.

In his book *What Is Literature?* Sartre describes it thus:

> The belief which I accord the tale is freely assented to. It is a Passion, in the Christian sense of the word, that is, a freedom which resolutely puts itself into a state of passivity to obtain a certain transcendent effect by this sacrifice. The reader renders himself credulous; he descends into credulity which, though it ends by enclosing him like a dream, is at every moment conscious of being free ... reading is a free dream. (Sartre, J P., [1948] 1988, p. 50).

We can see how reading leads the reader into a potential space where he can move between the 'me' and 'not me', between the internal and the external world and between reality and imagination. In so doing the reader manages to temporarily shed the limiting cloak of his fixed identity and is free to transcend his boundaries.

Pessoa describes the rereading of familiar books as one of the ways of transcending into a dreamlike state. The 'transitional object' described by Winnicott needs also to be a particular object (not 'a nappy' but a very specific nappy), one that is very familiar, recharged daily by the psychic investment of the infant. It is so familiar that if, for example, the infant's mother launders the nappy that, for the infant is the transitional object, the response is likely to lead to a catastrophic response. The infant has become so familiar with the texture of the transitional object's cloth, the smell absorbed every day that in his phantasy contained the mother's smell as well as his own and so forth. Even the dirt stuck to it is evidence of it being the one and only object with which it was possible, like Alice in Wonderland, to pass through the secret opening and into the transitional space between the infant and his mother, between the experience of being met with reality and inventing it.

Similarly Pessoa describes the advantages of the familiar book: it is a safe place into which one can delve without over taxing one's mind. Paradoxically, new reading, supposedly liberating the reader even more, in fact requires him to concentrate, which keeps him too conscious and alert – much like the walker treading an unfamiliar path who has to be more vigilant than if on a regular walk. Contrastingly, in reading the familiar book the reader can dive in effortlessly and get lost as he hoped, easily becoming merged with the familiar in the text, and so drift away from being just himself and away from the text being just what it is (like the infant merging with mother). Moreover, Pessoa prefers a text that moves along narrow and clear pathways, that lend a sense of security and maximum familiarity. 'I can only find repose in reading the classics. Their very narrowness, through which their clarity finds expression, brings me a kind of comfort' (Pessoa, F., [1982] 2017, p. 203). Thus, for him, reading the classicists with whom he is so familiar seems like listening to a lullaby releasing him into a dreamlike state.

Pessoa also claims that the transcendence occurring in the context of reading fiction is, paradoxically, what makes life real. Winnicott distinguished between the 'real self' and the 'false self' by assessing an individual's ability to express the entire range of his personality's and psyche's facets spontaneously without being afraid that these will destroy his surroundings. The 'true self' can create and animate the encounter with a work of art in a lively and fruitful way. The 'false self' leaves the 'true self' in a kind of concealed psychic capsule and only encounters the world through the rules and customs that guarantee him quiet interpersonal relations devoid of any conflict and tension. However, the price of such existence is a sense of unconscious falsehood and the narrowing of the freedom of the self to create, enrich his identity and find meaning in his life.

In a similar vein, Pessoa claims that in a dreamlike state there is a representation of truth that triumphs over the 'truth value' of the imposed reality. Pessoa describes it thus: 'I'm so used to feeling what's false as true, and what I dream as vividly as what I see, that I've lost the human distinction – false, I believe – between truth and falsehood' (ibid., loc. 2545). In reading literature Pessoa finds an answer to the puzzling link between the truth and reality:

> All literature consists of an effort to make life real. As everyone knows, even when they act as if they did not, in its physical reality, life is absolutely unreal; fields, cities, ideas are all totally fictitious, the children of our complex experience of ourselves. All impressions are uncommunicable unless we make literature of them. (ibid., p. 229).

According to Winnicott, the 'false self 'conducts an overly cautious psychic life that, generally speaking, is not challenged by drives or threatened by internal destructiveness. But a certain extent of destructiveness is imperative in order to create and grow in an authentic way. One needs to destroy the familiar and the customary in order to create and discover the new.

For Pessoa what is generally considered false – dreaming, imagining, literature – heals falsehood and introduces the true. It is evident in poetry, where the poetic freedom from the chains of logic and realistic reason releases the reader to enjoy 'falsehood', which enables him to transcend beyond the banality of thought and life.

2. Liberation through the language of literature

Pessoa as reader and writer relates to language in a very personal and intimate way. The text is for him an-other with whom he has relations, ranging from very good to very bad. His metaphors cover the entire gamut of relations: from a mother who can be hugged all the way to the criminal who has to be punished for writing a poorly worded sentence. For Pessoa, reading a well-articulated text is a highly emotional experience:

> I tremble if I hear someone speak well. Certain pages in Fialho or in Chateaubriand make life tingle in my veins, make me quietly, tremulously mad with an unattainable pleasure already mine ... make me shiver like a branch in the wind, in the passive delirium of something set in motion (Pessoa, F., [1982] 2017, p. 295).

Pessoa yearns for a live language in which he would be able to create whatever rules of existence come to his mind without any grammatical laws standing in his way. He senses an analogy between grammatical and existential rules and between transcending language and the possibility of transcending beyond the boundaries of his identity. He expresses fury towards the language when it fails to do its work appropriately namely doesn't allow him to dream his way out of the confines of his identity.

> My fatherland is the Portuguese language ... What I hate, with all the hatred I can muster ... is the poorly written page of Portuguese itself; what I hate, as if it were someone who deserved a beating, is the bad grammar itself ... For orthography is just as much a living thing as we are (ibid., p. 296).

The writing would be judged by him to be bad if written superficially and incorrectly or if it merely expresses and is not creative, reveals without being inventive. Bad writing is for him the fate of the person who is chained by cultural law without having succeeded to create himself. The words used by someone who is loyal to syntactical rules fail to produce live symbols of the described but rather make oddments that lack the breath of life. Contrastingly, if the writer is endowed with the ability to symbolize in a way that transcends the confines of syntax and common language, he offers the reader an opportunity to experience a live and emerging self. Not every reading is an opportunity for such transcendence. On the contrary, there are readings that will only repeat and further emphasize the infuriating boundary of the imposed identity. Only a creative use of language that modifies its rules and uses it playfully and openly will assist Pessoa and every other reader in their efforts to escape from the slavery of linguistic identification.

Pessoa stresses the importance of another component that has eluded many researchers dealing with reader responses. He reflects on the influence of the *style of writing* on the reader's experience. I intentionally term this 'style' and not 'skill' because Pessoa looks for styles of formulation in which there is something from the language of dreams that he so cherishes. Writing of this kind transports the reader to open horizons and doesn't only involve linguistic juggling but a connection between the emotion, the relation and the word. In its bosom Pessoa rests or alternatively is open to possibilities.

Psychoanalysis deals with the link between language, symbolization, process of thought and dreaming. Its conclusions can shed additional light on Pessoa's poetic 'debate' revolving around those very same topics.

Symbol formation, dreaming and the developing self

Freud contended that in the unconscious things appear as they are, without representation in language, whereas in preconscious and consciousness there is a link between the 'thing' and its representation in language (Freud, S., 1915). In a series of articles Melanie Klein (1929, 1930), portrayed the ability to form linguistic symbols as a central and necessary component in mental development. The term 'symbol formation' is directed first of all at the ability to express experiences linguistically and lend them a name. Klein's ideas on symbol formation lay the foundations for a theory of thought and creativity in the psychological sense.

Klein argued that in addition to cognitive development psychological growth is required to enable linguistic symbols to evolve, and gradually to become more complex so as to include abstract and metaphorical dimensions. For Klein, the verbal symbol is not only the linkage of a signified to the linguistic signifier but is loaded with emotion and is unconsciously connected to a relation towards an internal object.

The development of the ability to form symbols is a critical element in mental health and the development of the 'self'. This ability enables the child to think about himself and about the other, to decipher relations, to communicate, to play, to create and explore the world. Klein suggested the term 'symbolic equation' (1930), later developed by Hanna Segal[4] to describe the primitive way in which the infant identifies and senses his psychological-somatic experiences during his primary development. The symbolic equation ignores the separation between subject and object, and the thinking function is at a rigid, and primitive level (Sanchez-Pardo, E., 2003, p. 10). For example, in the infant's mind there is no distinction between a stomach ache and the mother so that in phantasy the mother appears as the cause of pain in a concrete, absolute and most threatening way. Forming a symbol that is a symbolic alternative to the thing itself (let's say mother or stomach) contributes to the understanding of the separation (this is mother; she is not me/my stomach; she is my mother; therefore I have to call her 'mother'). To be able to assign a name to anything one has to recognize it as separate from me. Therefore naming things involves a process of mourning due to them being separate from me. This process is inherent to the acquisition of language (Durban J. and Roth M., 2013, p. 83). At the same time, calling something by name also helps overcoming the loss and the separation. This is because my ability to call my mother by the name 'mother' makes it possible to protect the connection between us. As the cognitive and psychological development progresses so the use of symbols is richer, more abstract and more complex.

The psychoanalyst Wilfred Bion (1962), further developed these ideas and claimed that the development of thinking takes place in the framework of comprehensive relations (the mother's and the infant's psyche) and as an outcome of the maternal 'reverie' that, as previously said, is a kind of psychic dreamlike state of the mother towards the infant's raw experiences. Bion spoke of three levels of internal work: He related Freud's term 'dream-work' (Freud, S., 1900, pp. 277–338) to psychological work carried out at the unconscious level; the term 'reverie' to psychic work carried out at the preconscious level; and conscious work that links dreaming to language and to wakeful thinking. Bion was interested in the dream-work that occurs during wakefulness and not in sleeping, the former, in his view, being responsible for psychic transformation and development.

The dream-work of the literary language

We can now understand Pessoa's enchantment with literary language since literary writing can be transformative for the reader not only due to its contents, its tone or the linguistic skill that it demonstrates, but also for the quality of the thinking process that is expressed in it and affects its readers. This quality is expressed in the structure of symbols and the linguistic richness. Pessoa's reason for turning to literature resembles the motive of a patient turning to psychoanalysis described by Thomas Ogden thus:

A person consults a psychoanalyst because he is in emotional pain, which unbeknownst to him, he is either unable to dream (i.e. unable to do unconscious psychological work) or is so disturbed by what he is dreaming that his dreaming is disrupted. To the extent that he is unable to dream his emotional experience, the individual is unable to change, or to grow, or to become anything other than which he has been (Ogden, T., 2005, p. 11).

The similarity to Pessoa's wishes to dream about his emotional experience through reading and through the qualities of language is evident.

Like the infant who internalizes the mother's 'alpha functions' – the spontaneous working through in the mother's mind in relation to the infant's distress grants him both a container and meaning – so the reader of literature internalizes the literary dream-work. We almost never experience conscious situations that merge the various layers of our thinking simultaneously. Pessoa finds this simultaneity through the reading of literature. Thinking while reading is regulated by linguistic symbols that belong to awareness but at the same time it also maintains the quality of reverie – which is of sub-awareness – and the quality of unconscious dreaming. One part turns upwards towards awareness and the symbolic order, while the other part is pulled downward to the level of things before their shape is formed. In the context of such a reading, Pessoa succeeds in transcending the constant tendency to experience the world in the framework of the interpersonal and lexical grammatical rules. He longs for those moments of reading in which he can dream the text with a grammar that is idiosyncratic and free.

In a text that involves false thinking and the meaning is removed, leaving an empty representation, the reading experience can also lead to an opposite feeling. In such a reading the symbols are experienced as dead facts, or in the metaphor of the playwright Pirandello they are experienced as an empty sack:

The manager: Let's come to the point. This is only discussion.
The Father: Very good, sir! But a fact is like a sack which won't stand up when it is empty. In order that it may stand up, one has to put into it the reason and sentiment which have caused it to exist (Pirandello, L., 1921, p. 22).

In light of such language, which is accompanied by a lack of understanding, a misunderstanding or forced understanding, the reader is invited to indulge in pseudo thinking, which destroys the meaning and creates vacuous statements. Similar to Pirandello's metaphor one can think of such a language as an empty pregnancy sac from which psychic life cannot emerge. In such a situation the reader suffers what the psychoanalyst Ruth Riesenberg-Malcolm termed 'the phenomenon of not learning':

A false connection with the analyst and the interpretations in the sessions, which gives an outward impression of understanding and progress, while in fact the whole process lacks something real, does not feel genuine and seems to be going nowhere (Malcolm, R.R., 1990, p. 385).

This phenomenon is often characterized by staying close to and mimicking the therapeutic language while at the same time deliberately avoiding real thinking that exhibits openness and a readiness to change. Similarly, in a text that employs language in a way that is closer to false replication, an empty declaration or misunderstanding, narrows the reader's freedom of thought rather than broadening it. The reader becomes fettered by language's chains and his capacity to dream about his identity and expand its options is unconsciously attacked.

Three conditions for transcendence at the linguistic level

Pessoa presents three conditions for transcendence at the linguistic level: the use of grammar as an instrument and not as a law; not knowing – which leads to recreation; the 'power of transposition' – which makes it possible to move between different creative planes. Each one of these contributes to the transformative power of reading literature.

THE USE OF GRAMMAR AS AN INSTRUMENT NOT A LAW

Pessoa distinguishes between two types of symbol formation: that which is formed according to grammatical *laws* and that which is formed according to grammatical *rules*. He offers a description and an explanation of the conditions that make it possible for him as a writer and for the reader to transcend the confines of his routine thinking: reading a text that uses grammar as an instrument, not as a law. 'Analyzing myself this afternoon, I've discovered that my stylistic system is based on two principles ... first, to say what one feels exactly as one feels it ... secondly, to understand that grammar is a tool not a law' (Pessoa, F. [1982] 2017, p. 215). Pessoa differentiates between someone who obeys the laws of grammar because he is unable to think what he feels and 'the "supra grammaticam". Anyone who knows how to say what he wants to say is, in his own way, King of Rome. The title is regal and the reason for it impossible' (ibid., p. 216). In other words the writer who is faithful to the way in which he sees and feels things and not to the usual laws of grammar. That would allow Pessoa to say about his own writing: 'I would have spoken absolutely, photographically, stepping outside of all vulgar norms and beyond the commonplace. I will not merely have uttered words: I will have spoken' (ibid.)

Pessoa offers the following example. A man sees a girl with masculine gestures. An ordinary person would say that it was a girl who was acting out as a boy. Another would say that the girl was a boy whereas Pessoa would say: 'She's a boy' (ibid.). This is a clear example of the work of dreaming enabled by the text's language – in a dream and in literary language one can be male and female at one and the same time. One of the freedoms afforded by dreams described by Freud is the mechanism of 'condensation' (Freud, S., 1900, pp. 279–304) – a representation of hybrids of more than one signified. The mechanism of condensation is characteristic of dreams and unconscious thought. Pessoa's literary experience shows that when one can transcend the laws of grammar to the freedom of the dreamlike literary language, the reader is given an opportunity to transcend the boundaries of identity – in the example above, a transcendence of the boundaries of gender and physical identity. This process has a transformative potential. The reader can study himself in the mirror of the literary dream, where he can explore more options of being than those he actually experiences or has. In the wake of reflecting on the new states of self he has met in the literary mirror, he can return to his identity knowing himself in new ways. Both the reader and the written text have a responsibility to leave a space for the new, the unexpected and for everything that emerges in a creative and original way.

The example suggested by Pessoa touches on yet another psychoanalytic aspect: the resistance to boundaries and limitations that characterizes a perverted way of life. According to the definition of classical psychoanalysis, perversion doesn't acknowledge differences between genders, between generations and between roles. It aspires to create a sense that combines absolute control and all-encompassing free choice. Postmodernism led to the development of new views and conceptualizations that recognized the difference between biological gender and gender choice. This view democratizes sexuality and gender and comes close to the freedom so desired by Pessoa. In his writing it is evident that he considers the mental, the sexual, the gender and the linguistic to be linked.

In a further absurd example in an imagined conversation between a man and woman, Pessoa describes an invented friend who had taken his own life because he could not stand the heavy responsibility he all of a sudden felt for a grammatical trial he was conducting: he was trying to find a way to not complete sentences without anyone noticing. His woman friend tells him that he doesn't understand anything about the friends he didn't have because it was inconceivable that such a person would commit suicide with a revolver (Pessoa, F., [1982] 2017, p. 380).

Together with the narrator and his interlocutor we as readers also calculate our demise retrospectively in an attempt to find our way between reader and writer, logic and insanity, beginning and end. In so doing we participate in Pessoa's 'ideal' reading, which involves the stretching and widening of language's boundaries in terms of contents and form, like a sentence that has no end.

'NOT KNOWING' THAT LEADS TO RECREATION

Pessoa reveals a further imperative also linked to the use of grammar as an instrument rather than a law – the 'demand' to forgo a priori knowledge on the part of both writer and reader. The following discussion relates to the ideal of the reader's not knowing the language of the text.

Pessoa enjoys the possibility of not knowing how a word is to be structured or how the syntax is to be built. He sees as a writer, and has experienced as a reader, the privilege of renewing language as an individual's possibility for omnipotent creation:

> If I wanted to talk about my simple existence, I would say: 'I exist.' If I wanted to talk about my existence as a separate soul, I would say: 'I am me.' But if I wanted to talk about my existence as an entity that both directs and forms itself, that exercises within itself the divine function of self-creation, I would have to invent a transitive form and say, triumphantly and ungrammatically supreme, 'I exist me.' (ibid., p. 216).

The number of times the existence of the 'I' is mentioned in the above quote, reflects the intensity involved in forming the self in the process of the linguistic creation. In order to complete the process of creation and link the self to its being, Pessoa also plays with the words 'to be' in the most ungrammatical way, declaring himself to be 'triumphantly and anti-grammatically supreme.' He turns 'to be' into a transitive verb and discusses 'amming myself'. In this example, Pessoa endows the exemplified subject with a double meaning: by transcending the grammatical law he creates himself both through the linguistic form and through its contents. So, for a moment, he is indeed 'I exist me', which is to say he achieves a momentary being of birth and formation. The text created is not known in advance but rather occurs in the present, is hatched as a new 'being' that he so yearns for all the time: 'write words as if they were my soul's salvation' (ibid., p. 245). This both inspires the freedom to transcend beyond the known and expected, and the actualization of that freedom. It is also an omnipotent phantasy of being the creator of oneself, with no mother or father, with no law and no god. It is a desire to be freed of all influence, even primordial, and to repeatedly lose any other influence met along the way.

In a short and intriguing article mentioned previously, the psychoanalyst Wilfred Bion wrote that the analyst has to meet the patient in every analytic hour without memory and without desire (Bion, W., 1967). This is of course a utopian demand but posits a dramatic tension with the classical psychoanalyst's endeavour to know. Bion emphasized the importance of the idea that the analyst would agree to be in a state of 'not knowing' as the ultimate means to reach real knowledge. According to Ogden, with foreknowledge, 'the past eclipses the present, and the present is projected into the future ... Not knowing is a precondition for being able to imagine' (Ogden, T., 2005, p. 15).

This is very different if one allows himself not to know:

> In this state of mind, one is capable of marveling at the mystery, the utter unpredictability, and the power of the unconscious ... The imaginative capacity in the analytic setting is nothing less than sacred. Imagination holds open multiple possibilities experimenting with them all in the form of thinking, playing, dreaming and in every other sort of creative activity. (Ogden, T., 2005, p. 17).

Pessoa's writing about grammar buttresses this view and shows that through literary language the reader becomes linked to the mystery of existence on the one hand and the mystery of the unconscious on the other.

> Civilization consists in giving an inappropriate name to something and then dreaming what results from that. And in fact the false name and the true dream do create a new reality. The object really does become other, because we have made it so. We manufacture realities (Pessoa, F., [1982] 2017, p. 240).

Here Pessoa touches on the virtually oxymoronic link between 'being' and 'word'. He does so in an attempt to entrap that which is being formed within the borders of a few black-on-white letters. To escape from this he has to be ready to take a risk: not to know how to form a word or what the appropriate syntax of the word should be, and not to know which paths the thoughts of the reader will be pursuing while he is reading. In doing so he links himself to an experience not known in advance and thus transformative in its essence. Like analysts and patients, readers who would prefer to know where they are heading are liable to miss the surprises and innovations on their way.

Pessoa thought,

> It might be useful to place at the end of my book, when it's published, underneath any 'Errata', a few 'Non-Errata' and to say: the words 'this uncertain movements' on page so-and-so is correct, with the noun in the plural and the demonstrative pronoun in the singular (ibid., p. 214).

This reaffirms Pessoa's wish to leave grammar and syntax to his own judgment or more correctly to his non-judgment; to the direct experience 'unconsidered' by him. He concludes by saying: 'But what has that to do with what I was thinking? Nothing, which is why I let myself think it' (ibid.). What I 'thought' in the past is like a dead thought, an empty declaration, material already endlessly chewed over so that there is nothing nurturing about it. Contrastingly, grammar that we know not what form it will take, leads to a freedom that enables things to be created in language and establish innovative and original thinking. This freedom is conceptual, experiential and grammatical. As such it transcends the boundaries of the language that dictates identity and ways of self-definition. Pessoa's liberty not to know how the syntax or the grammar is supposed to be formed has profound implications for the 'syntax of the self'.

ACTIVATING THE POWER OF 'TRANSPOSITION'

Pessoa describes prose's powerful capacity for what he terms 'transposition',[5] as one of literary language's greatest strengths (Pessoa, F., [1982] 2017, p. 293). For Pessoa the term 'transposition' signifies prose's capacity to overcome the human limitation, which decrees that we understand through our senses, define through thinking and, in art, have the capacity to be creative along defined linear pivots. It is impossible to paint in sounds, or think via emotions According to Freud, a thing cannot be some other contradictory thing or simply different in substance and quality, other than in the realms of the unconscious. In Pessoa's view it can only be so in the realms of prose. Only through writing, argues Pessoa, is it possible to cross these boundaries so that only prose enables us to transcend beyond the most fundamental limits of human existence. As mentioned, according to Freud the unconscious contains a unique system of the 'primary process'. We can learn about the way primary process works in the language of dreams. A thing can also be its opposite, two essentially different things can be condensed into one representation. Alternatively, a representation can stand for something other than what it usually stands for. Finally, time's linearity and the rules of logic don't apply to it (Freud, S., 1900, pp. 277–338). Even though Freud saw a clear link between the secret of literature's magic and the three areas of a child's mind – play, daydreaming and dreams – he didn't put his trust in literature's ability for transposition but rather focused on the fact that in the creative space, as in the dreaming space, gratification is achieved when it is linked to the fulfilment of unconscious desires (Freud, S., 1908).

Pessoa examines the opportunity for transcendence in the course of reading from a different perspective: rather than focusing on the writing's content, he concentrates on what he sees as the power of prose to facilitate transcendence by employing a particularly sophisticated level of language. In a very unique occurrence of simultaneity, prose realizes the unconscious' primary ways of functioning in tandem with the conscious secondary symbolic order. According to Pessoa, this is not only because prose can render with words, colour, form, rhythm, structure, reality, sentiments and the like. Literature's unique virtue is that it also captures realms of expression that cannot reside together in any other space. In order to demonstrate this, Pessoa uses oxymoronic metaphors such as, 'We would allow sunsets to be sunsets, taking pains only to understand them verbally, communicating them through an intelligible music of colour' (Pessoa, F., [1982] 2017, p. 293).

And he continues:

> There is prose that dances, sings and recites to itself. There are verbal rhythms with a sinuous choreography, in which the idea being expressed strips off its clothing with veritable and exemplary sensuality. And there are also, in prose, gestural subtleties carried out by a great actor, the Word, which rhythmically transforms into its bodily substance the impalpable mystery of the universe (ibid., pp. 330–334).

Pessoa's eulogy to literature describes its rare capacity to touch the mystery of the universe but at the same time illustrates no less powerfully its own mysterious virtue. Prose is capable of containing and embodying the form of the unconscious and all the forms of expression of art and of the body, of movement and of ideas, of extension in space and of compression of material. Thanks to the literary virtue of transposition, there is an interchange between the mystery of prose, the mystery of existence and the mystery of the unconscious of both writer and reader, of the writer and reader as one.

The reader of such a text gains what the psychoanalyst J.R. Lifton has called 'experiential transcendence', which can be aroused by a work of art (Lifton, J.R., 1973, p. 7). Pessoa describes the experiential transcendence aroused by literature thus: 'To feel everything in all possible ways; to be able to think with the emotions and feel with the intellect ... in short, to experience all sensations inside oneself, stripping them down to God' (Pessoa, F., [1982] 2017, p. 200). And adds:

> And that's why I often write without even wanting to think, in an externalized daydream, letting the words caress me as if I were a little girl sitting on their lap. They're just meaningless sentences, flowing languidly with the fluidity of water that forgets itself as a stream does in the waves that mingle and fade, constantly reborn, following endlessly one on the other. That's how ideas and images, tremulous with expression, pass through me like a rustling procession of faded silks amongst which a sliver of an idea flickers, mottled and indistinct in the moonlight (ibid., p. 295).

Pessoa describes his experience as reader and at the same time he also arouses in his readers a transcendental experience beyond their routine ways of experience and use of language. The experience he describes clearly illustrates Donald Davidson's linguistic view that 'Metaphor is the dream work of language' (Davidson, D., 1984, p. 245). Pessoa expands this depiction to encompass all of literature's actions.[6] It is evident from what Pessoa writes that literature's extensive freedom to symbolize, personifies for him the continuous movement and innumerable possibilities of existence. Literature is always a source of existential truth that Pessoa so yearns to be a part of; to be able to constantly change too, to flow like water, to be a forgetful wave whose ripples burst their banks, continually morphing into other formations. These are the moments during which he feels that he is at long last fulfilling the impossible ideal to be freely open to all possibilities. Then, as he unerringly points out throughout his book, he always and inevitably loses his idyll and reverts to those routines of human existence that chain him again to the delineated forms of the self.

And perhaps, in the end, the way in which Pessoa's writings were left to be found by his readers contributes to the fulfilment of the morphological and creative claim that reading and writing are supposed to transcend the suffocating boundaries of the one identity of the self. His writings were discovered in a large wooden chest in which there were more than 27,000 written pages in which the writings of more than 70 independent 'heteronyms' – all invented and created by Pessoa – expressed numerous developed identities where we would expect to find just one.

3. Transcendence through identification

In Chapter 3, seven forms of reader identification with literary characters were presented. I now wish to examine the significance of the process of identification in a new light – that of the reader's transcendence beyond his otherwise immutable personal identity.

In their book *Constructing Therapeutic Narrative* (1997), Haim Omer and Nahi Alon argue that the stories told by patients in the course of therapy are highly significant as powerful narratives about themselves. For all the negativity they contain, they are stories that the patient has repeatedly retold to himself and others until in his mind they represent the actual events of his life. Rather than creating a new story, the task of the therapist is to fashion a narrative that is close enough to the patient's world as to be accepted by him as his story. At the same time, the new story must be sufficiently different from the old one so as to enable the patient to recognize new meanings and new possibilities.

This perspective is also relevant to the act of reading: The literary text offers an alternative to the reader's story. If the literary story has the power to be close enough and at the same time sufficiently different from that of the reader, it has the capacity to be transformational. The literary researcher George Poulet views the reader's transcendence from his boundaries as being achieved through borrowing the consciousness of the character in the text:

> Whatever I think is a part of my mental world. And yet here I am thinking a thought which manifestly belongs to another mental world, which is being thought in me just as though I did not exist. Already the notion is inconceivable and seems even more so if I reflect that, since every thought must have a subject to think it, this thought which is alien to me and yet in me, must also have in me a subject which is alien to me ... Whenever I read, I mentally pronounce an I, and yet the I which I pronounce is not myself (Poulet, G., 1969, p. 56).

Indeed the processes of identification with the literary text's characters are bound up with the reader temporarily freeing himself from the confines of his identity in order to experience an alternative world written by another subject. In addition, it is up to the reader to introject the physical, psychic and mental world of the book's characters through his imagination. This process leads to a temporary transcendence from the dominance in the life of the reader of his ways of thinking, feeling and employment of language. While he is immersed in reading, the reader unconsciously experiences these alternative ways of existence that challenge his habitual modes of living, lending an opportunity of working through and self-reflection.

Transcendence through identification in Luigi Pirandello's *Six Characters in Search of an Author*

Luigi Pirandello was an Italian writer who won a Noble prize for the audacity and innovation of his writing. In his play *Six Characters in Search of an Author* Pirandello, in a manner that is both rebellious and amusing, puts the spotlight on the universal preoccupation with self-identity. Indirectly the play also sheds light on the reading experience because it deals with fictitious characters who have neither an author or a play. This is how Pirandello illustrates the fact that every character we identify with in the course of reading is someone else's fiction. In addition he enlightens us as to our own tendency as readers to relate to a character as a 'real' independent other, in the absence of which it wouldn't arouse in us identification and an emotional response. In so doing, he also raises the possibility that we ourselves maintain the illusion of a crystallized identity when in fact it is fictitious. In contrast to an individual's existential experience of being imprisoned in the narrow ID of gender, age, the family into which he was born, the era in which he lives and such like, Pirandello's play shows that identity is contingent and more flexible than we tend to realize.

The characters in Pirandello's play are divided between supposedly real people and characters declared to be fictitious. In the course of the play these two groups converse with each other. The father, a character that is presented as a fictitious written character (as opposed to the supposedly 'real people' in the play), talks to the play's production manager/director who, unlike the 'father' plays the role of a 'real' person. Remonstrating against this real manager, the fictitious father tells him he simply wanted to show him 'that one is born to life in many forms, in many shapes, as tree, or as stone, as water, as butterfly, or as woman. So one may also be born a character in a play' (Pirandello, L., 1921, p. 10). The manager attempts to argue, telling the 'father' that fictitious characters don't have an independent existence nor do they have dealings with real people. Against this, the father insists on the important role of characters in the life of an individual precisely because it constitutes an ordered and fixed identity, written from beginning to end, thus reflecting (by contrast) the versatility and fragility of human identity.

> Father: A character, sir, may always ask a man who he is. Because a character has really a life of his own, marked with his especial characteristics; for which reason he is always 'somebody'. But a man – I'm not speaking of you now – may very well be 'nobody'. But only in order to know if you, as you really are now, see yourself as you once were with all the illusions that were yours then, with all the things both inside and outside of you as they seemed to you – as they were then indeed for you. Well, sir, if you think of all those illusions that mean nothing to you now, of all those things which don't even seem to you to exist anymore, while once they were for you, don't you feel that – I won't say these boards – but the very earth under your feet is sinking away from you when you reflect that in the same way this you as you feel it today – all this present reality of yours – is fated to seem a mere illusion to you tomorrow?
> Manager: (without having understood much, but astonished by the specious argument). Well, well! And where does all this take us anyway?
> Father: Oh, nowhere! It's only to show you that if we (indicating the characters) have no other reality beyond the illusion, you too must not count overmuch on your reality as you feel it today, since, like that of yesterday, it may prove an illusion for you tomorrow.
> Manager: (determining to make fun of him). Ah, excellent! Then you'll be saying next that you, with this comedy of yours that you brought here to act, are truer and more real than I am.
> Father: (with the greatest seriousness). But of course; without doubt!
> Manage: Ah, really? ...
> Father: If your reality can change from one day to another ...
> Manager: But everyone knows it can change. It is always changing, the same as anyone else's.
> Father: (with a cry). No, sir, not ours! Look here! That is the very difference! Our reality doesn't change: it can't change! It can't be other

than what it is, because it is already fixed forever. It's terrible. Ours is an immutable reality (ibid., pp. 60–61).

The constancy of the fictive character highlights the impermanence of human identity. The opportunity of entering another character, taking on its particular features, its traits, its age or character, doesn't resemble any kind of meeting between people in real life. An encounter between people always consists of a meeting between two sets of consciousness that change from one minute to the next, and the multifaceted diversity of the traits and appearances in different moments and situations makes them impossible to pin down. Identity is not uniformly united and fixed over time so that one can never capture the identity of an-other. Contrastingly, as Pirandello does through the father's statements, identification with the fictive character is an encounter with a known identity. Identifying with it momentarily facilitates taking a rest from the continuous change and the constant struggle to establish and crystallize the identity of the 'self'. At the same time identification with the character arouses anxiety because it casts doubt on whether one can trust human identity – be it mine or an other's – and depend on it as a real entity.

The reader's identification as a means of individuation

The encounter with the exquisitely portrayed literary character gives the reader a sense of identification with a more clearly defined existence than his own. The 'self' constantly changes – its memories fade, its desires are hidden and frequently evaporate or are fulfilled and consequently change their form. Contrastingly, the clearly defined written character enables the reader to momentarily identify with a clearer existence than his own. The written images will also frequently assume larger dimensions than in real life – featuring fearless heroes and alluring lovers, like the Greek and Roman sculptures that were fashioned in such a way as to appear to be greater than the real people they were meant to represent. But even when one is talking about the anti-hero or a secondary character, their clear and fixed colours are a part of what enables identification with them.

One of the roles of the literary character is to reflect the versatility of human identity. But in an absurd way Pirandello also proves the very opposite: A person cannot change and acquire every identity he may desire. The phantasy of being able to change identity is fallacious in two contradictory ways. The first is that an individual is confined within the boundaries of the one fate allotted to him. The second is that a person constantly changes, which doesn't allow him to hold on to any fixed identity. The dreams of yesterday are today's forgotten memories. And today's life events will tomorrow assume a different complexion. In contrast to the reader, the literary character is fixed, stable and offers him an anchor in 'live' colours that do not fade. Conceivably, it is in this feature that a part of the secret magic of rereadings is hidden. We will always be meeting up with the same character with its unchanging nature and traits, age and name, invariably awaiting us. If only momentarily, our identification with the literary character gives us the illusion of a clear, crystallized and permanent sense of identity.

Furthermore, a temporary identification with the literary characters hands the reader a borrowed character to dwell in. In Pirandello's play, the father having explained that 'Ours is an immutable reality' has the following exchange with the manager:

> Manager: That is quite all right. But what do you want here, all of you?
> Father: We want to live.
> Manager (ironically). For Eternity?
> Father No, sir, only for a moment ... in you (Pirandello, L., 1921, p. 11).

The reader's encounter with the characters gives him a life within them and them a life within him. Thus, for a while, through identification with them, he escapes the shackles of his identity and at the same time gains an opportunity to sharpen his sense of identity.

Literary projective identification and the transcendence of self

In a number of Klein's writings she uses literary works as an inspiration for her ideas (Klein, M., 1929, 1955, 1963). The phenomenon of projective identification is explored by Klein in her paper 'On Identification' (1955), through her reading of the novel *If I Were You* by the French writer Julien Green (Green, A., 1949). She uses the experiences of the novel's hero to illustrate the mechanism of projective identification. I shall briefly describe Klein's insights, as these shed light on the way in which this mechanism facilitates the literary reader transcending beyond the confines of his identity.

A young man named Fabian deeply resents being imprisoned within a restricted identity caused in the main by his penury, awkwardness and lack of success with women. The Devil does a deal with him resembling the pact reached between Mephistopheles and Faust in Goethe's literary work, except that in Green's novel the allure stemmed from the hero's ability to penetrate and metamorphose into people in whom he chooses to live. The secret formulation that will allow Fabian to transform into another person includes his name, Fabian. The allusion to his name is also important to his ability to escape from the characters when he wants to return to his original identity.

Green's novel and Klein's interpretation are an enlightening illustration of the reading experience. Like the reader of literature, Fabian, the hero, metamorphoses into all sorts of characters with traits he envies with such evident greed. However, these transformations always end up as a disappointment. Time and time again it turns out that the surrogate character and Fabian share a number of characteristics, which, for Fabian, proves to be a frustrating experience. That is to say, the character does not differ from his own to the extent that he had wished. Disappointed, Fabian repeatedly discards the character he has intruded and proceeds to his next 'victim'. So he continues until at the end of the story he returns home and to his old self, which has remained the same and yet different. At the end of his voyage into several other characters, he returns home (and at the same time wakes up from a three-day coma into which he had slumped, feeling elated and loving. He reaches a complete reconciliation with his mother, his dead father and himself, after which he is ready to die happily.

Perhaps the reason why Klein chose to explain the mechanism of projective identification through a literary text, was because of its power to illustrate how, across the chain of projective identifications, the hero experiences a process of developmental transformation. At the end of her paper Klein writes that:

> Whereas in childhood he had not been able to overcome these anxieties and to achieve integration, in the three days covered by the novel, he successfully traverses a world of emotional experiences which in my view entails a working through of the paranoid-schizoid and the depressive positions. As a result of overcoming the fundamental psychotic anxieties of infancy, the intrinsic need for integration comes out in full force. He achieves integration concurrently with good object relations and thereby repairs what had gone wrong in his life (Klein, M., 1955, p. 175).

Here Klein draws attention to a significant psychic development on the part of the hero, following him actively (and literally) projecting himself into different characters (just as the reader does). Klein stresses that these identifications lead to a better integration between paranoid-schizoid and depressive anxieties and between childhood needs, drives, painful memories and lost hopes, and the newly learned mature capacity to find peace within the self and in the face of one's fate.

From projective identification to the formation of the reader's self

Much like Fabian in Green's novel, every reader in the course of his reading metamorphoses into different characters, momentarily nearly forgets his name, almost loses his identity but then again returns and chooses 'to slip out' of the previous character and into the next. On every such occasion he consciously and unconsciously gains a new perspective of the other, the self and what's between them. In this sense literature is not only a place of temporary refuge and an opportunity for an illusory transcendence from the boundaries of the 'self'. It is also a process of reflection and development at the end of which the reader, like Fabian, retrieves parts that he projected on to the character, which he can now re-introject and re-evaluate. The novel analysed by Klein exemplifies a double process that the reader of literature also experiences: On the one hand, Fabian explores his characteristics within the container of the other; on the other hand, he explores the other in his internal container. Like Fabian, when the reader returns to his original name and identity he is the same as he was but also slightly different, after having observed himself as an-other and the other as himself. This simultaneous process contributes to the development of the ability to read the subjectivity of the other and at the same time reformulate the 'self'.

In Pessoa's *The Book of Disquiet* ([1982] 2017) this idea is beautifully illustrated by the author's thoughts about a couple of imaginary characters he saw in a café. In writing about them he imagines their responses when they read 'about themselves' in the future.

> Were they ever to read these pages, I'm sure they would recognize what they never said and would be grateful to me for having interpreted so accurately not just what they really are, but what they never wanted to be. (Pessoa, F. [1982] 2017, p. 41).

The reader who returns to himself from his 'visit' into the literary other – understands himself in new ways. Reading enables him to 'meet himself' through the literary characters, to discover traits that had escaped his self-awareness and capabilities that he hadn't thought were part of his lot in life. Like Moliere's reader of prose who never knew himself to be such, so literature's mirror of images enables the reader to discover himself as a more complex and richer figure than he had previously realized.

The researcher Orly Lubin describes the way in which a reading experience of this kind contributes to the formation of the self:

> The way in which I comprehend the world and my place in it, and within that the components of me as a subject, the very same things that characterize the ways in which I work and think and understand myself and the world, are an outcome of the images acquired from culture, that is to says texts. The subject, that is the 'self', to the extent that it is an outcome of contact with different discourses in culture, is fashioned, formulated, become, validated, changes through encounters with different sorts of discourse; every such encounter is not merely a moment of understanding but a moment of representation of the subject, a moment of the ceaseless process of its alteration ... the

fluidity of the subject, which is to say the changing way in which he perceives himself, corresponds with the fluidity of the encounter between reader and text, and with the ability of the reader to examine and be examined and re-examined *de novo* against the text at every moment. If so, the subject is the same thing that ... returns and is formed and goes and changes, never stable, never final, permanent and fixed. There is, therefore also a sense in thinking about a change which is a liberating change, and about the act of reading as an action that can take part in the process of liberation (Lubin, O., 2003, pp. 15–16).

As a result of these continuous processes of modification the reader who encounters a text is never the same 'self' between one reading and another. Even if the same person reads a certain text one more time, the reading experience will never be identical.

The psychoanalyst Rivka Eifermann exemplifies this in her fascinating account of her various readings of the story *Little Red Riding Hood*. Each separate reading was accompanied by self-analysis (Eifermann, R. R., 1997). This experiment enabled her to recall anew, discover and decipher in a profound way, subtleties in her childhood relations with her mother. Eifermann describes how different readings of the same story aroused different understandings that opened up in every reading by the same reader. Her experience testifies the extent to which every reading is a new event. It corresponds with previous readings and is influenced by them, but at the same time every reading is like an encounter of a new 'self' with a new text. The way in which new memories and new meanings were opened up sheds light on the two aspects of reading: the meaning of the text changes in light of the transformation of the reading 'self', and the reading 'self' changes in light of the 'new' text revealed to him. In the course of the encounter with the characters and the understanding of their perspectives, their existential coping and their internal language, the reader gains an opportunity to reformulate his individuality and his relations with the other.

A psychoanalytic reformulation in light of the reader's identification

The reader's identification with the literary characters should surely force us psychoanalysts to re-examine our precepts about identification and containment. We are used to see total identifications as belonging to more primitive, sometimes pathological, states of mind. And yet we see that the reading of a book that sweeps the reader into the story leads him momentarily to a confusion of identities or to total identification. One example of this out of many can be found in Sartre's book *The Words* in which he describes with a certain degree of irony how he had become so identified with the character that he was surprised to discover that the author had a different continuation than he had in mind: 'I turned the page. My error was demonstrated to me in black and white: the sororicide had to be acquitted' (Sartre, J.P., [1964] 1981, p. 55).

In the same vein Klein demonstrates in her article 'On Identification' (1955) that in order to achieve transformation and development the process of reading has to include a temporary total immersion in the literary character. In the case of Julian Green's character Fabian, only his momentary transcendence from all of his characteristics (both his physical traits, mental state and concrete life situation) achieved his desired experience of 'being an-other'. On his return from his visit to the domains of the other he has the opportunity to re-examine the characteristics of his own identity. In this sense Klein's illustration contributes to the understanding of the reading experiences described by Sartre, Pirandello and Pessoa in a slightly different way than do the descriptions of Winnicott and Bollas in relation to the transitional space. Klein highlights the idea that the moment in reading during which the identification is briefly total is essential if the self is to experience a significant transformation. This idea is in line with the notion previously mentioned, that projective identification also serves a communicative function. For example, Ogden writes that:

> The interpersonal facet of projective identification involves a transformation of the subjectivity of the 'recipient' in such a way that the separate 'I-ness' of the other-as-subject is (for a time and to a degree) subverted: 'You [the "recipient"] of the projective identification] are me [the projector] to the extent that I need to make use of you for the purpose of experiencing through you what I cannot experience myself. You are not me to the extent that I need to disown an aspect of myself and in fantasy hide myself (disguised as not me) in you.' The recipient of the projective identification becomes a participant in the negation of himself as a separate subject, thus making 'psychological room' in himself to be (in unconscious fantasy) occupied (taken over) by the projector.
>
> The projector in the process of projective identification has unconsciously entered into a form of negation of himself as a separate I and in so doing has become other-to-himself; he has become (in part) an unconscious being outside of himself who is simultaneously I and not I. (Ogden, T., 1994).

Ogden maintains that in the process of both subject and object being deprived of their identity a third subject is created: 'the subject of projective identification'. This third subject is assembled from the projector and the receiver and at the same time he is neither of them. The successful analytic process, Ogden argues, 'Involves the reappropriation of the individual subjectivities of analyst and analysand, which have been transformed through their experience of (in) the newly created analytic third' (ibid., p. 101).

Ogden's description of the process of projective identification (following Klein and Bion) sheds new light on the experience described by Sartre. The narrator in Sartre's *The Words* reads a book and in the course of reading for a moment becomes identified with the hero who proposes cutting off the accused's head. He discards his identity as a reader and takes on the hero's identity as the warrior protecting his beloved. The reader having invaded the character assumes the identity of a 'third subject'; a hybrid of both the reader and the character and yet not identical to either of them. One could say that he has become the hybrid that is 'the subject of projective identification' of the reading. The psychoanalyst Emmanuel Berman writes in this context that '[t]he development of the idea of projective identification (by Bion, Ogden, and others) as not merely an inner fantasy, but an actual interpersonal process, may make it particularly valuable in understanding the emotional undercurrents of writing and reading' (Berman, E., 1993, p. 8). In Sartre's *The Words* the experience of the narrator who is also a reader becomes an interpersonal process. He shoots the bad guy, he is the lover of the imaginary beloved and so forth. The reader's wish is not only to take on the character he is identified with, but to also enter an unconscious process in which he projects on to the character elements of his mind (anxieties, death drive, love, insecurity, heroic aspirations and so on). He does this so as to learn from the literary character new ways of managing his experiences and his identity. He not only has 'become' the character but also allows the character to 'be him' and so he experiences more possibilities of 'self'. As Pirandello wrote: 'Literature indeed! This is life, this is passion!' (Pirandello, L., 1921, p. 20).

The study of the writings of Pessoa and Sartre leads to different perspectives of reading and the connection between them sheds light on the complex process that involve identifying with the text's characters. Pessoa describes the reading experience as dreamlike whereas Sartre describes it as very 'real'. From these two perspectives one can understand (a) that one type of reading creates movement characteristic of the paranoid-schizoid position, which involves intense projective identification; (b) that a second type of reading occurs in the context of the potential space, which leads to the evolution of the depressive position characterized by the growing ability to distinguish between the 'self' and the 'other'. Yet again – the two types seem to complement each other and the movement between them creates a whole process of reading. If so, not every reading of a book is characterized by a dreamlike state of the kind typifying the potential space described by Winnicott. In order for the reading to be effective, it would seem that what is needed is a temporary, powerful and overwhelming influence. Only after being immersed in it for a time can one be extracted from it – as in the literary metaphor in Green's story about Fabian who extracted himself from the characters he had entered by remembering his name. The voyage into the character and the retreat from it back to the reader's identity is the infrastructure of the reflective process. The integration between the experience of identification in the bosom of 'the third subject' (the hybridization between the reader and the character) and the study of it from a distance upon the return to the boundaries of the 'self' is what facilitates the transformation of the reader.

From this we can deduce another important trait – the reading experience mixes movement between projective identification and empathy. The psychoanalyst Ogden writes about the distinction between empathy and projective identification:

> Empathy is a psychological process (as well as a form of object-relatedness) that occurs within the context of a dialectic of being and not-being the other. Within this context (Winnicott would say, 'within potential space'), one plays with the idea of being the other while knowing that one is not. It is possible to try on for size one identification and then another (i.e., to play with the feeling of being the other in different ways), because the opposite pole of the dialectic diminishes the danger of being trapped in the other and ultimately of losing oneself in the other. Projective identification, on the other hand, can be understood as a psychological-interpersonal process (a form of defense, communication, and object-relatedness) occurring outside of the dialectic of being and not-being the other, i.e., outside of potential space (Ogden, T., 1985, p. 227).

An accepted claim in psychoanalytic writing about the act of reading is that it takes place in the transformative transitional space in the context of aesthetic experience and empathic capacity. However, the literary examples presented thus far exemplify both 'playful' and total identifications. In light of this it would seem that reading's transformative power is to be found in the movement between two possibilities: The first is for the reader to collapse into a total experience leading to a transcendence of the 'self' through being lost in the other, thus blurring the boundaries and creating an absolute identification between 'self' and 'other, as in Pessoa's words: 'After a matter of minutes, I would become the person writing, and the words on the page would be nowhere to be found' (Pessoa, F., [1982] 2017, p. 235). The second rather involves the joy of the reader in knowing the difference between self and other, reality and imagination, and enjoying the playful encounter between them.

This idea influences not only the understanding of the processes of reading but also sheds light on the psychoanalytic process. Descriptions of reading can help in broadening the psychoanalytic understanding of the working of the mechanism of projective identification. If this mechanism is perceived as a primitive defence mechanism without which a containing object is liable to be destructive, literature raises a new possibility: this mechanism can contribute to developmental processes through the very fact of its activity and not only out of an encounter with an actual containing object. According to this understanding the projective identification mechanism also serves the person being hosted (in phantasy) by the mind of the other to engage in a special kind of self-examination and development.

In addition to the longing to transcend the boundaries of identity I will present in what follows the second plane of transcendence in reading literature, which is the longing to transcend beyond the menacing boundaries of the body and death.

Notes

3 Pessoa's theory of literature has a close affinity to the philosopher Martin Heidegger's idea of Dasein, the primordial essence of 'being', and to his view of art as not appropriated by 'everyone', but rather emerges from nothing that 'is' [present]. Its power, he argues, lay in its ability to reveal ('aletheia'). For more, see Heidegger's 'On the Origin of the Work of Art' ([1950] 1993, pp. 143–212).
4 The term 'symbolic equation' was further developed by Hannah Segal (1950, 1957).
5 The concept of transposition was also used by the philosopher of hermeneutics William Dilthey ([1927] 2002, pp. 235–251), to describe the peak of the encounter between an individual and an artistic creation. Dilthey sheds light on the transcendence that such an encounter facilitates from a different perspective, describing it as a transcendence towards an encounter with the human spirit, which is beyond both the particular reader and the artistic creation: 'Each verse of a poem is converted back into life through the inner nexus [Zusammenhang] in the lived experience from which the poem proceeded. Possibilities, which lie within the psyche [Seele], are called up by the external words which are apprehended by means of the elementary functions of understanding ... Innumerable paths open into the past and into the dreams of the future; innumerable trains of thought proceed from the words that are read ... Expressions of lived experience contain more that the creator was conscious of and remember more ... On the basis of this transposition there now appears the highest form in which the totality of psychic life is effective in the understanding creation or re-experiencing (*nachbilden oder nachahmung*) ... Understanding per se [*an sich*] is an inverse operation to the course of development itself. A fully sympathetic reliving [*vollkommenes Mitleben*] requires that understanding go forward along the line of the events themselves. It proceeds, advancing constantly, with the course of life itself. Thus the process of self-projection and transposition is broadened. Thus we proceed with the history of the time, with an occurrence in a distant land or with something that takes place in the psyche of someone near to us. Its completion is attained where the event is transmitted through the consciousness of the poet, artist or historian and now lies before us, fixed and permanent, in a work ... The sequence of scenes in a play renders it possible to re-experience fragments from the course of life of the persons who appear. The

narrative of the novelist or historian, which follows the historical course, brings about a re-experiencing in us. But what does this re-experiencing consist of? We are here interested in what the process yields. Accordingly we won't offer a psychological explanation ... We focus on the important contribution of this re-experiencing to our appropriation of the human world' (Dilthey, W., [1927] 2002, pp. 234–236).

6 Different kinds of literature give rise to this experience in a variety of ways. It is however beyond the scope of this book to try and depict their differing influence.

References

Berman, E. (Ed.) (1993). *Essential Papers on Literature and Psychoanalysis*. New York and London: New York University Press.

Bion, W.R. (1962). The Psycho-Analytic Study of Thinking. *International Journal of Psychoanalysis*, 43, pp. 306–310.

Bion, W.R. (1967). Notes on Memory and Desire. In: E.B. Spillius (Ed.) *Melanie Klein Today: Developments in Theory and Practice, Vol. 2: Mainly Practice*. London and New York: Routledge, pp. 17–21.

Bollas, C. (1979). The Transformational Object. *International Journal of Psychoanalysis*, 60, pp. 97–107.

Bollas, C. (1987). *The Shadow of the Object: Psychoanalysis of the Unthought Known*. New York: Columbia University Press.

Davidson, D. (1984). What Metaphors Mean. In: *Inquiries into Truth and Interpretation*. Oxford: Clarendon.

Dilthey, W. [1927] (2002). *The Formation of the Historical World in the Human Sciences*. R.A. Makkreel and F. Rodi (Eds) Princeton, NJ and Oxford: Princeton University Press.

Durban, J. and Roth, M. (2013). Introduction to 'The Importance of Symbol Formation in the Development of the Ego'. In: J. Durban and M. Roth (Eds) *Melanie Klein: Selected Papers*. Tel Aviv: Bookworm.

Eifermann, R.R. (1997). Countertransference in the Relationship Between Reader and Text: A Case Study and Retrospect. *Common Knowledge*, 6(1), pp. 155–178.

Freud, S. (1900). The Interpretation of Dreams. In: J. Strachey (Ed.) *The Standard Edition of the Complete Psychological Works of Sigmund Freud, Vol. IV*. London: Hogarth Press, pp. 1–338.

Freud, S. (1908). Creative Writers and Daydreaming. In: J. Strachey (Ed.) *The Standard Edition of the Complete Psychological Works of Sigmund Freud, Vol. IX*. London: Hogarth Press, pp. 141–153.

Freud, S. (1915). The Unconscious. In: J. Strachey (Ed.) *The Standard Edition of the Complete Psychological Works of Sigmund Freud, Vol. XIV*. London: Hogarth Press, pp. 159–215.

Green, J. (1949). *If I Were You*. New York: Harper & Brothers.

Heidegger, M. [1950] (1993). The Origin of the Work of Art. In: *Martin Heidegger: The Basic Writings*. London: Routledge, pp. 143–212.

Klein, M. (1929). Infantile Anxiety Situations Reflected in a Work of Art and in the Artistic Impulse. In: *Love, Guilt and Reparation and Other Works 1921–1945*. London: Vintage, pp. 210–218.

Klein, M. (1930). The Importance of Symbol Formation in the Development of the Ego. In: *Love, Guilt and Reparation and Other Works 1921–1945*. London: Vintage, pp. 219–232.
Klein, M. (1937). Love, Guilt and Reparation. In: *Love, Guilt and Reparation and Other Works 1921–1945*. London: Vintage, pp. 306–343.
Klein, M. (1946). Notes on Some Schizoid Mechanisms. In: *Envy and Gratitude and Other Works 1946–1963*. London: Vintage, pp. 25–42.
Klein, M. (1955). On Identification. In: *Envy and Gratitude and Other Works 1946–1963*. London: Vintage, pp. 141–175.
Klein, M. (1963). Some Reflections on the Orestheia. In: *Envy and Gratitude and Other Works 1946–1963*. London: Vintage, pp. 275–299.
Lifton, R.J. (1973b). The Sense of Immortality: On Death and the Continuity of Life. *American Journal of Psychoanalysis*, 33(1), pp. 3–15.
Lubin, O. (2003). *A Woman Reading A Woman*. Haifa: Haifa University Press.
Malcolm, R.R. (1990). As-If: The Phenomenon of Not Learning. *International Journal of Psychoanalysis*, 71, pp. 385–392.
Ogden, T.H. (1985). On Potential Space. *International Journal of Psychoanalysis*, 66, pp. 129–141.
Ogden, T.H. (1994). The Analytic Third: Working with Intersubjective Clinical Facts. *International Journal of Psychoanalysis*, 75, pp. 3–19.
Ogden, T.H. (2005). What I Would Not Part With. *Fort Da*, 11(2), pp. 8–17.
Omer, H. and Alon, N. (1997). *Constructing Therapeutic Narrative*. Tel Aviv: Modan.
Pessoa, F. [1982] (2017). *The Book of Disquiet*. London: Serpents Tail.
Pirandello, L. (1921). *Six Characters in Search of an Author*. New York: Dover Books.
Poulet, G. (1969). Phenomenology of Reading. In: *New Literary History I*. Baltimore, MD: Johns Hopkins University Press, pp. 53–68.
Sagi, A. (2009). *The Human Voyage to Meaning: A Philosophical-Hermeneutical Study of Literary Works*. Ramat Gan: Bar Ilan University Press.
Sanchez-Pardo, E. (2003). *Cultures of the Death Drive: Melanie Klein and Modernist Melancholia*. Durham, NC and London: Duke University Press.
Sartre, J. [1948] (1988). *What Is Literature?* Cambridge, MA: Harvard University Press.
Sartre, J. [1964] (1981). *The Words*. New York: Vintage Books.
Segal, H. (1950). Some Aspects of the Analysis of a Schizophrenic. *International Journal of Psychoanalysis*, 31, pp. 268–278.
Segal, H. (1957). Notes On Symbol Formation. *International Journal of Psychoanalysis*, 38, pp. 391–397.
Winnicott, D.W. (1953). Transitional Objects and Transitional Phenomena: A Study of the First Not-Me Possession. *International Journal of Psychoanalysis*, 34, pp. 89–97.
Zoran, R. (2000). *The Third Voice: The Therapeutic Qualities of Literature and Their Applications in Bibliotherapy*. Jerusalem: Carmel.
Zoran, R. (2009). *The Letter's Imprint: Reading and Identity within the Bibliotherapeutic Dialogue*. Jerusalem: Carmel.

Further reading

Eifermann, R.R. (1993). Interactions Between Textual Analysis and Related Self-Analysis. In: E. Berman (Ed.) *Essential Papers on Literature and Psychoanalysis.* New York and London: New York University Press, pp. 439–455.

Ogden, T.H. (2004a). The Analytic Third. *Psychoanalytic Quarterly*, 73(1), pp. 167–195.

Ogden, T.H. (2004b). This Art of Psychoanalysis. *International Journal of Psychoanalysis*, 85(4), pp. 857–877.

Chapter 9

Transcendence beyond the boundaries of human vulnerability and mortality

Literature enables the reader to transcend the boundaries connected to the body and its finiteness. These boundaries are associated with the body's inevitable tie to time, place and the imperfection of its existence. At the core of these is the ultimate fear of death. First let us look at the fear of death from a psychoanalytic and philosophical perspective.

Death anxiety: a psychoanalytic perspective

One of man's greatest fears, perhaps his central anxiety, is the fear of death. In his paper 'Beyond the Pleasure Principle' (1920) Freud suggests that we are born with two basic drives that operate in a dialectic relation with one another: the life instinct and the death instinct. Against the instinct to live is the death drive, which Freud explains as deriving from the urge of the organism to return to an inorganic state of not being. Nevertheless, the death drive is not identical to the wish to die. We experience the death drive as a force inside the psyche-soma that is liable to drive it to death. Such an experience arises, for example, during an extreme physical distress, frustration, rage and so on. Aside from its involvement in the tendency to suicide, the death drive mainly arouses in us either aggressiveness (trying to rid ourselves of this force) and/or a fear of death.

A literary example of the death drive in the Freudian sense – an inner movement towards not being – can be found in the following words by Pessoa:

> Leaning over the balcony, enjoying the day, looking out at the diverse shapes of the whole city, just one thought fills my soul – the deep-seated will to die, to finish, no more to see light falling on a city, not to think or feel, to leave behind me, like discarded wrapping paper, the course of the sun and all its days, and to peel off the involuntary effort of being, just as one would discard one's heavy clothing at the foot of the great bed (Pessoa, F., [1982] 2017, p. 365).

Pessoa's description helps us to understand an aspect of the death drive that tends to be forgotten: the tendency to imagine our death is by no means necessarily destructive and/or suicidal. Sometimes it is, but on other occasions it is simply the yearning not to be, to halt the effort that living exacts from us, to stop the movement. As Pessoa says, to remove the heavy suit of the involuntary life instinct – that endless effort of being.

Freud reached the idea of the death drive in stages. His formulation of the concept was aided by the painful confrontation with the massive casualties in the course of World War I.

A year after the outbreak of World War I, in an article titled 'Thoughts for the Times On War and Death' (Freud, S., 1915), Freud argues that we are unable to imagine our death and that every attempt we make to do so leads to the discovery that we are still in attendance in the present as observers. This led Freud to conclude that humans are unable to believe in their death or, in other words, they believe in their immortality. Freud linked the death drive to the biological inclination to return to a state of pre-being and to the yearning for Nirvana and homeostasis.[1] Both Freud and Klein regarded the death drive as the moving force behind the activation of an individual's defence mechanisms. Freud also linked the acts of destruction between people and countries to the projection of the death drive away from them and on to the other.

A year later, in a short requiem-article entitled 'On Transience' (Freud, S., 1916, pp. 303–307), Freud described a walk in the countryside with two friends, one of them a young but already famous poet. The poet (later identified as Rilke) was deeply disturbed by the fact that the beauty surrounding their summer walk would be gone when winter came. Freud writes comments on the falsity of the refusal to recognize the transience of things and emphasizes precisely the opposite view: The fact that things change not only doesn't harm their beauty, it can even reinforce the secret of their fascination in the present.

A third paper in the series, 'Mourning and Melancholia', was published by Freud in 1917 and came to be regarded as a seminal work. In this article Freud deals with man's difficulty in bearing loss and his ways of coping with it. He describes how an individual attempts to preserve the lost object in his psyche be it a person close to him or other things of value such as the loss of his homeland. In the same article Freud distinguishes between normal and pathological situations of mourning, the latter being termed by him 'melancholia'. Pathological states of mourning typify a person who has had an overly ambivalent relation with the lost object and cannot therefore bring the process of mourning to a close in a normal way. In pathological mourning the individual denies the principle of reality and the loss that he has experienced. He is critical of himself when, in fact, the tirade is unconsciously aimed at the lost object that now dwells within him.

Melanie Klein continued to develop the concept of the death drive arguing that it is the principal moving force behind anxiety. From birth, the death drive is immediately sensed as an instinctive experience of potential destruction that is translated at the psychic level as a fear of annihilation by another because his own destructiveness is projected on to the other. Klein claimed that in opposition to the death drive powerful defence mechanisms of splitting and projective identification are triggered. Klein linked mental representations of the death drive to the infant's somatic experiences such as suffocation, difficulties in swallowing, digestion, etc., which are experienced in phantasy as an active danger of annihilation by a persecutory object who comes to the infant in order to destroy him. Klein expanded Freud's concept of the existence of a dialectic between the death drive and the life drive and gradually developed an alternative view. According to Klein there is in fact a representation of death in a person's unconscious. Although excessive death anxiety disturbs the developmental processes, in a more balanced situation representations of death can even contribute in that they motivate a person to create, enrich his personality and broaden his horizons. A philosophical view of the fear of death will deepen the understanding of the link between the fear of death and the development of the 'self'.

Death anxiety: a philosophical perspective

The philosopher Martin Heidegger writes about the connection between the fear of death, the experience of time and the processes of formation of the 'self' (Heidegger, M., [1927] 1996, p. 96). He suggests that the knowledge of death is a compelling force in psychic development. According to Heidegger, our knowledge of death and the ability to recognize it enables us to examine our existence in a way that differs from that of someone who is immersed in his daily life as a continuous present, is not conscious of his immanent death and is therefore also not aware that the uniqueness of his life resides in 'being there' ('*Dasein*'). The recognition of death facilitates a process of individuation, in other words, a process of forming the self in a reflective way. Such a person transcends the habit of the in-authentic *Dasein*, whose main concern is to reduce the distance between himself and the other and to remain immersed in the familiar and in the meanings designed by the surroundings of which he is a part, an environment that lends him a sense of certainty. When this subject is prepared to face the fact of his future death he is ejected from the conventional and has the unique opportunity of experiencing his individuality. Thus *Dasein*, who is 'being there', gets to connect to his existence in an authentic way (ibid., p. 232).

The researcher Joel Pearl adds that according to Heidegger the difference between the possibility of death and other possibilities does not derive from death being the last possibility in a chain of possibilities. The difference stems from the fact that death is a possibility to which one cannot posit any alternative. When *Dasein* understands death in this way, death appears in his world as individuation's most extreme possibility. And as such it awakens the *Dasein* into an authentic existence (see Pearl, J., 2011, p. 71).

Both the psychoanalytic and the philosophic perspectives show that our encounter with the subject of death leads to contradictory psychic reactions. On the one hand, positions of avoidance, defence, a false attempt at dealing with the issue. On the other hand, a direct, honest, profound confrontation with death as an existential fact, which, once recognized, increases the subject's ability to undergo processes of authentic personal development and to search for meaningful pathways in his life. As we shall soon see, the literary space merges the two: It enables a recognition of death and simultaneously transcends it via the unique phantasies and psychic experiences that are enabled in the process of creating or being exposed to the works of art and literature. In what follows I shall present literary evidence demonstrating the reader's use of literature to transcend beyond physical boundaries and beyond the fear of death.

The fear of death and symbolic immortality

Robert J. Lifton (1973) is a psychoanalyst who researched the psychological impact on those who survived the dropping of an atom bomb on Hiroshima in 1945. In his view humans have 'intermediary knowledge' of the idea of death. In dealing with the fear of death an individual transcends beyond it via what Lifton describe as a 'formative process' of symbolization (ibid., p. 4), which is to say by conducting symbolic relations with the components of life. In the course of this 'formative symbolization' an individual maintains his links with his brothers and his own history, both past and future. The symbolic representation stems from a universal drive that exerts pressure on the individual to maintain continuous symbolic relations with the various components of life beyond time and space, and therefore also beyond death.

Lifton claims that the fear of death embraces three psychic representations: stasis, disintegration and separation. In dealing with the fear of death we apply various forms of coping, which enable us to transcend beyond the death anxiety. These states of transcendence are termed by Lifton 'symbolic immortality'. He lists five ways of experiencing symbolic immortality, which, as I will show, are powerfully awakened in the course of reading, through: descendants; spiritual transcendence; creativity; surviving dangerous conditions[2]; and an experiential transcendence.

Lifton suggests that the psychic state of experiential transcendence is attained in the context of a variety of human situations and activities such as singing, dancing, giving birth or through an encounter with a work of art or an intellectual composition. In such situations, according to Lifton, a new symbolic order reigns. Upon his return from this experience an individual is likely to sense that he differs in some way from the person he was when the experience began. Lifton sees in this situation a representation of death and rebirth, which is central to the attainment of psychic transformation. This experiential transcendence includes a feeling of a continuous present, which is experienced as inseparable from the past or the future and is comparable to 'eternity' and mythical time.

Reading literature as a transcendence beyond symbolic death

Although the therapeutic use of texts is mainly manifested to the practice of bibliotherapy (Zoran, R. 2000, 2009), it is also at times employed in psychoanalytic therapy, when the patient takes the initiative and describes a significant reading experience. In many instances the patient uses a description of his reading experience to inform the therapist of his unconscious psychic coping with his fears of death be they in relation to him or those close to him.

That, for example, is what happened during clinical work with a war orphan experiencing a difficult process of mourning following the death of his father (Palgi, P. and Durban, J., 1995, pp. 223–243). The boy created a split between the figure of the therapist, which in his eyes was human and vulnerable; and literary characters (such as James Bond, biblical characters and others), which he viewed as heroic and eternal. In their article Palgi and Durban mainly discuss the advantages of figures formed in a culture as collective symbols that the reader employs both in relation to their role in the story as well in relation to the use already made of them by the collective. The collective as an 'extended reader' passes on to a particular reader the projections and the transference towards these figures as part of a cultural heritage. In the case cited above, the split between the figure of the human therapist that arouses fears of vulnerability and death (lest he should die as did the father) and the employment of literary characters representing an alternative of eternity and immunity. This example shows how once he loaded these characters with features of 'symbolic immortality' they become for him objects that diminish fear and that he can use in the mourning process.

I have to point out that in the context of the reading of literature the word 'symbolic' is directed at the characteristics of the text and not at the reader's psychic process. In effect, there is a twofold process at work here: The literary characters are loaded with symbolic immortality. Through identification with the characters, the reader experiences a phantasy of immortality that he can experience at a primitive concrete level or at a symbolically creative level depending on the psychic process he goes through while reading.

Evidence of symbolic immortality in Semprún's book *Literature or Life*

As we saw earlier, Semprún writes about the voyage of confrontation he endured while a political prisoner in Buchenwald concentration camp and that he continued after his release. His descriptions expose the nature of experiencing an intimate daily encounter with death.

> I'm struck by the idea ... that I have not escaped death, but passed through it. Rather: that it has passed through me, that I have, in a way, lived through it ... I have wandered along its paths, losing and finding my way in this immense land streaming with absence, All things considered, I am a ghost (Semprún, J., 1994, pp. 14–15)

Openly and in detail Semprún describes the wakeful relations he conducted with language, literature and reading. He even engages in a dialogue with himself in the guise of another author writing in various periods of time as well as a discourse with other writers, philosophers, poets, composers of literature and thinkers, who occupy a significant space in his consciousness and in his life. He is writing in the language of *ars poetica*, a language informed by knowledge of the written word, its roles, its prices and its qualities. Semprún even goes so far as to consciously link writing and not-writing to life and death. Semprún is evidently also a reader who conducts extremely insightful relations with materials he has read and even with their authors. He has a keen memory of his extensive readings and in this sense returns and reads from memory even years after letting the physical text go. This ability proves to be very helpful during his time in the concentration camp as he leafed through pages of books etched in his memory. Semprún's descriptions of internal encounters with the substance of his reading and its authors are woven into his story as companions inextricably linked to his voyage – a representation of symbolic immortality. Contrary to Barthes' tidings about the 'death of the author' (1967) there are no dead among Semprún's friends – quite the reverse. They live and revitalize life. As he copes from one minute to the next with the threat of death it is these companions who come to his rescue.

Three powerful stories in Semprún's book evidence an individual attaining experiential transcendence in three encounters with a text: an encounter with a person who reads; an encounter with someone who sings a song with which the narrator is familiar from childhood days; and an encounter with a dying man intoning the Kaddish. The text enables the narrator and whoever is at his side in these encounters to broaden their horizons beyond the partial nature of somatic and material existence and discover a link to the human, the psychic and the spiritual.

The first story involves one of the most heart-rending episodes in Semprún's book and is linked to his encounters with his friend and revered teacher Halbwachs. In these meetings Semprún is seen accompanying his mentor as Halbwachs' life gradually ebbs away. He tells us how little by little Halbwachs 'no longer had the strength to utter a single word. He could only listen to me, and only at the cost of superhuman effort. Which is, moreover, the nature of man' (Semprún, J., 1994, p. 18). As Semprún spoke to the dying Halbwachs, he 'would smile, gazing at me like a brother' (ibid.). This sentence recurs in the book every time Semprún meets up with his old teacher. And what did he talk to him about? It is no accident that they mostly talk about Halbwachs' books, his lectures from university days, the spiritual assets with which he enriched Semprún's life when he was a student at the Sorbonne. One day the moment comes. As he arrives for a visit Semprún immediately sees that Halbwachs is in the last few moments of his life. He is alarmed and searches for a safe space in the face of such imminent death. In this fragile moment the answer comes to Semprún from the reading experiences stored in his memory. He writes:

> Then, seized with panic, not knowing whether I might call upon some god to accompany Maurice Halbwachs, yet aware of the need for a prayer, trying to control my voice and pitch it properly despite the lump in my throat, I recited a few lines by Baudelaire. It was the only thing I could think of,
> 'O death, old captaine, it's time, let's weight anchor'
> His eyes brightened slightly, as though with astonishment. I continued to recite. When I reached the line
> 'Our hearts, which you know are filled with light'
> a delicate tremor passed over the lips of Maurice Halbwachs.
> Dying, he smiled, gazing at me like a brother.

And in the next line Semprún adds, 'There were the SS as well, naturally' (ibid., pp. 22–23). These Spontaneous thoughts clearly show Semprún in the grip of the terror of the imminent death of his mentor and he makes the comparison between 'the need for a prayer' and Baudelaire's poem. The poetic prayer renews the bond between the two and Halbwachs' last gaze at Semprún expresses fraternity.

What is the nature of this bond formed with a text? An affiliation that doesn't revolve around any kind of spontaneous personal saying but around a text? The narrator describes the affinity between him and his friend based on their mutual sentiment towards a poem that for both of them has a meaning beyond its actual contents even though it has to be said that its contents as a poem about parting has its own significance. The bond between them immortalizes their humanity. The memory of the text contains a recollection of an essence beyond the body. The death continues but the soul, the psyche, the consciousness, the spirit, reach beyond death and cannot be reduced to the dimensions of the body; this is an experiential transcendence towards a reparational remembrance of the thinking, reflective, reading, consciousness. Baudelaire's poem of parting places the current traumatic farewell in a universal context and alleviates the solitude, alienation and helplessness surrounding the circumstances of this death.

Baudelaire's poem mediated the moments of Semprún's parting from Halbwachs and the latter's parting from life. It gave Halbwachs one more opportunity to smile, to look directly into the eyes of another person and be rescued from the absoluteness of the body via the awakening of the psychic, interpersonal and spiritual space.

The second story by Semprún about an experiential transcendence describes two people singing. One is a German soldier singing the popular Spanish song *La Paloma* and the second a Jew who the narrator and his friend came upon when they searched for survivors among the piled up bodies on the day the camp was liberated. Because the Jew was dying he was found chanting the prayer for the dead in Yiddish. The intertwinement of the two stories is chilling and emphasizes even more poignantly Semprún's sentiment towards a person who has a song in his heart. These stories are a clear example of an experiential transcendence that occurs owing to the link between the literary text, the human dimension and the holistic nature of existence. This link enables a person to transcend beyond the body as a decisive sign of his essence.

In the first description, both Semprún's and his friend's guns are aimed at the young German soldier who is unable to see them. It was obvious to both of them that they had to shoot him. Until he burst into song in a 'pleasant blondish voice': 'My hand began to shake. It had become impossible for me to shoot at that young soldier singing 'La Paloma'. As though singing the melody from my childhood, that refrain so full of nostalgia, had suddenly made him innocent' (ibid., p. 33). Semprún testifies that having been exposed to the humanity of the soldier who was capable of singing the song prevented him from reducing and dehumanizing the soldier by shooting him in cold blood. Moreover, this turn of events turns the soldier into an *innocent*. What is the crime of which he is suddenly innocent? The crime of inhumanity? Semprún writes that the soldier is innocent of any crime, not only of having been born in Germany under Hitler but 'fundamentally innocent, in the fullness of his existence, because he was singing "La Paloma"' (ibid., pp. 33–34).

'In the fullness of his existence' marks the turnabout evidencing an experiential transcendence. The song transformed the reductive form of his existence (soldier, enemy, murderer), turning him into a person who can yearn, learn, remember, sing – just like Semprún himself.

This description is intertwined with the depiction of the Jew who chanted the prayer for the dead in Yiddish: 'It would take me several lifetimes to tell all that death. Telling the story of that death right through to the end would be an endless task' (ibid., p. 35). In a literary twist of a story within a story, a kind of free association in the middle of the story about the Jew who chanted, Semprún remembers yet another kind of singing:

> It was there, one memorable night, that Darriet and I, taking delicious drags on the same cigarette end, discovered a mutual taste for Jazz and poetry. Shortly afterward ... we'd been trading poems: Darriet had just recited some Baudelaire for me; I was giving him Paul Valery's 'La Fileuse'. Miller ... recited some verse by Heine, in German. And then, to the great joy of Darriet, who marked time to our performance by waving his hands around like an orchestra conductor, Serge Miller and I together declaimed the song of the Lorelei ... We screamed out the end of the poem amid the defeating roar of dozens of pairs of wooden clogs ... After which, we ran off at top speed as well, heading for Block 62 in a kind of thrilling, unutterable happiness Kneeling next to the dying Jew, I have no idea how to keep him alive, my Christ of the Kaddish (ibid., p. 41).

Now comes the retrospective intertwining with Halbwachs and Baudelaire. Semprún describes how he took the Jew chanting the Kaddish in his arms and writes:

> I had taken Maurice Halbwachs in my arms, too, that last Sunday ... I slipped an arm under his shoulders and leaned over his face, to speak to him as closely, as gently as I could. I had just recited to him that poem by Baudelaire, the way one says a prayer for the dying. Halbwachs was no longer able to speak. He had gone even farther into death than that unknown Jew over whom I am now bending, who still has the strength – the unimaginable strength – to recite for himself the prayer for the dying, to accompany his own passing with words that celebrate death, that make it immortal, at least (ibid.).

The significance Semprún attributes to poetic, religious and chanted texts is evident. In his view, such texts enable a person to transcend their boundaries, creating an abundant space for spiritual existence that reaches well beyond those narrow boundaries. The texts indicate a closeness and an affinity between friends. They have the power to arouse powerful emotions, apparent in how Semprún and his friends 'read' Heine's *Loreley* within the camp's walls from the depths of their hearts and with 'indescribable excitement and joy'. The texts also have the power to immortalize the dying man intoning the Kaddish – enveloping him in a shroud of symbolic immortality even if he were to meet his death as his prayer ends.

We, the readers, are exposed to Semprún's witnessing and become witnesses ourselves. The 'small' human stories Semprún offers us, testify as would a thousand witnesses, to the power of the written and read word to create a distance between a person and his body, between a person and his worldly finiteness. The word has the power to preserve for him a human image and a spiritual space of existence where immortality resides sufficiently 'to at least make him eternal'.

The final relevant story appears towards the end of the book and presents a final version linking poetry, death, body's finiteness and friendship. Semprún recounts how he stood at the grave of Cesar Vallejo, the poet whom he loved, and was reminded of the poem's words, 'Do not die, I love you so!' But the corpse, alas! Continued dying' (ibid., p. 192). The very same poetic words that had come to his rescue in his sorrow when Morales died in his arms three months earlier in one of the wards in Buchenwald. And here he is once again facing the corpse of Vallejo the poet, standing at his grave, reading the words of the dead poet from memory – evidence of the eternity of the word and of Vallejo's own immortality, represented by the aliveness of his poem inscribed on the gravestone.

Until now I have been describing the use of reading to transcend the boundaries of the body and death in the extreme circumstances of incarceration in a concentration camp. Such situations accentuate the significance of symbolic immortality in the midst of reading and the power of literature to also mediate in the most ephemeral and harshest moments of existence. However, the literary evidence shows that the yearning to transcend the boundaries of time, place, partialness and finality are aroused in every person including those who lead temperate lives and is part of people's attraction to of literature. For the purpose of illustration I shall in the main be relying on Sartre's book *The Words*.

The reading of literature as a transcendence towards 'symbolic timelessness'

The fear of death is not only the lot of those who have suffered a trauma that has brought them closer to it. Reading enables us all to cope with the issue of finiteness, which, in the framework of fiction, enables us to reflect and from time to time offers us experiential transcendence and contact with the fantasy of symbolic immortality described by Lifton. In his article 'Thoughts for the Times on War and Death' (1915) Freud wrote that the thought that there will be nobody to take our place paralyses us and that we tend to remove the subject of death from our minds. Freud saw the resort to literature and art as means of making sure that death is a factor one can play with, overcome and deny its finality.

It is an inevitable result of all this that we should seek in the world of fiction, in literature and in the theatre compensation for what has been lost in life. There we still find people who know how to die – who, indeed, even manage to kill someone else. There alone too the condition can be fulfilled which makes it possible for us to reconcile ourselves with death: namely, that behind all the vicissitudes of life we should still be able to preserve a life intact. For it is really too sad that in life it should be as it is in chess, where one false move may force us to resign the game, but with the difference that we can start no second game, no return-match. In the realm of fiction we find the plurality of lives which we need. We die with the hero with whom we have identified ourselves; yet we survive him, and are ready to die again just as safely with another hero (Freud, S., 1915, p. 291).

Freud's words suggest that the reading of literature also involves transcending the boundaries of time. It facilitates a momentary enactment of the reader's yearning to transcend beyond the limits of present time in which a person is trapped. Similarly to the concept of 'symbolic immortality' coined by Lifton, I wish to suggest the concept of 'symbolic timelessness' in order to characterize this yearning. The philosopher of hermeneutics Hans Gadamer described the reading experience as a 'fusion of horizons' (Gadamer, H., 1960, p. 130). This is a dialogue that takes place and mediates between the time and tradition from which the reader meets the text with the time and tradition in which the text was created; a fundamental encounter between present and past. If, while reading, the reader can connect to any point in time that is outside the borders of his life then by this mental act he will have released himself from the bondage of present time. The reading also connects the reader to readers drawn from every period in the past, the present and even those who will read the book in the future. As far as the writer is concerned, it is obvious that every reading of his book will be at some future time relative to the period in which it was written. However, the new claim here is that this phantasy is also embedded in the mind of those readers who pass the book on from hand to hand across generations. Thus the reader connects into symbolic timelessness that stretches from an unlimited past to an unlimited future – a phantasy of continuity for ever more.

Sartre's *The Words* ([1964] 1981), which assisted us in previous chapters, offers very special literary evidence because in it the author elaborates on his relations to language and literature through an autobiographical prism. He recalls his experience as a child who grew up into complex, rich and formative relations with words, reading and writing; shaping his identity and consolidating his self-image.

The book was published in the year in which Sartre was nominated for the Noble Prize for Literature, which he refused to accept for ideological reasons. Thus, even though it describes the reading experience in the early years of his life, he is in fact nurtured by his experience as a creator and a highly skilled reader and writer.

The book is divided into two parts according to the order of events in his encounter with language. The first part is titled 'Reading' and the second 'Writing'. Sartre's evidence about his relations to reading crisscrosses the two parts of the book since even after he enters the twists and turns of his relations with writing he still remains and continues to forever be a reader.

The life story of the hero of *The Words* begins with the threat of death looming over father and son that ends with the death of the father. Immediately after his birth, baby Jean Paul and his father became ill. Both were in the throes of death until Sartre's father actually died while the infant recovered. Sartre denies the importance of his father's death and the importance of the internalized father figure. In this he also seeks to deny the tension between his bold vivaciousness as a child and his awareness of the constant menace of finality. From the very beginning of the book and to its end – though he doesn't relate to the anxiety about the terminality of existence – the hero deals with the limitations stemming from being imprisoned in the present. In reading literature he is searching for a remedy to counter the massive presence of transience in his inner world, a presence he vehemently denies. The hero also does attempt to become acquainted with his father's image in the reading space as he rifles the pages of various books and discovers one in which his father's scribbles appear, from a lost time when he was reading the very same books.

The death object: a psychoanalytic perspective

The psychoanalyst J. Durban describes our internal relations with a 'death object'. He writes: 'From early infancy on, every individual; needs to cope with two unresolved riddles: the riddle of one's birth and that of one's death' (Durban, J., 2017, p. 87), and 'The death object serves as a creative, internal unconscious attempt to represent death and to form various pacts and relationships with this object' (ibid., p. 95). This entity is personified within cultures by such symbols as the angel of death, Satan, a zombie or a vampire and can also be found personified in children's imaginations and dreams in the form of dark and scary human-like images. Every individual's phantasy about the 'death object' will have its own particular nature in line with his internalizations and his psychic and somatic structure. According to Durban the death object is created in the child's phantasy as representing all the experiences of annihilation and threat felt during his development from the moment of his conception, through his existence in the womb, his birth and his life thereafter. The death object is shaped according to the sum of all the child's experiences that are what Durban calls 'equivalents of death', such as separation, sleep, pain, a lack of continuity, the loss of or disappearance of the object and situations of serious existential or physical deprivations. In his phantasy the child creates a death object and establishes a kind of relation and undertaking with it as a defence against death. A simple conscious example would be 'I will be a good boy and you will not take my father', and numerous other conscious and unconscious deals and relations with the death object take place in our order to prevent our finiteness.

Symbolic immortality, timelessness and spacelessness in Sartre's *The Words*

The danger of death, threat and anxiety are all liable to manic defences, characterized by omnipotent denial of vulnerability and helplessness (and not necessarily with any sense of exaggerated elation as might be inferred from the common meaning of the word 'mania'). Melanie Klein described the manic mechanisms (Klein, M., 1940) as one of the most powerful means against entering the depressive position in which the limitations of existence are recognized, as is the 'otherness' of the other. The subject who does enter the depressive position is due to take responsibility for his life and the lives of others. For the most part manic defence is accompanied by the elimination of neediness, of the importance the other and, in pathological cases, this nullification is bolstered by a display of contempt and brutality towards the significant other so as to demonstrate the separateness and non-dependency of the 'self'.

Jean Paul Sartre as the hero of his autobiographical book *The Words* repeatedly affirms the evident advantages of his father's death. For example, he expresses joy at the fact that in his death his father granted him freedom and led him to no longer having a 'superego', since he supposedly had no father image.

It is only by reading between the lines, in his encounter with the books he inherited from his father, that a more ethereal attitude comes to light, which enfolds yearning, curiosity and pain, but is also accompanied by a defensive manic contempt: 'I later inherited some books that had belonged to him ... He read bad books, like all his contemporaries' (Sartre, J.P., [1964] 1981, p.19). Sartre's first encounter with his father's identity didn't come about through his family because, as he put it, 'No one in my family was able to make me curious about that man' (ibid.). Instead, the father and son are introduced by books! This is the first identifying feature of the link between the son's search for his father and the son's turning to books with the yearning to transcend beyond the present reality. Sartre the son denies his need for his father and the pain of his loss but this denial is indirectly undermined by his preoccupation with the possibility that the living and the dead can pick up the same book, read it each in his own time, and so develop a dialogue or at least a kind of acquaintance between them. Sartre meets his father in a reading within a reading: 'In the margins, I came upon indecipherable scribbles, dead signs of a little illumination that had been alive and dancing at about the time of my birth' (ibid.). The touching and frustrating attempt to understand 'the indecipherable scribbles' that were the most first-hand remnant he had of his father's 'voice,' is immediately replaced by an omnipotent blunt denial of his longing for a father, 'That defunct was of so little concern to me that I sold the books' (ibid.).

The psychoanalyst Andre Green described the negative mechanisms that retain the affinity to a missing object by negating the representation of the object itself:

> Negative hallucinations can also apply to representations. In these cases representations are not only repressed, they are suppressed, that is no longer available to be represented in a way different from repression or splitting. Repression keeps the representation as far as possible from consciousness. It is conserved in the mind though out of reach, impossible to awaken to memory, but still there. In the case of negative hallucination the thoughts, some capital thoughts are lost, because they have been erased. There is no trace of their ever having existed or of their 'underground' performances (Green, A., 1998, pp. 658–659)

Sartre creates a negative hallucination – a relation with no content – where a representation of the father was supposed to be found. It is important to understand that the death of a father, even if it is a father we have never met, does not at all demand the erasure of his representation in our internal world. For the most part the very opposite is the case. When Sartre reads a book that was formerly read by his father, he is momentarily released from this unconscious defence and tries to read the comments scribbled by his father. In these scribbles the son sees evidence of a life that once was. But alas, despite his efforts the scribbles remain indecipherable and so remain 'dead signs'. There is an unbearable frustration caused by the unfulfilled potential of having come so close to reading a text handwritten by his father, almost like a sudden and unexpected feeding directly from the palm of his hand, which eventually met the father's undecipherable handwriting. Sartre thus returns to his previous tenor, which emphasizes the advantages of his father's absence. Reading the unreadable scribbles in his father's handwriting becomes altogether too much like the negative hallucination that took the place of the father from the outset. The reading that yearned to transcend the fetters of time and death became an act of investment in an absent father.

Nevertheless, after this very personal testimony Sartre continues to deal throughout his memoir with books as a potential wellspring for transcendence beyond the confines of time. In the framework of reading, books provide him in phantasy two attributes needed by him: symbolic immortality and symbolic timelessness. His unconscious death object was consolidated following the danger of imminent death and through the penetration of the real death of his father in his early infancy. It is therefore clear why he so needed the phantasies of immortality and timelessness. Sartre likened books to ancient signifiers of perpetuity that represented for him continuity from time immemorial and for ever more and as constituting a means of transcending human finiteness. Symbolic timelessness not only ensures his continuity but also enables him to move freely and limitlessly forwards and backwards along the dimension of time. It is for good reason that Sartre likens books to prehistoric megalithic stones and calls them 'ancient monuments' (ibid., p. 41). The literary works free him from the confines of present time of personal human existence.

When Melanie Klein founded the method of psychoanalysis for children she claimed that children attribute human features to animals and belongings and that these become part of their inner 'world of objects' (Klein, M., 1926, 1929). As a demonstration of this, Sartre testifies in *The Words* that his relations with books as a child resembled relations with people. As was described in Chapter 3, in the framework of the personification of these monuments, he attributes to them a live gaze that they give him while he reads. Sartre's books look at him. There is a reversal of roles here that serves the reader's need to be seen by what the book represents to him and not only to read it. The other's look is needed, and supplied by the books. The psychoanalyst Thomas Ogden relates to the role of the other's look thus:

> Paradoxically, 'I-ness' is made possible by the other. Winnicott (1967b) describes this as the infant's discovery of himself in what he sees reflected in his mother's eyes. This constitutes an interpersonal dialectic wherein 'I-ness' and otherness create one another and are preserved by the other. The mother creates the infant and the infant creates the mother (Ogden, T., 1986, p. 209).

One can see the phantasy of symbolic timelessness in three processes described by Sartre, two of them connected to gazing.

First, he testifies that the book is an object that existed before him and will exist after he has gone and so constitutes for him a magic carpet on which he transcends beyond his time and place:

> I began my life as I shall no doubt end it: amidst books ... I disported myself in a tiny sanctuary, surrounded by ancient, heavy-set monuments which had seen me into the world, which would see me out of it, and whose permanence guaranteed me a future as calm as the past (Sartre, J.P., [1964] 1981, pp. 40–41).

The book that existed before him and would continue to exist after him is like an overview that gives him both perspective and peace. The otherness of the book whose boundaries stretch beyond the space of time and place in which the living Sartre reads and works establishes his awareness of himself as a continuous being that preceded him, and that will outlast him.

Second, Sartre creates an identity between the book and the writer. At yet another time of reading he again has a confusing experience of a bidirectional vision in which he stares at the writer who stares back at him through the windows of the book's pages (ibid., p. 64). We can see that this time the writer also transcends the confines of his death and is resurrected by the reading. The physical characteristics of the book become the physical characteristics of the writer in the eyes of Sartre the child: 'Flaubert was a cloth-bound, odourless little thing spotted with freckles' (ibid., p. 63).

Third, Sartre also grants the writers an eternal life. Thus for instance he says: 'In my sight, they were not dead; at any rate, not entirely. They had been metamorphosed into books' (ibid., p. 63). The authors' immortality is described in a morbid, ironical and yet romantic way. He admires them and is aided by them; he views them as somewhat exalted but also as having experienced their immortality as a prison in which they are trapped by him, given to his capricious usage and denied the right to eternal rest. Thus, for example, in the segment mentioned in a different context in the previous chapter, Sartre writes about books: 'I did not yet know how to cut the dead into pieces, but I did subject them to my whims ... Those garbled figures were my dolls, and I pitied that wretched, paralyzed survival which was called immortality' (ibid., p. 66). Here the phantasy of immortality links up with the phantasy of timelessness. The dead live a life of eternity, and their bodies metamorphose into books and thus are not lost to the world. At the same time one can identify the fragility that inherently accompanies the phantasies of timelessness and immortality and the way in which they are attacked in the text by the intrusion of the morbid associations represented by paralysis and the figures of the dead.

Every reader has an important role in immortalizing his books' writers. The books immortalize their authors, but no less importantly the readers immortalize them by discovering them and breathing new life into them across the generations long after they have been written and after the writers have passed. As said, through *The Words* Sartre refers to the cathedrals and old libraries, megaliths and statues, graves and pantheons – all symbolizing the books as monuments that lend their writers immortality. But this is dependent on the act of reading. According to Sartre it can only happen if assiduous readers invest in reading an ancient manuscript. When Sartre is preoccupied with immortalizing himself as a future writer, he fantasizes about how as yet unborn children will weep over him in the future as readers. The phantasy of timelessness also undermines the linearity of the dimension of time, which moves from the past to the future. So, for example, when Sartre imagines the tears his readers will shed over him he writes: 'I saw my death through their eyes; it had taken place, it was my truth: I became my own obituary' (ibid., p. 209). If so, it is not only the writer who bestows immortality and timelessness upon the reader but also the readers who bestow timelessness and immortality upon the author. The imagined tears to be shed by his future readers constitutes a paradoxical reflection of Sartre's death and immortality at one and the same time: They lament his death yet in doing so they again and again return him to life.

Reading also arouses another phantasy, that of the ability to transcend the confines of space, which I term 'symbolic placenessness'. It is relevant both to the writer and to the readers. The reader is able to cross the boundaries of the place in which he is reading as he tours the story's various sites. From the writer's perspective Sartre describes how readers across the globe will enable the author to dominate geographical areas that will mark the extent of his immortal importance:

> I was consecrated, illustrious. I had my tomb in Pere Lachaise Cemetery and perhaps in the Pantheon; an avenue was named after me in Paris, as were public squares in the provinces and in foreign countries. Yet, at the core of my optimism I had a sneaking feeling that I lacked substance (ibid., p. 207).

This lack of substance described by Sartre testifies to the fact that the use of literature as a means to omnipotent transcendence beyond the boundaries of time, place and death, is accompanied by a concealed and continuous fear of certain features of reality that include helplessness, partialness and finality. The power of literature to transport the reader beyond this reality is at the heart of its attraction while the lack of substance referred to by Sartre is part of the concealed pain and anxiety that we feel at exactly at the same time as we enjoy the reading.

Retrospective illusion

An additional feature of symbolic timelessness aroused by reading is termed by Sartre as 'retrospective illusion'. He writes: 'My grandfather had brought me up in a state of retrospective illusion ... that mirage is born spontaneously of culture' (Sartre, J.P., [1964] 1981, p. 198). The narrator describes the special relation of time between the reader and the book's hero:

> His life belongs to us; we enter it at either end or in the middle; we go up and down the course of it at will. The reason is that chronological order has exploded. Impossible to restore it. The personage runs no further risks and no longer even expects the tickling in his nose to end in sneezing. His existence has the appearance of an unfolding, but as soon as we

try to restore a bit of life to it, it relapses into simultaneity ... That's the mirage: the future more real than the present (ibid., p. 199).

Sartre describes a difference between the chronological and linear way in which we experience time in our actual life, advancing from the past to the future, and the experience of time during reading in which all directions are possible, each one of which leads to a different experience. The experience of time in the course of reading has two facets. On the one hand, the tension while reading stems in part from our identification with the story that simulates reality and so we attribute to it an advance from past to future just as time progresses in life. On the other hand, in reading there are various multidirectional chronological layers. We know and yet deny that we begin where the end already exists, for we always begin to read a book in which the last page has already been written. Perhaps we choose not to turn to that last page (even though it is known that some readers won't read a book without first looking at its epilogue), but the ending is already there. The narrator's viewpoint might be of 'the one who knows' the end of the story in advance, or that of one who doesn't know its ending. As for the writer, with whom the reader also has transference relations, it is as if he owns all the story's 'times'. The story's content can also move in every direction both forward and backwards in time. Finally, we too as readers can leaf through the book eyeing parts of the story and even read it again and so return the future to its past and vice versa.

The narrator's identification with the characters and stories in Sartre's *The Words* is at times so intense that the freedom afforded to the reader by the text has been reversed to the point that he feels imprisoned within its walls while once again both the direction of time and that of the gaze are confused:

> I would find myself on the other side of the page, inside the book ... I was being seen, from death to birth, by those future children ... I shuddered, paralyzed by my death, which was the true meaning of all my gestures. Ousted from myself, I tried to go back up the page in the opposite direction and find myself on the reader's side. I would raise my head, I would ask the light for help ... I could not get out of the book. I had long since finished reading it, but I remained a character in it (ibid., pp. 204–205).

The anxiety of death and finality is one of the most fundamental features of an individual's mind and one of the deepest motivations to the activation of defence mechanisms and the withdrawal from reality. At the same time, it is also an essential bedrock of development, mourning and psychic growth. In Sartre's book one can see the two psychic characteristics linked to the fear of death: On the one hand, we saw how defence mechanisms are activated as denial and omnipotence expressed in phantasies of symbolic immortality, symbolic timelessness and symbolic placenessness. On the other hand, one can also find in Sartre's literary evidence the way in which the fear of death is the driving force in recognizing his limitations, helping him to move beyond the depressive position described by Klein, which is bound up with psychic maturity and genuine, modest and responsible encounter with reality. Thus, for example, when Sartre deals with the life expectancy of his literary hero, it helps him to relate to his own existence and mortality:

> The reader is not fooled; he has leafed through the last chapter to see whether the novel has a happy ending; he knows that the pale young man leaning against the mantel has three hundred and fifty pages to go ... of love and adventure. I had at least five hundred ... I pitied my grandmother; she would certainly not reappear in the second part. As for me, I was the beginning, middle, and end gathered together in a tiny little boy already old, already dead (ibid., pp. 243–244).

Alongside what had begun as a desire on the part of the reader to demolish the boundaries of reality and reject any recognition of them, a new insight is gradually constructed: The reader becomes a reader of his own existence. Literature facilitates a temporary sojourn in that area of timelessness and phantasies of immortality. Via his reflection, the reader works through his anxieties vis-à-vis the finality and fragility of existence. Through identification with the characters and the movement between times, he comes to understand that within him is contained the future that he will leaf through in his life, will encounter his limitations, will weep over his finiteness and will praise what he received or contributed during his life. For the reader, the literary story personifies the future 'self' and thus reveals that there are numerous possible ways in which the inner and external lives can develop.

Symbolic timelessness and retrospective reparation

The phantasy of symbolic timelessness gives an opportunity to make reparation over events whose time has supposedly passed. According to Klein, a person is born with the drive to make reparation. In the paranoid-schizoid position the reparation phantasies are manic and grandiose, such as the phantasy of timelessness that reverses the arrow of time and erases the destruction and harm inflicted upon reality. On the other hand, one of the significant achievements of the depressive position lies in the movement of the psyche from its attempts to deny reality to its recognition of the complexity of reality and towards the understanding that the mind of the 'self' and of the 'other' includes good and bad, construction and destruction.

This position – which recognizes the partialness and the harms that stem from others, from reality and from the inner world – lead a person to the path of reparation. Out of the drive to make reparation a person finds within himself the powers of active creativity.

A moving example of the unconscious wish to make personal reparation aroused in the midst of reading appears towards the end of the book *The Words*. We remember Sartre's early desire as an orphan to get to know his father through the words that he had scribbled in the margins of the book that the young Jean Paul by chance found in the library but was disappointed to discover that his father's handwriting was indecipherable. This desire returns many pages later in the book, and appears implicitly when Sartre glides across the space of symbolic timelessness and imagines himself to be a writer whose last manuscript is found by readers in the future. Now, Sartre imagines that his handwriting is indecipherable and that in the distant future when readers find the last of his creations they will say 'But it's illegible!' (Sartre, J.P., [1964] 1981, p. 205). This phrasing much resembles what he at the time wrote about his father's handwriting: 'In the margins, I came upon indecipherable scribbles' (ibid., p. 19).

But in contrast to the devaluative action taken by Sartre in selling the father's books with the illegible scribbles, by which he tried to deny and rid himself from the wish to come to know his father, he now imagines that his readers will be assiduous, tireless researchers. One cannot know whether Sartre the writer was aware that in this part of the book he was trying to heal the pain of his inner child who appeared at the beginning of the book. But there can be no doubt that in the narrator's phantasy his future readers will behave differently to him and will insist upon repairing the estrangement between him and them and so indirectly also between him and his inner father. The description of his future eager readers divulges the complementary, unconscious aspect of his relation to his father's 'illegible scribbles', namely, the yearning to decipher them as a code to a riddle in which the missing key to know the father figure would be found. The reparation is not only expressed in of the devotion which his readers lend to the illegible scribbles but also that they, unlike Sartre, succeed in deciphering the writing and discover the concealed figure of the father. Moreover, Sartre imagines that after all their efforts his readers will discover that behind his scribbles a masterpiece is concealed: 'And then, one day, out of love for me, young scholars would try to decipher it; their entire lifetime would not be enough to restore what would, of course, be my masterpiece' (ibid., p. 205). In the phantasy that his readers will find a masterpiece behind the illegible scribbles there is a reparation of the internal father object.

This is one example of an experience of retrospective reparation. It can occur as a result of every event in the text that goes back in time and links up to events in the reader's past that have remained unresolved and for the most part repressed and seeking consolation. In these literary events the reader can find an opportunity to transcend the finiteness of his life's events and through them to imagine another development to his story and to bestow a new interpretation and meaning to his past experiences. Reading also transports the reader to times in the distant future within the boundaries of his life or even beyond those boundaries and enables him to imagine the realms of possible reparation that will occur in his future or even after his time. Apart from consolation he can also find in the literary text an inspiration for further reparations in his life. Sartre's text is an excellent example of such a reparation.

Redemptive literature: a religious quality

An additional transcendence that occurs in the framework of reading literature is the reader's transcendence from experiencing himself as a lacking-being by a momentary affiliation with literature. The hoped for redemption in our encounter with books often assumes a religious quality. Sartre repeatedly equates between the reader's encounter with books and a religious encounter. He first experienced this in his early encounter with his grandfather's library even before he was able to read. He identifies a special quality in the way in which his grandfather approached books that to Sartre appeared to resemble the way in which someone engaged in reading holy texts would behave. Thus, for example, he says: 'My grandfather ... handled those cultural objects with the dexterity of an officiant' (Sartre, J.P., [1964] 1981, p. 41). When his grandfather shows him a series of 'stout volumes bound in brown cloth', which he took part in their publishing, Sartre felt proud to be '[t]he grandson of a craftsman who specialized in the making of sacred objects, who was as respectable as an organ-maker, as a tailor for ecclesiastics' (ibid., p. 42).

And elsewhere Sartre writes:

> I had found my religion: nothing seemed to me more important than a book. I regarded the library as a temple. Grandson of a priest, I lived on the roof of the world, on the sixth floor, perched on the highest branch of the Central Tree (ibid., pp. 59–60).

The linkage between literature and religious objects and between writers and priests is interlaced throughout Sartre's book. He also frequently describes the act of reading itself as a religious event: 'I became a Catharian, I confused literature with prayer' (ibid., p. 179).

Not only is literature described in religious terms, it is portrayed as a mission and a means to redeem humanity. The moment of redemption in reading links into the religious aspect in two ways: Reading sometimes arouses religious-like feelings of elation and mercy and also serves as a religious salvation from existential confusion and human evil. One can assume that this feeling of salvation is connected to the phenomenon described in the previous chapter, termed by the psychoanalyst Bollas as a 'transformational object' (a work of art for instance), which evolves from the transformational effect the mother has on the infant, leading to 'aesthetic moments' in adulthood. In Bollas' formulation the mother involves herself in a myriad of acts of caring for the infant in the course of which she transfers to him some of her culture and transforms his inner landscape. In later life as an adult, he encounters similar 'aesthetic moments' in poetry, in painting or in a breathtaking view, which become for him a 'transformational object'.[3]

The excitement that books and literature ignite in Sartre is not merely a reflection of childlike confusion and emotional arousal. It is an elation that testifies to the human yearning for transcendence from the daily existential dimensions of the body, mind and spirit. This experience links up with a subject's profound yearning to join a much bigger space that has the power to really alter him, relieve his solitude and enrich his life.

On the one hand, the idealization of literature relates to that same profound yearning to undergo a transformation in the wake of reading and, on the other hand, it is linked to the feeling of belongingness and worth felt by the reading 'self' who seeks refuge under literature's mighty wings. The young and sensitive Sartre also identifies the disposition towards idealization vis-à-vis literature among the adults around him, which still further intensifies the relation of idealization that he himself feels for the literary work. His need for the world of religious concepts stems from his search for an appropriate context for such a level of sublimity and elevation. At the same time the relation of idealization also conceals his feelings of smallness.

The reader's feelings of inferiority begin to surface in what Sartre terms as his lacking-being. Occasionally when it becomes insufferable he uses the two primitive defence mechanisms of splitting and projection and turns the tables so that he idealizes himself as belonging to literature yet at the same time projects the feelings of insignificance onto his 'future readers':

> What solitude! Two billion men horizontal, and I, above them, alone on the watch-tower. The Holy Ghost was observing me … The Holy Ghost and I held secret meetings: 'You'll write,' he said to me. I wrung my hands: 'What is there about me, Lord, that has made you choose me?' – 'Nothing in particular.' – 'Then, why me?' – 'For no reason' …'Lord, since I'm such a non-entity, how could I write a book?' – 'By buckling down to it.' 'Does that mean anyone can write?' 'Anyone. But you're the one I've chosen' (ibid., pp. 185–186).

In phantasy Sartre the writer is a son of God or at least chosen by Him. Thus the reader is pulled in two opposing directions. From one perspective he experienced himself as the common man, small and simple, dependent both on the idealized writer and the idealized power of literature. On the other hand, the reader momentarily merges with literature and thus gains its idealized qualities in phantasy.

Realistic transcendence in reading literature

Literature also evokes idealization because it truly does possess the power to impart knowledge. By reading, the reader can transcend his means of coping and the extent of his knowledge and so broaden the scope of his mental existence and his orientation in the world. It is no accident that the texts of human history became the birth right of those who were 'entitled to it' – those with hegemonic power over society. Within the book in phantasy as well as in reality – the guarantee of knowledge, power and control resides.

In the historical novel *Pope Joan* by Donna Woolfolk Cross, the fact that Joan learns how to read is the launching pad for a voyage that transcends gender, fate and possibilities. The novel shows how the attempt to deny the right to read is part of a desperate stand to protect a position of strength.

> The canon [Joan's father] stepped out of the darkness. Instinctively, Joan moved to hide the book from him, but it was too late.
> His face, lit from below by the unsteady flame, was ghastly, terrifying.
> What wickedness is this?
> Joan's voice was a whisper. 'A book.' 'A book!'
> He stared at it as if he could scarcely believe the evidence of his eyes. 'How do you come by this? What are you doing with it?'
> 'Reading it. It, – it's mine, it was given to me by Aesculapius. It's mine.'
> The force of her father's blow caught her by surprise, knocking her off the stool. She lay on the ground in a heap, the earthen floor cool against her cheek.
> 'Yours! Insolent child! I am master in this house! (Cross, D.W., 1996, pp. 55–56)

Idealization of literature is thus not only a defence mechanism against one's sense of insignificance and dependence, but also derives from a profound recognition of literature's ability to instil wisdom and liberate the reader from his limited consciousness and reality. Given that every individual 'only' lives his own life and is 'only' able to draw on his personal experience, literature offers a unique opportunity to transcend beyond this particular experience.

Let us return to Gadamer's idea as to the nature of an encounter that fuses the reader's horizon to the horizon that dictated the writing of the literary work. Every encounter with a tradition that exists in the context of historical awareness includes the tension between the text (which represents the tradition and the past) and the present. According to Gadamer, we put a question to the text and engage in a dialogue with the literary work that is inevitably biased by basic assumptions and prejudices embedded in the reader's present tradition and are thus unavoidable. The dialogue between the meanings and interpretations that the reader brings forth on the one hand, and the text on other, continues until a unity of meaning appears (Gadamer, H., 1960, pp. 265–311).

Sartre excitedly writes: 'I was allowed to browse in the library and I took man's wisdom by storm. That was what made me' (Sartre, J.P., [1964] 1981, p. 48). And literature does indeed transcend the limitations of time and place and in doing so links the reader to a feeling of omniscience; he can move between multiple minds, different periods of time and diverse cultures. He takes command of a certain imaginary infinite library that can enlighten a single person of the accumulative truths of all the people over every period of time. So reading is the key to both instilling wisdom in people and getting to know the world. As such, reading is also accompanied by a sense of having made contact with the great secret, with the unknown and the mysteries of the universe. Books turn from being the fount of knowledge about the universe to having knowledge of the unpredictable, of that which cannot be either explained or deciphered. One of the more beautiful of Sartre's description looks into the reading of two contradictory perspectives: The book as a personal property over which there is complete control as with a domestic pet, and the book as a gateway to the great mysteries of the universe: 'Books were my birds and my nests, my household pets, my barn and my countryside. The library was the world caught in a mirror' (ibid., p. 49). In a certain sense the book is perceived as a person, perhaps the wisest of people, who shares with Sartre his living modes but at the same time transcends their boundaries to spaces that go well beyond his daily routine, reach beyond the reader's grasp and that he cannot put his hand on. As such the book is the fount of magic, great attraction and fascination. In Sartre's experience it was sometimes overwhelming:

> Our visitors would leave, I would be left alone, I would escape from that graveyard of banalities and go back to life, to the wildness in books. I had only to open one to rediscover the inhuman, restless thinking whose pomp and darkness were beyond my understanding, which jumped from one idea to the other so quickly that I would lose my grip on it a dozen times a page and let it slip, feeling lost and bewildered (ibid., pp. 52–53).

Paradoxically the encounter with the live guests, because of its banal nature, was tantamount to death, whereas the encounter with books was enlivening. From this description by Sartre it is clear that he prefers to lose his way in reading to the graveyard of banality.

Literature's precedence over life

If literature transcends beyond life's private space it is no wonder that Sartre bestows it with supreme precedence over other experiences in life. Sartre the child prefers to play with the characters in the books he reads than with children of his own age. He prefers to nurture an image of a 'reader' instead of his identity as Jean Paul the child who doesn't understand himself. He feels that he 'lives' inside reading and later on also in writing. He describes these dwellings as being lifted above the residents who are not able to read and write in the meaningful way that he is able to. He grew up on the sixth floor in *Rue Le Goff* in Paris. Sartre describes the height of the dwelling and the high level of literature, which for him will forever be the 'right floor' for mental and spiritual habitation, the only place where he is able to breath. Thus, for example, he writes:

> I had only to climb a molehill for joy to come rushing back: I would return to my symbolic sixth floor; there I would once again breathe the rarefied air of belles-lettres; the Universe would rise in tiers at my feet and all things would humbly beg for a name; to name the thing was both to create and take it (Sartre, J.P., [1964] 1981, p. 59).

The literary text has precedence over reality and Sartre lives among the books' pages and not between people and reality's extra-literary demands. Here too the paradox wherein the written text is endowed with life and taken from life itself.

> In Platonic fashion, I went from knowledge to its subject. I found more reality in the idea than in the thing because it was given to me first and because it was given as a thing. It was in books that I encountered the universe: assimilated, classified, labelled, pondered, still formidable; and I confused the disorder of my bookish experiences with the random course of real events (ibid., p. 50).

Elsewhere he expresses this so: 'I found the human heart, of which my grandfather was fond of speaking, insipid and hollow, except in books' (ibid., p. 55).

I conclude this chapter with Fernando Pessoa's poetic portrayal of literature's supremacy over daily life: 'Perhaps my destiny is to remain forever a bookkeeper, with poetry or literature as a butterfly that alights on my head, making me look ridiculous to the extent it looks beautiful' (Pessoa, F., [1982] 2017, p. 325)

Notes

1 It was not until 1920 that Freud was able to characterize the death drive in his article 'Beyond the Pleasure Principle'.
2 This view is well illustrated in a sentence written by Semprún following his experience in the Buchenwald concentration camp: 'Perhaps I have not simply survived death, but been resurrected from it' (Semprún, J., 1994, p. 15).
3 '[By] ... this anticipation of being transformed by an object ... the adult subject tends to nominate the object as sacred' (Bollas, C., 1979, p. 99).

References

Barthes, R. (1967). The Death of the Author. In: D. Lodge (Ed.) *Modern Criticism and Theory: A Reader*. New York: Pearson Education, pp. 145–150.
Bollas, C. (1979). The Transformational Object. *International Journal of Psychoanalysis*, 60, pp. 97–107.
Cross, D.W. (1996). *Pope Joan*. New York: Three Rivers Press.
Durban, J. (2017). Facing the Death-Object: Unconscious Phantasies of Relationships with Death. In: M. Erlich-Ginor (Ed.) *Not Knowing Knowing Not Knowing*. New York: International Psychoanalytic Books, pp. 85–114.
Freud, S. (1915). Thoughts for the Times of War and Death. In: J. Strachey (Ed.) *The Standard Edition of the Complete Psychological Works of Sigmund Freud, Vol. XIV*. London: Hogarth Press, pp. 273–302.
Freud, S. (1916). On Transience. In: J. Strachey (Ed.) *The Standard Edition of the Complete Psychological Works of Sigmund Freud, Vol. XIV*. London: Hogarth Press, pp. 303–307.
Freud, S. (1917). Mourning and Melancholia. In: J. Strachey (Ed.) *The Standard Edition of the Complete Psychological Works of Sigmund Freud, Vol. XIV*. London: Hogarth Press, pp. 237–258.
Freud, S. (1920). Beyond the Pleasure Principle. In: J. Strachey (Ed.) *The Standard Edition of the Complete Psychological Works of Sigmund Freud, Vol. XVIII*. London: Hogarth Press, pp. 1–64.
Gadamer, H.G. (1960). *Truth and Method*. London and New York: Continuum.
Green, A. (1998). The Primordial Mind and the Work of the Negative. *International Journal of Psychoanalysis*, 79, pp. 649–665.
Heidegger, M. [1927] (1996). *Being and Time*. Albany: State University of New York Press.
Klein, M. (1926). The Psychological Principles of Early Analysis. In: *Love, Guilt and Reparation and Other Works 1921–1945*. London: Vintage, pp. 128–138.
Klein, M. (1929). Personification in the Play of Children. In: *Love, Guilt and Reparation and Other Works 1921–1945*. London: Vintage, pp. 199–209.
Klein, M. (1940). Mourning and Its Relation to Manic-Depressive States. In: *Love, Guilt and Reparation and Other Works 1921–1945*. London: Vintage, pp. 344–369.
Lifton, R.J. (1973). The Sense of Immortality: On Death and the Continuity of Life. *American Journal of Psychoanalysis*, 33(1), pp. 3–15.
Ogden, T. (1986). *The Matrix of the Mind: Object Relations and the Psychoanalytic Dialogue*. Lanham, MD: Jason Aronson Books.

Palgi, P. and Durban, J. (1995). The Role and Function of Collective Representation for the Individual During the Mourning Process: The Case of a War-Orphaned Boy in Israel. *Ethos*, 23(1), pp. 223–243.
Pearl, J. (2011). *A Question of Time Between Philosophy and Psychoanalysis*. Ramat Gan: Bar Ilan University Press.
Pessoa, F. [1982] (2017). *The Book of Disquiet*. London: Serpents Tail.
Sartre, J. [1964] (1981). *The Words*. New York: Vintage Books.
Semprún, J. (1994). *Literature or Life*. London and New York: Penguin Books.
Zoran, R. (2000). *The Third Voice: The Therapeutic Qualities of Literature and Their Applications in Bibliotherapy*. Jerusalem: Carmel.
Zoran, R. (2009). *The Letter's Imprint: Reading and Identity within the Bibliotherapeutic Dialogue*. Jerusalem: Carmel.

Further reading

Klein, M. (1946). Notes on Some Schizoid Mechanisms. In: *Envy and Gratitude and Other Works 1946–1963*. London: Vintage, pp. 25–42.
Klein, M. (1948). On the Theory of Anxiety and Guilt. In: *Envy and Gratitude and Other Works 1946–1963*. London: Vintage, pp. 25–42.
Klein, M. (1957). Envy and Gratitude. In: *Envy and Gratitude and Other Works 1946–1963*. London: Vintage, pp. 176–235.

Part III

From psychic equilibrium to psychic change
The dialectic forces of literature

Introduction

The reading experience creates a space of internal dialectic movement. Literature involves and creates in the reader an encounter, a confrontation and even a struggle between opposing forces, causing a mobilization from psychic equilibrium to psychic change (Joseph, B., 1989). This aspect – which has not to date been discussed in the context of reader research – appears to be one of the most active and influential processes that occur in the course of literary reading. For the sake of clarity it is important to understand that these dialectic tensions exist in our mind independently of the reading of literature. However, since these internal dialectics also characterize the literary text, the process of reading stirs them to movement and life in the reader, thus paving the way to the mobilization of previous defensive psychic equilibriums and enabling transformation and reintegration. It is interesting that in certain cases reading literature serves and preserves 'pathological' solutions to the dialectic struggles taking place in the reader's psyche, whereas others lead to a significant transformation and new integration between these dialectic forces.

In the literary works I have assembled four psychic equilibriums between four dialectic tensions were very clearly awakened in the reader's mind, allowing for meaningful psychic change.

Each of these dialectics manifests a tension between forces in the human mind that battle and pull in different directions. The more integrated the dialectic forces are, the more the mind is free to move between the different tendencies with a minimum of anxiety and tension and in greater accord with psychic and existential demands. Part III will exemplify how literature awakens and mobilizes previous internal 'arrangements' between these dialectic forces, creating a potential basis for working through the anxieties beneath them thus leading towards better integration than was hitherto possible.

The psyche as a dialectic space: a psychoanalytic perspective

The human mind is organized as a multidialectic structure, in which various forces pull in opposite directions. This feature is the primary source of the psyche's constant dynamism.

Freud's psychoanalytic theory is known as a 'dynamic theory of drives' because it is based on a dynamic dialectic between dominant forces such as: the life drive vs the death drive, the pleasure principle vs the reality principle the 'id' vs the 'superego' and so on. All of these and others are part of the overarching dialectic between the unconscious and the conscious. The repressed seeks to be discovered and gain relief whereas the preserving ego seeks to repress, particularly when a drive that triggers conflict is involved (such as a sexual drive aimed towards a morally inappropriate object).

There is an additional dialectic movement to be considered: the unceasing movement between the self and the object. Freud argued that this movement is secondary to the primary narcissistic urge of self-satisfaction (Freud, S., 1914), i.e. that it is rooted in the need to satisfy the drives. His follower, Melanie Klein, thought otherwise, arguing that there is a primary inclination of the self towards the object, which exists from birth and creates a dialectic tension between the self and the object from the very beginning of life (Klein, M., 1937). Klein maintained that the tensions between the life drive/death drive and between love/hate are fundamental motivational forces, adding to these the dialectic movement between the paranoid- schizoid and the depressive positions as well as the movement between the inner world (the world of unconscious phantasy) and the real world. In Klein's perspective the psychic mechanisms are also characterized by a dialectic process: between, for example, introjective identification and projective identification, splitting and integration, idealization and devaluation, etc. This multidialectic weave spawns additional dialectic tensions and creates 'tugs of war' between the different forces in the mind. The developmental movement and structuring of the psyche is never complete because the integration is never final. Over a lifetime each of the dialectic forces pull in their own direction in line with the external and internal circumstances. Nevertheless and at the very same time, the mind always seeks to find balance and equilibrium (Freud, S., 1920). Various psychic equilibriums function as a kind of compromise between these internal struggles. The healthier the mind is, the more flexible and benign is the psychic equilibrium between these internal forces. On the one hand, it maintains a good-enough balance between the different demands, and on the other, enables playful movement according to the changing needs. Under excessive and pathological anxiety we find two opposing internal solutions: either the psychic equilibrium is more rigid or it is liable to become tempestuous and unstable.

In what follows I shall describe four dialectics that were found to be particularly active in the course of reading literature and therefore have the potential to mobilize internal forces so that they create an opportunity to work through and transform previous psychic equilibriums and facilitate psychic change.

References

Freud, S. (1914). On Narcissism: An Introduction. In: J. Strachey (Ed.) *The Standard Edition of the Complete Psychological Works of Sigmund Freud, Vol. XIV.* London: Hogarth Press, pp. 67–102.

Freud, S. (1920). Beyond the Pleasure Principle. In: J. Strachey (Ed.) *The Standard Edition of the Complete Psychological Works of Sigmund Freud, Vol. XVIII.* London: Hogarth Press, pp. 1–64.

Joseph, B. (1989). *Psychic Equilibrium and Psychic Change: Selected Papers of Betty Joseph.* London and New York: Tavistock/Routledge.

Klein, M. (1937). Love, Guilt and Reparation. In: *Love, Guilt and Reparation and Other Works 1921–1945.* London: Vintage, pp. 306–343.

Chapter 10

The dialectic between the present and the absent

The literary evidence used in this chapter is concerned with the search for an absent (and longed-for) text. Both in Poe's 'The Purloined Letter' ([1844] 2011) and in James' *The Aspern Papers* (1888), the absent text is a metaphor for a key to a salvation we search for from birth to death. Psychoanalysis describes an individual's post-natal quest for the lost natal paradise, that 'one thing' that can be projected on to various signifiers: *the* one and only relation, *the* professional achievement, *the* promised land, etc. (Lacan, J., [1959–1960] 1992). This movement is represented in three central paradigms: the yearning to unite with a longed-for other; the desire for knowledge; and the search for a spiritual domain. The first paradigm – union with an-other – is symbolized, for example, by the lost Garden of Eden of the womb; the mother's breast (Bion, W., 1967; Klein, M., 1963); the oceanic feeling; mythical figures combined with one another (such as Chimera in mythology), and by the divine other – God. The second paradigm, the desire for knowledge, is symbolized by ancient monuments, keys, spectacles, barometers and the like (Freud, S., 1919, p. 229). The third paradigm – the search for the spiritual domain – is represented by, for example, religious symbols (Sartre, J.P., [1964] 1981, p. 57) and metaphysical symbols such as the 'yin and yang' representing nature's two opposing and complementary forces in ancient Chinese philosophy. The dominant search in the first paradigm emphasizes relations, the second concerns the search for meaning and the third emphasizes the path. There is no contradiction between the three. Rather, they interlink and at times complement one another. The overlap between paradigms is exemplified when the longed-for unity relates to an omniscient object, for instance a god, an omnipotent mother or father.

The developmental background to the pursuit of the absent stems from the fact that the survival of the infant is dependent on a breast full of milk. According to Klein, from this moment an instinctive dynamic erupts, at first a longing for the 'good breast', then followed by the greedy pursuit of that 'desired absent'. Greed is aroused both in moments of frustration and while waiting for gratification as well as by feelings of inferiority and dependency. Envy might also be aroused towards the breast, involving a possible urge to destroy it (and in so doing also destroy the needy self), if only not to feel the pain, the dependency and the lack. The dialectic tension triggered by this lifelong dynamic is between the powerful urges towards the object, which typify the paranoid-schizoid position on the one hand, and the depressive anxiety of destroying the loved object that evokes a desperate wish to protect the attacked object on the other. This dialectic tension sets in motion a developmental process at the end of which an individual can become more responsible for the conflicting forces active within him. That being said, this tension is never completely settled and resolved.

This enduring process of lack that arouses a longing for the absent and that an individual copes with from the moment of birth leads him to the symbolic order – i.e. to language. In Klein's words, 'not only does symbolism come to be the foundation of all phantasy and sublimation but, more than that, upon it is built up the subject's relation to the outside world and to reality in general' (Klein, M., 1930, p. 221). The word symbolizes what is absent; it represents the absent and at the same time takes its place. In Julia Kristeva's words: 'Upon losing mother and relying on negation, I retrieve her as a sign, an image, a word' (Kristeva, J., 1987).[1]

Reading literature necessarily includes both 'presence' and 'absence'. The characters and the author are simultaneously there and not there, and the words also constitute a substitute for the missing objects. Thus, reading swamps the reader's inner coping with the two forces in his psyche pulling in opposite directions: His attempt to *complement the lack* as against the necessity and wisdom of *coming to terms with the lack*.

There are two central aspects of the dialectic between the present and the absent that arise in reading:

1. The writer as a present-absent

The French psychoanalyst Andre Green (1978) explained the 'absent' as an inherent part of the forms of communication in reading and writing: The author writes to the reader who is absent at the time of writing and the reader reads the author's words when the latter is absent. Green points to the connection between this situation and that of the patient on the psychoanalytic couch, where the analyst sits behind the couch and is absent from the analysand's field of vision. This absence advances the possibility of projecting representations from the patient's inner world on to the present-absent figure of the analyst, instead of these representations being subdued by the manifest presence of the analyst's 'real' figure. In these three situations, reading, writing and analysis, the absent is also present and the present is also absent. As the analysand experiences the analyst in line with the transference relations towards him, so the reader is free to attribute to the writer qualities and characterizations in line with his transference relations towards him.

2. The absent as a motive

The literary text always deals with the absent (or a variety of absentees) the stimulant for the story's plot – a longed-for beloved, a hoped for holy chalice, etc. As in life itself, were it the case that heroes lacked nothing, there would be no motive for their active part in the story, be it about relationships, love, war or any other subject. The absent is, in this sense, the lack that has to be complemented. However, in certain instances it is up to the hero and the reader to come to terms with its absence. This is a dialectic between the incomplete and the complete. On the one hand, this dialectic involves the hero, and in his footsteps the reader, holding on to the phantasy of the complete and the perfect that is characterized by splitting and by a denial of lack. On the other hand, it arouses the psychic preoccupation with the depressive pain of incompleteness that is inherent to human existence.

Literary examples of the absent-present dialectic

In exploring this subject I have chosen two literary works that involve an absent text and in which the entire plot focuses on its acquisition. In a number of highly influential literary works, as is the case in the two works presented below, the plot is driven from start to finish by a search for some longed-for written material that the story's hero is never able to find. In some scenarios the literary quest is accompanied only by the investigative aspects of the search, whilst at other times it shapes the novel's plot and even sentences to death some of the characters who pine for the text. A longed-for and absent text of this kind becomes a paradoxical symbol because even though we are told that it is written, its very absence is evidence that its content is not the crux of the matter. The reader develops a strong relationship of curiosity, passion and tension with a text, even though he does not know nor will he ever know its contents.

The author as the owner of the longed-for 'absent' in Edgar Allan Poe's story 'The Purloined Letter'

Edgar Alan Poe's story 'The Purloined Letter' is an example of a literary text in which absence is at the heart of the tale. This example has been explored and debated to an unprecedented extent in literary research so that it has become some sort of a 'philosopher's stone' in relation to the question of 'the absent'. The story's heroes are the narrator, his friend Dupin and the Prefect of the Parisian Police, Monsieur G–, whose name is concealed, a concealment emphasized by the dash after the first letter of his name, indicating the *missing* letters. The conversation between the three revolves around a riddle: a highly confidential letter was stolen by Minister D– (whose name is also concealed by the same literary signifier) from a 'personage of most exalted station' (Poe, E.A., [1844] 2011, p. 209). The latter is also not identified by name but we are given to understand in what follows – and subsequently discover – that it is the Queen. No one knows the contents of the letter but it is described as 'a certain document of the last importance' (ibid., p. 208), stolen from the royal bedroom. The tension between the importance of the document and its unrevealed contents is maintained throughout the story. The urgency of finding it is not driven, as one would expect, by knowledge of its dangerous contents but rather by the mystery surrounding it and the fantasies it arouses among those involved in the matter. This particular set of circumstances in Poe's story focuses attention on two unconscious characteristics of reading.

The first of these is the yearning for the absent literary text. Paradoxically and ironically, the interest in reading in Poe's story revolves around the desire to discover the contents of the stolen letter. At least in part this yearning is directed at what was allegedly written rather than at what was *actually* written. Given the absence of the text, 'what was likely to have been written' arouses in each reader a different unconscious phantasy about the longed-for entity. Every reader projects his own yearnings on to a text before it is read so that it is suffused with transference relations of wishes, curiosity and desire to find in the text what the reader misses and lacks. At the same time he is anxious that in the end he will be left longing, partial and lacking.

The second unconscious characteristic of reading is the reader's transference relations towards *the author as the owner* of the longed-for absent. An exploration of Poe's story reveals a vicious circle between the reader and the writer – the reader attributing to the writer the ability to 'steal the letter from him'; the very private letter that reflects the reader's image and tells his story. This arouses in the reader an idealizing transference towards the writer (perceived as his owner), accompanied by a strong wish to re-own his image, thus a strong desire to get hold of the text. In other words, the reader wants to repossess 'the letter' that has been stolen from him and that tells *his* story. He pines for the writer, whose ability to steal reflections he so admires, and asks him to return his reflection. Except that according to Poe's ingenious story, the writer who allegedly 'stole' the reader's reflection has no such letter and all he can return is the image of the reader searching for his reflection in the mirror held up to him by the author, represented by Monsieur Dupin. Despite the letter remaining concealed, the process of searching for it, imagining it and exploring its possible contents and reflections are all significant to the reader's development. Poe's irony shows that something of importance is not necessarily to be found where we think it has been hidden.

I wish now to turn Poe's philosopher's stone one more time, trying to read the mysterious, absent purloined letter as reflecting the character of the reader, of the writer and the relations between the two vis-à-vis the forces of the present and the absent.

The irony in Poe's story

Poe's language is highly ironic and invites the reader to be skeptical about the excessive importance attributed to the longed-for text (perhaps a reflection on the over-importance we attach to any text we read).

> 'It is clearly inferred,' replied the Prefect, 'from the nature of the document, and from the non-appearance of certain results which would at once arise from its passing out of the robber's possession; that is to say, from his employing it as he must design in the end to employ it.'

And it continues:

> 'Be a little more explicit,' I said.
> 'Well, I may venture so far as to say that the paper gives its holder a certain power in a certain quarter where such power is immensely valuable.' (Poe, E.A., [1844] 2011, p. 209).

The reader's longing is reflected in various views filled with that same sense of yearning: First there is the viewpoint of the story's assorted characters – the Queen who desperately needs to get the letter back and is, as the addressee, its 'lawful' reader; Minister 'D–' – who stole the letter and is certainly not legally entitled to read it; the police prefect and Dupin who are engaged in searching for the stolen object; and then there is the narrator monitoring all these developments from the sidelines, becoming curious himself. At another level we, Poe's readers, attach ourselves to the viewpoints of all these characters and, adopting our own perspective, join them in the search for the desired letter even though we too don't have a clue what its content really is, so that our phantasies vis-à-vis 'the absent' combine with those of the story's characters.

The irony in Poe's writing is punctuated by his portrayal of the naivety of the approach adopted by the Queen, the Prefect and the narrator when compared to the patronizing condescension, sophistication and supposed omniscience of the Minister especially when compared to Dupin's approach. The gap between the Prefect's dramatic temper and the level headed, almost amused approach displayed by Monsieur Dupin is evident, as he tells the Prefect that: 'Perhaps it is the very simplicity of the thing which puts you at fault … Perhaps the mystery is a little too plain … A little too self-evident' (ibid., p. 208).

Dupin's ironic comment goes to the heart of the issue of 'the absent' and every query to the Prefect can be understood as questioning its nature: Are we to launch a complex search for it or is it in fact to be found right under our noses, visible for all to see? And is it absent because of a trait inherent to its nature or is it thought to be absent only because of the blindness of the observer? The letter, and analogously, the literary text, exists in terms of its actual words and syntax, but we project on to it a quintessential text that is the product of our phantasies. We believe that this text is the author's exclusive property. We long for it but never fully own it. In Poe's story the reader is invited to rummage through the 'thief's' room and belongings but the letter, that letter of the utmost importance stolen from the Queen's bedroom, will never be found by him. Poe's irony serves to expose the deceit at play wherein the reader is being invited to engage in a foolhardy search for the inherently absent.

As said, 'The Purloined Letter', exemplifying a literary text focusing on 'absence', has been the subject of such keen debate in literary research that it has become a kind of 'philosopher's stone' whenever it's enigma is explored from either a psychoanalytic, philosophic or literary perspective. And yet it would appear that for all the exploration and debate it makes no difference whether the absent is understood as the signifier of the mother's phallus as interpreted by Marie Bonaparte (Bonaparte, M., [1933] 1949), of the elusive unconscious (Lacan, J., [1959–1960] 1992), of the intertextual literature (Derrida, J., 1980) or of the enigmatic area of meaning (Felman, S., 1993, pp. 300–322). Dupin and the Prefect, Bonaparte, Lacan, Derrida and Felman and also we the readers have one thing in common: we are all sucked into the black hole of the absent text.

The reader's character according to 'The Purloined Letter'

SPLITTING I: THE DETECTIVE READER VS THE NAÏVE READER

Dupin the detective is presented as the 'great victor' in Poe's story. In finding the letter he hits the jackpot and follows this victory with long explanations of the reason for his ascendency over both the Prefect and even over the Minister (who fooled the Prefect but could not fool Dupin). In psychoanalytic language we can describe this as the rhetoric of splitting and manic superiority. It is evident in many ways in the story. The splitting begins with the crime of replacing the 'utmost important letter' by an 'unimportant letter'. Her Majesty the Queen was ingenious in concealing the letter 'open as it was, upon a table' (Poe, E.A., [1844] 2011, p. 209). The Minister who steals the letter leaves in its place 'his own letter – one of no importance – upon the table' (ibid., p. 210). A swapping of texts: both are openly placed on the table, there for all to see. One letter is charged with increased importance by stressing the superfluity of the second letter. The thief has rights over the unimportant letter since it is his in the first place, while as far as the letter of the utmost importance is concerned, 'he had no claim' (ibid.).

It would appear that the numerous splits in the story between important and unimportant, idealized and despised, genius and imbecility, appropriate and inappropriate, entitled and guilty etc., serve the gradual construction of splitting in the reader's mind. This, as he becomes captivated by the idealized side and increasingly wants to disassociate himself from the ridiculous, worthless side, against which the character of the Prefect struggles in vain, so gracelessly and pathetically.

This splitting also re-enforces the importance of the absent text as well as the importance of anyone who has access to it. The dependency on whoever or whatever it is that holds the keys to the absent becomes increasingly marked. By now we don't remember that the story apparently began with infidelity in the Queen's court. Nor do we sympathize with the failing efforts of the Prefect – the industrious, hardworking, experienced man who works in the service of the state and attempts to repair the damage. Throughout the story he is called 'the Prefect' until the moment when Dupin gets a big fat check from him and in return hands him over the stolen letter. This is how the narrator describes the scene:

> This functionary [i.e. the Prefect] grasped it in a perfect agony of joy, opened it with a trembling hand, cast a rapid glance at its contents, and then, scrambling and struggling to the door, rushed at length unceremoniously from the room and from the house, without having uttered a syllable) (ibid. p. 215).

The narrator is contemptuous of the man who has been demoted by him to the rank of a functionary whereas he is amazed and fascinated by Dupin's ability to identify with the opponent in a cold, patronizing Sherlockian manner: 'In the present instance I have no sympathy – at least no pity' (ibid., p. 223). Yet readers are invited to identify with the narrator and be excited by the sophisticated way Dupin uses pragmatic identification in order to overcome the barriers blocking the path to the absent text. While we, the readers, are invited to participate in this identification, we overlook the fact that it is us that detective Dupin is ridiculing, mocking us for searching without noticing the obvious.

SPLITTING 2: THE APPROPRIATING READER VS THE CURIOUS READER

By the very nature of splitting, no single one of its parts reflects the wider complex picture so that the splitting, though necessary as a defence against pain, does not lead to processes of developmental integration. The split between the poetic genius (Dupin) and the idiotic reader (the Prefect) presented by Poe does not reflect in any one of its sides a complete picture and this may explain why neither one of them ends up actually reading the purloined letter (for the story ends without telling us the contents of the letter). Such an outcome may contain the hint that a reading by a detached, compassionless investigator, in fact constitutes only a partial reading of the human story. An empathic reading is accomplished out of both intellectual and emotional involvement alongside a recognition of 'the otherness of the other'. This means that we can never achieve a full reading of the other, be he a literary character, the unconscious, the patient or the analyst.

A further splitting between two kinds of reading that stands out in Poe's story is the split between the appropriating reader and the curious reader. The story informs us that Dupin and the Minister specialize in appropriating the text of others for themselves. They covet the text of others and feel they are superior to them in reading their faces (value) and their minds, and thus it is in their ability to steal their text (the Minister from the Queen, Dupin from the Minister). From a psychoanalytic perspective one can view this as greed, which denies the absent and uses manic defences of arrogance and negation towards the other in order not to feel his separateness and of being in need of him and his treasures. The appropriating reader is facing the literary 'letter' like an infant who gorges and appropriates for himself the mother's treasures (the milk and the good breast are 'his', while denying that he is small, separate, dependent and lacking).

Contrastingly, the studious, curious reader accepts the challenging psychic task of recognizing the lack. The curious reader turns to the 'other' out of a position of longing, which recognizes his own partiality and his need of the other/writer. He isn't greedy in a destructive and manic way but rather desires due to 'epistemophilia' (Freud, S., 1909, 1917a, Klein, M., 1930 for example) – a natural inquisitive instinct that recognizes that the other and the world possess values that he wishes to discover. Just as no one gets to read the contents of the purloined letter even after it is found, so the 'depressive' reader – in Klein's terminology analogous to a more developed reader – makes an unpleasant discovery. He finds out that after reading a story and after all the efforts he has made to gain control of it, the text's contents remains out of reach. Thus an honest reading that establishes meaning is one that devotes itself to the process as opposed to a reading that tries to covet and obtain the ultimate contents of the text. A text as a property can only be pocketed in the realms of phantasy.

These two kinds of reading are analogous to two forms of analytic listening. One is that of the analyst who while listening to the patient tries to precede him and to understand him more fully than the patient understands himself. This resembles Dupin's description of his smart 'see it coming' moves. In this kind of listening the analyst supposedly achieves an ascendency over the patient while exposing him to himself by way of false knowledge; of a presence that is devoid of any absence and that presents an illusion of possessing clear, stable and existing knowledge. Contrastingly, the analyst can be open to the patient's voice, while he also remembers that the unconscious is always illusive and therefore all we can ever do is to listen to our inner thoughts and feelings in the face of a presence that includes inherent absence (the unconscious). We need to realize and accept the fact that we cannot grasp everything and we have to cope throughout our lives with aspects that are beyond our intellectual, emotional and spiritual reach. When an analyst engages in such a 'reading' of the patient's text it will be characterized by compassion aroused by facing the boundaries of the possible and yet with an openness towards a live encounter to the utmost extent possible. He will read the patient's text in an attempt to be as open as possible to the patient's efforts to learn about himself, his analyst and his world. He will offer himself as an object of transformation not in the sense of making whole that which is lacking and making present that which is absent, but rather in the sense of accepting and coping with constantly encountering the partial in tandem with the ongoing experience of creativity and reparation. This type of listening also creates a different dynamic where the analytic couple unites in a mutual voyage of exploration that involves continuous searching bound up with inevitable mourning. It furthermore involves a continuous mourning bound up with continuous discoveries of meaningful revelations.

The character of the author

Poe's text has four 'authors': the author of the work (Poe), the Queen who is the author of the absent and much sought after letter, Dupin the poet, and Minister D– who stole the letter and who wrote the alternative letter to be left on the table in the Queen's bedroom. An examination of the relation between these characters as authors creates a complex image of a writer.

The first complex relationship is between Dupin and the story's author, Poe. This is hinted at in the description of Dupin as writing poems, similarly to Poe himself. In addition, Dupin explains that his method of writing is connected to a method that an 8-year-old child had introduced him to. This method, he says, 'lies at the bottom of all the spurious profundity which has been attributed to Rochefoucault, to La Bougive, to Machiavelli, and to Campanella' (Poe, E.A., [1844] 2011, p. 216). As with these well-known authors, 'profundity' is also said to be an attribute of the four authors in the story in so far as their ability to sense the other and identify his next move is concerned. This resembles Dupin's skills as he deciphers the moves of the thief who stole the letter and so identifies him. A further hint of the close resemblance of character between Dupin and Poe is the fact that the story takes place in Dupin's 'book closet,' an allusion perhaps to Poe's own library and writing room. In addition, Dupin protests that '[i]t is safe to wager that every public idea and every accepted convention is sheer foolishness, because it has suited the majority' (ibid., p. 218).

196   From psychic equilibrium to psychic change

For example, the thought that hiding something far from sight when you are trying to ensure that no one will find it is presented here as decidedly naïve. Poe tempts the narrator, and through him us the readers, to wish to be counted among the elite, ironically described throughout the book in glowing terms as those who know how to hide something of value from everyone.

Dupin's high regard for the simple elementary skills of investigation are made known by the scorn he displays for the reverse approach that involves searching in highly concealed places and ignoring the obvious even though we generally think that the former is the more ingenious. Dupin stands this argument on its head by suggesting that the search in an unusual place constitutes an act of conventional thinking. The tactic of searching in unconcealed places is stressed three times in succession at the very beginning of the story:

> 'Perhaps it is the very simplicity of the thing which puts you at fault,' said my friend. 'What nonsense you do talk!' replied the Prefect, laughing heartily.
> 'Perhaps the mystery is a little too plain,' said Dupin.
> 'Oh, good heavens! Who ever heard of such an idea?'
> 'A little too self-evident.'
> 'Ha! Ha! Ha – ha! Ha! Ha! – Ho! Ho! Ho!' roared our visitor, profoundly amused, 'Oh, Dupin, you will be the death of me yet!' (ibid. p. 208).

Dupin does indeed 'kill him' symbolically in solving the mystery, by stripping the Prefect of his honour, his money and in effect making him utterly redundant.

A further complex relation between two of the authors of Poe's story is that between Dupin and Minister 'D–' – who stole the letter. Dupin stresses the importance of the Minister's combined skills as mathematician and poet. These skills give him a power that mathematics alone doesn't; a mathematician follows a conventional pattern of thought whereas being also a poet opens up for the Minister new ways of thinking. Dupin expresses his judgment of this amalgam of skills by saying that conventional thinking turns physics into metaphysics and interferes with the distinction between facts and pagan myths. The image of the minister/poet/mathematician/thief is characterized as being that of an unrestrained sophisticate, bold daring genius.

Dupin and the thief can be viewed as twin characters. A number of signs point to this interpretation: their names both begin with the same letter; both of them employ the same skill of reading and guessing the next move of the other thus trapping him. Dupin testifies that 'D' – knows him like the palm of his hand; and finally when he took the stolen letter from the Minister, Dupin writes a single sentence in the substituted letter that was left in the Minister's apartment: 'Such a baleful scheme, while not worthy of Atrée, is worthy of Thyeste' (ibid., p. 223).

With these words the story ends. Nothing is added by Poe leaving it to the reader to discover that in Greek mythology Atrée et Thyeste were the twin brothers sons of Pelops who killed their half-brother, were exiled and subsequently fought each other for the throne of Mycenae. Following numerous unprecedented and violent intrigues, Thyeste was able to murder his brother and become the unchallenged rule of Mycenae. Twins, like the two sides of the split in the author's psyche; the curious side and the appropriating side, the modest learning side and the greedy thieving side.

The author stealing the text from the reader

As we can see, the story represents an ambivalence towards the author – he appears as a creator but at the same time he possesses a destructive power. He is an eccentric and admires genius but he also steals letters that are not his, peeps into bedrooms where he seizes texts that he daringly and unscrupulously appropriates. He invades the psyche of the other, studies it via identification but without empathy; by subterfuge, coldly and glaringly. The author resembles a detective who sees what others don't even though the information is staring them in the face. Nor does he follow conventional patterns of thought. Unlike the real thief, the detective operates under the maxim that 'a thief who robs a thief is exempt from punishment', yet he resembles the thief because he himself steals. Moreover, he is the monster twin of the thief because he is prepared to kill his 'brother' for the sake of the monarchy. By way of analogy the author is the dangerous twin because he kills his br(other). He is also like a mirror returning a reflection. In fact, he is a murderous twin – a mirror that steals the reader's reflection and returns it to him as a present in return for a cheque.

Having said that, we cannot manage without the author of literature. He returns to the Queen what she lost. On the psychic level this implies that the author is needed by the reader because through the text he returns the reader's 'self' so he can become re-acquainted with its lost parts.

This need on the side of the reader creates a powerful transference towards the author as someone who possesses the 'big lack' – a paradigmatic lack, the fundamental lack felt by every person during their lives. In Poe's story it is represented by the letter. This lack, according to Poe's story, is so fateful that if we were to lose control of it, it has the power to destroy us. If, however we are able to retrieve it, we ourselves will be saved and we may even, through it, save another. Even a text of which the intended reader is Her Majesty the Queen is in fact a text that only the author can hand her. In this sense the author occupies a position above that of the monarchy.

The paradox is that the author is the actual writer of the letter that everyone is searching for. It is possible that there is in this a childlike quality or playful capacity that is personified within Poe's story of an 8-year-old who mimics the facial expressions of a child with whom he is playing and in doing so penetrates the mind of that 'other' and by way of analogy, the mind of the reader.

Two dialectic tensions referred to at the beginning of the chapter are both in action here: The tension between the 'self' and the 'other' and the tension between the 'present' and the 'absent'. This twofold dialectic moves circuitously. The stolen letter is the author's text, which has been stolen from the reader in the first place, and is now returned to him. But according to Poe's story it is also never returned to him because although the letter was handed back we are not aware of a single reader of the story who actually read it and that includes us its readers.

It is because the text of the letter is absent that it becomes the heart of the story and its generator. If we pay close attention we will discover that the letter in fact belongs to no one. The text supposedly belongs to the reader or in this instance the Queen. But as we saw, the only one who can lay his hands on the text is the author. However, if the author steals the text from the other then it isn't his property either. Because the author is always writing the story of an-other the text does not belong to him either, since the text actually tells the story of the reader. The author wrote our text, the text of us the readers. That is the stolen letter, and it was stolen from us.

The reader facing the author as a mirror

After exploring the character of the author that emerges from the story of 'The Purloined Letter' let us now fathom what happens to the reader within its framework. Both Lacan (1949, pp. 1–7) and Winnicott (1971, p. 149) include in their writing the metaphor of a mirror reflecting the individual's image. The thinking of both these writers offers an important contribution to the understanding of the structure that emerges from reading Poe's story. Lacan points out that the mirror (which can be the mirror of the mother's eyes or an actual mirror) does not return a 'real' reflection of the child. The image reflected in the mirror is a unifying illusion of a homogeneous figure whereas the child facing it is, in fact, fragmentary and constantly changing.

Winnicott describes the child reflected and sees himself in his mother's eyes, when 'what she looks like is related to what she sees there' (Winnicott, D.W., 1971, p. 149). In other words the reflection he sees includes his image plus his mother's response to him. In a continuation of this, the psychoanalyst Heinz Kohut spoke of the essentialness of a mirroring 'self-object' in early object relations and of mirror transference in psychoanalysis. The subject needs the self-object's mirroring as part of the establishment of the self and structuring feelings of vitality and meaning in his existence (Kohut, H., 1984). Poe's reader faces these mirror paradigms. He sees his reflection through the eyes of the author, but the purloined letter that he will never read (because it cannot appear in any text) is his 'real' reflection. From a psychoanalytic perspective, and perhaps also a physical one, this is an oxymoron because the reflection functions in a way that is foreign to the organism reflected in it. The mother and the author never return to the child or the reader, a reflection of his very owns 'real' self, which is in constant movement and change. The original letter in Poe's story remains hidden until the end, or in other words is endlessly written and endlessly evades being read. The mother and the author return to the child or the reader goes back to his constantly changing self, reflected in a misleading coherent mirror image.

In his book *The Detective as a Cultural Hero*, David Gurevich discusses the difference between the 'modern view' on the one hand, promoting the detective's ability to expose an object that is there for all to see, whereas on the other hand, in postmodern thought the searched-for object remains hidden. Gurevich explains that

> [p]ostmodernism views the detective not as a character in pursuit of a deeply buried secret but rather as one observing flat objects across the surface of a 'Thousand Plateaus' (Gilles and Deleuze) of the visible. The modern view is focused on the rhetoric of discovering 'the truth'; postmodernist thinking on the other hand attaches itself to the mysterious, undecipherable character of indifferent objects upon the field of observation (Gurevich, D., 2013, p. 351).

In this sense one can view the reader as facing the 'purloined letter's mirror'. Dupin's action returns to the reader his reflection: A subject who disregards the obvious because he is deeply immersed in the narcissistic manoeuvres of his thinking, moving time and again to what he already knows. He is not open to the discovery of anything in a new light.

The naïve reader submits to the text whereas in Poe's description the author is a calculating and estranged genius. He does not necessarily offer a flattering mirror but the reader in his narcissistic self-preoccupation is not choosy. He reads in order to read how the text reads him. Every reflection fascinates him and is extremely important to him so that he is highly dependent on the author and the text at hand. We admire the author and follow his thinking and his moves in amazement. We have transference love relations towards him because we believe him to be in possession of 'the secret', or, in Lacan's words, 'the subject who is supposed to know' (Felman, S., 1977, p. 134).

Permanence vs change in the reading experience

'The Purloined Letter' is a permanent absent. Around it there are ongoing processes and change. A search and a failure to find, a further search and a further disappointment; the search is unflagging and in the end even when the detective/thief/author, finds the letter he can only tell us about the way in which it was found. The letter remains forever a mystery. It is an illusion that is important for the reader and motivates him. The reader delves into the story in order to reach this illusion believing that he will shortly be able to read it. In fact it is destined to remain the permanent absent signifier; it is an important source of curiosity, movement and growth. At the end of every reading of a literary letter we look for another book in our continuing search for the absent that is permanently in our mind. Like with the negation of the letter that was there for all to see, so negations and negations of negations in the labyrinth of literary mirrors create the process of establishing the reading subject in a continuous and infinite dialectic movement of reflections.

The enigmatic nature of the text is understood as an area of meaning, which Felman suggested also be termed 'the indecipherable'. A transformative reading is therefore one that will lead to an understanding by the reader of the changing nature of the 'self', the illusive quality of the unconscious, and the illusion involved in the pursuit of 'the' existential absent. In contrast to the appropriating reader who in fact is in a state of repetition compulsion of false reading, the curious reader will find himself mourning the partialness and the fact that there will always be islands in his psyche and in his life that will remain an indecipherable text, but he will also – precisely because of that insight – become richer, more creative and more vital.

We will now examine an additional and more tempestuous example of a reader's refusal to recognize these insights in Henry James' *The Aspern Papers*.

The destructive cycles of the reader's envious phantasies: illustrated in Henry James' *The Aspern Papers*

Lacan termed 'phantasm' the human illusion about 'a thing' that if it were only reachable would make the individual complete, in need of nothing. The phantasm is every subject's private myth regarding a certain thing lacking, which had he possessed it he would 'have it all' – property, name, appearance, certain relations and so forth. The individual believes that the phantasm can be realized. He moves along the chain of signifiers from one signifier to another in his search after the missing part. One of the imagined ways of resolving the quintessential lack is by joining the 'big Other' as Lacan termed it; that 'radical otherness' that he cannot gain hold of. This 'Other' is also embodied in the otherness of the language, which mediates and represents the longed-for yet unattainable object. This 'big Other' may be projected on to the omniscient parent, and in later life towards the image of God. It might also be connected to an image of an admired figure such as the analyst in therapy or the literary author (Lacan, J., [1959–1960] 1992).

According to Melanie Klein, the root of the quest for the absent is embedded in early childhood by the infant's absolute dependence on the mother's assets, which arouse the infantile feelings of theft and loss. These feelings are expressed paradigmatically in the experience of weaning, which is liable to trigger greed and destructive envy characteristic of the paranoid- schizoid refusal to accept life's inherent partiality. Alternatively, these feelings may lead to depressive mourning, which will lead to the development of the ability to create and the wish to repair the fundamental pain and lack in the self and in the other.

The literary evidence from *The Aspern Papers* exposes an attitude of greed on the part of the reader that is not restricted to the literary text's 'good breast' and the author.[2] His greed drives the reader (represented by the hero of the story) crazy and is accompanied by destructive envy. Envy is characterized by the extent to which the fact that the assets belong to the other is insufferable, to the extent that it leads to murderous destructiveness directed towards these desired assets. In phantasy (and in reality) envy is so strong that it destroys the 'good breast' even at the price of relinquishing the nourishment it offers (Klein, M., 1957, pp. 241–304). In day-to-day life envy is seen in situations in which a person will harm someone who is generous and kind to him, triggered by the envy at the plentitude possessed by the other, which enables him to share his good fortune.

Like Poe's *Purloined Letter* Henry James' *The Aspern Papers* is also a story involving a text being pursued by the hero who is unable to reach and reveal its contents until the very end of the story. The same is true of us, its readers. The frenetic and unbounded quest drives the plot that has the hero engaged in a fatal chase after the text he so longs to possess. His odyssey is so impulsive, greedy and envious, that at the bitter end it leads to the destruction of both the longed-for text and the woman to whom the text belonged. In his voyage of conquest the hero too suffers a severe setback and is left impoverished and robbed of the very object of his desire. As we shall see in what follows, the absent text in James' story functions as a phantasm – like 'the thing' the reader believes he lacks in life and that will bring him perfect happiness. The process the hero experiences involves a dramatic struggle between presence and absence – the two sides of the dialectic – which eventually leads to the insight gained from the story's bitter ending: namely that the 'whole' is not defined by 'having it all' but rather by coming to terms with the inherent partiality of human existence.

Henry James' hero is a literature researcher working on a biography of an admired long-dead American poet named Jeffry Aspern. We are told that Aspern had written numerous letters and poems to a woman who refuses to hand them over to anybody. The character of the researcher is possessed by a private phantasm shaped in the conscious fantasy of him getting hold of everything the poet ever wrote, including in particular those missing texts. I shall gradually follow the movement of the text as step by step it reveals the unconscious phantasy of reading as a way of making whole and present that which is partial and absent.

The plot

The narrator is also a writer, writing a biography of yet another author – Aspern – and is therefore, perhaps above all else, to be considered a reader. The hero longs to put his hands on the poems and letters that he knows the poet wrote to his one-time lover – a 150-year-old virgin named Juliana Bordereau. Juliana lives in a dilapidated castle on a godforsaken canal in Venice with her niece Tita, a spinster well past her prime. In a correspondence between them the narrator fails to convince the very old woman to hand over the letters. In his eagerness to get hold of the texts he decides to invest the best part of his money and masquerades as a tourist who wants to live in her house for a while: 'I am prepared to roast all summer – as well as hereafter' (James, H., 1888, p. 7), he says, as he presents his cunning plan to his friend Mrs Prest. His secret strategy is to deceive the old lady and her niece in all sorts of ways: first, to go by a fictive name; second, to capture their hearts by making their withering garden bloom; and third, by courting the lonely and elderly unmarried niece. All means can and must be used on the way to attaining the desired text written by the author's admired 'other'.

Unlike the plot of 'The Purloined Letter' in which the detective is convinced that the thief won't destroy the letter, as it is his means of blackmailing the Queen, the story of *The Aspern Papers* is driven inter alia by an anxiety harboured by the narrator who informs us that he 'had perfectly considered the possibility that she would destroy her papers on the day she should feel her end really approach. I believed that she would cling to them till then' (ibid., pp. 23–24). The letter's owner is not a writer. She too is a 'reader', being closely watched by yet another reader who feels robbed and envious because the text is in her possession. The narrator projects on her phantasies involving erotic relations between her and the text of which, in desperation, he was willing to be a voyeur, in a way similar to the infant's phantasy of his parent's unification in what is named in psychoanalysis as the 'primal scene': 'I think I had an idea that she read Aspern's letters over every night or at least pressed them to her withered lips. I would have given a good deal to have a glimpse of the latter spectacle' (ibid., p. 24).

The narrator's friend and confidant, Mrs Prest, is disappointed by his wastage of time and money trying to establish relations with the niece and the old woman instead of being bold and 'simply taking' the text:

> She reproached me with wanting boldness, and I answered that even to be bold you must have an opportunity: you may push on through a breach but you can't batter down a dead wall. She answered that the breach I had already made was big enough to admit an army and

accused me of wasting precious hours in whimpering in her salon when I ought to have been carrying on the struggle in the field ... 'They'll lead you on to your ruin,' she said before she left Venice. 'They'll get all your money without showing you a scrap' (ibid., pp. 26–27).

Mrs Prest's role in the story resembles that of the Greek Choir. She tells us what will be and even tells the hero that he will never attain his desire, but her warnings fall on deaf ears reassured by self-justifications:

> My eccentric private errand became a part of the general romance and the general glory – I felt even a mystic companionship, a moral fraternity with all those who in the past had been in the service of art. They had worked for beauty, for a devotion; and what else was I doing? That element was in everything that Jeffrey Aspern had written, and I was only bringing it to the light (ibid., pp. 29–30).

Jeffry Aspern is omnipotently described as a messenger of God, and therefore whoever gets to his letters will become involved in a 'love story', 'mystic companionship' and 'moral fraternity' with the Divine Other. The story's hero, who considers himself Aspern's most faithful reader, is immersed in religious ecstasy. As a zealous believer, doubt is not an option.

> I hold it singular, as I look back, that I should never have doubted for a moment that the sacred relics were there; never have failed to feel a certain joy at being under the same roof with them. After all they were under my hand – they had not escaped me yet; and they made my life continuous, in a fashion, with the illustrious life they had touched at the other end (ibid., p. 30).

The transference relations towards 'the papers', which here assume the importance of a religious text or a sacred relic, is accompanied by a psychic explanation: The character's view is that touching the sacred text transforms his life into a continuum of that magnificence. He is 'touched' by it by placing his hands on the text. It's impossible to miss the erotic, fetishistic approach to 'the papers'. The phantasmic quality in the reader's transference relation is magnified by the fact that he attributes holiness to a text that he has not read, is not aware of its contents and without even having had a single shred of evidence confirming its existence.[3]

The transference relations that combine love, betrothal and religious relations are expressed in a conversation between the researcher and the niece in which he suddenly reveals his love for Aspern the poet. He was curious to know whether in her response she would disclose her and her Aunt's secret, as he says:

He is my poet of poets – I know him almost by heart.
'Oh, by heart – that's nothing!' she murmured, smiling. 'My aunt used to know him ... He used to call on her and take her out.'
I continued to stare. 'My dear lady, he died a hundred years ago!'
'Well,' she said mirthfully, 'My aunt is a hundred and fifty.'
'Mercy on us!' I exclaimed, 'Why didn't you tell me before? I should like so to ask her about him'
Oh, you should have come twenty years ago: then she still talked about him.
'And what did she say?' I asked eagerly
'She said he was a god' (ibid., p. 43).

Then, when the hero asks the niece whether the old lady has a portrait of the author he adds, 'A portrait of the god. I don't know what I wouldn't give to see it.' To which she replies, 'I don't know what she has got. She keeps her things locked up' (ibid., p. 44).

The portrait of God, of the ultimate Other, is under lock and key. We read the words 'locked up' and imagine hearing the sound of the key being turned, emphasizing the futility of the hero's attempt to reach the object of his desire. The lady is a 150-year-old spinster possibly under the spell of eternal life and the author is her past, her love, her memories, he is her god and that of all his readers of which the narrator is one. And wherever there is a god, a devil also resides. Getting to the desired text involves the employment of strategies and deception. The narrator deceives the old lady and her niece by giving false information as to his identity and the reason for him being in Venice. Further into the story he convinces the niece to deceive her aunt so as to get to Aspern's documents. There is good reason for her Aunt choosing to name him as 'The devil' when he wrote to her prior to his visit asking for the text he so wanted; a mirror image of the narrator's image of her as a demon who in the narrator's fantasy is liable to commit the 'horrible sacrilege' (ibid., p. 59) of burning the holy papers.

The presence of the text's two readers sitting opposite each other again constitutes the image of monstrous twin readers – this time the narrator and the old lady. An additional similarity to Poe's story lies in the respective roles of the man and the woman: The woman is in possession of the author's love letter, which the man is keen to put his hands on. Both of their psychic splitting defence mechanisms are primitive and extreme. Both readers regard the author as a god and see each other as a devil. One desires to steal the text from the other. They resemble two infants at war over the mother's breast ready to kill one another to gain sole sovereignty over the object of their desires. However, the letters and poems are under lock and key and driving the frustrated readers out of their minds.

Her doing this made me think I was right ... the Aspern papers at that moment languished behind the peevish little lock of the secretary. It was hard to remove my eyes from the dull mahogany front when I reflected that a simple panel divided me from the goal of my hopes (ibid., p. 70).

In the end the hero can no longer restrain himself, enters the old lady's room one night, a lamp he is carrying illuminates the *escritoire*. It is the novel's climax: 'If I have candidly narrated the importunities, the indelicacies, of which my desire to possess myself of Jeffrey Aspern's papers had rendered me capable ... I think it was the worst thing I did' (ibid., p. 80). The old lady wakes up and for the first time since the beginning of the story exposes her eyes.

I almost let my luminary drop and certainly I stepped back, straightening myself up at what I saw. Miss Bordereau stood there in her nightdress, in the doorway of her room, watching me; her hands were raised, she had lifted the everlasting curtain that covered half her face, and for the first, the last, the only time I beheld her extraordinary eyes. They glared at me ... 'Ah, you publishing scoundrel!' ... I went toward her, to tell her I meant no harm. She waved me off with her old hands, retreating before me in horror; and the next thing I knew she had fallen back with a quick spasm, as if death had descended on her (ibid., pp. 81–82).

Here the narrator actualizes his irresistible drive with catastrophic consequences. The old lady dies, but not before showing him her incandescent eyes and sharing her cruel laconic summation of him as a 'publishing scoundrel'. All the sublime descriptions of art and beauty, of the cosmic love story, mystic companionship and moral fraternity are insultingly devalued by the old lady's words and the mirror she places in front of him as he becomes a 'publishing scoundrel'. The hero flees the castle and loiters through Venice as if lost. Nonetheless, after an interval of 12 days he decides to return to the castle.

The supposedly lofty longing for the text is unmasked as a ridiculous, pathetic pursuit of some printed material; not a holy chalice, not prestige, not the completion of life's mission; simply a text on to which the phantasm had been projected. And the reader is forced to accept that his lifetime pursuit of the absent was a pointless chase. This instead of humbly accepting the partiality of life, the right of the other to their privacy and property, the fact that one is never going to be able to 'devour' the other in their entirety and that one must bear separateness and partiality and create a 'whole' from what exists while forging meaning from what is absent. That is the opportunity that James' literary character and we his readers are offered to work through the psychological and existential dialectic between the absent and the present, between the partial and the complete.

Even when it seems there are no more peaks to conquer, James manages to surprise us. Towards the end of the story there is yet another dramatic twist. The innocent, kind and moral Miss Tita, who till then hadn't known the meaning of chicanery, gives the hero as a present the portrait of Aspern his admired poet, which he had wanted to buy from the old lady a few months earlier. Only then does she surprise him by saying she felt the old lady wanted to tell her something at the end:

> If you were not a stranger. Then it would be the same for you as for me. Anything that is mine – would be yours, and you could do what you like. I couldn't prevent you … You could see them – you could use … I would give you everything – and she would understand, where she is – she would forgive me!
>
> 'Ah, Miss Tita – ah, Miss Tita,' I stammered … What in the name of the preposterous did she mean if she did not mean to offer me her hand? That was the price – that was the price! (ibid., pp. 92–94).

Miss Tita had become the owner of the text and as such she had acquired the power of possession. Yet at the same time she too is living a phantasy and her lack – as is allegedly proper for a heroic middle-aged spinster – is a husband. She wishes to strike a deal: by using the narrator's longed-for lack she seeks to attain her own desired lack – marriage to the narrator. The narrator finds himself confronting the question of whether getting hold of the text is indeed worth any price and how the value of the text is to be estimated.

At first his answer is 'no'. He leaves the castle and again finds himself stricken and confused wondering between the canals of Venice. At one point he gazes at the statue of the Venetian military tactician and strategist Bartolomeo Colleoni, perhaps symbolizing his transference relations towards the author, and tells us that:

> I found myself staring at the triumphant captain as if he had an oracle on his lips … But he continued to look far over my head, at the red immersion of another day … He could not direct me what to do, gaze up at him as I might (ibid., p. 96).

As long as he is awake he remains determined not to marry Tita in exchange for the letters. But then he falls asleep. As he sleeps so too does his common sense while his urges are wide awake with the result that:

> During my sleep a very odd revulsion had taken place in my spirit. I found myself aware of this almost as soon as I opened my eyes; it made me jump out of my bed with the movement of a man who remembers that he has left the house door ajar or a candle burning under a shelf. Was I still in time to save my goods? ... For what had now come to pass was that in the unconscious cerebration of sleep I had swung back to a passionate appreciation of Miss Bordereau's papers. They were now more precious than ever, and a kind of ferocity had come into my desire to possess them. The condition Miss Tita had attached to the possession of them no longer appeared an obstacle worth thinking of ... and for an hour, that morning, my repentant imagination brushed it aside. It was absurd ... renounce so easily and turn away helpless from the idea that the only way to get hold of the papers was to unite myself to her for life (ibid., p. 97).

And then comes Henry James' one more and this time final, twist, as poor Miss Tita's sense of her failure produces an extraordinary transformation in her:

> Now I perceived it; I can scarcely tell how it startled me. She stood in the middle of the room with a face of mildness bent upon me, and her look of forgiveness, of absolution, made her angelic. It beautified her ... and while I was still the victim of it I heard a whisper somewhere in the depths of my conscience: 'Why not, after all – why not?' (ibid., pp. 97–98).

However, Miss Tita surprises him:

> 'I have done the great thing. I have destroyed the papers.'
> 'Destroyed them?' I faltered.
> 'Yes; what was I to keep them for? I burned them last night, one by one, in the kitchen.'
> 'One by one?' I repeated, mechanically.
> 'It took a long time – there were so many.' The room seemed to go round me as she said this, and a real darkness for a moment descended upon my eyes. When it passed Miss Tita was there still, but the transfiguration was over and she had changed back to a *plain*, dingy, elderly person (ibid., pp. 98–99).

The story ends with an admission by the hero to his confidant Mrs Prest that he had hung the admired author's portrait above his writing desk and that 'When I look at it my chagrin at the loss of the letters becomes almost intolerable' (ibid., pp. 99–100).

Was that insight genuinely gained and assimilated into the character's mind? One cannot be certain. Apparently in his admiring reader's eyes the papers remained precious.

This is a story about a reading in which the words, which are supposed to be a *substitute* and to function as signifiers for 'the things in and off themselves' are perceived to be '*the* thing'; an asset that is wished to be devoured and owned rather than internalized, worked through and forging a personal meaning. Nevertheless, the picture above the narrator's desk is, after all, a symbol, a representation and is a substitute for an absent object of desire. This conceivably implies that there was at least partial psychological progress and that a new psychic equilibrium had been achieved regarding the need to let go of the greedy desire to have it all. Instead there was a depressive acceptance of the existential terms that come with the benefit of joining the symbolic order.

Before leaving James' hero in his gloomy room I wish to use what was described in order to highlight two phenomena: 'repetition compulsion' and 'the aesthetic conflict', both aroused in the reader of *The Aspern Papers* in response to the absent. Both phenomena are linked to the conflict between the force that seeks to complement the lack and the force that aims at coming to terms with it. Both are activated by and are relevant to other dialectic equilibriums that will be discussed later in the chapter. In the context of Henry James' story, these two phenomena respond to the inherent lack of the literary text – which also represents the object of the author, who is never taken under complete subjugation by the reader.

Repetition compulsion: a psychoanalytic perspective

Freud takes up the subject of 'repetition compulsion' in a significant way in his article 'Remembering, Repeating and Working-Through' in which he describes this phenomenon thus:

> We may now ask what it is that he in fact repeats or acts out. The answer is that he repeats everything that has already made its way from the sources of the repressed into his manifest personality … while the patient experiences it as something real and contemporary, we have to do our therapeutic work on it, which consists in a large measure in tracing it back to the past (Freud, S., 1914, pp. 145–156).

Freud argues that transference relations are the most efficient means by which to treat repetition compulsion. One can see that Freud's description can also be applicable to a large extent to the reading of literature:

> We render the compulsion harmless, and indeed useful, by giving it the right to assert itself in a definite field. We admit it into the

transference as a playground in which it is allowed to expand in almost complete freedom and in which it is expected to display to us everything in the way of pathogenic instincts that is hidden in the patient's mind. Provided only that the patient shows compliance enough to respect the necessary conditions of the analysis, we regularly succeed in giving all the symptoms of the illness ... The transference thus creates an intermediate region between illness and real life through which the transition from the one to the other is made (ibid., p.154).

Freud's second reference to repetition compulsion was in his article 'Beyond the Pleasure Principle' (1920). In it Freud presents the death drive and its psychic derivative – hatred – and reveals the significance of repetition compulsion as representing the death drive's inclination to return to the inorganic state that preceded life, to the absence of existence that precedes existence.

Additionally, in this complex article Freud describes repetitiveness and illustrates it paradigmatically by a 'fort-da' ('gone-there') game, which he coincidently happened to observe in a little child, where the child threw a wooden reel with a piece of string wound round it as far away as he could, saying something like 'gone' (i.e. lost), then pulled it back, joyfully hailing something like 'there' (i.e. found). In this activity the little boy time and again returns to the source of a repressed distress and hopelessness over feeling abandoned by his loved object. Repetition compulsion has an active hold on the source of pain and anxiety and creates a certain experience of being in control over it, especially with the invention of the second part of the game – when it's in his power to let go of the object but even more so to then retrieve it.

Melanie Klein (1940) saw the appearance of repetition compulsion as a primitive means of defence against the recognition of lack and absence, of finitude, partiality, dependency and the ultimate embodiment of them all – death. In the framework of the paranoid-schizoid position, in situations in which hatred and the death drive overcome love and the life drive, the activity of repetition compulsion paradoxically works against itself. In the attempted battle against the absent or death through repetition compulsion there is a freezing of movement and thus a manifestation of the death and absence that the subject is trying to avoid. This is a struggle against death that decrees psychic death. According to Melanie Klein there is a continuous dialectic movement between the life drive and the death drive. Moreover, repetition compulsion also provides a recurring opportunity to turn the futile effort to own the object, control it and unite with it into a productive attempt at internalizing the good object in recognition of his separateness. Only the latter may lead to the consolidation of the 'self' and a renewed movement of processes of integration, reparation and creativity.

The dual track conflict: at-oneness vs separateness

The psychoanalyst Frances Tustin described the way in which an infant in normal development moves along a dual track, from a situation in which he is 'flowing-over-at-oneness' in union with the mother, to situations in which he becomes aware of his separateness from the mother and from the world (Tustin, F., 1994, pp. 2–23). The infant faces three central possibilities: the most pathological option described by Tustin, is an autistic freeze due to a refusal or an inability to endure the separation. A second option, described by Klein in relation to an infant in the paranoid-schizoid position, is for the child to be so consumed by greed vis-à-vis the object that he seeks to control – the body of the mother, by projective and intrusive identification. These two forms of identification satisfy three greedy demands: appropriation (the mother's body in my ownership and mine), territory (I am the only one in the mother's body or it is only in me) and exclusivity (accompanied by murderous instincts towards competitors – the father's penis and other babies in the mother's body, and in a more complete way – towards the father and brothers). A third way of being rescued from the dual track of at-oneness vs separateness that constitutes an opening to reparation is described by Klein and Meltzer. They stress the possibility of unifying oneself with a desire for knowledge that goes beyond the desire to control and possess the object (Klein, M., 1930, Meltzer, D. and Williams, M.H., 1988).

The voyage of the 'self' that involves the recognition of the separateness of the object is heading towards reparation (Klein, M., 1937). This voyage too involves repeated returns to the areas of pain but this time in order to find a new, more fertile path to coping. In contrast to the aggressive union of the paranoid-schizoid position, in the depressive position, which stems from a better integration of the psyche, the individual recognizes that he is lacking and seeks to return to internal and external painful states out of a feeling of mature guilt and responsibility and out of a desire to repair the damaged object and self. The process of working through in therapy is also achieved by repetitive returns to the roots of anxiety and pain in order to enable recurring reflections and interpretations. These repetitions, again and again, in the midst of the transformative container of the analytic space, gradually enable turning denial and possessiveness in the face of partiality into creative acceptance of the lack as an inherent and even formative part of human nature.

An observation of the actions of the hero in James' story that take place along the continuum between pathological repetitiveness and repetition for the sake of reparation enables us to learn a great deal about the dynamic of the greedy reader.

Three sources of the author's powers of seduction: magical thinking, alpha function and the aesthetic conflict

Magical thinking

The fountainhead of magical thinking is in the pre-verbal stage of early development. To feel protected the infant has to phantasize that he possesses the magical power to create whatever and whoever is needed by him. Alternatively he has to imagine that his object has the magical power to save him from everything bad. In the realms of magical thinking the rules of logic are nullified. One of the sources of a writer's capacity to 'seduce' the reader into a state of pathological dependence is to be found in his power of magical thinking. Despite the fact that in normative development magical thinking is a regular part of infancy, remnants are evident in every adult. In our phantasies, which we often fear, we can create and kill by merely thinking. The literary author creates and kills by simply writing. Moreover, he is eternal because he dwells in his writings and in the minds and hearts of his readers for years after his death. In *The Aspern Papers*, the magical phantasy that ownership of the author's writings is like an antidote to death, is personified by Juliana, who owns the papers, reaches the advanced age of 150 and then loses the drug of life when the narrator comes to take the papers away from her. The magical power of clinging to the author as if to an amulet evaporates and she dies.

Behind the hero's obsession there is a longing for reparation. However, it is a longing for a magical reparation, as if by an act of sorcery – a yearning for the immediate completion of everything he lacks through the appropriation of the literary text. In fact, magical reparation cannot repair anything. Because of its denial of reality it is wrapped up in destructiveness. An example of its destructive power is expressed in the hero's stubbornness, loss of judgment and the suffering he brings upon himself that he experiences as unavoidable: wretched lodgings in Venice, the loss of all his money and even a readiness to marry the ageing, ugly, lifeless spinster.

Alpha function

Another source of a writer's ability to 'seduce' the reader is linked to the power of words in early development. The words of the mother while the infant is suffering, even if spoken to herself, are a means of calming both her and the infant. Such words both relieve the frustration and lend it meaning. From a psychoanalytic perspective the narrator's unconscious is 'justified' in searching for the author whose words will change everything and restore all to a state of perfect harmony. In phantasy the reader is returning to that same early mother/infant experience, whereas now it is an encounter with the writer, who is said to possess the knowledge, power and means to rise above the misery and reach realms of beauty and reparation. Moreover, in early development and subsequently, the infant not only listens to the mother's words but also learns from her how to use words himself as a means of achieving tranquillity, meaning and development. Bion (1962) terms as 'alpha-function' the mother's ability to use her inner thoughts and words to contain and transform the child's experiences. Bion argues that the alpha function is internalized together with the mother's handling of the infant's anxiety.

The literary writer is like a wizard with words. In James' novel for instance, Aspern the poet (like the writer James himself as well as others) deals with psychic materials that arouse anxiety in him, works them through in a creative and productive way to produce an aesthetic creation. The ability to be creative is considered one of the most developed ways of achieving psychic reparation. It includes a process of 'creative mourning' (Ogden, T., 2000, pp. 65–68). The reader follows the author out of a desire to learn from him how he metabolizes psychic materials to create a literary work.

There is a moment in the novel when the spinster, Miss Tita, offers herself to the narrator in exchange for the papers, a move that interrupts the hero's inclination to repetition compulsion; he leaves the castle, meanders around the canals of Venice, reflects, lost in thought: 'I wandered about … to the continued stupefaction of my gondolier, who had never seen me so restless and yet so void of a purpose' (James, H., 1888, p. 96).

The hero almost reaches the point of convincing himself that his is an overblown obsession, that he has to give up, surrender, come to terms with the lack. His doubt is even expressed orally. That day he doesn't eat, as if for a moment he has put a halt to the voracious greed that knows no bounds.

> He [the gondolier] reminded me that I had not lunched … I told him that that day, for a change, I would touch no meat. It was an effect of poor Miss Tita's proposal, not altogether auspicious, that I had quite lost my appetite (ibid., p. 96).

This is the one and only scene in which the soft voice of the depressive position can be heard; a lone moment in which the hero halts his predatory inclinations seeking to devour the literary object in order to override the lack and instead pays heed to feelings of despondency and helplessness. But with nightfall he swiftly falls back on the manic drive to fill the lack and leaps up from his bed questioning whether he will be in time to salvage his property (ibid., p. 97).

From here the way to setting fire to the valuable papers proves to be short.

In the end it is the aging, spinsterish and gullible niece – the novel's only character intent on making contact and who recognizes her dependency – who rescues the hero from his dizzying confusion. She is not trapped by magical projections towards the absent papers and thus burns them as her aunt requested her to do. Against his will she liberates the hero from his repetition compulsion. He is forced to confront the existential truth that his psychic wholeness is from now on dependent on his readiness to accept the partiality of life and, as a keen reader, of the literary treasures in his hand. The narrator will from now on have to bear the fact that he will never read everything written by the admired author thus, by analogy, recognize that one cannot take everything from the object and that we cannot be completely fulfilled and satisfied. That is actually the source of our search, our learning and our openness towards the new and the other. Moreover, this is also the foundation of the ethical position, which, out of compassion, recognizes lack and deficiency as the heritage of us all and thus no longer gnaws with envious greed and without pangs of conscience at the imagined perfection of the other.

Henry James lit a match and resolved the imbroglio. This violent solution of burning the literary text simultaneously created an unsettling and liberating cure. Now instead of loss there is space for symbolization. The picture of the author hanging above his admiring reader's desk at the end of the novel symbolizes what he had previously sought to attain in concrete form. Literature returned to being a symbol and a representation instead of a tangible asset in the form of a set of holy papers. And yet the hero's understanding is only partial since he continues to mourn the loss of the valuable papers, admitting to his friend Mrs Prest, that when he looks at the picture above his desk his 'chagrin at the loss of the letters becomes almost intolerable' (ibid., pp. 99–100).

The aesthetic conflict

An additional source of the author's seductive power is linked to a psychic mechanism activated at the very beginning of life when encountering beauty and absence, termed in psychoanalysis as 'the aesthetic conflict'.

The psychoanalyst Donald Meltzer described the young infant's 'aesthetic conflict', which in later life stretches to the artistic space thus: The infant is overwhelmed by the mother's beauty and is filled with love and inspiration. At the same time, he is assailed by her enigmatic separateness, which he senses as inaccessibility. The combination of beauty and mystery confronts the infant with a particularly difficult challenge. He has a feeling of extreme beauty combined with ugliness and evil, and it arouses anxiety. So consumed is he by the longing for beauty that it becomes unbearable for him to discover that the mother's enigmatic quality is out of his control and conquest even though in fact the enigmatic aspect is an essential part of her aesthetics (Meltzer, D. and Williams, H., 1988, pp. 124–132).

Meltzer argues that the aesthetic conflict is a fundamental factor in the development of creativity, of art and of the relation towards them. Meltzer's concept of the aesthetic object is highly relevant to the standing of the absent text in both Poe's 'The Purloined Letter' and in James' The *Aspern Papers*. The absent text resembles the mother's mysteriousness as does the aesthetic capacity of the author. In the hero's phantasy in James' novel, the Aspern papers are imbued with the sublime and the divine, the beautiful, the virtuous and with pure love. The written is a love letter. The writer is a god. The reader is moved by an emotional and instinctual storm towards this mighty object. Juliana, the 150-year-old lover of the author, and the hero, the author's biographer, both recognize the stupendous beauty of Aspern's creation, which turns into a fetish for each one of them. The papers become the signifier of *the* creation, of *the* thing, of *the* truth, of *the* ultimate beauty. At the same time they also lead to ugliness, hatred and great anxiety. Even if no one reads them – Tita has testified that it had been a long time since the old woman had read them – having them in one's possession signifies an affinity to the holy and the beautiful so that neither the 150-year-old Juliana nor the hero is prepared to give up a claim on owning them – a claim that they are both unable to restrain.

It is important to understand that literature's aesthetic object like that personified by *The Aspern Papers*' narrator's desires is not merely characterized by its textual beauty. It holds the secret of existence. It contains everything; it is the source of everything; and in phantasy the connection to it is a link with omniscience and with the eternal. But it forever includes an overwhelming enigmatic, elusive and inaccessible quality that not only adds beauty and splendour to the aesthetic object but also arouses profound anxiety and pain, denied by the phantasy of exclusive possession.

The literary reader represented by the hero in James' story resembles a demanding and greedy infant who wants to dominate his mother's body and ensure that no rival is able to exert a right over her. He wants to do this via 'intrusive projective identification', which is to say an uninvited invasion of the mother's body in order to appropriate her inner treasures – symbolized in the author's text. This is a violent movement that erases the capacity to really learn and acquire knowledge. It is a movement that also undermines the ethical position that recognizes the other in his otherness and separateness.

Inspired by Jacques Derrida's book *The Postcard* (Derrida, J., 1980) the researcher Michal Ben-Naftali ([2000] 2015) writes that by its very nature a written text already transcends the phantasized symbiosis because it is positioned outside the duo of reader and writer. On the oedipal level psychoanalysis explains this by noting that symbiosis occurs only between two. Therefore, the pairing between the written text and the writer keeps the reader out so that he becomes an excluded 'third'. Ben-Naftali writes that according to the 'pathology of addressing' (like addressing a letter to the reader):

> The post card must be incorporated, it must be swallowed and saved as was done in the Resistance, a crypt, as it were, sealed to and from communication. Ingesting the post card is not just a metaphor of the lovers' symbiosis. It is a bodily enactment of the idea of love perceived as address. The lover mourns the beloved, a beloved who resides under his skin, is with him all the time, the addressee of his words, object of emulation. (Ben-Naftali, M., [2000] 2015, p. 38).

In Freudian and Kleinian terms this represents melancholia rather than mourning (Freud S., 1917b; Klein, M., 1940). The opportunity to mourn the separateness of the loved one will, in fact, bear the capacity to feel compassion for him as part of loving him. However, the refusal to recognize his separateness under any circumstances activates the merciless gluttony.

In James' story, the greedy reader is determined to complete the lack, to incorporate the 'absent' for the sake of the longed-for feeling of 'perfection'. Paradoxically, the repetitive pursuit of that perfection ensures the perpetuation of the painful contact with the absent and missing. Only a process of mourning the lack of an opportunity to completely conquer the aesthetic object can lead to a transformation in the wake of which the reader will pick up a book with an attitude of openness, which is made possible precisely as a result of a recognition of partiality. In a reading of this kind, though the pain will not disappear, it will nonetheless make room for processes of growth, curiosity, liberation and even elation, inspiration and creativity.

The literary evidence gleaned from James' story reveals three kinds of reading awakened in the face of literature's 'aesthetic conflict'. The first involves the avoidance of the aesthetic object as manifested in the stance adopted by Tita, the old lady's niece. The second kind of reading involves a paranoid-schizoid effort to capture the aesthetic object as exemplified by the attitude of the hero – Aspern's biographer. In this kind of reading, the recognition of the aesthetic value of the text arouses a desire in the reader to conquer and incorporate it as means of controlling it by gaining exclusive possession of it. A third type of reading, which is inversely hinted at by the tragic ending of James' novel, is a recognition by the reader of the text's aesthetic value, which, in fact, stems from its transcendental dimensions. Such literary reading is accompanied by a recognition that we are in an eternal process of learning in which there is this painful pleasure derived from the dimension of infinitude in our lives. This recognition is likely to derive from a better integration between the two sides of the dialectic vector – the present and the absent. Instead of the text being in Julia's possession or that of the hero, it is to be the heritage of all and yet belong to no one. In this sense, the endings of both 'The Purloined Letter' and *The Aspern Papers* suggest that the attempt to capture the text by theft, for no clear reason results in there being no real encounter with it. We cannot plumb the depths of its meaning nor can we take off and fly skywards on its wings. In fact, the recognition of the aesthetic paradox, of which beauty stems in part from it being enigmatic, is what facilitates a profound immersion in the process of reading that can never be exhausted.

Notes

1 For further discussion see Amir, D. (2014, pp. 2–3).
2 In his article 'Some Unconscious Factors in Reading' (1930) the psychoanalyst James Strachey wrote about the oral aspects of reading, illustrating this facet with metaphors linking reading to oral experiences.
3 There are additional similarities between the real author – James – and the novel's author – Aspern. For example, they both become literary creators when they arrive in Europe from America. As the narrator tells it: 'I went with him – I tried to judge how the Old World would have struck him. It was when literature was lonely there [America] and art and form almost impossible, he had found means to live and write like one of the first; to be free and general and not at all afraid; to feel, understand, and express everything' (James, H., 1888, p. 34). However, since this book's focus is on the phenomenological reading of the texts, the autobiographical aspects of this story are not dealt with here.

References

Amir, D. (2014). *Cleft Tongue: The Language of Psychic Structures*. London: Karnac Books.
Ben-Naftali, M. [2000] (2015). *Chronicle of Separation: On Deconstruction's Disillusioned Love (Essays)*. New York: Fordham University Press.
Bion, W.R. (1962). *Learning from Experience*. London: Tavistock.
Bion, W.R. (1967). *Second Thoughts*. London and New York: Routledge.
Bonaparte, M. [1933] (1949). *Life and Works of Edgar Allan Poe*. London: Imago.
Derrida, J. (1980). *La Carte Postale: De Socrate a Freud Et Au-Dela*. Paris: Flammarion.
Felman, S. (Ed.) (1977). *Literature and Psychoanalysis: The Question of Reading: Otherwise*. Baltimore, MD and London: John Hopkins University Press.
Felman, S. (1993). The Case of Poe: Applications/Implications of Psychoanalysis. In: E. Berman (Ed.) *Essential Papers on Literature and Psychoanalysis*. New York and London: New York University Press, pp. 300–302.
Freud, S. (1909). Notes Upon a Case of Obsessional Neurosis. In: J. Strachey (Ed.) *The Standard Edition of the Complete Psychological Works of Sigmund Freud, Vol. X*. London: Hogarth Press, pp. 153–320.
Freud, S. (1914). Remembering, Repeating and Working-through. In: J. Strachey (Ed.) *The Standard Edition of the Complete Psychological Works of Sigmund Freud, Vol. II*. London: Hogarth Press, pp. 145–156.

Freud, S. (1917a). Introductory Lectures on Psycho-Analysis. In: J. Strachey (Ed.) *The Standard Edition of the Complete Psychological Works of Sigmund Freud, Vol. XVI*. London: Hogarth Press, pp. 241–463.

Freud, S. (1917b). Mourning and Melancholia. In: J. Strachey (Ed.) *The Standard Edition of the Complete Psychological Works of Sigmund Freud, Vol. XIV*. London: Hogarth Press, pp. 237–258.

Freud, S. (1919). The Uncanny. In: J. Strachey (Ed.) *The Standard Edition of the Complete Psychological Works of Sigmund Freud, Vol. XVII*. London: Hogarth Press, pp. 217–255.

Freud, S. (1920). Beyond the Pleasure Principle. In: J. Strachey (Ed.) *The Standard Edition of the Complete Psychological Works of Sigmund Freud, Vol. XVIII*. London: Hogarth Press, pp. 1–64.

Green, A. (1978). The Double and the Absent. In: A. Roland (Ed.) *Psychoanalysis, Creativity and Literature: A French-American Inquiry*. New York: Columbia University Press, pp. 271–292.

Gurevich, D. (2013). *The Detective as a Cultural Hero*. Tel Aviv: Ministry of Defense.

James, H. (1888). *The Aspern Papers*. London and New York: Macmillan & Co. [Kindle Edition].

Klein, M. (1930). The Importance of Symbol Formation in the Development of the Ego. In: *Love, Guilt and Reparation and Other Works 1921–1945*. London: Vintage, pp. 219–232.

Klein, M. (1937). Love, Guilt and Reparation. In: *Love, Guilt and Reparation and Other Works 1921–1945*. London: Vintage, pp. 306–343.

Klein, M. (1940). Mourning and Its Relation to Manic-Depressive States. In: *Love, Guilt and Reparation and Other Works 1921–1945*. London: Vintage, pp. 344–369.

Klein, M. (1957). Envy and Gratitude. In: *Envy and Gratitude and Other Works 1946–1963*. London: Vintage, pp. 176–235.

Klein, M. (1963). On the Sense of Loneliness. In: *Envy and Gratitude and Other Works 1946–1963*. London: Vintage, pp. 300–313.

Kohut, H. (1984). *How Does Analysis Cure?* Chicago, IL: University of Chicago Press.

Kristeva, J. (1987). *Tales of Love*. New York: Columbia University Press.

Lacan, J. (1949). The Mirror-Stage as Formative of the I: As Revealed in Psychoanalytic Experience. In: J.A. Miller (Ed.) *Écrits: A Selection*. New York and London: W.W. Norton, pp. 74–81.

Lacan, J. [1959–1960] (1992). The Ethics of Psychoanalysis. In: J.A. Miller (Ed.) *Écrits: A Selection: Book VII*. New York and London: W.W. Norton, pp. 1–330.

Meltzer, D. and Williams, M.H. (1988). *The Apprehension of Beauty*. London: Karnac Books Ltd.

Ogden, T.H. (2000). Borges and the Art of Mourning. *Psychoanalytic Dialogues*, 10(1), pp. 65–88.

Poe, E.A. [1844] (2011). The Purloined Letter. In: *The Complete Works of Edgar Allan Poe*. Orange Sky Project [Kindle Edition], vol. II, loc. 4185–4506.

Sartre, J. [1964] (1981). *The Words*. New York: Vintage Books.

Strachey, J. (1930). Some Unconscious Factors in Reading. *International Journal of Psychoanalysis*, 11, pp. 322–331.

Tustin, F. (1994). The Perpetuation of an Error. *Journal of Child Psychotherapy*, 20(1), pp. 3–23.
Winnicott, D.W. (1971). *Playing and Reality*. London: Tavistock.

Further reading

Derrida, J. (1967). *Writing and Difference*. London and New York: Routledge.
Lacan, J. (1955). The Purloined Letter. In: J.A. Miller (Ed.) *Écrits: A Selection, Book II*. New York and London: W.W. Norton, pp. 11–48.

Chapter 11

The dialectic between the familiar and the uncanny

The uncanny according to Freud, Lacan and Heidegger

The 'uncanny' ('*unheimlich*') is a concept that became a useful linguistic coin for thinkers in the fields of philosophy, cultural studies, literature, architecture and more. In this chapter we shall see how reading literature revives the dialectic tension between the two opposing psychic and existential forces of the 'familiar' and the 'uncanny', with the aid of Shai Agnon's short story 'Friendship'. Before reviewing the literary evidence I shall explain the concept of the 'uncanny' as understood by Freud, Lacan and Heidegger. Each of them highlights different aspects of this concept, which are particularly relevant to the reading of literature.

Freud's uncanny

Freud described the concept of the 'uncanny' in an article devoted to the subject published in 1919. This is one of the forms of anxiety that preoccupied Freud throughout his life. The uncanny is a foreign element that bursts into the most familiar and destabilizes it; the uncanny is actually a part of the familiar, which has been repressed. When we are unexpectedly exposed to the uncanny it arouses acute anxiety and distress.

Freud himself saw the uncanny as related to aesthetics and illustrated it via a literary work, noting that:

> It is only rarely that a psycho-analyst feels impelled to investigate the subject of aesthetics, even when aesthetics is understood to mean not merely the theory of beauty but the theory of the qualities of feeling ... But it does occasionally happen that he has to interest himself in some particular province of that subject ... The subject of the 'uncanny' is a province of this kind. It is undoubtedly related to what is frightening – to what arouses dread and horror (Freud, S., 1919, p. 219).

Freud's article on the 'uncanny' was published in the wake of the horrors of World War I and was closely followed in 1920 by the publication of his paper 'Beyond the Pleasure Principle' in which Freud presented the idea of the death drive. As a literary example of the phenomenon of the uncanny Freud uses E.T.A. Hoffman's story *The Sandman*.[1]

Freud adds two examples from his personal experience. In one of these he describes a tour through a small Italian town. While there he kept on returning to a street where prostitutes were touting for business. Freud was distressed by his encounter with the repressed – with the part that was unconsciously forcing him to return to the area from which his conscious sought to withdraw. The second example offered by Freud, describes a heart-rending night-time moment in a train when the door to the toilet opens and Freud thinks that an old man in a turban has mistakenly come into his room. But when he gets up to approach the stranger he discovers to his utter amazement that the figure he was seeing was in fact nothing other than a mirror image of himself. For a moment the familiar image had become foreign, intruding into the most routine of scenes and arousing a dread of the 'uncanny'. Additional paradigmatic forms referred to by Freud involve situations accompanied by a strangely repetitive sign, for example the number 62 that appears again and again in the course of one's day (in addresses, stations, etc.). These situations of unexplained repetitions, which arouse an uncanny feeling, are personified, according to Freud, in the phenomena of the 'double' in both reality and art. Freud argues that such situations are connected to the early phase of development during which we hold on to an animistic and magical perception – the origin of adult superstitions. In addition, Freud claims that an uncanny feeling is also linked to the dread of the repressed and of death, which, according to Freud, is not accepted by the unconscious. The distress that accompanies inexplicable repetitiveness is linked to repetition compulsion and to the refusal of the 'self' to be cognizant of the existence of the repressed and of death.

Finally, Freud connects the uncanny to fearing the female genitalia: 'This *Unheimlich* [i.e. "uncanny"] place, however, is the entrance to the former *Heim* [home] of all human beings, to the place where each one of us lived once upon a time and in the beginning. There is a joking saying that "Love is home-sickness"' (Freud, S., 1919, p. 245). It is therefore the most primary and familiar that is the first to be repressed and thus becomes uncanny, arousing distress when re-encountered. The distress or the dread, a subject Freud also deals with extensively in his article 'Inhibitions, Symptoms and Anxiety' (Freud, S., 1926) does not stem from an external object; its earliest paradigm is the caesura of birth, which is experienced as an anxiety of losing the object, when in fact it has no object.

The uncanny is the unfamiliarity that erupts into the most familiar, the most intimate and the most known of all. The child in his home, in his bed with his father, his mother, the fellow with his fiancée, the old man in the train compartment – is confronted by a foreign element that blurs the border between external and internal reality so that the familiar becomes foreign and threatening.

Similarly, when in art and literature conditions of comfortable familiarity are created, followed by an unanticipated catastrophic intrusion, the ontological status of the intrusive threat becomes unclear, uncanny, so that we don't know if it was a consequence of psychic illusion or evident reality. According to Freud the uncanny contributes to the understanding of art, part of whose power and magic for us resides in its ability to introduce us to the uncanny.

Lacan's uncanny

Lacan devoted his tenth seminar (Lacan, J., 1962–1963) to an in-depth study of Freud's concept of the uncanny. He describes the sudden invasion of the uncanny as the intrusion of the 'real' order into the 'imaginary' and 'symbolic' orders. Lacan likens the uncanny to a disruptive fissure in the continuous and united self-image that the subject acquired during the 'mirror stage'. That is the stage mentioned earlier, during which the subject stands in front of the mirror, or in front of his reflection in his mother's eye. The unconscious foreignness of the 'familiar' reflection stems from the fact that his real image of the constantly changing fragmentary body is absent from the complete and coherent reflection visible to him in the mirror. The mirror is veiled by the imaginary, so that it seems to the subject that he is looking at a full and reliable reflection of himself. The uncanny is the moment at which the 'real' bursts in and the veil of the imaginary is removed from the mirror, so that the subject meets himself as an object, very close to him being 'the thing' (*'das ding'*), which is not included in the signifier: a primary object that has no symbolic representation. The uncanny is totally foreign to the subject and yet he feels that it touches him in the most intimate way. The uncanny reveals the subject to himself as object and so exiles him from his subjectivity. This is a moment in which the phantasm that protected the subject from anxiety gives way to the uncanny. According to Lacan, the subject is likely to react in various ways in light of the intrusion of the real: he can act in accordance with the command of the real, as did Nathanael – the hero in Hoffman's *The Sandman*, which Freud used in his paper on the uncanny – who jumped to his death because of his identification with the eyes that were supposed to jump out of their sockets. Alternatively, the subject can try to rehabilitate the phantasm as in the famous case of 'the rat man' treated by Freud (Freud, S., 1909). An additional option facilitated in the context of psychoanalytic therapy is to meet yourself as object for moments, use the gap created between 'the real' and 'the imaginary' and ask whether you do indeed identify with what crystalized as a phantasm in the course of your life. As formulated by Lacan, the subject's encounter with the uncanny enables him to explore the question as to whether he really wants what he believed to be his utmost/ultimate desire.

Heidegger's uncanny

The philosopher Martine Heidegger expands his study of the concept of the uncanny in his magnum opus *Being and Time* (Heidegger, M., [1927] 1996). In the discussion of his concept of 'Being there' ('*Dasein*'), Heidegger argues that a subject has no existence in isolation from the world in which he lives because 'being there' is always also 'being with' ('*Mitsein*'). This means that there is an ontological relationship between 'being there' and 'others', those who in fact are nobody because they are not a particular other. From the outset the subject is immersed in the 'them'. This is a primary ontological condition of his existence. Heidegger writes:

> In falling, *Dasein* itself as tactical Being-in-the-world is something from which it has already fallen away. And it has not fallen into some entity which it comes upon for the first time in the course of its Being, or even one which it has not come upon at all; it has fallen into the world, which itself belongs to its Being (ibid., p. 231).

However, there is yet another mood, a state of anxiety, which makes it possible for *Dasein* to recognize the structure of his existence: 'That which anxiety is anxious about is Being-in-the world itself. In anxiety what is environmentally ready-to-hand sinks away, and so, in general, do entities within-the-world. The "world" can offer nothing more, and neither can the *Dasein*-with of Others' (ibid., p. 233). Anxiety is thus linked to the collapse of the familiar illusory feeling of 'being with', a feeling that leads an individual to forget death, finality and the limitations that characterize his life. 'Anxiety, therefore, opens the possibility for *Dasein* to acknowledge its own existential structure' (Pearl, J., 2011, p. 46). The uncanny involves a feeling of existential distress from which the individual will again flee to the apparent familiarity of 'being with'. Thus the uncanny has a formative role in an individual's coping with his life. Avi Sagi stresses the importance of

> the existentialist perspective which lends a meaning to the role of death in a person's life. Death reinforces the fragility of existence, in Heidegger's words 'the possibility of the impossibility of any existence at all'. As a result of this recognition, every moment in a person's life assumes a particular meaning and value since it is impossible to live life for ever (Sagi, A., 2009, p. 81).

This conceptualization also has ethical implications. The recognition of the subject, which, according to both Freud and Heidegger, is linked to the acknowledgement of death, leads to the recognition of the other. The philosopher Emmanuel Levinas linked familiarity to welcoming and hospitality as concepts connected to responsibility towards the other (Levinas, E., [1961] 1991). Sagi suggests that this formulation of the ethical stand negates the aspect of the subject's sovereignty. Sagi offers the concept of 'self-retreat', which describes an insistence on the following two vectors: 'the subject and the presence of what there is "there". These two vectors produce an open dialectic which seeks to simultaneously maintain both the subject as a sovereign-being and what is present there' (Sagi, A., 2012, p. 297).

Moments of exposure to the uncanny aspect of existence thus have the potential for emotional and ethical development, because they expose denied aspects of our being that arouse deep anxiety due to the otherness of the other, the foreign in the familiar self, sexuality and death.

The familiar and the uncanny in Agnon's story 'Friendship'

'Friendship' (Agnon, S., [1932] 1970, pp. 120–125) is one of the stories in an anthology titled *The Book of Deeds* by the Hebrew writer and Nobel prize laureate S.Y. Agnon and is considered to be one of his most daring modernistic works. This period in Agnon's writing is characterized by a surrealist dreamlike and uncanny style. In his book *The Mask of the European Novel and Story* the literary researcher Baruch Kurzweil considered *The Book of Deeds* to be 'the main key to the real understanding of Agnon the poet' (Kurzweil, B., [1973] 1987, pp. 69–89). Kurzweil recognized an original force in the writing of this anthology. He stressed the unique stylistic and experiential features of the stories included in this collection expressed in three central 'unreal' characteristics: a blurring of periods of time; a synoptic perception of place (i.e. a merging of places, for example between Jerusalem and a German city); and erasing the difference in principle between life and death. In these stories Kurzweil sees finely and skilfully drawn compositions. He identifies the sophisticated way in which Agnon is accepting and at the same time rejecting the confessional nature of these stories, emphasized by the fact that they are all written in the first-person singular:

> As if someone … wanted to emphasize in a mixture of seriousness and unfathomable irony: Be aware that here I will be writing about myself and only about myself and should you think that what is written is about me then you are nonetheless mistaken since I am different, completely different (ibid., p. 70).

Alongside the personal view, Kurzweil sees in all the stories included in *The Book of Deeds* part of the overall fabric of Agnon's writing, which lays stress on the tension between a loss of direction and the attempt to 'return home' to the bosom of God.

The literary researcher Ariel Hirschfeld rejects the idea that Agnon's *Book of Deeds* can be said to be 'surrealist' or 'uncanny'. He argues that these stories invite readers to spend time in their company and to surrender to them without them being classified by any unique characteristics. Nevertheless, while rejecting Kurzweil's proposed categorizations, Hirschfeld does recognize these stories' uniqueness both in relation to the body of Agnon's literary work as well as in relation to literary works in general. Similarly to Kurzweil, Hirschfeld point to aspects linked to the breakup of realism, which lend these stories their odd and special traits reminding one of the realms of the uncanny:

> The sequence of events which create the plot in [*The Book of Deeds*'] stories are not subject to the assumptions of realism; the dead come into the world of the living and interfere with their lives; concepts of time conflict and undermine the sense of continuity; and, most significant of all, the accepted notions of cause and effect give way to twists and turns that appear to be puzzling, occasionally frightening and always strange. Agnon mixes different kinds of representation in the stories ... and their continuity and endings are a long way off from what one would expect in the course of a realistic story (Hirschfeld, A., 2011, p. 201).

Agnon's tale 'Friendship' is a short story that conforms to the above characteristics. For example, the story begins by presenting self-restraint as an introduction to a confession written in the first-person singular and features a mixture of places (between a German city and Jerusalem[2]) and discontinuities of time. The story's reader is unsure about which of the events he is experiencing are real and which are imaginary, what is the result of circumstance and what is due to psychic collapse. Because the narrator speaks in the first person the readers are caught up in the same quandaries and share the same confusion. The entire story is steeped in the tension between a loss of direction and the attempt to return to the authority of a higher power. According to Kurzweil the supreme authority is God though one can think of it in other senses such as the return to the familiar, a return to the known or to the subject's sovereignty over his world.

Agnon's 'Friendship': a precis of the plot

The story begins with the return of the hero's wife from a trip. He accompanies her to the house of a neighbour, Mrs Klingel, because he doesn't want neighbours to bother them in their own house. Just as he becomes increasingly embittered by Mrs Klingel's search for respect and by the bother of being in the company of people with whom he has nothing in common, the hostess turns to his wife and says, 'You were away, my dear, and in the meantime your husband spent his nights in pleasure' (Agnon, S. Y., [1932] 1970, p. 121). Mrs Klingel then jokingly tells the now furious husband that, 'I am not telling your wife that pretty girls came to visit you' (ibid., p. 123). Exploding with anger the husband hurls abuse at her and they leave the house. He questions himself as to why he blew up in such a way and is troubled by his wife's gloom. After speaking to a writer acquaintance he realizes that his wife had left. Now deeply distressed he takes out a letter from his pocket, reads it and then tears it up. In that instant he forgets where he lives. His wife, meanwhile, has disappeared from sight. Panic stricken he searches for answers with a number of approaches and meetings linked to language (the meaning of which will be discussed in what follows). Finally he bumps into an old friend who is by then blind. The blind man tells his son that the hero is his friend and asks him to show him where his house is. The story ends with the hero mysteriously reporting that, 'I found myself standing by my home' (ibid., p. 78). And we the readers aren't really sure whether he actually wandered away from his house or whether the entire story was nothing other than his phantasy.

Reading the reader of 'Friendship'

At first glance: the slide to the uncanny

Agnon's story exposes the vivid tension between the familiar in its physical and metaphoric sense and the uncanny in the physical and psychic sense. The story line has the hero 'descending' from the pole of the familiar into the dread of the uncanny. When he loses his way he tries to anchor himself in language and reading. The more he rejects the suggestion offered by symbolic, narrative language so the language and the hero's psyche increasingly descend into a state of complete collapse. On the face of it the hero has fallen victim to the external *control* of the uncanny and all he wants is to return home. But I will seek to show how the uncanny element subverts *from within*, and the way in which its personification in the story sheds light on how the reading of literature confronts readers with the tension between the presence of the uncanny and the desire to feel 'at home' in both their outer and inner world.

At first the narrator is exceedingly happy that his wife has come back home and that he is whole again. But then the sense of home is so rapidly undermined in so many different ways, shattering the illusion that the familiar is based on a continuous, eternal and secure foundation. From that point on, the experience of the uncanny increasingly gains control of the character as an existential fear. This dread is characterized by profound confusion, undermining the most basic foundations of thought, such as knowledge of a geographical place, linguistic orientation, somatic stability, faith in the other and the faith of the subject in him.

At second glance: self-exile from the familiar (heimlich) to the uncanny (unheimlich)

A psychoanalytic perspective reveals the false impression of the hero's passive stance as he 'suddenly' finds himself in the very heart of the uncanny. Patients often tell their stories as if something had occurred 'externally' to them 'in reality', and they are merely subject to its mercy and responding to it. A patient can honestly describe an acute anxiety of losing the significant relationships in his life or the (transference) relations with the analyst. However, what he doesn't know is that the anxiety stems also from ambivalence, an inner force that hates the dependency, the neediness and the plenitude of the object, leading to harmful unconscious phantasies regarding these very relations. Similarly, a psychoanalytic reading of Agnon's story reveals that below the surface the hero's ambivalence towards the familiar and his unconscious contribution to the eruption of the uncanny are prominent.

From the very first sentence of the story it is evident that the hero is immediately ambivalent about his wife's return. Why should a man who is overjoyed by the return of his wife become instantly saddened by the prospect of neighbours arriving and why should he flout her return by encouraging her to immediately desert it? The same can be said about the severity of his response to the facetious accusation of infidelity, which might imply the existence of a personal indictment, evidencing an unconscious identification with the accusation.

As the hero stops on the street to talk to his acquaintance the writer, his wife who he'd been so happy to welcome back leaves him there. He pays no attention to the fact that she has disappeared. From the moment of her disappearance, he becomes amnestic to one specific detail: he cannot remember his home address. In other words, he is unable to remember how to get back to his wife. This amnesia is at the core of the phenomena of the uncanny. And yet Agnon invites his readers to experience this forgetfulness as an external happening, just as the hero experienced it. And as we now see, it turns out to have been a subterfuge of his psyche, which can be understood as an unconscious motivation, expressing his ambivalence towards returning home to the safe bosom of his wife. By his conscious words and efforts the hero hopes to remember the name of his street and return to his wife and home. However it is *his* psyche that keeps back from him the small piece of information that would have made this possible.

In Lacan's terms the story's hero is assailed by the intrusion of 'the real'. The mirror doesn't return to him the reflection he had expected; his life partner and his home. Instead it introduces him to the experience that nothing which is familiar and known can be taken for granted. The home, including the relations in it, is not a solid fact but rather a choice to be realized. It is not an existential given but rather a contingent possibility in which the subject dwells as a fortunate guest. The roof over his head that it provides is in doubt and given to being infringed.

The fate of language in the uncanny state: disassembling the narrative to its linguistic parts

The distress and anxiety of Agnon's hero gathers pace and the attempt to return home occurs via an illuminating encounter with language. However, as the hero tries to regain his secure state through language we witness a process of decline in the levels of symbolization used by him. At first he turns to the high, metaphorical level of symbolization when talking to a teacher and journalist, though in his formulation there is an evident sarcasm towards the writer: 'A Hebrew teacher who had gone abroad and come back rich; now he spent his time stuffing the periodicals with his verbiage' (Agnon, S.Y., [1932] 1970, p. 121).

A moment later the hero reads a letter in the same spirit of rejecting texts, and then he tears it up:

> While I was walking, I put my hand in my pocket and took out an envelope or a letter and stopped to read: 'The main trial of Job was not that of Job, but that of the Holy One, blessed be he. He, as it were, because He had handed over His servant Job to Satan's power. That is, God's trial was greater than Job's. He had a perfect and upright man and he placed him in the power of Satan.' After reading what I had written, I tore up the envelope and the letter, and scattered the pieces to the wind, as I usually do to every letter, sometimes before I read it and sometimes at the time of reading (ibid., pp. 121–122).

From that moment on the hero's way of talking about himself hints at him being in a state of confusion, perhaps even psychotic.[3]

> After I had done this, I said to myself: I must find my wife. My thoughts had distracted me and I had strayed from the road; I now found myself suddenly standing in a street where I had never been before. It was no different from all the other streets in the city, but I knew I had strayed to a place I did not know. By this time all the shops were locked up and little lamps shone in the windows among all kinds of commodities. I saw that I had strayed far from home, and

I knew I must go by a different road, but I did not know which (ibid., pp. 122–123).

The hero's attempts to orientate himself through the language continued to wane. At first he tries to be helped by Dr Rischel a philologist. He then once more puts his hand in his pocket trying to find the address on the envelope but remembers that he had torn that one up, and two other envelopes in his pocket turn out to be of no use because neither envelope carries the home address. He retreats into an attempt to move in an associative and arbitrary way amid the words in his mind and starts 'reciting aloud names of towns and villages, kings and nobles, sages and poets, trees and flowers, every kind of street name. Perhaps I could remember the name of my street – but I could not' (ibid., p. 121). A final attempt takes place in the post office, the domain of arbitrary regulation. But even there he doesn't find what he is looking for. At the post office he loses his temper and ends up shouting for someone to help to 'get to' his wife, all of this in the face of the jeers of a crowd of onlookers and a sniggering post office clerk who simply closed his window and left the premises.

The hero collapses as he faces up to infinite distance opened up between him, his house and his wife. In his attempts to find a remedy to his sense of a loss of reality, of confusion and the spread everywhere of the uncanny feeling, the hero turned to texts. Not a single one of these approaches returns him home either psychically or physically. Indeed, quite the reverse may have been the case. Agnon may be hinting that written words are confusing like the story of God's experiment of Job – go look in your reading for the way back home and you will discover that your house becomes increasingly distant. The uncanny defeats the familiar.

Coming back home

It is as if the final chord of the story is taken from a different musical scale. The language is replaced by relations, but in a way that is tenuous and hardly convincing. The person who finally helps the hero to return to his house is an old friend who, with the passage of time, has become blind. The hero addresses his old friend with a mixture of blame and love to which the friend responds with friendship dispatching his son to lead the lost hero back to his home. The blind man (through his son) opens the hero's eyes and he sees himself 'standing beside my home' (Agnon, S.Y., [1932] 1970, p. 125).

The irregularity of this final act is marked. In a way that is detached from what happened till now, it is a relationship that leads to reparation. Moreover, for the first time, there is no mention of language and reading as a means of returning a person to his home. On the contrary, from

Agnon's short and somewhat frightening story, it is clear that rather than reading – leading a person back to his house – it is the return to a position of affinity with the other (human or divine), which includes memory, yearning, nostalgia, guilt, affection, desire and solicitation. Having discovered that all the language people he had consulted turned out to be unreliable and all the attempts at reading were in vain, it is perhaps for the best that the hero's friend is blind, so that words do not disturb his eyes and that they remain open towards the familiar and the friendly in existence; and vis-à-vis human relations.[4] Although this is a reasonable interpretation of this development, a strict analysis of the gaps in the text casts a sceptical light on the romantic ending planted by Agnon at the end of the story as well as the romantic interpretation it prompts.

The vague phrasing 'and I saw myself standing beside my house' makes one wonder. The hero doesn't say 'I found my home' but rather 'I saw myself standing beside my home'. The formulation hints at the possibility that the hero never wandered far from the house and that his whole story is a wild illusion that suffers from the rejection of the inner and existential narrative embodied in his comment about his habit of tearing up letters either before or during his reading of them.

An echo of this idea of a journey that doesn't involve leaving the place is to be found in the way in which psychoanalytic treatment is conducted. As the patient tells his story to the analyst he doesn't move from his place, while all his inner voyages and his transference relations offer him a platform to observe his dialectic movements between the familiar (*heimlich*) and the uncanny (*unheimlich*). The analyst is supposed to forego the human inclination to focus on the external reality and instead to look inwardly into the patient's mind, and also into his own. The analyst and the patient attempt to work through the anxieties involved in the dialectic between the familiar and the uncanny in a way that will make it possible to weave an internal envelope as a replacement to the one that was torn in the course of the patient's psychic history. Like the hero in Agnon's story, the patient is unaware of the fact that he repeatedly tears his psychic envelopes and rejects the opportunities he has 'to return home', because his anxieties and defence mechanisms interfere. Only when the patient ceases to tear up the messages written in his free associations, does he begin to feel, in some cases for the first time, a profound sense of home and connectedness.

The letter: the interpretive key

Among the diverse barren linguistic attempts by the hero at 'finding his way', 'the letter' that he reads and tears up ranks above all as an interpretive key. First, it stands out among all other as the only detailed narrative in the story. The letter was written by the hero to himself and even sent to himself. Second, immediately after his reading of the letter the twofold tearing up takes place – of the letter and of the familiar state of the hero's consciousness. The hero doesn't convey to us his reflections about the letter's contents but through the act of tearing up and scattering the shreds he hints that he refuses to devote himself to what the letter aroused in him at the time of reading. Later it becomes clear that the tearing up of the letter was a fatal mistake as he realizes that had he not torn up the letter he would have known how to get back to his home, because his address was on that specific envelope.

In the reader's experience there is in this story an unsolvable duality of reading vs tearing up. On the one hand, the narrator does tell us what he has read; an interpretation of the biblical story of Job, one of the most dramatic stories about testing the power of belief and one of the great mythologies relating to human suffering. On the other hand, and in total opposition to this weighty subject matter, there is the act of tearing up and the disposing of the letter. Acting out in the service of the wish to undo and disregard, instead of scrutiny that might have led to insight. Just as if it had been hinted to the reader that he was now falling victim to a divine hoax that forces God to hand him over to Satan – a message that the reader chooses to ignore in a demonstrative way. The reading doesn't awaken the hero from his dormancy to see the connection between his quarrelsome and impulsive behaviour in relation to the existential anxiety rising within him. Rather it causes him to violently erase all trace of this acknowledgement by tearing up the letter. The question arises as to why the reader of the letter lost his way once he had torn it up.

The 'Agnonian'/literary envelope, in its concrete and functional sense, is reminiscent of the psychoanalytic concept of the 'psychic envelope' (Anzieu, D., 1987). Psychoanalysis assumes that the psyche is experienced by individuals as wrapped by a psychic envelope analogous to the skin wrapping the body. The psychic envelope supports the psychic structure and is even an indication of its quality.[5] In Agnon's story the reader pays no heed to the letter's text but stresses his desperate dependence on the envelope and the address on it as an external representation defining his identity and status in the world.

The role of the letter's contents is also dualistic. On the one hand, since it was created in the most private manner possible – the letter was written, mailed, read and destroyed by the hero, and was then forgotten – therefore its content is uncertain. On the other hand, this is a text that has more validity than any other, not only because it is the only text in the story containing a narrative content but also because it addresses a universal story – the biblical account and its interpretations. Let us explore the threat to the sense of the familiar that stems from the letter torn up by the hero.

The negation of the text by the act of tearing up the envelope and the letter conveys a powerful relation towards it. In his article 'Negation'

Freud argues that the negation of something suggests that it had previously had a psychic representation because otherwise it would not be possible to negate it (Freud, S., 1925).

What the story's hero wishes to negate by tearing up the letter can be interpreted in a number of ways: The negation of the letter can be seen as a representation of the confusion with respect to faith. In the context of the crisis of faith referred to by Kurzweil, at this dramatic moment in the story, the fracture, the doubt, the confusion, the reflections of heresy, are all intermingled. In the course of his attempt to return to his house, the hero is invited to the biblical story and the house of faith, including the shared and the private to be found there. Yet he turns his back on that invitation. The text's negation highlights an existential confusion. The text in the envelope touches on the general story of Job, while at the same time we are told by the hero that it is he who wrote 'the story' in the letter. So it would seem that the most personal and the most universal were written with the same ink. The reading confronts the reader with the possibility that his most internal and private experiences are represented by a universal language and common experience. A tension is aroused between the illusion of the reader being master of his mind, his body and his fate, and the uncanny element in his life that stems from the recognition that even what is most private for us is immersed in the universal human experience. This recognition undermines the sense of ownership and exclusivity because it bears witness to the encounter between the personal and the collective identity, and the encounter between individual and common language (Amir, D., 2014, p. 8). Every reading of a literary text bears witness to the fact that we are not the exclusive creators and masters of time, body, the other, life and death and the unconscious, nor of the language in which we express ourselves. And yet there is in this also a potential source of comfort. Reading of literature, and certainly reading of the story of Job, enables the reader who genuinely devotes himself to it to find shelter under the roof of humanity's shared fate.

Job's message

The choice of Job's story as the subject matter of the letter is, in fact, an interpretive key to the story. Job's story is a paradigmatic story about the familiar that turns into the uncanny, a story in which all sense of the obvious from any and all perspective is infringed, and that exposes its hero to indescribable suffering. Agnon's hero faces the crucial question: What is he to do with the message revealed to him as a reader? Will he fall back on primitive defences of denial and acting out? If he does so he will lose his ability to use symbolic language as a developmental capacity (Klein, M., 1930). Will he succeed in being aided by the text's tidings to engage in a depressive contemplation of life's fragility? Literature offers the reader a bridge over which he can cross from the position of denying the anxiety to a position of mourning and reconciliation with the circumstances of his existence. The psychoanalytic assumption is that out of a readiness to mourn the loss of false omnipotence with honesty and compassion an individual can reconstruct the sense of the familiar in his mind and in his life.

In the story 'Friendship' the hero, as the reader of the letter, rejects literature's tidings; he rejects the message of the letter he reads and is thus condemned to eternal exile in the realm of the uncanny. He fiercely repudiates the story according to which God may condemn Job, every Job, to a life of terrible suffering. This message arouses in him an unbearable existential anxiety. He retreats from language, from sanity, from the royal road and thus ignores the profound and threatening insight about a subject's existence in the world; that nothing is guaranteed and that the most deeply rooted alliance, such as that with his wife, and even with his god, cannot guarantee that he won't be handed 'into the hands of Satan'. The notion of 'Satan' can be understood in a number of different ways. Satan may appear as a transcendental force; it can derive from the power of the unconscious; or it can be experienced as a 'satanic' dimension of life, in the sense of the inherent suffering in a person's world. As the biblical story illustrates, we can all feel that we have been delivered into the hands of Satan as was Job as we face a host of situations involving suffering – the loss of loved ones, enfeeblement of the body, impoverishment, illness and death.

Because the story's hero refuses to linger in the text's transitional space and consider how it illuminates his existence, he finds himself oscillating between dissociation and psychic disintegration in the course of which he loses all that seemed familiar and safe: his memory, his way, the significant relationships in his life (to God and his wife) and his home.

One of the most distinctive consequences of the hero's attitude in Agnon's story is the profound loneliness to which he succumbs, which soon turns into total isolation. Indeed the reader who immerses himself in Job's letter, which is in many ways also literature's letter, comes face to face with loneliness as a fundamental aspect of human existence. Melanie Klein titled the last paper written in her lifetime 'On the Sense of Loneliness' (Klein, M., 1963). The paper suggests that loneliness is liable to lead to mechanisms of isolation and denial but that it can also lead to a recognition of the continuous existential tension between the sense of loneliness and the sense of connectedness manifested in the emotion of longing. Such a recognition makes it possible to bear the loneliness and move from it towards a significant and deep connection with the other where a part of its import lies in the latent dialectic between 'togetherness' and 'aloneness'. The reader's rejection of the text's tidings in Agnon's story results in his isolation from both his world and from himself. Because he is unwilling to recognize that 'aloneness' is an existential fundament he becomes isolated from himself and stripped of his means of association, which would have offered him the solace of 'togetherness' instead of the dictates of loneliness. In order to confront the psychic challenge involved in 'belonging' to his wife, his god and his fate, the reader has to acknowledge the inevitable tension between the familiar and the uncanny as an inherent part of belonging, where the longing is always a part.

There is an echo in Agnon's story 'Friendship' of the reader's bidirectional movement between the known and the foreign: As the reader is confronted by the anxiety of the foreign and uncanny, he turns to literature – the known and familiar. However, the reading of a known story in turn raises a renewed confrontation with a dialectic tension in the mind and in existence between the element of the familiar and that of the uncanny because reading is akin to meeting our reflection in the literary mirror. The literary text contains information that tells us that the uncanny is an inseparable part of the familiar.

The story invites the reader to transform their reading position, crossing over from reading literature through the prism of the paranoid-schizoid position that mobilizes psychic mechanisms in order to tear up the literary letter – to reading through the lens of the depressive position, a position that doesn't negate literature's letter but rather delves deeply into it, works it through and is enriched by it. Such a reader will feel the way in which the literary letter erodes the illusion that a person can be rooted and integrated in his surrounding and home, protected from violations of any kind. Literature exposes the reader to his ontological lack of confidence. It undermines the illusion he held about the infinite nature of the familiar in his mind and in his existence. But that is also literature's power. In the context of the protected space of reading, the reader may gradually find a more integrated and balanced psychic equilibrium between the familiar and the uncanny, because literature offers him an opportunity to contemplate and reflect on the terms of his life, including its partiality, sufferings and finality. It is then that he can also more fully appreciate and cherish beauty, true love and creative reparation (Roth, M., 2018). As is apparent from the accounts by Freud, Lacan and Heidegger, this moment opens an individual up to his broad existential experience and enables him to become an introspective being, genuinely present in his world. Reading is relevant to our lives from beginning to end because 'self-formation and self-creation are not a unique action; they are a life time's mission which only ends with a person's death' (Sagi, A., 2009, p. 21). Indeed, the recognition reflected in the pages of every book that nothing is obvious is liable to lead the reader into a life characterized by meaning and gratitude.

Notes

1 Hoffman's tale *The Sandman* ([1816] 1952) is the story of a young boy, Nathaniel, who, in his childhood was sent to bed with the warning that the Sandman would

come during the night and 'throw handfuls of sand in his eyes so that they jump out of his head all bleeding'. One evening Nathaniel witnesses an argument with the family lawyer, Coppelius, which leads him to believe that Coppelius is, in fact, non-other than the Sandman! In the course of the argument Nathaniel hears Coppelius/the Sandman call out 'here with your eyes!' and lets out a scream whereupon the Sandman attacks him. During another visit to the family home by the lawyer a year later Nathaniel's father is killed by an explosion. Now a young man, Nathaniel becomes engaged to be married and lives in another town. One day he encounters an itinerant optician by the name of Coppola who he believes is his childhood's phantom of horror when the optician offers him 'eyes' by which the optician actually meant a spyglass. He buys it and looks through the spyglass at the window of the house opposite where the mechanic is assembling a doll named Olympia. He believes that her eyes had been put in place by Coppola the Sandman. Nathaniel falls in love with Olympia and forgets all about his fiancée. One evening Coppola and the mechanic have an argument about their handiwork and the former throws Olympia's eyes dripping with blood in Nathaniel's direction, saying that Coppola had stolen them from Nathaniel. The young man becomes crazed and exclaims, 'Faster faster faster – rings of fire – rings of fire! Whirlabout, rings of fire round and round! Wooden doll, ho! Lovely wooden doll, whirl about' – a reminder of the event in which his father had died. Following a prolonged illness Nathaniel recovers. During an outing in town with his fiancée they climb up a high tower. Nathaniel looks through Coppola's spyglass and once more has a fit of madness and wants to throw his fiancée to the bottom of the tower, chanting 'Faster faster faster – rings of fire – rings of fire!' Among the people assembling below they see Coppelius, the sight of whom may have triggered Nathaniel's fit of madness. He flings himself to his death from the parapet and the Sandman disappears.

2 Kurzweil identifies the German city by way of the European tramcar and the street names of Humboldt Strasse and Westend Strasse (Kurzweil, B., [1973] 1987, p. 73).

3 This state is reminiscent of the way in which Freud described the uncanny state of mind, as he walked around a city in Italy, lost his way and found himself repeatedly returning to the same street.

4 The blind old man is also reminiscent of Tiresias, the blind prophet in Greek mythology. Among other legends surrounding him, Tiresias was able to see the future and the essence of things more clearly than those around him who were fully sighted. This ability of his to 'see' despite his blindness emphasizes the blindness of those with sight who are not able to see what is in front of them.

5 The motif of the psychic 'envelope' that functions as the psyche's protective container has been the subject of a number of canonical essays and books. Two of the most important of these are *The Skin-Ego* by Didier Anzieu (1987) and *Psychic Envelopes*, also by Didier Anzieu (1990).

References

Agnon, S.Y. [1932] (1970). Friendship. In: *Twenty-One Stories*. New York: Schocken Books.

Amir, D. (2014). *Cleft Tongue: The Language of Psychic Structures*. London: Karnac Books.

Anzieu, D. (1987). *The Skin-Ego*. London: Karnac.

Anzieu, D. (1990). *Psychic Envelopes*. London: Karnac.

Freud, S. (1909). Notes Upon a Case of Obsessional Neurosis. In: J. Strachey (Ed.) *The Standard Edition of the Complete Psychological Works of Sigmund Freud, Vol. X.* London: Hogarth Press, pp. 151–318.
Freud, S. (1919). The Uncanny. In: J. Strachey (Ed.) *The Standard Edition of the Complete Psychological Works of Sigmund Freud, Vol. XVII.* London: Hogarth Press, pp. 217–255.
Freud, S. (1920). Beyond the Pleasure Principle. In: J. Strachey (Ed.) *The Standard Edition of the Complete Psychological Works of Sigmund Freud, Vol. XVIII.* London: Hogarth Press, pp. 1–64.
Freud, S. (1925). Negation. In: J. Strachey (Ed.) *The Standard Edition of the Complete Psychological Works of Sigmund Freud, Vol. XIX.* London: Hogarth Press, pp. 233–240.
Freud, S. (1926). Inhibitions, Symptoms and Anxiety. In: J. Strachey (Ed.) *The Standard Edition of the Complete Psychological Works of Sigmund Freud, Vol. XX.* London: Hogarth Press, pp. 87–175.
Heidegger, M. [1927] (1996). *Being and Time.* Albany: State University of New York Press.
Hirschfeld, A. (2011). *Reading S. Y. Agnon.* Tel Aviv: Achuzat Bayit Books.
Hoffmann, E.T.A. [1816] (1952). *The Sandman.* London: Pan Books.
Klein, M. (1930). The Importance of Symbol Formation in the Development of the Ego. In: *Love, Guilt and Reparation and Other Works 1921–1945.* London: Vintage, pp. 219–232.
Klein, M. (1963). On the Sense of Loneliness. In: *Envy and Gratitude and Other Works 1946–1963.* London: Vintage, pp. 300–313.
Kurzweil, B. [1973] (1987). *The Mask of the European Novel and Story.* Jerusalem and Tel Aviv: Schocken.
Lacan, J. (1962–1963). Anxiety. In: J.A. Miller (Ed.) *Écrits: A Selection: Book X.* New York and London: W.W. Norton.
Levinas, E. [1961] (1991). *Totality and Infinity.* Dortrecht: Kluwer Academic.
Pearl, J. (2011). *A Question of Time Between Philosophy and Psychoanalysis.* Ramat Gan: Bar Ilan University Press.
Roth, M. (2018). True Love as the Love of Truth. *Psychoanalytic Perspectives,* 15, pp. 186–198.
Sagi, A. (2009). *The Human Voyage to Meaning: A Philosophical-Hermeneutical Study of Literary Works.* Ramat Gan: Bar Ilan University Press.
Sagi, A. (2012). *Facing Others and Otherness: The Ethics of Inner Retreat.* Tel Aviv: HaKibbutz HaMeuchad.

Chapter 12

The dialectic between the symbolic order and disorder

Reading literature raises the reader's inner struggle between two opposing forces to the surface: the force that seeks inner order and sensible existence and the force that seeks to subvert that order both because of the unconscious' traits and because of the unanticipated and unorganized aspects of existence itself. Reading is revealed as accomplishing an action and its reverse: it arranges and dismantles the symbolic order, exposes the madness and organizes it at one and the same time. It thus offers a transformational space for the internal psychic equilibrium between these two opposing forces.

The symbolic order and disorder in a poem by Yair Horowitz

I shall exemplify the dialectic between the symbolic order and disorder with one of the poems from Yair Horowitz's collection of poems *Caged Bird*,[1] by exploring the reading experience of the poem's two characters – one of whom reads a poem aloud to his friend.

Fluttering Corridors

In the spare-time between awakening and breakfast
My neighbor in room and illness (a Jew
Of Czech origin and Hungarian accent)
Recites in my ears
A poem by a poet who had tuberculosis
And died at the age of 24.
Quiescence and comfort in poetry.
A day will come when our lines
Will also bring quiescence and comfort.
So simple is the thought
And the sentiment so inexplicable
    (Horowitz, Y., 1987, p. 41).[2]

The poem's opening lines are very detailed and clearly set in terms of time and space. The character who reads the poem (in Horowitz's poem) is a man in hospital. He shares his room with another sick person who is described by his religious affiliation, roots and accent. These depictions link us more closely to the character so that we are able to get to know him more intimately. They share a room in one of the hospital's wings – not dead (as is the poet whose poem they read) but also not enjoying the indifference towards the soma, which is the privilege of the able bodied. Sagi notes that 'illness has an ontological significance ... in the individual's standing in existence, in his coping with the question of existence' (Sagi, A., 2009, p. 103). The disease raises the question of existence because it is inevitably a station between life and death. Even if the illness is located close to the central station with the sign 'life' hoisted above it and even if it is close to the final station above which the signpost 'death' flutters in the wind, it signifies one way or another the potential exhaustion of the body until its finality. The poem's heroes are thus forced to be aware of the body's burden and its limitations.

The poem's narrator relates that his roommate, with whom he also shares illness and the intermediate station, is reciting to him a poem by a tubercular poet who died at the age of 24. This exquisitely sensitive moment contains two pivotal components – reading poetry and knowledge of the poet's death. It is a moment that is shared between two and, at the same time between three partners. One patient reads a poem to another patient, which was written by a third patient – a poet now dead. Since both these readers are ill, there is an affinity between them and the illness suffered by the poet that led to his death. In the context of transference relations of us readers, knowing that we are also reading a poem written by the poet Horowitz, a further affinity is created between the poet Horowitz and the tubercular poet – the potential illness and death of both of them. It is interesting to note that Horowitz lost his father when he was only 8 years old and he himself suffered from heart disease. Sickness and death constituted key elements of his poetry.

After directly referring to death, the seventh line of the poem marks a change as the narrator's voice, which until now spoke in the first person, becomes blurred just as we reach the first piece of emotive evidence. It is not personally articulated, nor subjectively. The narrator doesn't say, 'I felt quiescence and comfort from the poem's words'. Instead he adopts an impersonal position and describes/declares a general rule: 'Quiescence and comfort in poetry'.

In the following two lines the narrator refers to one of the reasons why poems are the source of quiescence and comfort. It is because poetry outlives the poet: 'A day will come when our lines / Will also bring quiescence and comfort.' Poetry is immortal and eternal. It facilitates an imaginary connection between the mortal poet and those who read his poetry after his death. Poetry makes it possible for the poet to continue being a good object for his readers even after he has gone, when his words will induce quiescence and comfort.

Immediately after that, in the last two lines, a mystery: 'So simple is the thought / And the sentiment so inexplicable' – the psychic equilibrium in all its glory: On the one hand, the supposedly simple thought, while on the other hand, there is the inexplicable sentiment. Conceivably this line is there to also explain the earlier line – 'Quiescence and comfort in poetry'. The inexplicable sentiment felt by the hospitalized patient who faces the stations of life moving inexorably along a one-way track from birth towards death is comforted by the simple form of the text. Formed lines, rhyming, rhythm, stanzas, the aesthetics of poetry, of a short story, of a novel. Simple comfort, simple thought, and yet the sentiment demands explanation.

The symbolic order vs the psychic and existential disorder

The mind constantly copes with the disorderly boundaries surrounding a subject's emotional and psychic aspects – boundaries that threaten to spread and expand: nameless anxieties, fear of death, sexual urges, the pain of solitude, dependency, envy, exhilarating love, tormenting guilt, shame, pride, self-doubt, excitement. All these and others appear in the mind undefined, shapeless, so that there is no way of knowing where they come from or where they are heading; who their internal narrator is and how and when they will turn to the next emotion. There is a ceaseless struggle between the individual attempting to control the boundaries on the one hand, and the boundaries that control him on the other; between their autonomous and dominating appearance and the attempt to contain them, understand them and use them in the formation of the self.

In contrast to the boundless features of the unconscious, literature offers the reader order and form. First the external shape: a poem such as that of the tubercular poet's poem and Horowitz's poem is printed on a page. The spaces between words and lines are fixed. The poem has a clear beginning and end. It is written from the top to the bottom of the page and the collection of poems is arranged to run from the beginning of the book to its end. The author, the publisher, the year of publication and where the book was published are all known. A network of comforting, clear-cut features.

The features of the literary or poetic character are also constant whereas the character of the reader is always changing. This is part of the solace that appears in the poem – inviting the reader to the illusion of the coherence of the self, embodied in the literary happening. For a moment he can live the illusion that like the literary hero he too is constant and cohesive in terms of his identity and characteristics.

Creativity and the symbolic order: a subversive view

Postmodernist thinkers such as the French philosopher Michel Foucault cast doubt on 'the problematic nature of the word "work" and the unity it designates' (Foucault, M., 1969, p. 302). Foucault raises a difficult question by asking, 'What, for instance, were Sade's papers before he was consecrated as an author? Little more, perhaps, than rolls of paper on which he endlessly unravelled his fantasies while in prison' (ibid). This line of thinking suggests that the literary work is perceived as a consolidated unit with a beginning and an end only for the sake of convenience and appearances, but that in fact every written text is always delineated by an artificial contour and is a part of a longer, endless text. The text is also in correspondence with a host of other texts with which it is engaged in an endless intertextual dialogue, or as Foucault termed it in 'transcursive position' (ibid., p. 309). In Roland Barthes' radical definition, even the author of the text is 'dead' in the sense that 'the writer can only imitate a gesture forever anterior, never original' (Barthes, R., [1967] 1977, p. 4), because it too is the product of other texts that it has incorporated and that invade the sovereignty of his own text. Thus postmodernist thinkers express 'the murmur of indifference: "What matter who's speaking?"' (Foucault, M., 1969, p. 314), and seem to swap the discussion about the 'author's work' with discussion of 'discursive practices' (ibid., p. 299).

This description stems from the morphological power of the work, which it emphasizes also by a process of elimination. Whether or not we agree with them, all these 'illusions' gain their power from the form of the text that is organized, defined and associated with the author. When a reader picks up a book he exchanges the complex and unravelled field of the internal world with a perfectly clear and well-defined field: a book that has a name and title, a date of publication and a publisher who takes responsibility for its morphology and linguistic accuracy.

To return to our example, the formal construction of the text in Horowitz's poetry is thus twofold. First, there is the outward form. Second, there are the thematic rules relating to a poem or a story, stemming from the deepest regions of the mind. While the psyche's story is complex, obscure and constantly changing, the character of the tubercular poet remains unaltered. Even if the poet is describing an emotional confrontation, as stormy as it may be, his description will still appear in a certain form and succession and so it will stay. Though the meanings the reader attributes to it will change, the singular poetic choice made by the poet establishes the emotional content in a firmly set narrative sequence, including emphasized meanings and a given resolution. To a great extent its path is also fixed, in that it moves from entanglement to resolution within the framework of a plot that has a beginning and an end, as against the life of the psyche whose 'plots' remain unresolved while the individual is still alive and, fortunately, do not crystalize into a fixed form. All of these are captured by Horowitz's words 'quiescence and comfort in poetry, 'So simple is the thought / And the sentiment so inexplicable'.

Literature undermines the order

Alongside the organized dimension described above, a closer scrutiny sheds light on reading from an opposite angle in which literature undermines the order, facilitating a temporary visit to the chaotic realms of madness and the loss of borders. The literary formalization of a text does not, at first, expose the dialectic struggle between order and the breach of that order, between reason and madness, which the written work raises in the reader's mind. After all, at the same time as the reader is invited to share the illusion of the order of the morphological and narrative structure, he is also invited to project into it – like the patient does into the analytic container – his internal world over which in daily life he meticulously maintains order and control. The conscious by definition never gets to know its unconscious and so is always exposed to the tension between the act of ordering and the chaotic bubbling beneath the surface. Reading forgoes the good order in two senses: First, the text itself is an unknown other and we devote ourselves to an encounter with it without taking control of its course. Second, the involvement of the unconscious in the process of reading also plunges into the world that is below the organized surface of the conscious. This too is one of the reasons why we become excited whenever a book sweeps us far beyond our daily psychic and practical routines.

Five literary characteristics that arouse the dialectic struggle between order and disorder

In Horowitz's text one can find five meaningful expressions of the dialectic struggle between the symbolic order and disorder (Felman, S., 1977, pp. 94–207): the prologue; reading as a repetitive event; transference relations breaching the textual order; the absent and the unconscious; and the absence of an external vantage point.

I. The prologue

The prologue lends the text a context offering readers an opportunity to orientate themselves before delving into the text's 'situation' as they would into a situation in real life. The reader enters a specific location – a room in the hospital – and time – during a period of illness and immediately after breakfast. The narrator's roommate reads the poem to his neighbour and personifies a split of the character of 'the reader' into two parts. The part that reads and the part that listens to what he reads. This split is reminiscent of the childhood experience of listening to the story being read by the parent to their child in a period in life when the confusion between reality and imagination is at its height and the intra-literary reality mingles with the parent–child reality, all fused with a welter of instincts, imagination and feelings.[3]

The prologue also reveals to the reader the identity of the text's authoritative speakers. For instance, in the case under review here, the Hungarian roommate tells the narrator that the poem he was reading him is that of a tubercular Czech poet who died at the age of 24.

As the literary researcher Yael Renan shows, one of the ways of defamiliarizing the familiar is by 'removing or undermining an organizing framework' (Renan, Y., 1973, p. 346), such as undermining the prologue by an unanticipated continuation of the story itself. As Renan notes, 'When the representation is habitual and autonomous, the signifier becomes 'transparent'. The dismantling of the autonomous connection between the signifier and the signified defamiliarizes both' (ibid., p. 347). The prologue representing 'the hospital' arouses in the reader of the poem a familiar signified – beds, helplessness, passivity and the erasure of personal characteristics such as name and cultural capital (education, intellect, style of speech and dress etc.). However, instead of this what we get is the unexpected sequel, a nameless patient reads a poem to another patient. The fate of the Czech poet whose poem the roommate reads to his friend is the habitual fate of those who belong to the world of hospitals – a tubercular person who died. But suddenly this becomes mixed up with poetry, wrecking the good order that separates art from disease, poetry from body. As we have seen with the entry of the 'real order' into the 'imaginary order' and the intrusion of the uncanny into the familiar, 'the removal out of the normal, natural and anticipated domain leads to the removal of everything concealing reality from us' (ibid., p. 343). The prologue is terra firma or the prop, the symbolic order, the reading. The undermining of these props in what follows leads to the revelation of the meaning.

2. Reading as a repetitive event

Felman reminds us that in every text the narrator is recounting 'a story that has already happened', and that in this sense we are, on the one hand, captive of the illusion of participation in a live and emergent moment and, on the other hand, participants in a repetitive feature that the work triggers. Felman stresses that the reader doesn't reflect on the text from outside but is rather an inseparable part of it and acts it out (Felman, S., 1977, pp. 94–207). According to Felman no one remains outside the literary text. This is so of the writer, the narrator, the heroes, the literary critic and the reader. They are all active participants in its realization and the establishment of its meaning (ibid.).

In Horowitz's poem one can detect a number of repetitions. The tubercular poet wrote a poem about an event or thought that passed through his awareness. He wrote it down and repeated it in a poem. The neighbour who recites it must have first read the poem to himself and then returned and read it to the narrator. The narrator in turn creates another repetition by recounting to us the experience of listening to the poem and the thoughts and feelings that the reading aroused in him. We the readers are next in line. We listen to the narrator and look into the repetitive hall of mirrors he has revealed to us. According to Felman the moment we become aware of the fact that there are differing readings of a text, the illusion of it recounting a coherent event is lost and it is exposed as a chain of narrative voices, a chain of its readings. Every reader of the tubercular poet's poem charges it with different meanings, different emphases, infuses it with different projections of his psyche, reads it at a different moment in time and on a different occasion. The subjective meaning changes his reading. The emphasis on the act of reading as part of the impact of the text lessens the sovereignty of the text as a constant that creates clarity and thus brings 'quiescence and comfort'. It is for good reason that the narrator testifies that the reading is accompanied by an 'inexplicable emotion'. If the emotion were to be explained there would be no place for the reader's subjectivity. His creativity in relation to the text gives him the privilege and perhaps even the obligation to infuse it with a meaning of his own and so, in Sartre's words, to 'create it again' (Sartre, J.P., [1948] 1988, p. 40).

Felman argues that an unowned narrative of a story resembles the structure of

> the unconscious, itself a sort of obscure knowledge which is, precisely, authorless and ownerless, to the extent that it is a knowledge which no consciousness can master or be in possession of, a knowledge which no conscious subject can attribute to himself, assume as his own knowledge (Felman, S., 1977, p. 128).

The neighbour who reads the tubercular poet's poem, the narrator who reads the poem 'second hand' and we, the readers of Horowitz's poetry are all part of the narrative of the story so that the narrative has no owner and master. From a psychoanalytic perspective repetitiveness has three crucial aspects, which appear in Horowitz's text, two of which have been referred to in other contexts in this chapter: blind repetition compulsion; from repetition to reparation (Durban, J. and Roth, M., 2013, p. 28) and afterwardness (*nachtraglich*) (Laplanche J. and Pontalis, J.B., 1973, loc. 3029).

There are three forms of literary repetitions:

Blind repetition compulsion

Freud coined the term repetition compulsion to explain the inclination of the unconscious drive, which impels an individual to repeatedly trigger an experience involving pain linked to repressed emotions. The recurrent reading of a poem is another way of being repeatedly in touch with the element arousing fear from which it is impossible to become detached both because of its fascination and because of the individual's unconscious need to control it via repeated encounters. Thus, for example, through the recurrent reading of the verse of the cited poem, the three patients in Horowitz's creation return time and again to coping with the fear of death.

Felman argues that the reader conducts within himself a 'blind repetition' of the text. According to Felman the transference effect of the reading is one in which the reader constitutes a signifier to the text's signifier. He participates in a live drama and he himself is an actor unconsciously trapped by the rhetorical power of the text. This is an essential part in the text's rhetorical force (Felman, S., 2003, p. 31). The idea emphasizes the compulsive aspect of the repetition that occurs during reading and that is not yet transformative but solely repetitive.

Repetition as an opportunity for reparation

The return to the source of inner anxiety through reading enables the reader to search for psychic and creative gateways to reparation in the protected space of the text that he had been unable to confront directly. The patients sharing the room and readings of the poem meet up with their fear of death but do so this time through relating to art, to the meaning of existence symbolized within the poem's words, as well as to the immortality of words and art as means of transcendence beyond the finitude of the body. We know for sure that the character who hears the poem read by his neighbour links it to death from the one piece of information we are given: his roommate points out that the poet was ill and died young. Such a return to anxiety via a poem exemplifies the transformation enabled by way of repetition compulsion. Reading helps one to experience and explore new ways of reconciliation, rehabilitation, meaning, creativity and reparation in the world of the individual. In this sense the transformation that occurs while reading may also serve as an opening to ethical development because it distances the compulsive repetition of the 'negative' drives in favour of a search for benign ways of achieving reparation.

Retrospective repetition and afterwards repetition

Understanding the reading of the poem as a repetitive event also means that the act of reading involves an admixture of periods of time, since the reading in the present arouses the relevant moments of reading in the reader's past – be it in his psyche or in the reality of his life. Two crucial ways of mixed times occur during reading, each of which mobilizes a psychological transformation.

The retrospective aspect allowed by the repetitions of the reading experience is exemplified, for instance, in the way that the sick character in the hospital who reads the tubercular poet's poem gains, through the poetic work, a *retrospective look* at his illness, his attitude to life and death, to others and to himself. Every reading reconstructs aspects of the reader's inner and real world on two levels. First, there are repetitions of events on the narrative level – loves, infidelities, losses, hopes and so on. Variations of these subjects, which the reader meets in the literary work, occurred in the course of his life. Moreover, they had already appeared in his conscious and in his unconscious. Second, there is a repetition on the level of the hero's psychic mechanisms, which reflect mechanisms activated in the reader's psyche, such as denial, projection, envy, gratitude and so on. From both these perspectives, reading by its very nature is a recurring event that highlights what has already happened. That is its great power. Due to the power of the recurrence of the events in the relatively protected space of the literary work, the text is likely to facilitate a reading *de novo* of events in the past and, psychic or real-life events, and retrospectively endow them with new meaning.

The second aspect of repetition involves an 'afterwardness' transformation. Felman stresses that the poem is a repetitive event that has already occurred and one to which we return and now encounter in a new developmental phase. Following this idea, we can borrow Freud's radical idea of *'nachtraglichkeit'*, translated as 'deferred action' or 'afterwardness', which suggests that old events may be rewritten and gain new meaning not only in retrospect, but also as if re-experienced due to a new event, which illuminate aspects of the older event that could not be felt and recognized at the time it was first experienced (Freud, S., 1918). The same phenomena can be applied to the reading situation in which also

> experiences, impressions and memory-traces may be revised at a later date to fit in with fresh experiences or with the attainment of a new stage of development. They may in that event be endowed not only with a new meaning but also with psychical effectiveness (Laplanche, J. and Pontalis, B., 1973, loc. 3032–3034).

The poetic experience has also the power to create a fusion between inner time periods. In the event of a transformative reading we return to ourselves from the reading in a way that differs from how we began the reading – either as a former experience is rewritten as traumatic or as liberating. In both cases one can imagine that past experiences that were consumed by excessive anxiety can borrow the poet's pen and afterwards rewrite them anew and differently. Sometimes the previous impression of our fate changes in light of the freedom created in the textual space. So not only does the reading experience shed a new light retrospectively, it also transforms our memory-traces 'afterwardly'.

3. The reader's transference undermines the textual order

Shoshana Felman argues that the acting out of the unconscious is always an acting out of a story. In this sense all the textual stories and narratives hint at the transferential structure:

> Both senses of the term 'transference' in Freud's text – transference ... as the repetitive structural principle of the relation between patient and analyst, and transference as the rhetorical function of any signifying material in psychic life, as the movement and the energy of displacement through a chain of signifiers (Felman, S., 1977, p. 137).

A variety of transference relations are activated in the context of reading. When we carefully listen to the poetic text during this fragile moment of morning in hospital we find ourselves in a room of mirrors where 'the movement and the energy of displacement' imply the mobilization of various transference relations. The diversity of ways of reading a poetic situation stems, in effect, from the multiplicity of our transference relations; towards one character – the narrator; towards two characters – the narrator and his roommate; towards three characters – the narrator, his roommate and the tubercular poet who died young; towards four characters – the narrator, the roommate, the tubercular poet and the poet Yair Horowitz. Every one of these characters offers readers the opportunity for different transference relations and at every moment of reading a different aspect of transference is activated according to the way the literary story meets our unconscious phantasies and our internal relations.

For example, the narrator might listen to the poem's reciter like an anxious child listening to a poem being read to him by a wise father who's already 'read' the life story's ending (the death of the poet) and softens his message with rhymes. At the same time the narrator can also arouse the inner child in the reader who is worried about his father, while this time he agrees to be the object who takes care of his father's anxiety, which is contained by the act of reading, and so achieves quiescence and comfort. The roommate, here in the position of the 'random other', can also arouse different transference relations. For a moment he can be the reader's elderly father at his bedside. At another moment he can represent that same reader's enlightened father who endows him with his goodness and reinforces his resilience in the presence of life and death. This profundity and richness of transformational events is in marked contrast to the poem's 11 lines, which are ordered, structured, answer to the rules of scale, rhythm and rhyme, in which even their breach is intentional and ordered. A part of the fascination for the literary creation lies in the resemblance between the reading and the psychic experience – both struggle between the orderliness and richness in an attempt to turn the feverish movement of unconscious phantasies, drives, doubts and transference relations into a story that possesses order and logic.

4. The 'absent' vs the 'unreadable' in Horowitz's text

As with the purloined letter and Aspern's lost papers, so the contents of the tubercular poet's poem that we are told about in Horowitz's poem is actually excluded from the text. The textual absent functions as a constant representation of the concealed unconscious and of the unknown aspects of life in general, at the end of which is 'the great unknown' – death. We know that it will come but know nothing of its nature. The dead poet mentioned in Horowitz's poem is in the position of 'the one who knows', since he is, after all, both a poet and dead. However his knowledge is concealed, excluded from the poem. Thus, 'the unreadable' part in life and in the text gains representation. But there are two meanings to the unreadable: one is that it is out of sight and reach, and the other is that it cannot be ordered and understood. Literature introduces the reader to both meanings. As the writer Vladimir Nabokov noted, 'it is chaos, and to this chaos the author says: "go!"'(Nabokov, V., 1980, p. 2).

The words of the fictive father in Pirandello's play *Six Characters in Search of an Author* clarify why disorder subverts the act of reading:

> The father: I say that to reverse the ordinary process may well be considered a madness: that is, to create credible situations, in order that they may appear true. But permit me to observe that if this be madness, it is the sole *raison d'être* of your profession, gentlemen. (The actors look hurt and perplexed) (Pirandello, L., 1921, p. 9).

Shoshana Felman asks:

> How can we read the unreadable? This question ... grounded in contradiction, it in fact subverts its own terms: to actually read the unreadable, to impose a meaning on it, is precisely not to read the unreadable as unreadable, but to reduce it to the readable, to interpret it as if it were of the same order as the readable ... Our task would perhaps then become not so much to read the unreadable as a variant of the readable, but, to the very contrary, to rethink the readable itself, and hence, to attempt to read it as a variant of the unreadable ... to ask not what does the unreadable mean, but how ... in what way do the letters escape meaning (Felman, S., 1977, pp. 142–143).

The chain of signifiers positioned like a column of soldiers on the poet's page or across an entire book is entwined with the emotional, the psychic, the unconscious – the very essence of which excludes them ever being fully explained. Felman posits that the deep meaning of the text lies in the dialectic between the explicable and the inexplicable parts of the literary text, which parallels the dialectic between the conscious and the unconscious. This is not a dialectic between equals, nor is it intended to decipher the unconscious. Rather it draws its significance from the various levels of order in the psyche as well as in the literary work.

The elusive meaning is revealed as an important part of the general meaning. The attempt to lend meaning to something that eludes meaning, to impose discipline on the text, resembles attempting to impose the conscious upon the unconscious or the symbolic order on the 'real' order.

Every poetic or literary text outlines an artificial contour taken from a bigger story, whose borders are always limitless, stretching all the way to infinity. We too, the readers of Horowitz's poem, are unknowingly exposed to many other meanings that elude us, a phenomenon that is of crucial significance for both the text's characters as well as for the poem's readers.

The gap between the knowledge and meaning that are comprehensible to the reader and the variety of meanings and details eluding him is expressed in the real and concrete layers of knowledge that are absent from the literary text, as well as in the psychic and existential layers that are 'there' but can't be captured. So, for example, we will never know what else happened between the time the patients in hospital awoke and had breakfast. We will never know what the roommates looked like, what their illnesses were, what was the colour[4] of their pyjamas or when they were supposed to be discharged from the hospital. We will never know what happened prior to the poem's prologue or what happens once the last line has been penned. But these are just the unknown concrete details. These are not the only things to remain permanently unknown: we will never know what their emotions were, what it is they yearned for, what their internalized object relations are or what anxieties keep them awake at night and swallow up their days. And even had an especially assiduous and ambitious author wanted to tells us everything he knows and was prepared to devote his whole life to such a venture, he would still be unable to convey to us what is 'written' in his unconscious, or tell us about his future, his sense of death or explain the riddles of existence that are as mysterious to him as they are to us all.

5. The absence of a vantage point beyond the literary text

Literature has no exterior. It has no external fulcrum to lean on; no tower that can be climbed which is not embedded in the text being read by the reader, exactly in the same way as it is impossible to try and locate oneself outside of language and separate yourself from it (Felman, S., 1977).

We read Horowitz's poem in the same way as the patient in the poem reads the tubercular poet's verse. And just as he is a captive so we too are captives of the text's impact on him as well as on us. We all play a part of the text. As Sartre notes in his book *What Is Literature?* the extent of dedication to the text is a matter of individual choice but it always involves an act of generosity of gifting oneself to the text.

In Sartre's words:

> Thus, reading is an exercise in generosity, and what the writer requires of the reader is not the application of an abstract freedom but the gift of his whole person, with his passions, his prepossessions, his sympathies, his sexual temperament, and his scale of values. Only this person will give himself generously; freedom goes through and through him and comes to transform the darkest masses of his sensibility. And just as activity has rendered itself passive in order for it better to create the object, conversely, passiveness becomes an act; the man who is reading has raised himself to the highest degree. That is why we see people who are known for their toughness shed tears at the recital of imaginary misfortunes; for the moment they have become what they would have been if they had not spent their lives hiding their freedom from themselves (Sartre, J.P., [1948] 1988, p. 58).

The romantic nature of Sartre's description of the act of reading suggests that the reader is a willing participant, as if his reading is entirely based on acts of freedom and generosity. But from the moment the reader whose devotion to the text is based on generosity submits himself to it, he finds himself compelled to act it out with no possibility of remaining on the outside. He has already become involved in the text, and now it is no longer solely because of his generosity. From the moment he applied himself to the reading he also became involved in ways over which he has no control, ways that are opened up within him by the echo of his internal object relations and his transference relations that have already assumed a life of their own. Furthermore, as we saw earlier, the reader is exposed to the difficult and troubling experience of the uncanny as an inseparable aspect of literature's textual material. Thus, aspects of his unconscious elude any form of salvation offered by the symbolic order. This is one of the hidden and threatening messages embedded in the act of reading. The reader has to face the fact that he is not the master of his inner world (the 'sentiment so inexplicable') and is not the sovereign of his fate. At the very same time, this lends the reader a unique opportunity to become familiar with these characteristics in his existence and to gradually open himself up to the meaning of what eludes meaning. The reading experience makes 'the stranger' gradually accepted as a part of the family and constitutes a significant part of the reader's grounded view of himself in his life's journey.

The text's orderly form appears on two levels: The first is its formal shape and the second, the narrative order of its content, which has a beginning, a middle and an end that don't change their positions. It has an inner causality and regularity. Often it even has a measure of justice and compassion about it, arrangements that are better than those written for us by the creator of life's texts. The language's symbolic order alongside the morphological and narrative order of the poem, the story or the novel that lends the reader a degree of *quiescence and comfort*, can be likened to a small well-kept house encircled by a fine fence. However, as we 'read' into it and explore it carefully, we realize that we also become exposed to the other side of the dialectic. We know nothing about the depths of the ground upon which the literary 'house' rests, nothing about its surroundings and its landscapes, all of which are beyond delineation. When we look into the structure through the psychoanalytic prism it unveils the ever-dynamic and in many ways chaotic life beneath the surface of the orderly lines of words. Literature's power lies, among other things, in that it exposes the reader to the existential dialectic tension and struggle that we are constantly faced with, between the 'fine order' of literature on the one hand, and the variability and constant movement in psychic life on the other hand, represented in the literary work, mobilized by it as well as lending it meaning. Included within this are the meanings of all aspects that refuse to be reduced and confined by the symbolic order.

Notes

1 In Yair Horowitz's anthology of poems *Caged Bird*, there are 18 poems identified by the order in which they appear in the cycle.
2 Translated by Shulamit Lapid.
3 An illustration of this childhood experience is to be found in Sartre's book *The Words*. Jean Paul the child is amazed to discover that the characters his mother had been telling him about 'were to be found in the book': 'She raised her eyes from her sewing: "What would you like me to read to you, darling? The Fairies?" I asked incredulously: "Are the Fairies in there" ... I simply could not believe that someone had composed a whole book to tell about that episode of our profane life, which smelled of soap and eau de Cologne' (Sartre, J.P., [1964] 1981, pp. 45–46).
4 A unique attempt at achieving congruence between the broad parameters of life, the unconscious and the literary text, was undertaken by Marcel Proust. He devoted decades of his life to the writing of *In Search of Lost Time*, and as he testifies in the book: 'I understood that all the material of a literary work was in my past life, I understood that I had acquired it in the midst of frivolous amusements, in idleness, in tenderness and in pain, stored up by me without my divining its destination or even its survival, as the seed has in reserve all the ingredients which will nourish the plant. Like the seed I might die when the plant had developed and I might find I had lived for it without knowing it' (Proust, M., 1927, loc. 49037).

References

Barthes, R. [1967] (1977). The Death of the Author. In: S. Heath (Ed.) *Image – Music – Text: Essays*. New York: Hill & Wang, pp. 142–148.

Durban, J. and Roth, M. (Eds) (2013). *Melanie Klein: Essential Papers*. Tel Aviv: Bookworm.

Felman, S. (Ed.) (1977). *Literature and Psychoanalysis: The Question of Reading: Otherwise*. Baltimore, MD and London: John Hopkins University Press.

Felman, S. (2003). *Writing and Madness*. Standford, CA: Stanford University Press.

Foucault, M. (1969). What Is an Author? In: D.B. Bouchard (Ed.) *Language, Counter-Memory, Practice: Selected Essays and Interviews*. Ithaca, NY: Cornell University Press, pp. 113–138.

Freud, S. (1918). From the History of an Infantile Neurosis. In: J. Strachey (Ed.) *The Standard Edition of the Complete Psychological Works of Sigmund Freud, Vol. XVII*. London: Hogarth Press, pp. 1–124.

Horowitz, Y. (1987). *Caged Bird*. Tel Aviv: HaKibbutz HaMeuchad.

Laplanche, J. and Pontalis, J.B. (1973). *The Language of Psychoanalysis*. London: Hogarth Press [Kindle Edition].

Nabokov, V. (1980). *Lectures on Literature*. (Ed.) F. Bowers. New York: Harcourt Brace Jovanovich.

Pirandello, L. (1921). *Six Characters in Search of an Author*. Mineola, NY: Dover Books.

Proust, M. (1927). *In Search of Lost Time: Complete Edition*. New York: Modern Library [Kindle Edition].

Renan, Y. (1973). Hearing the Waves' Sound: Defamiliarization: Reviving the Reality Perception in the Literary Work. *Siman Kria*, 2, pp. 341–361.

Sagi, A. (2009). *The Human Voyage to Meaning: A Philosophical-Hermeneutical Study of Literary Works*. Ramat Gan: Bar Ilan University Press.

Sartre, J. [1948] (1988). *What Is Literature?* Cambridge, MA: Harvard University Press.

Sartre, J. [1964] (1981). *The Words*. New York: Vintage Books.

Chapter 13
The dialectic between 'continuous doing' and 'emergent being'

Introduction

Reading literature expresses and arouses the *psychic-equilibrium* between the tendency for 'continuous doing' and that for 'emergent being'. Continuous doing enables us to construct our lives – to respond to bodily needs, to encounter the actual world, to survive, to learn and to form both practical and mental links and relations.

Emergent being, on the other hand, involves an individual's openness to novelty, to the unknown and to the ever-changing shapes and creations in his psyche and in his existence. After clarifying these concepts from a psychoanalytic and philosophical perspective, I shall be using three works to exemplify the employment by the reader of literary texts to work through and to reach a new and better integration between these conflicting forces that the reading stirs into movement.

The tendencies toward 'continuous doing' and 'emergent being': a psychoanalytic perspective

The psychoanalyst Donald Winnicott distinguished between two fundamental psychic states – being and doing (Winnicott, D.W., 1971). Winnicott termed the initial phase of development unintegration – assuming it had not been disturbed by exaggerated tensions and impingements by the physical or environmental reality. During the phase in which the infant is utterly dependent and in circumstances in which he has complete trust in his mother as a secure environment, this situation is characterized by relaxation, contentment and a presence of openness on the one hand, and by 'primitive agonies' on the other. At one extreme the infant is in a state of 'emergent being'. He is unafraid of going-on-being as he is without having to catalogue, define, signify, verify, activate, convey, symbolize or know. In Winnicott's words 'It is only here, in this unintegrated state of the personality, that that which we describe as creative can appear' (ibid., p. 88).

At the other extreme, the absolute dependence and psychic unintegration arouse unthinkable primitive anxieties that continue in later life as an amorphous threat stemming from impressions gathered without any actual experience; impressions that exist but that are unconscious and inaccessible to consciousness.

The 'unintegration' state, unknowingly involves a kind of spellbound devotion to 'going-on-being'. However, physical anguish, frustration and the mother's impingements allow reality to insinuate itself, arousing the infant to sense his own reality and to gradually distance himself from the entirely open primary state. From then on he is destined to a continuous movement and struggle between a state of 'emergent being' on the one hand, and a variety of forms of doing on the other hand, ranging from productive and creative doing, needed and adaptive doing, defensive doing aimed at lessening anxiety and lastly pathological doing embedded in a collapse of the psychic structure and replaced by a pathological organization.

Out of all these forms of doing the most significant movement to the developing self. which creates and enjoys his creation is the movement between unintegration and creative doing.

Winnicott argues that the creative employment of unintegration is dependent on a facilitating environment. Such an environment, Winnicott claims, contributes to the gradual development from total dependence to relative dependence and eventually to psychic integration and to the 'capacity to be alone' (Winnicott, D.W., 1958, pp. 167–177; 1974, pp. 102–104). At first the infant is 'alone' in the presence of another who protects the still weak 'self'. In the course of time the presence of the object is internalized and enables this aloneness that is vital to psychic development:

'It is only when alone (that is to say, in the presence of someone) that the infant can discover his own personal life. The pathological alternative is a false life built on reactions to external stimuli' (Winnicott, D.W., 1958, p. 175). In a normal situation the infant will gradually move from subjectivity to objectivity and from symbiosis to separateness. This development takes place in the course of the establishment of the 'potential space', that critical 'third zone' between the 'me' and 'not me', internal and external world, fantasy and reality.

Because of these developments the 'self' is able in later life to withdraw to a paradoxical state of 'connected-aloneness', which is characterized by relaxation, openness and a profound connection to both the inner and outer world. This withdrawal facilitates engaging in a creative process and to the endowment of meaning in a way that Winnicott links to the freedom from false knowledge.

A further and crucial phenomenon connected to primary unintegration is its menacing sibling – the fear of disintegration. According to Winnicott, psychic disintegration is a means of defence against returning to the primary state of unintegration. Paradoxically, in order to put up a defence against disintegration the mind disintegrates so as to avoid experiencing the unbearable anxiety. In his famous formulation Winnicott explains that 'a fear of which destroys his or her life, has already been' (Winnicott, D.W., 1974, p. 10). Even though this is an experience that has already happened in the past, it hasn't been experienced consciously because it happened before there was an experiencing 'self'.

Throughout life the 'self' continues to fear this breakdown and at the same time long for it. This experience goes to the heart of the beginning of development and also to the essence of the capacity to be fully open and creative. In the words of the psychoanalyst Sarah Volker:

> The search after breakdown is not only the path of the mind to its cure but also its path to its very being/essence/itself. The gravity toward breakdown is also the strength of the core of the self, since in the heart of its breakdown, in that short moment of being, despite the infinite pain – an individual sense himself for who/what he really is (Kolker, S., 2009, p. 291).

Winnicott notes that 'sanity is liable to become a prison, charged with fear or denial of madness, fear or denial of the innate capacity of every human being to become unintegrated, depersonalized, and to feel that the world is unreal' (Winnicott, D.W., 1945, p. 140). The tendency for 'emergent being' thus pulls the mind in these two competing and related directions: towards threatening disintegration and towards longed-for creativity.

The psychoanalyst Shmuel Erlich (2003) contends that every experience is by its very nature dual and is formed between the mode of 'doing' and the mode of 'being'. Erlich notes that our existence's mode of 'doing' enables us to construct our lives – to respond to bodily needs, to encounter the actual world, to survive, to learn and to form both practical and mental links and relations. Alongside this the importance of the mode of 'being' derives from it being 'inherently involved in and silently underpins our sense of aliveness as well as connectedness with everything – relationships, nature, life, ideals and values – without which our psychological life is seriously impoverished and hampered' (Erlich, S., 2003, p. 114). In her book *On the Lyricism of the Mind* Dana Amir suggests that integration between the emergent and continuous facets creates the 'lyrical dimension of the psyche', meaning that we are able to experience ourselves as having boundaries, depth and meaning and that the self has the freedom to withdraw from the limitations of its actual existence (Amir, D., [2008] 2016, p. xiv).

The emergent and the continuous tendencies of the mind: a philosophical perspective

The emergent and the continuous tendencies are relevant to three existential affinities: the affinity to the dimension of time, to death and to art and reading. These will be examined considering the ideas of the two existential philosophers Heidegger and Kierkegaard.

1. The affinity to the dimension of time

The researcher Joel Pearl analyses the difference between Freud and Heidegger's concepts of time (Pearl, J., 2011). Freud relates mainly to an individual's linear relationship to time. Heidegger, on the other hand, sees *Dasein* – the individual in a state of 'being there', as 'thrown' (*Geworfen*) into the world. He stresses the horizon of possibilities ready in future time. At the same time, he looks from the vantage point of *Dasein*'s future – backwards to his present, thus infringing the linearity of time. Heidegger relates to time as part of his distinction between 'being there' that is invested in continuous daily life and 'being there' of *Dasein* that is invested in the emergence of his self-individuation. Pearl portrays the differences between these two positions towards time thus:

> A self-individuation *Dasein* maintains a different relation to time than that of a *Dasein* immersed in average everydayness. These modes of relating to time are in fact two distinct modes of being in the world. In the life of the *Dasein* immersed in everydayness, the past and the future accompany a continuous present in which the subject dwells, a continuous present which passes through the future and becomes the past. In contrast, the life of the self-individuation *Dasein* consists of a temporal movement arising from a future which has-been and which emerges again and again into the present. The subject who does not live in light of temporality sees time as an axis of instances which unfold themselves from the moment its life begun to the moment it ends. In contrast, the subject who does live in light of temporality beholds time as a dynamic occurrence, maintaining that its own existence can never be reduced to a sequence of instances. The *Dasein* immersed in everydayness sees time as a linear succession because its worldview is constrained by the interpretative framework of the 'they'. The self-individuated *Dasein* regards time as a movement which cannot be represented along a linear timeline, seeing that the perspective from which it observes time is itself a dynamic position, from which the temporal occurrence is only visible as a constant movement between paths of time (ibid., pp. 68–69).

Heidegger noted that an individual is steeped in assumptions already reached by others and interpretations that flow from them. An interpretation is seen by Heidegger not as new knowledge added to an existing understanding. Rather it is an elaboration of the possibilities opened up by that understanding. An authentic understanding reacts to the world and is therefore not actually a new invention but rather a primordial understanding of the possibilities opened up by existence. But when the interpretation derives from 'them' – the society and its dictates, *Dasein* fails to open to primordial understandings and new possibilities, thus determining the mode of existence of continuous doing in a direction that is not authentic (Heidegger, M., [1927] 1996, pp. 361–364).

On the other hand, the emergent being's mode of existence can be linked to the non-linear relationship to time, which addresses the horizon of the present rather the actual present. The concept of 'in the blink of an eye' clearly describes the position in time of the emergent presence. This concept serves both Kierkegaard and Heidegger in their illustration of what Sagi has described as

> the moment at which reality is indeed seen in a new, deeper and more original light. The blink of an eye does not relate to the present moment (*dem Jetzt*); it relates to the gaze of the eye which captures reality itself in its entirety (Sagi, A., 1991, p. 105).

The simultaneity of the momentary and the general, the transient and the encompassing, embodied in the blink of an eye is portrayed even more acutely by Kierkegaard when he declares:

> And now the moment ... It is brief and temporal indeed, like every moment; it is transient as all moments are... And yet it is decisive and filled with the Eternal. Such a moment ought to have a distinctive name; let us call it the Fullness of Time (Kierkegaard, S., [1843] 2003, p. 18).

The illuminating distinction made by Sagi between identification and identity (Sagi, 1991, p. 75) described in Chapter 8 can also be applied to the difference between continuous doing and emergent being respectively. When reading a book one can adopt the position of 'identifying' the text, when reading is an act of conscious learning. But one can also become immersed in the text in a way that opens the reader to new possibilities, and thus establishes *de novo* his 'identity'. The difference between 'identity' and 'identification' has a powerful affinity to one's relation to time. An open reading uses the opportunity to transcend beyond identified time and establish an identity in the moment of the experience and the creation. The meaning of an open reading is that the psyche is open to possibilities of whose existence it was unaware before. The integration between identifying time along a linear axis and the experience of time as an axis of instances and movements, involves a continuous tension and creates a psychic equilibrium between the eternal and the finite facets of our existence.

2. Attitude toward death

An individual's recognition that his death is the endpoint of his life decisively influences his capacity to exist in time and opens him up to emergent possibilities. On the other hand, existence within the given track dictated by a person being-in-the-world of 'them', leaves him distanced from the creative and open potential of what one can be receptive to when acknowledging one's own death.

Pearl (2011) discusses two temporal affinities to death in Heideggerian thinking. One such link mounts a defence against death as an imminent possibility in an individual's life and activates an attitude of negating possibilities, locating it in an unknown future or as a known event that happens only to others. This results in an estrangement between the individual and his death. A different attitude regards death as part of the structure of 'being there' and enables the individual to establish his self-individuation as a temporal perspective that comes from the future (death) to his past and into his present, accepting it as a continuation that is finite. This temporal movement that recognizes its own finiteness enables to create an alternative contextual story of one's life, differing from the account that others dictated to him; a story of a 'self' written in time (ibid., pp. 70–72). This is a liberation from the concept of time determined only by the continuous doing.

The fear of death – when it is no longer possible to deny it – undermines the status quo of continuous doing and compels the individual to examine his existence. Death is an 'otherness' that when accepted as such it expands the self and changes the psychic equilibrium between existence's mode of continuous doing and its mode of emergent being.

The literary text includes 'otherness' as an immanent aspect; both the otherness of the text itself and of its creator. The text offers itself to the reader who can either open up to it as an enlightening otherness or protect himself from it as a representation of the ultimate otherness of death. The reader who regards deviation from continuous doing as a threat is liable to immerse himself in the text as representing the routine and the known-in-advance and thus avoid exposure to the facet of otherness that is mysterious and threatening. In effect, the reader can adopt one of three perspectives as outlined by Sagi in the context of ethics in his book *Facing Others and Otherness* (Sagi, A., 2012):

1. Levinas' perspective, which sees the presence of the other as coercive and obliging. In this context the other and death are equally threatening.
2. Husserl's perspective, according to which the transcendental-self establishes the object and is liable to take steps in order to free himself and seeks an 'exist for himself'. The intermediate perspective outlined by Heidegger, Maurice Merleau-Ponty and Jean-Luc Marion. According

to this view the subject has a formative role in the appearance of the object while at the same time the object is predefined by itself and its existence is not dependent on the subject.

From these three perspectives one can deduce the position of the individual vis-à-vis death as well as the position through which the reader encounters the text. The third position enables the individual to cope with the concept of death and the fear of it by recognizing that this 'other' appears without any dependence on him, without his involvement and is beyond his control. However, at the same time this view leads to the recognition that it is the other who lends the 'self' the possibility of shaping the way in which he takes on both his encounter with death and his fear of it. The third attitude is the one that will lead to the fruitful link between the vivid and creative aspects of the reading-self and to his readiness to allow the text to appear as an object in its own right, independent of the reader's subjectivity. These perspectives are reminiscent of views expressed by Melanie Klein who saw the confrontation with the facet of death in a person's psyche a crucial basis for two opposite orientations: a defensive withdrawal in an attempt to outwardly project the threat of death and thus be rid of the anxiety of it that characterizes the paranoid-schizoid position. This as opposed to recognizing it in the context of the depressive position, leading to psychic development and creativity: 'Though the rejected aspects of the self and of internalized objects contribute to instability, they are also at the source of inspiration in artistic productions and in various intellectual activities' (Klein, M., 1958, p. 89).

The French philosopher Maurice Blanchot, who was profoundly influenced by Heidegger, likens death to night and distinguishes between two affinities to death: One is defensive, adopted by, as he puts it:

> Those who think they see ghosts are those who do not want to see the night. They crowd it with the terror of little images, they occupy and distract it by immobilizing it – stopping the oscillation of eternal starting over (Blanchot, M., [1955] 1982, p. 143).

On the other hand, there will be those who will dare to be in touch with the night as the appearance of 'everything [that has] disappeared' (ibid.). Blanchot also emphasizes a non-linear time involved in this link to death:

> One never dies now, one always dies later, in the future – in a future which is never an actuality, which cannot come except when everything will be over and done. And when everything is over, there will be no more present: the future will again be past. This leap by which the past catches up with the future, overstepping the present, is the sense of human death, death permeated with humanity (ibid., p. 144).

Blanchot describes death as being 'like my invisible form, my gesture, the silence of my most hidden secret' (ibid., p. 105). Articulated in a poetic and dense way Blanchot likens the affinity to death to our attitude toward a secret. Every attempt to reveal the secret would distance it, whereas recognizing its secrecy lends it meaning. The paradox of the ear being attuned to death, but refrains from deliberately approaching it, is like an opportunity to open oneself up to one's own possibilities without having to fall back on the influence of the *others* and of the 'already known'.

Since it is out of our reach, Blanchot terms death as 'The other night':

> The other night is always the other, and he who senses it becomes the other. He who approaches it departs from himself, is no longer he who approaches but he who turns away, goes hither and yon. He who, having entered the first night, seeks intrepidly to go toward its profoundest intimacy, toward the essential, hears at a certain moment the other night – hears himself, hears the eternally reverberating echo of his own step, a step toward silence, toward the void. But the echo sends this step back to him as the whispering immensity, and the void is now a presence coming toward him (ibid., p. 149).

Blanchot's metaphor likening death to night gives life an image of daylight and yet one that is willing to recognize everything concealed within it including the darkness of night. The emergent self's life is alert to death's silence, to the secret of the end, which becomes a fundamental facet in the emergent being. This is an active, dreamy silence, that occurs from minute to minute, unlike the 'continuous doing' that travels in linear time among the known and familiar and is flooded by a shadowless neon light.

The presence of death in a mind that tries to deny it is similar to a dreamless sleep. On the contrary, Death's presence in a mind that opens itself to finitude is expressed in a dreaming sleep and a dreaming wakefulness (Ogden, T., 2003), which is also willing to contain the anxiety bound up with the recognition of the ontological fragility of the human existence.

3. The relation to art and literature

Heidegger's writings about creativity and art in general and about the written work in particular emphasize the power of a work of art in revealing the space of Alethia, which transcends the bounds of the ordinary. The writer is not the inventor of the exceptional, but he is the one who has the capacity to find it and express it in words. This idea reminds one of what the psychoanalyst Bollas terms 'the unthought known' (Bollas, C., 1987, pp. 277–283), which he links to unconscious processes. Here, however, we can also apply it to the 'unthought known' that emanates from the truth of the world as in a state of inspiration, enabling the creator to be like a pipe that comprehends existence without 'knowing' it and knows it without thinking.

As the following literary examples will show, the written creation can liberate the reader from the ordinary and open him up to the emergent being. Blanchot defines this reading as 'a genuine' reading and it is clear from what he writes that such a reading occurs in the tension between the gravitational force of continuous doing and the transcendental force of the emergent being.

The reading is not a conversation; it does not discuss, it does not question. It never asks of the book, and still less of the author: 'What exactly did you mean? What truth, then, do you bring me?' A genuine reading never questions the genuine book. But neither does it submit to the 'text'.

> Only the non-literary book is presented as a tightly woven net of determined significations, a set of real affirmations ... But the book which has its origin in art has no guarantee in the world, and when it is read, it has never been read before. It does not come into its presence as a work except in the space opened by this unique reading, each time the first and each time the only (Blanchot, M., [1955] 1982, p. 174).

Let us now consider three literary works, in each of which we find the reader's engagement with the dialectic tendencies of continuous doing as opposed to the emergent being. Like every reader, each character in these books uses his reading experiences in a different and unique way in order to work through and transform an old psychic equilibrium between doing and being with a new, more integrated one.

Chapter 13a

First illustration
Aharon Appelfeld's book *The Man Who Never Stopped Sleeping*

Aharon Appelfeld's book *The Man Who Never Stopped Sleeping* (Appelfeld, [2010] 2017), exemplifies the way that reading serves the attempt to reorganize and renew the facets of emergent being and continuous doing in an individual who withdraws from a traumatic reality into a kind of psychic death that is expressed in incessant sleep. This character uses his reading experiences to revive the two tendencies that were tied in a deadlock and create a renewed and better integration between them.

The Man Who Never Stopped Sleeping is the story of Erwin Aharon, an adolescent who survived the Holocaust, his name a clear hint that this is Aharon Appelfeld's autobiography. He was named at birth Erwin, survived the Holocaust and then, having spent several months in a displaced persons camp in Italy, arrived in Palestine two years before Israel declared its independence in 1948. In the book, once the war had ended, its hero, Erwin, finds he unable to stop sleeping, a slumber over which he has no control even during the day; a kind of 'not being' that manifested itself in a situation of existential sleep. Gradually the youth is able to extricate himself from this soporific state. He wonders between languages, fields of battle and sacrifice, changing definitions of self, until he finally emerges as a fledgling writer.

The first few pages of the book describe an extreme form of existence, a psychic state analogous to deadness that dwells on both tendencies of being and doing. This is a powerful literary example of a dreamless sleep as the consequence of trauma and an existential crisis. The book begins with the following words:

> At the end of the war, I became immersed in constant slumber. Though I moved from train to train, from truck to truck, and sometimes from wagon to wagon, it was all in a dense, dreamless sleep. When I opened my eyes for a moment, the people looked heavy and expressionless ... The refugees carried me and supported me. Sometimes I was forgotten, and then someone remembered me and went

back to pick me up ... Sometimes it seems that I'm still in that darkness, drifting and being borne along. What happened to me during those days of sleep will probably be unknown to me forever. Sometimes a voice that spoke to me comes back, or the taste of a piece of bread that was shoved into my mouth. But aside from that, there is just darkness.

... In the evening a man approached, nudged me, and called out loud, 'What are you doing here?' I didn't open my eyes and didn't bother to answer him. But he kept shaking me and bothering me, so I had no choice but to say to him, 'I'm sleeping.' 'Did you eat?' asked the man. 'I'm not hungry,' I replied. My body knew that kind of annoyance. All along the way people tried to wake me up, to shove bread into my mouth, to speak to me, to convince me that the war was over and that I had to open my eyes. There were no words in me to explain that I couldn't open my eyes, that I was trapped in thick sleep. From time to time, I did try to wake up, but sleep overpowered me ... As I was being carried forward, a hand touched me, and when I didn't react, the hand shook me again ... 'Leave me alone. I want to sleep' ... 'You mustn't sleep for such a long time.' 'My weariness isn't done. Leave me alone'.

The man asked my age, and I told him.

'I'm sixteen years and nine months old.'

'What do you want to do now?' he asked, as if he were a relative and not a stranger. 'I don't know yet.'

That night I woke up and found a tray of fruit and a note. The note said, 'Hello, my young friend. Tonight, I'm leaving the camp and setting out. I wish you a fine awakening and a life of alertness, activity, and the ability to love.' The note was signed, 'Your friend who looks like your uncle Arthur.' I read it again and again, and tears flowed from my eyes (Appelfeld, A., [2010] 2017, pp. 3–6).

This segment illustrates withdrawal from both modes of existence, emergent being and continuous doing. The latter for instance was supposed to arouse hunger and make the hero eat, but he sank into a kind of indifference to both body and mind alike. This is a comprehensive withdrawal that makes death part of the here and now. It exemplifies/illustrates the way internal deadness is used to avoid the fear of death and the pains of life.

At the end of this account we are told that the hero is waking up to life by reading. The stranger's attempts at conversation didn't stir him. But reading the letter he left him did indeed wake him up, tears streaming from his eyes. He read it and then read it again. Thus, ends the first chapter of Appelfeld's book, the next begins with 'I overcame the bonds of sleep and rose to my feet'.

From impermeable reading to permeable reading

Appelfeld's hero engages in a gradual, cautious voyage of revival that is peppered with anecdotes about his journey to the new words he was leaning in Hebrew. Clashing with the encounter with Hebrew is his longing for his mother's (and father's) tongue, which keeps returning to memory and dreams. These are accompanied by her voice and warmth, alongside his father's, a tormented writer. The dialectic movement between 'not being' at the beginning of the novel, and being; and between continuous doing and renewed openness to the emergent being, is embodied in the hero's different kind of readings.[1]

Erwin starts by learning the new language – Hebrew – by continuous doing:

> The language drills got harder by the day. Everything was oral, without notebooks or books ... As we ran; we recited the poems of Rachel, of Leah Goldberg, and of Nathan Alterman. And here and there, a verse from the Bible (Appelfeld, A., [2010] 2017, p. 29).

Then the hero meets a new teacher by the name of Slobotsky, a man who proves to be a teacher in the full sense of the word. Slobotsky introduces his pupils to the emergent being, as can be seen from his instructions to them:

> The Bible must be read attentively ... Many secrets are hidden in it. Too bad that my colleagues, the researchers, refuse to listen to its melodies. History and geography have their place, but the secrets are more important than they are (ibid., p. 78).

When these youngsters turn to studying the book of Samuel with Slobotsky, Appelfeld's hero is imbued with a vitality and movement that is a coming together of the arousal of the senses and the feeling in the moment of reading on the one hand, and the penetration of the past by way of the memory of both mother tongue and the maternal bosom on the other.

> But that first chapter of the book of Samuel made my body tremble as it had not for a long time. It seemed that the words Slobotsky presented to us were carved out, each word individually, and laden with secret content. I felt something similar when I saw for the first time the blue of the inner Carpathians. I was so astonished that I wept. Mother didn't know what to do and enfolded me in her arms (ibid., pp. 77–78).

The metaphor Erwin uses to describe his first sight of the 'inner blue of the Carpathians' – a poetic allusion to the depths of the mother's embrace – illuminates the primary and unique nature of a reading that involves the emergent being. The hero's being encounters the secret of the world and immediately trembles. This description evokes in my mind Pessoa's special formulation of situations in which the self connects to nature and in the blink of an eye becomes 'the size of what I see!' (Pessoa, F., 2017, p. 201).

Reading instils in every individual reader, in every situation, a different mode of coping. The effect of this is illustrated in the difference between Erwin's experience upon hearing the biblical chapter and that of his friend Robert. From Appelfeld's description one can gain the impression that the text did also influence Robert, but in an entirely different way than the overwhelming way to be found in Erwin's encounter with the text.

The facet of the emergent being does not detach the reader from the facet of continuous doing. The very ability of the hero to include in his experience memory of his mother and the comparison between his experience and that of his friend is linked to the mode of continuous doing that is common to everyone and that includes the shared language and norms of behaviour. The continuous doing facilitates a transition from the language of the singular (the personal experience) to the language of the plural. Nonetheless, in the blink of an eye both Erwin and Robert also experienced the transcendental quality of the language, each in his own way. Erwin and Robert's readings reveal the richness of the reading experience in opening the reader up to his personal psychology, his sensual memories and preferences, his historical contexts and the object relations from which his identity sprouted.

It seems as if Erwin Aharon's response to the chapter from the *Book of Samuel* also awakens in him the memory of the 'aesthetic conflict' described earlier, used by Meltzer to describe the conflict aroused in the infant when exposed to his mother's enigmatic beauty and otherness (Meltzer. D. and Williams, H., 1988, pp. 125–132). The hero's reading of the *Book of Samuel* raises the early memory (either real or in fantasy) in which the infant Erwin encountered his mother's 'inner blue', raised from the depths.

At a later stage in the story when the hero is wounded in Israel's War of Independence he is hospitalized and undergoes surgery a number of times. He dreams about his parents' home and in his dreams there is a discourse between him and his mother on reading in Hebrew and reading in general, which is a part of a reparatory process for his wounded body and mind. For example, he writes:

> 'I'm reading the Bible and am becoming attached to the words,' I told her. 'Are you religious?' She was alarmed. 'Don't worry. My faith is like yours and like Father's.' 'I'm glad,' she said, her eyes brightening ... 'I'm

recovering from my fractures. The recuperation is slow and long. But in the meantime, I'm getting to know my body and my soul, if I may say so. By the way, do we have Siddhartha at home?' 'A wonderful book. I'll send it to you. But where? I don't have your address.' 'It's very simple, Kibbutz Misgav Yitzhak, Palestine. That's my home now. Any mail you send will get to me, but I need Siddhartha like I need air to breathe' (ibid., p. 157).

The hero tells his mother that he is becoming attached to the words of the bible and her response is one of consternation in case this meant that he had become religious. He tells her about a reading accompanied by an experience of an emergent being, which widens his sense of identity. But his mother responds as if this was the kind of reading that establishes identity based on the narrowing and determining facets of continuous doing. The hero then describes how his recovery from his fractured bones – which are soon understood to also stand for psychological trauma – looks to reading as a healer of his somatic and psychic wounds, when he asks his mother to send him Hermann Hesse's book *Siddhartha*.

Siddhartha (Hesse, H., [1922] 1981) is the story of Siddhartha Buddha's voyage in search of enlightenment; in the context of a personal voyage such as Siddhartha's, an importance is attached to the understanding of non-linear time and the fullness of the moment, to viewing suffering as part of human existence and the awareness of the uniqueness of every experience as a primary experience that adds to one's knowledge of existence. In the present context, it is evident that the dialectic between the emergent being and continuous doing is connected to the psyche-soma dialectic, as the hero's need for a book equals his need for 'air to breathe' – a term usually applied to a somatic function. Though the hero's need is spiritual, it is clear to both him and us that psychic recovery would also help the body's process of healing.

And again, not only the private but also the shared is evidently required; the continuous and not only the emergent. His mother is familiar with the book he wants to read. Conceivably she had read it in German, and he may try to read it in Hebrew. But the fact that they share the reading of Hesse's *Siddhartha* is a function of the achievements of continuous doing, which facilitate sharing and understanding the experience of an-other through structured and common communication. These shared aspects of the continuous doing are not less important and are even necessary for the personal voyages of the heroes, Erwin Aharon and Siddhartha, to aid them in the healing process. The integration of the reader's early object relations with his mother and father, as well as integration between mother tongue and a new language, between his and her reading experiences, between shared knowledge and private revelations – will all combine to lead to the recovery of the reader's body and mind.

One of the central aspects that arouse the tension between continuous doing and emergent being is, as said, the awareness and fear of death. Appelfeld's hero faces death on numerous occasions.

> In about two months, on February sixteenth, I would turn eighteen. My years seemed long to me. Life before the war, in the ghetto, in the hiding place, wandering after the war, in Naples, sailing to Palestine, at Atlit, at work on the terrace and the orchards, at the advanced training –eighteen years couldn't hold it all ... I had read the Hebrew Bible that the hospital rabbi gave me when I was still in pain and half asleep. His untidy appearance and the way he muttered as he handed the book to me clouded my spirit. It appeared to be the way one gave this type of book to a dying man, so that he would say his confessions before he died.
> At the convalescent home, I read the Bible with my own eyes, and I was glad that I understood most of the words. The Binding of Isaac: the story was dreadful but was told with restraint, in a few words, perhaps so that we could hear the silence between them. I felt a closeness to those measured sentences, and it didn't seem to be a story with a moral, because what was the moral? Rather, it was intended to seep into one's cells, and there it would wait patiently until it was deciphered (Appelfeld, A., [2010] 2017, pp. 158–159).

Like Isaac the narrator had been 'bound' numerous times since birth and throughout his life he finds it difficult to open his eyes because the times of 'near-death' experiences (Joseph, B., 1982) brought death's all-consuming power too close to consciousness. When the rabbi gives him the bible, he feels that this is how the holy book is offered to a dying man. He describes his reading of the story 'The Binding of Isaac' as an attempt to work through the threat of near death. In remembering his mother's suspended attention (Freud, S., 1912) when reading stories to him he is looking for a way of a sustained reading, which enables him, as a reader, to experience the story's horrors without the need to reach any conclusions. In other words, he wants to linger in the text's potential space. Alongside the characteristics of the potential space as containing a playful movement between 'me' and 'not me' internal and external, reality and fantasy, one can also characterize it as a flexible movement between the open emergent being and the orderly continuous doing. If Erwin Aharon were to succeed in lingering in the story of Isaac with his eyes closed as his mother had suggested him to read, he could conceivably stop 'closing his eyes' both actually and symbolically. This would enable him to 'open' his eyes to new possibilities of life and meaning, of which he had been robbed because of having repeatedly experienced being 'bound'. Then, like Siddhartha, Erwin Aharon would be in a position to change the ordeal and transcend it in a way similar to that described by

Kierkegaard. In this process the work of art facilitates a transcendence beyond the 'self' and a return to it in a novel state. Thus, Erwin would be able to return from the story 'The Binding of Isaac' to his own near-death experiences and lend new meaning and significance to his existence.

In conclusion, we see that the post-traumatic structure of Erwin Aharon's psyche was not well integrated. Instead, the psychic equilibrium between the two facets of existence – emergent being and continuous doing – was in the grip of a deadly freeze. In the context of his reading experiences, there was a gradual change in this balance. The movement began with the reading of the note from the man in the woods who reminded him of his uncle Arthur; a note that brought tears to his opening eyes. Subsequently Erwin Aharon's learning Hebrew involves the awakening of the continuous doing. As his affinity to the Hebrew language grew closer, his longing for both his mother tongue and mother were split off. Gradually the reading in Hebrew also exposes him to the 'now-moment experience' characteristic of the emerging being. At the same time the splitting between his mother, her language, and Palestine and its language, decreases, as the narrative of the Hebrew text hurls him back to his mother's embrace in the blue of the Carpathian Mountains.

In contrast to the dreamless sleep that characterized the balance between the 'continuous' and the 'emergent' in the hero's psyche in the midst of the trauma of the war, Erwin Aharon gradually remembers his dreams and in them, the memory of a shared reading experience – that of Siddhartha's voyage – brings to life the internal good object of his mother. Finally, when he is wounded in the war and is once again confronted by the threat of death, he is aided by the story 'The Binding of Isaac'. The reawakening of his mother in his inner world helps him to understand that there is no need to 'do' anything about the recognition of death other than letting it be. As Blanchot would put it, the hero learns that there is no need to turn away from 'the other night'. In contrast to the pathological attachment to continuous sleep and frozen continuous doing at the beginning, reading the story of Isaac's ordeal and 'The Testing of Abraham by God', creates an opportunity for both a renewed working through of the reader's own 'testing' and the awakening of the good objects within him. This leads to a transformation in relation to the internal 'death object' (Durban, J., 2017). Thus, if at the beginning of the book Erwin Aharon is attached to sleep as a kind of defensive identification with death, then following his reading experiences a renewed movement is taking place in two senses: He becomes open to what has been revealed within the text and from within himself as well as to a renewed encounter between the personal language and the shared language of reality. A significant development has occurred in Erwin Aharon the reader, towards better integration and balance between continuous-doing and emergent-being facets of existence. He is capable of leading a life of mourning, longing, reparation and creativity.

Notes

1 I use the term 'reading' also when, for example, Appelfeld is listening to his teacher reading to him. This is in accordance with the understanding of situations of 'reading by listening', like in childhood bedtime-story telling, as those described in *The Words* (Sartre, J.P., 1964 [1981], see for example p. 48). For further discussion on passive reading see also Zoran, R. (2000).

Chapter 13b

Second illustration
Søren Kierkegaard's book *Fear and Trembling: Dialectical Lyric*

The book *Fear and Trembling: Dialectical Lyric* by the existentialist philosopher Søren Kierkegaard ([1843] 2003) illustrates the way in which reading helps an individual in his pursuit of new meaning and balance in his life as a believer. An equilibrium is created between continuous doing expressed by the extreme of blind obedience and emergent being, which is at the heart of complete faith.

The book's narrator embarks on a years-long voyage of repeatedly reading just one text. He has an intuitive belief that within that text he will ultimately discover the code to solving the riddle of Abraham – the textual hero of his life – and in doing so would be freed to establish a renewed integration between his worldly and spiritual life. On the face of it such a reading is a case of repetition compulsion. In fact, however, it serves as a beautiful example of a reading that contains hope, faith and devotion to a process, motivated by the reader's search for a longed-for transformation, which he believes that is to be revealed in the text.

Similarly to Appelfeld, for Kierkegaard 'The Testing of Abraham' is an especially important story. The story and its hero, Abraham, is the sole subject of Kierkegaard's book. Even though his text is considered to be essentially philosophical, I rely on the narrator's testimony when he says that the person who read the story of Abraham

> [w]as no thinker, he felt no need to go further than faith. To be remembered as its father seemed to him to be surely the greatest glory of all, and to have it a lot to be envied even if no one else knew. This man was no learned exegete, he knew no Hebrew; had he known Hebrew then perhaps it might have been easy for him to understand the story of Abraham (Kierkegaard, S., [1843] 2003, p. 46).

Based on this description by Kierkegaard I shall present a reading of *Fear and Trembling* as *literary* evidence of the reading experience in the story of Abraham. The narrator reads it time and again but is not comforted:[2] He said, 'Take your son, your only son Isaac, whom you love, and go to the land of Moriah, and offer him there as a burnt offering on one of the mountains of which I shall tell you' (Genesis 22:2, ESV). Appelfeld and Kierkegaard were not the only captives of this biblical story. It is a story that spurs a daring reading as evidenced by the multiplicity of referrals to it in the course of history by both religious and secular thinkers. It aroused various existential questions; near-death and sacrifice, loyalty, blind faith, the relation of father to son and the devotion of son to father, responsibility and submission, moral dilemmas, divinity and miracles. The story of the binding has been examined from a psychoanalytic perspective in a number of different ways: as expressing a child's fear of being castrated by his father; as paralleling the story of King Laius in Greek mythology, as well as a reconstruction of a childhood trauma experience by Abraham in which, according to the *Midrash* (biblical interpretations) he destroyed his father's idols and as a punishment was thrown into King Nimrod's furnace. His body was saved but not his soul, and so he makes his son suffer the same trauma as a means of coping with his own. The psychologist Avivah Gottlieb-Zornberg links this to Winnicott's concept of 'the fear of breakdown', arguing that we are not afraid of what will be but of what has already been. Thus, Abraham was a captive of what he had experienced in childhood hence his reconstruction of the threat as a means of coping with it (Gottlieb-Zornberg, A., 2009).

However, these psychoanalytic analyses miss the pursuit of new meaning in the biblical story – the prize so yearned for by Kierkegaard. The interpretive psychoanalytic reading of 'The Binding of Issac' exemplifies an element of the very fear Kierkegaard warned against; the tendency to read only what is already known in the text instead of seeking to discover it *de novo*.

Kierkegaard was aware of the dialectical nature of his reading: 'What I intend now is to extract from the story of Abraham its dialectical element, in the form of problemata, in order to see how monstrous a paradox faith is' (Kierkegaard, S., [1843] 2003, p. 53). Already in the opening pages of *Fear of Trembling* the dialectic movement between continuous doing and emergent being is evident as it is awakened by reading the biblical story and by its contents:

> There was once a man; he had learned as a child that beautiful tale of how God tried Abraham, how he withstood the test, kept his faith and for the second time received a son against every expectation. When he became older he read the same story with even greater admiration, for life had divided what had been united in the child's pious simplicity. The older he became the more often his thoughts turned to that tale, his enthusiasm became stronger and stronger, and yet less and less could he understand it. Finally, it put everything else out of his mind; his soul had but one wish, actually to see Abraham, and one longing, to have been witness to those events (ibid., p. 64).

This portrait by Kierkegaard of the reader illustrates two attitudes of his to the written text. There is the approach of the reader who chooses to read the 'known in advance'. The hero as the hero is worthy of adoration and the text repeatedly proves and approves that. That, it would seem, is the preliminary relation to the text of the reader in Kierkegaard's story. He is immersed in the world of meaning as he has come to know it in the context of his religious and ideological beliefs. The more he reads, the more he 'discovers' what was known in the first place. At the same time, beneath this repetitive reading there is a persistent desire to open oneself via a receptive reading to a novel experience. As long as this yearned-for experience fails to materialize, it troubles the reader and causes him to become engaged in a struggle and a repetition compulsion of reading the text time and time again.

Moreover, the reader becomes increasingly captivated by the text's wonderment, but the new meaning of the text remains as elusive as ever. Nevertheless, repetition compulsion also serves another purpose. It assists the reader in his search for an exit from the 'claustrophobic known' (Meltzer, D., 1992), towards the still unrevealed secret in the text that has the power to release him from the psychic system in which he is trapped.

With the passage of time though, the recurrent readings of the story by the narrator in Kierkegaard's book do not lead to a better understanding of Abraham's responsiveness to God's test. If anything, it lessens as he ages. He is unpersuaded by all the interpretations of the tormenting questions raised by the biblical text; how could Abraham possibly prefer to commit himself to the idea of faith in God at the expense of the actual relations with his son Isaac and the obligations that relation demands, including a father's responsibility to protect his offspring? The narrator is engaged in a believer's transference relations towards Abraham, which are parallel to Abraham's transference relations towards God. The reader 'believes' in Abraham but doesn't understand him: 'No one was as great as Abraham ... who is able to understand him?' (ibid.). He cannot understand his hero, nor can he doubt him. The more he doubts him, the more he is tormented, so he goes back to read the text again. In the course of this process the reading itself turns from being an experience and becomes a lifetime's voyage, which, in a certain sense, comes at the expense of real life because of Kierkegaard's desire to deepen his spiritual life and solve the riddle of faith. It is for good reason that Kierkegaard named his book *Fear and Trembling* – dialectical lyric. It is a dialectic between two forces pulling in different directions so that the reader is trapped in the eye of the storm spinning constantly in its cross winds consumed by fear and trembling. This maybe so because of a lack of equilibrium between the two forms of existence, when the weight of continuous doing lacks the gravity required to balance the spiritual path.

To the narrator, Abraham's blind faith seems sublime but at the same time beyond his understanding and capacity. There is a hint by Kierkegaard that his repeated reading stems from his refusal to believe that blind faith is a known given. He searches for the bridge towards that faith as an opening to the secret, so as to be at one with the emergent presence of existence and of God. The unintegrated balance between the facets of continuous and emergent damages both the narrator's quality of reading as well as damaging the quality of his life. His relations toward the biblical characters of Sarah or Abraham is a relationship of schizoid and compulsive attachment to mythology, to literature. These literary characters appear at the expense of real object relations in his life. In the following we see how the reader projects on to the literary characters his psychic state – his despair, his terror and his restlessness. He tries to observe the way in which they cope as a guide in his own existential struggle.

> I would like to present some poetic personages. By exercising the power of dialectic over them I shall keep them at extremes, and by waving the scourge of despair over them I should prevent them from standing still, so that in their anguish they might perhaps bring something or other to light (ibid., p. 87).

As for the aspect of compulsion and repetition, the narrator informs us that he has experienced a dynamic reading that animates the heroes and revives the encounter with them. As part of his voyage he casts despair into them so that he can track their mind in the face of his own existential anxiety. His yearning for the text's heroes is described in daring colours: 'His soul had but one wish, actually to see Abraham' (ibid., p. 56), and elsewhere: 'No, Sarah is the heroine. Her I would like to draw close to as I have drawn close to no other girl, or been tempted to draw close in thought to anyone of whom I have read' (ibid., p. 64).

The reader is eager to get closer to Sarah. He is supposedly talking about the 'Sarah' from the story of Tobias whose seven husbands died on their wedding nights and Tobias wishes to marry her. The name, of course, sends us back to Sarah, Isaac's mother. By expressing his desire to draw close to Sarah 'as I have drawn close to no other girl', Kierkegaard testifies to the fact that his longing for the mythological character surpasses his longing for any real character in his life.

In the same vein, the process of reading *Fear and Trembling* reflects the question troubling the author as to the meaning of devotion to God at the expense of the individual most close to you to the extent of being responsive to the request to sacrifice one's own son? The narrator is preoccupied with the question of whether the essence of faith in fact become embodied in life and in the relations with real characters. In the same way as analysts know that the patient's internalized object relations are awakened in relations with the analyst, so it is evident how the reader's internal object relations are influenced by a story he reads. Using Shoshana

Felman's expression, the reader of *Fear and Trembling* 'acts out' the text. After all, the narrator's attachment to Abraham resembles a sacrificial offering. For Abraham and Sarah's sake, he sacrifices the real beloveds in his life, and perhaps even himself.

Abraham's silence

Silence is an opening to all voices both from within and from the infinite horizon. It is an open space. In his anguish the narrator looks to silence as a key to understanding his hero. Abraham's silence attracts his attention because of the gap it creates in the very place where words of refusal and denial were supposed to appear. The gap it leaves torments him. The narrator is unable to bear the thought that Abraham's silence represents passive cooperation and therefore attributes his silence to a unique affinity to the ultimate certainty.

Abraham cannot be mediated, which can also be put by saying he cannot speak. The moment I speak I express the universal ... Thus while Abraham arouses my admiration, he also appals me ... the person who gives up the universal to grasp something still higher that is not the universal, what does he do? ... But now when the ethical is thus teleologically suspended, how does the single individual in whom it is suspended exist? He exists as the particular in opposition to the universal. Does this mean he sins? For this is the form of sin looked at ideally ... Then how did Abraham exist? He had faith. That is the paradox that keeps him at the extremity and that he cannot make clear to anyone else, for the paradox is that he puts himself as the single individual in an absolute relation to the absolute (ibid., p. 74).

Before we go on to explore Abraham's silence as a key to the reading of the narrator in *Fear and Trembling*, let us briefly review the meaning of silence from a psychoanalytic perspective.

The role of silence in the early development of language

At the beginning of life, the infant is invited to cross the bridge from the mother's language to the general language. The mother presents the infant to the father and so exposes him to the general. She reveals to him both the existence of a 'general' in the sense of a 'public' with which one must communicate as well as the 'general' in the sense of the 'law of the father' that dictates the language of communication. The father also creates a space in which there is a need for a language that was less needed as long as the symbiosis between the infant and mother lasted. It is the mother who first presents the word to the infant, but it is the father who defines the relation of the infant's language to the general language.

The psychoanalyst Dana Amir maintains that the mother's different ways of presenting the language lay the foundations for the child's use of language in different ways. The mother can expose him to a language that will serve him to question and enquire. However, in the event that the mother is unable to bear gaps and becomes anxious when confronted by them she could also teach the infant a pathological language that contains absolute knowledge instead of knowledge that always involves the existing space between the signified and its signifier; between the most private and that which can be communicated; between silence and words. Like the word, silence can also serve as a linguistic sign for certainty. In that event, silence can signify the redundancy of language as a system of communication and laws. Silence can signify the infant's total certainty and trust in the mother's understanding of him and his understanding of her. Alternatively, it testifies to his surrender to the mother's troubled inner world and her inability to accept the need for language stemming from her symbiotic tendency according to which the need for language represents a distance between the two. The usage of language does indeed create a distance between mother and infant and moves away from a situation of the 'two being as one', a situation in which words are allegedly not needed. Silence in relationships is prone to cause trouble, because the certainty signified by silence opens the way to misunderstandings, as opposed to a saying or even better a question that leads to an investigation of the mutual reality. A certain degree of anxiety is required so as to enable the capacity to cause symbols to develop, whereas a lack of anxiety (or an excess of it) leads to psychological muteness and limits the ability to use language for the purposes of coping and development (Klein, M., 1930).

The narrator in Kierkegaard's book is a meticulous reader who challenges Abraham's silence. Perhaps Abraham hadn't understood God's request? In the name of what certainty did Abraham think he was acting? What permits him to sacrifice his son? He uses the text in order to investigate the various possibilities and move between them given the freedom a reader has and his right to judge the characters and be sceptical about their motives even if he believes in them. By the way in which he goes about reading the text, the narrator is in effect doing the very thing that puzzled him by its absence in Abraham's action, an action that on the face of it was unquestioning, was not reversed in God's text and responded to by mute obedience.

In contrast to silence, psychoanalysis sees the very use of language as evidence of a process of mourning. First, because in speaking there is a separation from the symbiosis, from the phantasy of omnipotence according to which the other knows me, I know him and there isn't a distance between us that necessitates the use of words. Second and similarly, the appearance of the word also recognizes the fact that I need to give a name to things so that 'I' and 'the things' are not one and the same. This also involves a process of mourning.

The narrator assumes that Abraham doesn't need to say anything because he is not mourning. He is convinced that God is right and therefore also believes in the righteousness of his own action. He is sure of his consent. Kierkegaard deduces from the silence of the story's hero that Abraham completely waived any shred of doubt because of his faith in God. This is the hero's ultimate non-mourning and the reader looks at it with wonderment.

In the psychoanalytic sense, the process of mourning is needed and even essential for the purposes of transformation. The blind believer does not undergo transformation and development because he 'turns a blind eye' (Steiner, J., 2011, pp. 161–172) and therefore remains identical to himself in continuous doing of obedience and absolute knowledge that is not to be questioned. Kierkegaard's subversive reading presents a different kind of faith, which involves constant doubt and torment. Yet it is precisely this that leaves an opening for movement between the believer's continuous doing and his emergent being that is searching for a live link to the secret; to the otherness that is concealed among the words of the text.

After years of repeated reversions to the text and his voyage to the midst of numerous other literary heroes whom he compares to Abraham, the reader of *Fear and Trembling* is at long last exposed to a novel meaning of Abraham's silence. He recognizes that Abraham is a 'knight of faith' because even though he recognizes the value of belonging to the general – including his obligation as a father towards his son – the value of being subject to the general laws doesn't qualify him to be regarded as the kind of hero that has a standing among the general public. He is neither a tragic hero who speaks out and thus sacrifices himself to save someone else, nor is he a moral hero who is silent thus sacrificing himself to save another.

When the narrator in Kierkegaard's *Fear and Trembling* begins his reading of the story of the binding of Isaac, he is portrayed as a two-dimensional admirer of Abraham. Contrastingly the adult, developed reader, having delved more deeply into the text, laments Abraham's lot in life and understands that the test he had undergone was infinitely harder. He understands that the Knight of faith's test is one that never ends unlike the test of the tragic hero that ends when the decree materializes.

The knight of faith longs to return to the general but he is prevented from doing so because of his sublime faith. He is aware of the meaning and significance of 'moral' behaviour but is prevented from responding to its call. That is his test. Abraham's silence gets a new interpretation: it is not a heroic silence but rather the outcome of torment and fear stemming from the tension in which he is trapped – between his love and loyalty to his son and his faith in his god. Kierkegaard extracts from the story the existential moment of loneliness that comes with carrying the burden of a dilemma that no one can understand. In the end the silence is interpreted as an expression of the torment felt by Abraham, alienated from his son, from his community, as he is compelled to maintain silence over his readiness to respond to God's command despite knowing that this contradicts the heroic urge, the fatherly instinct and the moral imperative. The reading had led to a new understanding: 'The distress and anguish in the paradox consisted, as explained above, precisely in the silence; Abraham cannot speak' (ibid., p. 153).

The Abraham as read by the narrator at the beginning of the narrator's reading voyage is entirely different than the Abraham at journey's end. The reading experience gradually led him to a profound affinity to the mysterious character of the knight of faith and he interprets his course of action as rooted in a spirit that is silent out of torment and fear. This interpretation at long last refutes the reader's doubts. His hero's sublime power of faith is restored and with it restored is the reader's sense of faith and meaning.

Solving the mystery: the paradox of faith

In a brief segment at the end of his treatise Kierkegaard turns to the few words uttered by Abraham in reply to Isaac's question as to the whereabouts of the sacrifice: 'God himself will provide the lamb for the burnt offering, my son' (Genesis 22). The reader interprets his hero's saying thus:

> So far as I can understand the paradox I can also understand Abraham's total presence in that word ... So, after having made this movement Abraham has at every instant been performing the next, making the movement on the strength of the absurd. To that extent he utters no untruth, for on the strength of the absurd it is after all possible that God might do something quite different. He utters no untruth then, but neither does he say anything, for he speaks in a foreign tongue ... Abraham would in a straightforward sense be right to talk as enigmatically as he did, for in that case he himself could not have known what would happen (Kierkegaard, S., [1843] 2003, pp. 167–168).

The nature of the paradox revealed by Abraham's words finally puts the mind of the reader of the binding to rest because in that story is concealed the key to the riddle of his faith. On the one hand, Abraham must know that he is indeed sacrificing his son and in doing so expresses absolute faith and the absolute relinquishment. On the other hand, in telling Isaac that God will provide the lamb for the offering he is not lying nor is this an expression of a hidden hope for a last-minute change of plan. It is rather an enigmatic saying that holds/signifies its contradiction: the sacrifice of the son. Abraham's few words express a faithful truth that undermines the first truth of the submissive sacrifice. Abraham understands that the revelation will come not from him but from God. This represents a devotion to an ideal object whose idealness stems from him being sovereign of the constant emergent being and its translation into the continuous doing. This is a paradox because he believes that he is sacrificing his son and hands himself over to his god, but at the same time he also knows that God is not a concept the human mind can grasp. Abraham must have known that he doesn't really know what the divine moment held in store for him.

The moment of binding resembles an act undertaken on the spur of the moment when everything seems possible. At the very moment it embodies both the collapse into only one option and the potentiality of every possible option. 'Do first and understand later' (*Naase ve Nishma*), because it is beyond us to figure out the meaning of what we do in the realms of the Creator.

A new integration between the continuous and the emergent

The reading voyage embarked on by the narrator in Kierkegaard's *Fear and Trembling* proves to be a lifelong existential voyage to just one literary text. The reader gains the ability to use the text in order to work through existential anxiety, torment and solitude. The exploration of these emotions in the text's hero helps him to reflect on his own life and inject a personal meaning into it. The narrator's reading the story of the binding makes it a merged story of the child Isaac who is led to be sacrificed and of the child who reads Isaac's story and gradually grows up with it. The narrator describes the way in which the story continues to live in his mind, how it is every time revealed from a different perspective, revealing a further smidgen of doubt, of wondering, of questions about one's existence. This is a mode of reading that includes basic anxieties around relationships and death, a search for meaning and the usage of defence mechanisms – which are all personified both in the contents and in the process of reading. The reading takes place amid the tension between the blind repetition compulsion and the live encounter with the text, which seeks to transcend beyond the familiar and known to open the door to new possibilities. In this sense what the reader is looking for in the text is a compass rather than a place/datum point. He is looking for the 'basic mood' of the creation [*Grundstimmung*] as Heidegger terms it, which will lead him to the truth that will open up in the text's space of Alethea. This truth will prevail over all that is concealed by the familiar. Conceivably, this is the opening to the 'O' discussed by Bion (1965), which transcends beyond the world's knowledge that is understood through K (Knowledge) L (Love) and H (Hate). Abraham, in his paradox of belief, commits himself to the divine text in the knowledge that he was ignorant of its meaning and consequences and all that was left for him was to meet the outcome. In a similar way, every open literary reading takes into consideration the paradox that we read the well-known words but at the very same time we don't know what secrets and new meanings to these words might be revealed to us through this creation that portrays a world dreamed up by the poet.

The search for meaning by the reader is in constant movement. It is evident in Kierkegaard's reader and it also echoes our own repeated readings of Kierkegaard's text, and its time dimension is not linear. In Blanchot's words:

> The work does not endure over the ages; it is. This being can inaugurate a new age, for it is an appeal to the beginning, recalling that nothing is affirmed except through the fecundity of an initial decisiveness ... The true reader does not rewrite the book, but he is apt to return, drawn by an imperceptible pull, toward the various prefigurations of the reader which have caused him to be present in advance at the hazardous experience of the book. It ceases, then, to appear necessary to him and again becomes a possibility among others (Blanchot, M., [1955] 1982, pp. 182–183).

The biblical story fascinates Kierkegaard's narrator not only as a universal tale but also because it includes internal shadows that Kierkegaard is projecting into it (Sagi, A., 1991, p. 37). It is not only Abraham that he comes to know each time *de novo*, he also gets to know himself anew reflected in the images of his literary hero. In each turn into the text there is an alienation from the self, and in each return from the text there is a potential of further unification between the self and the world he lives in. Thus, by speaking of 'returning' there is an element of the past (that the reader turns to) but also a rebirth of the self, i.e. an emergence of being in the presence and towards the future (ibid., pp. 32–33).

An in-depth study of Kierkegaard's *Fear and Trembling* thus reveals that reading Isaac's story exposes the reader with/to his inner psychic equilibrium, a balance within which there is an evident effort to reach the horizon of the emergent at the expense of continuous doing. The reader explores the balance between the two facets in Abraham's mind. Gradually there is a transformation in the way in which he understands this balanced image towards which he is devoting the process of his maturation. In the wake of this prolonged semi-analytical process a new balance begins to develop within the reader. Though the reader is not yet inclined towards continuous doing, he nonetheless understands in a different way the positioning at the pole of emergent being as influencing aspects of relations, identity, ethics and faith. This new understanding creates potential for new integration between the facets of the continuous and the emergent in his mind.

Notes

2 The tension between personal relationships and faith preoccupies both the biblical character of Abraham, the narrator and the author Kierkegaard in his real life. According to his biographical details we know that Kierkegaard

struggled between his powerful wish to commit himself to marriage on the one hand, and his being a thinker and author on the other hand. Eventually, the study of such questions as identity, ethics, faith, choice and existence took precedence over a commitment to personal relations. This interpretation of the story of Kierkegaard's life point to a dialectic tension between the spiritual and intellectual journey. In his book *Fear and Trembling* Kierkegaard accompanies the story of his reading of 'The Binding of Isaac' with other reading experiences that serve him in his personal journey. These include mythologies, Shakespeare and other biblical stories that seek to promote emergent being and the commitment to relations that involves the 'continuous doing' in terms of investment in maintaining connection and commitment.

Chapter 13c

Third illustration
Otto Dov Kulka's book *Landscapes of the Metropolis of Death*

Otto Dov Kulka's book *Landscapes of the Metropolis of Death* (2013) illuminates the reading experience as a way of mobilizing a split between the emergent being that was trapped in the claustrum of a personal trauma on the one hand, and an excessive continuous doing that helped the self to remain anchored and even contributing in his world on the other hand.

Kulka was born in Czechoslovakia in 1933. When he was 10, he was transported to Auschwitz concentration camp. After World War II he became Professor of History at the Hebrew University in Jerusalem. Today he researches anti-Semitism in modern times stretching to its apogee with the implementation of Nazi Germany's 'Final Solution'. At the beginning of his book, Kulka writes that over the years he had maintained 'an attitude of strict and impersonally remote research, always conducted within well-defined historical categories, as a kind of self-contained method unto itself' (Kulka, O.D., 2013, p. xi). However, during the last decade of the twentieth century Kulka recorded what he termed to himself 'Landscapes of the Metropolis of Death' or 'Landscapes of Childhood in Auschwitz'. He claimed that these recordings were not to be considered historical testimony but rather

> the reflections of a person then in his late fifties and sixties, turning over in his mind those fragments of memory and imagination that have remained from the world of the wondering child of ten to eleven that I had once been (ibid.).

Kulka worked on these recordings and published them as a book in which his personal testimony as a youth in Auschwitz is published for the first time.

From Kulka's book it emerges that his reading of the works of Heinrich von Kleist and even more so the writings of Franz Kafka kindled in him an opportunity for a crucial change in the psychic equilibrium between continuous doing and emergent being in his mind and in his life – a transformation I shall describe in what follows.

In their book *Testimony: Crises of Witnessing in Literature, Psychoanalysis and History* (1992) Shoshana Felman and Dori Laub write that:

> The literature of testimony ... is not simply a statement (any statement can but lag behind events), but a performative engagement between consciousness and history, a struggling act of readjustment between the integrative scope of words and the unintegrated impact of events (Felman, S. and Laub, D., 1992, p 114).

Kulka's book offers a testimony of a trauma written many years after the event, a period during which Kulka took on the role of an 'objective' researcher and kept his private experiences apart from this preoccupation. It is only in his book that, for the first time, he 'introduces' the child to the researcher and the past to the present in a way that enables both Kulka and his readers to embark on these traumatic times from a different perspective – the perspective of a mind that remembers, struggles, creates. Kulka writes in the knowledge that he not only remembers but also imagines and even remembers imaginings and imagines memories. This testimony brings closer together Kulka's way of coping by the continuous-doing mode – which was very fruitful for the researcher of history – and his emergent being, which was reeling in the traumatic dungeon of its past, longing to be set free and to finally be worked through.

Unlike a conventional history book, Kulka's book adopts the form of a literary chronotope rather than telling it linearly (Bakhtin, M.M., 1975). It moves forwards and backwards between present time and space and that of the past. Kulka describes 'the eternal death of the child' (Kulka, O.D., 2013, p. 31), who is imprisoned in this traumatic claustrum from which there is no deliverance. Kulka the historian subjects this unique experience of time and space to a professional analysis. However, it is also presented in repeated dreams that always end in the same vicious circle. For most of his life after Auschwitz the narrator clearly biased in favour of the facet of continuous doing, which led him to great professional achievements. Nevertheless, Kulka recurrently describes how, split off from that contribution, a repetitive centrifugal movement takes place in his psyche, which tries disparately to pave the way to the mode of an emergent being – open, playful and free. Kulka describes the recurrent private, secret visit to the landscapes of the metropolis of death, for example in his dreams, as a visit to the familiar, to the extent that it feels comfortable and homely. Somewhat similarly to the struggle described by Semprún in his book *Literature or Life*, Kulka brings to light the dilemma as to whether to live the death – which would mean being connected to the inner truth and then die over and over again – or attempt to live detached from death, 'leaving it behind'. Paradoxically, the latter option condemns the self to psychic death because this entails discarding the psyche's most essential memories, leaving them depleted and devoid of affinity/connectedness/connection and meaning.

Kulka the historian functions within the fertile and adaptive mode of continuous doing, whereas the emergent being remains buried by '[t]he immutable law of the Great Death, the immutable law which recurs in that dream in infinite permutations, which in one place I called "the eternal death of the child"' (ibid., p. 60). The child's psyche had been too close to traumatic death; to the immutable law of death in the life of the camp, a certain death from which there was no escape. He continues to be preoccupied with it in a compulsive, repetitive, private and almost invariable way. Before coming to Kulka's reading experiences, which mobilized this balance of internal forces, let us begin with a description of the biographical circumstances. Kulka the child arrived in Auschwitz from Theresienstadt, where he was imprisoned with his mother in 'the Czech family camp'. It was only later that they became aware that they had been the beneficiaries of a strange miracle: everyone arriving in Auschwitz was immediately either sent to the crematoria or to hard labour. Only those who arrived from Theresienstadt were placed in this camp where their heads were not shaved nor were their clothes taken away. In due course it became known that this was the camp that was to be presented to the Red Cross as a refutation of the accusations levelled at the Nazis that they were engaged in the annihilation of the Jews. Kulka and the entire contingent of people who came with him and his mother didn't know that with the arrival of the next group, six months later, they would all be murdered. There would be no selection. That would be the fate of them all except for anyone who might by chance be ill, like Kulka the youth who was hospitalized on that particular day. That was why he didn't go down the stairs to the crematorium with all the others.

Kulka writes about his visit to the concentration camp years later as an adult. His first stop was the building that housed children and youths. Then he visited the hospital where Dr Mengele carried out his cruel experiments and where Kulka lay on that fateful day when he was saved and at the same time condemned to 'eternal death'. Only then does he enter the area where the remnants of the crematoria are to be found. About this eternal trap in his psyche Kulka writes:

> From here, the way to the third place was unavoidable, the place where I seemingly lived and remained always, from that day to this, and I am held captive there as a life prisoner, bound and fettered with chains that cannot be undone. Were it not so grating, I would say, 'like Prometheus bound'. But I am after all a child, who was bound with those chains as a child and remained bound by them throughout every stage of growing up. I say that I was bound and remained bound, or fettered

by chains, but that is because I was never there, because my foot never stepped into those courtyards, inside those buildings. I circled them as a moth circles a flame, knowing that falling into it was inevitable, yet I kept on circling outside, willingly or unwillingly – it was not up to me – all my friends, the butterflies, not all of them, but almost all of them, were there and did not come out of there (ibid., pp. 9–11).

Kulka's three transformative reading experiences

1. Transformative reading in Kleist's stories

The first movement towards Kulka's insight of the relations between the facets of emergent being and continuous doing in his psyche is activated as a consequence of him reading Heinrich Kleist's two stories *Michael Kohlhaas* (von Kleist, H., [1810] 2005) and 'The Earthquake in Chile' (von Kleist, H., [1807] 1993). Kulka provides us with no details about his experience reading these two stories but testifies that by reading them he had gained a new understanding of his tendency to repetition and acceptance of the immutable law of the great death.

> I made my way across the path, which I never crossed before, and I descended, as in those recurrent dreams in which I descend these stairs together with all my friends and all those who are close to me. It's the dream that always takes me back there, when I know that there is no way to avoid that place, that everyone is bound to arrive at that place because it is an inalterable law of the place, one from which there is no escape, and there is no chance for the fantasy we conjure up about liberation and an end, like playful childish fantasies, for an iron law leads everyone there and no one will escape from there. I also knew, because everyone died one night and I remained, I knew that at the last moment I would be saved. Not for any merit of mine, but because of some sort of inexorable fate … And however much I know that I must be caught, I always know, too, and that I must be spared. It's a kind of circle, a cycle of Tantalus or Sisyphus, or of whatever myth we choose to invoke that is germane here, which returns in an endless vicious circle to the same place (Kulka, O.D., 2013, p. 11).

The narrator discovers his double in von Kleist's story in which the heroes mount a far-reaching rebellion against a big law in force in their districts, but in the end they return to an acceptance of those same laws. Kulka finds an echo in this unavoidable return to the rule of the overarching law and its decrees. This movement, even though it was initiated by the heroes, is imposed on them. For Kulka this movement also represents a perspective that lends meaning to his countless internal visits to the immutable law of death. The text helps him to begin to apply meaning to his repetition compulsion, which consists of two crucial components: On the one hand there is a terrifying law that has been internalized and that has to rule for eternity. On the other hand, Kulka identifies the foundations of the rebellion and the desperate effort at resistance, which are also turning the wheel of repetition compulsion round and round.

2. Transformative reading in Kafka's 'In the Penal Colony'

The insight thus gained is broadened when Kulka reads Franz Kafka's short story 'In the Penal Colony' (Kafka, [1919] 1975b). In the story, an 'investigator-voyager' reaches a penal colony and discovers a system of law imposed by 'the colony's previous commandant'. This set of laws determines that every criminal shall discover his sentence when a machine engraves his fate on his body. After six hours of torture the inscription on his skin is revealed to him and he then discovers what his sentence is to be. There is no place for a trial, since the accused's guilt and sentence are known in advance. This is a law against which there is no appeal, a law from which there is no escape. As Kulka reads 'The Penal Colony', an incident in the concentration camp in which he saw prisoners being flogged to death, surfaces in his memory.

> I probably would not have recalled this incident, would not have engraved the scene and its import in my memory, had it not loomed before me again much later when I read Kafka's story '*In der Strafkolonie*' – 'In the Penal Colony' (ibid., p. 44).

In great detail Kulka then describes the situation he has recalled in which a prisoner had been flogged to death in front of all the other inmates who watched in complete silence. It is apparent that it wasn't the remembering triggered by the reading of 'The Penal Colony' that was transformative. Rather it was the insight that Kulka the child had become an investigator-voyager looking on from the sidelines at a law that is so absolute:

> That can exist without any connection to the strange landscape the traveller chances upon and can be transposed to the landscape of the camp on that foggy morning, in Auschwitz itself. And from Auschwitz itself, might infiltrate into every possible situation, as though it is an autonomous system, utterly divorced from any feeling of pity, repulsion, cruelty – even the distinction between victim and perpetrator seems to disappear here completely. This was the way I remembered that scene, that scene of violence-as-ritual, as part of the system, not of the Great Death or of the games of the small death, but of everyday life. The daily routine of the system functioning between the Great

Death and the liquidation of Auschwitz camp. But also Auschwitz under the dominion of a shadow of its 'glory' (ibid.).

Kafka's story permeates Kulka's selective amnesia and leaves him wondering how he could possibly have completely forgotten '[t]he violence, the cruelty, the torture, the individual killings' (ibid.). He claims not to have retained a memory of pictures of violence yet at the same time knows that:

> Actually, certain episodes of this kind do inhabit my consciousness. Earlier, I described, in passing, the piles of skeletons, the bodies – bones covered with skin – which were heaped up behind the barracks before dawn and which we children sidestepped, skirted, on the way to the youth barracks (ibid., p. 41).

The sidestepping over the skeletons became a psychological act of denial, part of the youths' mental effort to survive and avoid breaking down physically or mentally. But the price that had to be paid for this sidestepping was that the world had become arbitrary and reality was not negotiable. The language serving the self became a concrete language, a pseudo-language, devoid of emotion. The language had ceased to represent or arouse emotions because of the intensity of the trauma. Alternatively, it has prohibited emotion to appear, so as to be protected from its disintegrative potential. There is no room for emotion, for rebuke, rebellion, doubt, panic or pain. As Kulka noted, his defensive organization was 'An autonomous system, utterly divorced from any feeling' (ibid., p. 44). This is challenged when he is reading Kafka's story, which introduces him to a literary mirror of an absolutely arbitrary situation in which everyone is answerable to the immutable law of death without appealing against it, so that it creates a death sentence to the private language of the individual as well. Reading Kafka undermined the inner equilibrium between the overly efficient mode of continuous doing by Kulka the researcher and his private being that was spinning endlessly in an inner centrifugal unable to emerge as a responsive and reflexive being to the outer and inner life he was facing.

The reading experience and the insight that followed it enable Kulka to begin to search his memory for human moments that transcended the monotony of landscapes of the metropolis of death. These moments alluded to an emergent being that dared to assert itself in the midst of the hellish inferno and to voice arising from a neglected space of human values and protest.

And indeed, Kulka begins to remember voices that breached the atmosphere where the immutable law of death ruled. To his surprise he recalled several occasions when such voices had been heard. He remembered, for example, a conversation in the hospital in which two young men entertained themselves in order to divert attention from the horrors around them, talking of possible revenge against the Nazis, which they called 'Solution of the German Question'. Another memory was of the cries of three Russians as they were about to be hanged in the camp's yard: 'For Stalin! For the Homeland!' (ibid., p. 46). Instead of closing his eyes as he usually did when faced with such terrifying acts, this loud cry of defiance led him to suddenly think: 'You must look! You must engrave it in your heart! You must remember it and you must take revenge at the time of justice and retaliation' (ibid.). This memory was echoed in what he had experienced when reading Kafka. Faced with the text's mirror he is led to realize once more that he is a human being and that he must observe what is happening externally and internally in order to establish identity and meaning. So too in that moment in the concentration camp when Kulka the youth deviates from his usual habit of 'sidestepping' the traumatic event around him:

> This thought about justice being done transcends the immutable law which prevailed in that place. As though those cries ripped through the present of that time and revealed another dimension, utopian, but at least for a moment, a concrete reality because everyone heard, everyone listened, because everyone contemplated the revenge which there was called by its name. And I interiorized these things (ibid., p. 47).

Through this newly opened window in Kulka's mind following his reading of Kafka, more moments that transcended the immutable and arbitrary law of death keep returning from the repressed. One such moment had occurred really close to him and is described in a farewell letter written by his mother to his father when they were parted for ever in the camp. The letter is today in Yad Vashem's archives. In the letter she expresses her outrage at the cruelty they were being subjected to and demands 'to avenge the guiltless blood of the innocents' (ibid., p. 49). However, as Kulka points out, again with a degree of compulsiveness that is also reflected in his writing:

> This was actually an anomaly, a most rare anomaly within the system. Within the system as I remember it, as I experience it unrelentingly. It is the system of the immutable law of the Great Death, an immutability that is seemingly self-enclosed, beyond which lies nothing; and even when there is something like a spark of uprising, of illusion, of hope, such notions only float past here and there like motes on the surface of the grim consciousness that is innate within us. And remains with us afterwards, too, like that system enclosed within itself (ibid., p. 50).

Finally, Kulka remembers a young woman aged 20 giving three poems she herself had written to a Kapo standing at the entrance to the gas chamber as she was being led into the crematorium. The poems, the first of which was titled 'We the Dead Accuse!' Called for those responsible for these crimes to be brought to justice.

These transcendences recalled by Kulka following his reading of Kafka's 'The Penal Colony' are now understood by him as flickers of prayers, which were 'a kind of prayer after the "death of God"' (Sagi, A., 2011). A prayer 'expresses an essential aspect in the life of an individual: against reality and its forced nature is pitted a person's nature as someone who rejects this essentiality and transcends it by praying' (ibid., p. 101). These events were reminders that things should have been different, expressed on the rare occasions when the voice of the individual 'self' and the emergent being was heard. This voice called for a halt to the wilfully murderous acts of continuous doing that had become the 'language of the masses', a barbarian norm that children sidesteps so that they don't fall in.

In the penal colony of Auschwitz, Kulka the child learned that there was no room for prayer. Obedience to the big law was the only option. So, he also casts the memory of the violent and murderous scenes that his psyche was unable to endure into a fenced-off camp in his mind. The psychoanalyst Donald Meltzer describes the claustrum as a 'space of phantasy' in which the self is imprisoned defensively against experiencing overwhelming trauma and anxiety (Meltzer, D., 1992). Kulka's acceptance of the laws of the metropolis of death resulted in an entire part of his psyche being concealed and imprisoned in the claustrum of his mind from which nothing exited or entered. As time went by, when confronted by his double that he found in Kafka's story, Kulka begins to remember and with those memories the claustrum's ironclad, splitting envelope that protected him from breaking down during all those years begins to crack. Sagi points to the act of self-expression as a mental, spiritual and performative act that involves transcendence (Sagi, A., 2011). These moments of self-expression and transcendence surfaced in the memory of Kulka the investigator-voyager in Auschwitz's penal colony, who researched it every day as an historian but felt helpless and mute in relation to personal experience, cocooned in his childhood penal colony in eternal isolation. Reading Kafka began to mobilize his inner speech as he recalled the transcendent sayings of those who had been condemned to death, those who lay in the camp's hospital, his mother's farewell letter to his father, the act of a young woman as she was about to enter the gas chamber and even the memory of the child he once was, who for a moment in the camp's yard had dared to lift his head in an attempt to be present as an individual and now does so once again.

3. Transformative reading of Kafka's story 'Before the Law': a sub-dialectic – the particular vs the universal

Two obstacles stood in Kulka's way when it came to tell his personal story. The first, as said, was his submission to the law of the big death. This silenced his voice and clouded some of his memories and thus also parts of his psychic life. The one exception was the recurrent memory of the stairs down to the crematorium a path he was designated to tread but never did and therefore remained trapped in those memories for ever.

The second obstacle stemmed from an absolute alienation he sensed towards other accounts of the Holocaust and a feeling that the same would happen to his readers when he tells his own story. One of the distinct aspects of continuous doing is the splitting and lack of ability in achieving integration between the particular, personal event and the general. According to Kierkegaard, this reflexivity, which turns life into an object, is an indication that the word 'singular' has a double meaning in that it is both universal and particular. Only integration between the private (personal) and the general (universal) enables integration so that instead of an individual sensing his experience as idiosyncratic, singular and isolated, the single and special experience will turn into an experience that at least in its essential parts has meaning, can be talked about and communicated.

Writing about the threat of the communal language against the language of the individual Dana Amir notes that

> [i]t effaces the bird. It annihilates that unconverted freedom that cannot be transformed ... that freedom, shared by those for whom language it is not only roots but wings – not only to be the owner of 'a different story', but to be, at least for a moment, story-less (Amir, D., [2013] 2014, p. 29).

Not only did Kulka not want to tell his personal story he also absolutely avoided reading about, watching films, attending exhibitions or becoming familiar with any other kind documentation concerning Auschwitz. He didn't know exactly why this was so, other than his awareness of that experience of alienation that he felt every time he was exposed even a shred of such information. His story remained singular and isolated, unassimilated in the general account of the Holocaust. Consequently, Kulka was also unable to begin the process of working through and integration of his personal story within the general account and so remained trapped in the endless circularity of his own story.

Kulka's reading of Kafka's story 'Before the Law' (Kafka, F., [1919] 1975a) continued to breach the claustrum's shell that had cocooned him in eternal death and led to a dramatic transformation in his inner equilibrium between the singular and the general. This reading began when Kulka was invited to participate in a lecture delivered by a colleague on the subject of 'The Holocaust in Literature.' It was an invitation that he felt he had to accept. In advance of the lecture he uncharacteristically picked up a book about the Holocaust by an outstanding writer recording his memories. However, as he read the book he again felt that same alienation, finding no connection between 'his' Auschwitz and the Auschwitz described in the book. In despair he turned to Kafka. I quote his full, powerful testimony, which reads as if it was written in one stream of consciousness, so as to shed light on Kulka's usage of Kafka's story 'Before the Law':

> The only response I feel able to express is alienation; all that is authentic is the authenticity of the alienation. Therefore I ask: in what am I different? Something is wrong with me! And then, as so often, as almost always during periods of distress, I escape to Kafka, either his diaries or his other works. At that time, I again opened at the ending – I always open randomly – I opened at the ending of the wonderful story of the man standing before the Gate of the Law. This man who stands before the Gate of the Law actually asks the same question – and it is one of the last questions he asks, driven by his insatiable curiosity, as the gatekeeper jests. He asks: 'Tell me, after all this is the Gate of the Law, and the Gate of the Law is open to everyone.' To which the gatekeeper says: 'Yes, that is so.' Then the man says (if I remember the text correctly): 'Yet in all the years I have been sitting here no one has entered the gate.' And the gatekeeper nods his head and says: 'Indeed.' The man asks him to explain this puzzling fact, and the gatekeeper does him this one last mercy and says: 'This gate is open only for you, it exists only for you, and now I am going to close it.' Accordingly, everything I have recorded here – all these landscapes, this whole private mythology, this Metropolis, Auschwitz – this Auschwitz that was recorded here, which speaks here from my words, is the only entrance and exit – an exit, perhaps, or a closing – the only one that exists for me alone. I take this to mean that I cannot enter by any other way, by any other gate to that place. Will others be able to enter through the gate that I opened here, that remains open for me? It is possible that they will, because this gate that Kafka opened, which was intended for only one person, for K, Josef K., is actually open to almost everyone. But for him there was only one gate into his private mythology.
>
> I don't know whether this analogy is valid here, but this is the only meaning I can find for the puzzle of the occupation of my present with that past, which I experience constantly, in which I create constantly, to which I escape constantly, in which I create landscapes intermixed with scenes of childhood reality and time and of the onlooker, of the big boy looking with puzzlement at all this, and who, before it is shut – before

that gate is shut – asks these questions and, at least to this mystifying matter, seems to have found an answer at last. It's not much, a marginal thing, really, but it is impossible not to convey these things, not to puzzle over them, not to believe in them, for without that belief the whole memory of my childhood landscapes, the landscapes in which I always find freedom – my last but one freedom – would be los (Kulka, O.D., 2013, p. 81).

Since in the world of Auschwitz no God stood beside him, no law and no judge, Kulka feels condemned to his solitariness for ever. There is no one to turn to either outside or inside.[3] Kulka the child is left to his solitude surrounded by impenetrable walls. Until he read Kafka's 'Before the Law', he didn't think that he could transcend those walls. The story led him to a new possibility.[4] A different literary text about yet another personal holocaust of someone who sits at the Gate of the Law until the day of his death mobilized his reflection on his own Gate of the Law on the surface of which he was sitting for so many years. This is a reading experience that includes the paradox that is at the heart of the miracle of reading: Another's story tells the most private story of the reader. He suddenly feels recognized, touched, taken care of by the text and its author. He thus begins to search

> for individual language, for the singular details that have been subsumed and negated into generalities, into the communal, 'plural language'. What is plural language? An idiom that alienates, privileges sharing over individuality, and therefore fails to distinguish private essences ... It is a language ... which makes comparisons but does not differentiate, that evades the private and rejects any exception to the general as well as to the rule (Amir, D., [2013] 2014, p. 22).

As we saw in a previous context, Appelfeld writes that this is literature's imperative:

> Literature ... is, above all, obligated to practical precepts and its greatest practical obligation is towards the individual ... This individual whose unique countenance has been erased by the masses so that he becomes just another face in the crowd, this individual is the core and the essence of every literary vision. The moment this simple truth is revealed ... you learn to ask humbly. 'Who is this individual whose soul you wish to touch ... and his roots to reveal (Appelfeld, A., 1979, pp. 90–91).

Furthermore, in the context of the position of the 'self' after the Holocaust and the capacity of art to repair the egregious damage it inflicted, Appelfeld adds:

> The Holocaust was the cause of abominable injury in many areas of life but the undermining of the 'self 'was one of the most profoundly damaging of them all. The sense of insignificance is no stranger to man. However, during the period of the Holocaust this feeling reached unimagined dimensions. Who then will restore the demolished dignity of the 'self'? I'm not claiming that art is omnipotent, magical or pure faith. But one thing cannot be denied – its devotion to the individual ... His suffering and his fears and the sliver of light that occasionally shines within him. All true art unflaggingly returns and repeats that the world revolves around the individual ... the world of the individual, his personal name, his weakness or his supremacy is its great preoccupation. And when those who question this ask what has art got to do in a realm where one is demanded to do or to keep silent, I say to myself; who will set free from darkness the fears, the pain and the torment, the concealed beliefs, the sense of insignificance and of eternity from darkness. Who will liberate them from the gloom and lend them some warmth and dignity if not this art which takes such care in its choice of words, which is so cautious about every feeling and every hint of emotion (ibid., p. 98).

Kafka's story aroused the feeling in Kulka that if the private gate of Kafka's story's hero, K, is open to him as a reader, then he too doesn't have to be condemned to solitude until his death and that he too can share something of the pain, the sense of insignificance, the mourning that he is enduring. His reading of 'Before the Law' exposed him to the duality of the experience that however private it may be is also universal. It is at one and the same time nobody's and everybody's story. This led to mobilization of the mode of emergent being that erupted into the horizon of continuous doing of the historian Kulka who was so skilled in the general language. This flickering of present experience that traversed his inner barbed-wire fences led to the growth within him of hope that he can share his story after all, facing the gate of his life and death, a story that was no longer experienced as only singular but rather as personal, and the personal is also applicable to the general.

The absolute split between the historian Kulka's fertile continuous doing and the youth imprisoned in eternal death, spinning around in them repeatedly, had been transformed. Kulka begins to establish a new psychic equilibrium. Kafka's story had set in motion the dialectic between the emergent being and continuous doing by drawing Kulka's attention, in a mirror image, to the stagnation he was facing. Reflexively, Kulka observes the transformation in him following his reading of Kafka's story and writes about the previous equilibrium before he had crossed the gate of the traumatic law in order to create integration between the man of science who deals with the history of Auschwitz and the child locked behind its gates:

I have dwelt on the duality, the methodological distancing, and all the rest. Yet the truth, as it seems to me now, is that I only tried to bypass here the barrier of that gate, to enter it with the whole force of my being, in the guise of, or in the metamorphosis of, perhaps, a Trojan horse, intended, finally, to smash the gate and shatter the invisible wall of the city forbidden to me, outside whose domain I had decreed that I would remain (Kulka, O.D., 2013, pp. 82–83).

The dialectic between continuous doing and the emergent being undergoes a transformation when Kulka takes note for the first time of the product of his scientific research in terms of the emergent being. He intuitively understands that like any other defence mechanism, this was the best ad hoc solution found by the psychic system but that it had functioned in line with the law of repetition compulsion that is faithful to the discipline of the death drive. Nonetheless, that unknowingly enfolded within it also a wish to escape from the inner dungeon. The scientist was the child's Trojan horse – the child who sought to burst out of the walls of the claustrum, the wall of singularity to which he had condemned himself, which not only stood between him and the world but was also a barrier between him and his own being. From the moment that the child within the scientist emerged, a potential space began to show its signals. One of the signs of the opening to this potential space is Kulka's recognition that until then he had been living in a closed space without realizing that all this time he had been looking for a way of forcing himself out of it, 'for that rigorous "pure scientific" writing is fraught with tremendous "meta-dimensional" baggage and tensions, which are somehow time-transcendent' (ibid., p. 82). Kulka borrows Kafka's gate in order to face his own gate. In trenchant and at the same time exquisite words he closes the gate of his book in which a new light now flickers:

Was that my gate to the law? To the law of the world? One of the two massive iron doors of that gate, a gate that is open day and night? And now, as the gatekeeper said to the man, 'I am going to close it.' Yet it seems to me that story also tells, that in those moments it appeared to the man that beyond that gate there shone, or glowed dimly, a new light, such as he had never before seen in his life (ibid., p. 83).

In a general way one can describe the traumatic history in terms of the balance between continuous doing and emergent being. The traumatic images return and haunt the post-traumatic individual in both his waking hours and in his dreams. This experience severely damages the functioning of the facet of emergent being, which facilitates a live, open and reflexive existence. A person who has experienced trauma, as exemplified by Kulka, is likely to function in the axis of continuous doing in a beneficial way and, in the case of a powerful personality, even realize parts of emergent being that function in the adaptational areas of life. But a critical part of his psyche remains in the 'there and then' so that in this area he remains psychologically impoverished and is unable to be fully attendant in the present and open to the call of the experience that seeks to meet him. A reader and writer such as Kulka are needed in order to illustrate that these determinations are not final. Out of a profound insight Kulka shows that in retrospect, despite and alongside the detachment between the inner child and the man of science, between being and doing, between the past and the continuous present, there hides all the time the mind's secret effort to force its way out of the gate of the law of trauma towards prayer, towards the voice that seeks to transcend, which wants to continue to live, to create, to observe, to mourn what has happened and what came to an end and to achieve a renewed integration between all of these aspects of his internal and external life.

An individual's loneliness is an existential fundament that never vanishes, but it is not the same as the sense of solitude caused when isolated parts of the self are split off from others. The return of these parts to an integration with the rest of the psyche creates a new experience of self. With the solitude of the child from Auschwitz there begins a split between the absolute evil and the good,[5] between death and life, between the past and the present, between the frozen and the emergent, between the child and the adult. Now a psychic change was achieved, and the various parts of the mind that encounter each other *de novo* are able to contain one another, take care of one another and even allow meaningful others to meet them and take care of them in the space of the literary text, in the therapeutic space and in real life.

Kulka's reading liberated the besieged city in his mind and led to the reestablishment of the metaphorical inner witness.[6] With that another poetic miracle takes place: We too gain the privilege of reading Kulka's story.

Notes

3 Sagi writes, 'The death of God and the removal of his existence from the world are likely to lead man to himself as he discovers that he is locked in a life of loneliness behind walls which he cannot transcend' (Sagi, A., 2011, p. 98).
4 The psychologist Rina Lazar (1995) writes about 'defamiliarization' in literature and therapy and contends that change includes friendship with the stranger (both the external stranger and the stranger from within).
5 To gain an understanding of the dialectic movement as a curative means against absolute evil, see Roth, M. (2016b).
6 For further reading on the development in the forms of the internal witnessing of the narrator in Kulka's book, see Roth, M. (2016a). A Psychoanalytic View on the Witness 'Before the Law' of Trauma, and the Transformative Power in Reading Literature. *Maarag Journal*, 6, pp. 247–261.

References

Amir, D. [2008] (2016). *On the Lyricism of the Mind*. London and New York: Routledge.
Amir, D. [2013] (2014). *Cleft Tongue: The Language of Psychic Structures*. London: Karnac Books.
Appelfeld, A. (1979). *Essays in the First Person*. Jerusalem: Bialik Publishing.
Appelfeld, A. [2010] (2017). *The Man Who Never Stopped Sleeping*. New York: Penguin Random House.
Bakhtin, M.M. (1975). *Formy vremeni i khronotopa v romane* [Time's and Chronotope's Forms in a Novel]. Voprosy literatury i estetiki. Issledovaniia raznykh let. [The editor of this volume is listed as S. Leibovich, but it was actually put together by] S.G. Bocharov (Ed.). Moskva: Khudozhestvennaia literature, pp. 234–407.
Bion, W.R. (1965). *Transformations: Change from Learning to Growth*. London: Tavistock.
Blanchot, M. [1955] (1982). *The Space of Literature*. Lincoln: University of Nebraska Press.
Bollas, C. (1987). *The Shadow of the Object: Psychoanalysis of the Unthought Known*. New York: Columbia University Press.
Durban, J. (2017). Facing the Death-Object: Unconscious Phantasies of Relationships with Death. In: M. Erlich-Ginor (Ed.) *Not Knowing Knowing Not Knowing*. New York: International Psychoanalytic Books, pp. 85–114.
Erlich, S.H. (2003). Experience: What Is It? *International Journal of Psychoanalysis*, 84, pp. 1125–1147.
Felman, S. and Laub, D. (1992). *Testimony: Crises of Witnessing in Literature, Psychoanalysis and History*. New York and London: Routledge.
Freud, S. (1912). Recommendations to Physicians Practicing Psycho-Analysis. In: J. Strachey (Ed.) *The Standard Edition of the Complete Psychological Works of Sigmund Freud, Vol. XII*. London: Hogarth Press, pp. 109–120.
Gottlieb-Zornberg, A. (2009). *The Murmuring Deep: Reflections on the Biblical Unconscious*. New York: Random House.
Heidegger, M. [1927] (1996). *Being and Time*. Albany: State University of New York Press.
Hesse, H. [1922] (1981). *Siddharta*. New York: Bantam Books.
Joseph, B. (1982). Addiction to Near-Death. *International Journal of Psychoanalysis*, 63, pp. 449–456.
Kafka, F. [1915] (1975). The Metamorphosis. In: *The Great Short Stories by Franz Kafka*. New York: Schocken Books, pp. 67–134.
Kafka, F. [1919] (1975a). Before the Law. In: *The Great Short Stories by Franz Kafka*. New York: Schocken Books, pp. 148–150.
Kafka, F. [1919] (1975b). In The Penal Colony. In: *The Great Short Stories by Franz Kafka*. New York: Schocken Books, pp. 191–230.
Kierkegaard, S. [1843] (2003). *Fear and Trembling*. London: Penguin.
Kierkegaard, S. [1844] (1985). *Philosophical Fragments*. H.V. Hong and E. Hong (Eds). Princeton, NJ: Princeton University Press.
Klein, M. (1930). The Importance of Symbol Formation in the Development of the Ego. In: *Love, Guilt and Reparation and Other Works 1921–1945*. London: Vintage, pp. 219–232.

Klein, M. (1958). On the Development of Mental Functioning. In: *Envy and Gratitude and Other Works 1946–1963*. London: Vintage, pp. 236–246.
Kolker, S. (2009). Introduction to 'Fear of Breakdown'. In: E. Berman and D. W. Winnicott (Eds) *True Self, False Self*. Tel Aviv: Am Oved, pp. 187–291.
Kulka, O.D. (2013). *Landscapes of the Metropolis of Death: Reflections on Memory and Imagination*. London: Penguin.
Lazar, R. (1995). The Familiar and the Strange: The Dynamics of Change. *The Israel Journal of Psychiatry and Related Sciences*, 32, pp. 157–166.
Meltzer, D. (1992). *The Claustrum*. Perthshire, UK: Clunie Press.
Meltzer, D. and Williams, M.H. (1988). *The Apprehension of Beauty*. London: Karnac Books Ltd.
Ogden, T.H. (2003). On Not Being Able to Dream. *International Journal of Psychoanalysis*, 84(1), pp. 17–30.
Pearl, J. (2011). *A Question of Time between Philosophy and Psychoanalysis*. Ramat Gan: Bar Ilan University Press.
Pessoa, F. (2017). *The Book of Disquiet*. London: Serpent's Tail.
Roth, M. (2016a). A Psychoanalytic View on the Witness 'Before the Law' of Trauma, and the Transformative Power in Reading Literature. *Maarag Journal*, 6, pp. 247–261.
Roth, M. (2016b). The Restorative Power of Reading Literature: From Evil to Dialectics. In: R. Lazar (Ed.) *Talking About Evil: Psychoanalytic, Social, and Cultural Perspectives*. London: Routledge, pp. 181–199.
Sagi, A. (1991). *Kierkegaard: Religion and Existence: The Voyage of the Self*. Jerusalem: Bialik Institute.
Sagi, A. (2011). *Prayer After 'The Death of God': A Phenomenological Study in Hebrew Literature*. Ramat-Gan and Jerusalem: Bar-Ilan University Press and Shalom Hartman Institute.
Sagi, A. (2012). *Facing Others and Otherness: The Ethics of Inner Retreat*. Tel Aviv: HaKibbutz HaMeuchad.
Sartre, J. [1964] (1981). *The Words*. New York: Vintage Books.
Steiner, J. (2011). *Seeng and Being Seen: Emerging from a Psychic Retreat*. London: New Library of Psychoanalysis.
von Kleist, H. [1807] (1993). The Earthquake in Chile. In: S. Appelbaum (Ed.) *Five Great German Short Stories*. Mineola, NY: Dover Publications, pp. 5–33.
von Kleist, H. [1810] (2005). *Michael Kohlhaas*. New York: Melville Books.
Winnicott, D.W. (1945). Primitive Emotional Development. *International Journal of Psychoanalysis*, 26, pp. 137–143.
Winnicott, D.W. (1958). The Capacity to Be Alone. *International Journal of Psychoanalysis*, 39, pp. 416–420.
Winnicott, D.W. (1971). *Playing and Reality*. London: Tavistock Publications.
Winnicott, D.W. (1974). Fear of Breakdown. *International Review of Psychoanalysis*, 1, pp. 103–107.
Zoran, R. (2000). *The Third Voice: The Therapeutic Qualities of Literature and Their Applications in Bibliotherapy*. Jerusalem: Carmel.

Further reading

Heidegger, M. [1950] (1993). The Origin of the Work of Art. In: M. Heidegger: *The Basic Writings, Revised and Expanded Edition*. London: Routledge, pp. 143–212.

Kierkegaard, S. [1859] (1962). *The Point of View of My Work as an Author: A Report to History, and Related Writings*. New York: Harper Torchbooks.

Sagi, A. (1991). *Kierkegaard: Religion and Existence: The Voyage of the Self*. Jerusalem: Bialik Institute.

Sagi, A. (2007). *To Be a Jew: Brener: An Existentialist Jew*. Tel Aviv: Hakibbutz Hameuchad.

Sagi, A. (2009). *The Human Voyage to Meanin: A Philosophical-Hermeneutical Study of Literary Works*. Ramat Gan: Bar Ilan University Press.

Semprún, J. (1994). *Literature or Life*. London and New York: Penguin Books.

Chapter 14

Epilogue
The transformative power of reading literature

At the end of this journey through the labyrinthine complexity of the reading mind I want to briefly discuss a number of insights as to the transformative power inherent in the reading of literature.

But first two reservations.

The first relates to the limitations of a text's therapeutic power. The text's constancy, that anchor which facilitates the profound and multilayered movement between the reader's mind and the text's characters is, at the same time, reading's glass ceiling. This is because however much the literary characters alter their identity in line with the reader's transference relations and however much the reader's freedom to use these characters is expanded, they nonetheless remain enshrined in the letters chosen by the author and fashioned in the way the writer decided to create them. So, irrespective of the extent to which the reader may change as a result of his encounter with the literary characters they themselves will remain unaltered.

On the other hand, in real-life relations, including relations in the context of a therapeutic process, a part of the transformative power stems from the dynamic and emergent connection between two minds and the vivid unconscious dialogue between them. In such a setting, the 'self' as well as the 'other' change as a result of the encounter. The capacity to influence and induce change in the 'other' as part of their communication is an important element in the healing process and offers one an opportunity to achieve a crucial transformation in life. Psychoanalysts devote their professional lives; the sum total of their intellectual, emotional and moral resources, to 'reading the text' presented by their patients so as to help them free themselves from their anxieties and defences in favour of revealing new pathways to a life full of creativity and meaning. Therefore, before discussing literature's transformative power and the fascination of its multifaceted traits, modesty requires that we recognize the limitations of the reading experience as a basis for achieving psychic change. In the event of need, seeking help from a close person or from a therapeutic process may provide assistance that transcends beyond reading's power to heal.

The second reservation has to do with the variance in the transformative power of different texts. Not every reading leads to reflection and psychic development. Texts differ in terms of the kind of identification they trigger and are dissimilar in their suitability for a given reader who seeks to identify with them. Writing about books, Virginia Woolf notes that, 'Books differ ... each differs from the other as a tiger differs from a tortoise, a tortoise from an elephant. Our attitude must always be changing, it is clear. From different books we must ask different qualities' (Woolf, V., 1932, p. 4). And just as every book has a different quality so too every reader differs in his openness and capacity to use each reading in itself and reading in general.

Despite these reservations we have seen that reading possesses the power to mobilize the reader's psyche. This is the moment, before the reading of another book comes to an end, to conclude by delineating the roots of reading's transformative powers.

Multilayered identifications

The most basic magnate that draws the reader's psyche to a literary text is his identification with its characters and their experiences. This is the basis for the formation of the transference relations, the launch pad from which the reader transcends beyond the confines of his daily life and the motor that enables him to work through his psychic equilibriums. Great importance has to be attached to the movement between the different forms and levels of identification as the vivid platform for the creation of the reader's experience. This is a kind of practice in laboratory conditions that enables the mind to 'train' in the conduct of relations, psychic solutions and existential coping. The many layers of the various forms of identification possess three crucial traits: *types* of identification; the *movement* between different forms and different levels of identifications; and the *bidirectional nature* of the identification between the reader and the literary characters.

Forms of identification

The literary illustrations presented throughout this book revealed seven types of identification aroused during reading. These identifications range from primitive types (such as adhesive identification) to 'higher', more developed ones (such as internalized identification). Thus, 'form of identification' refers both to the 'type of identification' as well as to its positioning on the continuum between normal and pathological. As was evident from the literary examples, 'normal' and 'pathological' identifications do not appear in isolation from one another so that in the same reading the involved reader is likely to move from a 'pathological' kind of identification to a 'normal' one.

The distinction between normal and pathological identification can be made by questioning whether the type of identification helps the reader to work through his inner struggles or whether it involves a primitive identification and a denial of reality that can even reach the extent of a collapse of the reality testing by way of total merger with the literary characters.

One can assess the difference in the quality of the identification by the distance that separates the reader from the text's heroes and the reality in which 'they live'. One end of this range lacks the playful traits of the transitional space of the literary work, as described in Buber-Neuman's book *Milena* ([1976] 1997). In her reading experience in the solitary cell in which she was actually imprisoned in the Ravensbrück concentration camp she became one with the characters in Maxim Gorky's story *A Man Is Born*, and her imagination became the exclusive reality.

The other end of the range is characterized by the reader's ability to use reading's transitional space, which is to say to position himself on the pleasurable seamline between the 'me' and the 'not me', between reality and imagination and between the internal and external worlds. We saw an example of this in Semprún's identification with Malraux, which not only did not undermine his psychological functioning but rather aided the reader to return from a disintegrative moment and earn back his psychological strengths (Semprún, J., 1994). The latter kind of identification by the reader with a character in a book can be discontinued at any moment as, for instance, when the reader has to put the book down. And yet when the identification is active it can carry intense emotions, imagination and psychological efficacy.

Movement between the forms and levels of identification

'Books act as introductions to dreams' writes Pessoa (Pessoa, F., [1982] 2017, p. 235). Reading is indeed a simulation of concealed psychic situations. The most effective reading won't be the one that enables the reader to identify himself with the text in an absolute and limitless way. Nor will it be the reading that only settles in the transitional space of the literary work. The most effective will be the one that facilitates psychic movement between different types of identification. This movement activates an inner therapeutic function that is linked to an openness to primitive identifications no less than being open to the more developed identifications. In daily life our mind's more primitive aspects appear when we lose control, or they are repressed beneath the more developed personality. There is therefore a decisive advantage to the movement that literature enables the reader to enjoy. He is invited to withdraw to the primitive realms of his psyche and to climb back out of them, in the course of which a unique dialogue between the different aspects of the 'self' is created.

The significant power of reading's transitional space is thus reinforced by the movement between the transitional space to the mind's extremities and back. When the reader returns from his journeys to these internal frontiers, he has the opportunity to learn about himself by reading in which he can engage with others in a way he cannot allow himself to do in the cautious conditions of real life. This movement facilitates the establishment of an overarching reflexive position that observes these movements that are essential and inherent to psychic existence. It is in the power of this overarching position to enable the reader to be modest about the extent of his sovereignty over his ultimate fate. By his identification with literature's heroes who rise and fall, he learns that there are aspects of life that are not dependent on him such as the finiteness of life, the partiality of resources, the dependence on others, etc. He also humbly recognizes, through his identification with the literary characters, that we own both primitive and mature aspects, which we constantly move between, and so does the other, and that all we can do is to try and assume responsibility for the different layers and conflicting forces of the mind.

This acknowledgement emboldens the reader's sovereignty over his internal world and his fate because he can now retreat from literary fiction and return to his life where he is now able to perform on the basis of a greater awareness, responsibility and compassion. He becomes more equipped to search for novel pathways to reparation and creativity. The movement between types of identification and the development of the reader's overarching view are therefore likely to lead both to a recognition of the limitations of the subject's freedom in his world alongside the acknowledgment of the freedoms he still possesses, which lead to a new horizon of possibilities.

Bidirectional identification between reader, characters and author

The literary text as a lightning rod

The process of identification in reading is bidirectional. In effect, the text is experienced and conceivably functions as a lightning rod for bidirectional projections. Each of the sides, the author on the one hand and the reader on the other, turn into a container for the inner world of the other. On one side of the equation the reader and along with him the entire reading community, become a huge container for the riddles of one mind – the author's – that has turned its unconscious into literary gemstones. On the other hand, the author and his 'representatives' – the text's characters – are experienced as containing the reader's mind that projects his inner world on to them. The reader feels that he is containing and working through the real psychic challenges confronted by the text's heroes. At the same time, he feels that the coping shown by the characters also metabolizes and works through his own anxieties and pains. The room of mirrors lends the text an interpretive and transformative power.

A complete reading would include both the aspect of the reader as a container and as being contained. We have seen how this mutual process of containment and working through is likely to influence the internal psychic equilibriums so that they gradually become less polarized and more complementary. There is profound affinity between the psychic dialectics, which are aroused in reading: insanity needs order; the depth of meaning involves the subversive presence of the unreadable; the absent illuminates the present and its significance; the present always carries the shadow of the absent and it's importance; the homely encapsulates the uncanny, which deepens its compassion; the emergent being in the absence of continuous doing makes existence infinitely disintegrative and therefore endangers the self. The continuous doing without the emergent being, on the other hand, is akin to an infrastructure and a goal that lacks the aspect of dreaming and creativity. Reading literature aids these complementary forces to movement and mutual fertilization, which leads to further development and creativity.

For this multilayered movement to occur there has to be a difference between the subject and the 'reading subject'. The reading subject's behaviour differs from that of the subject engaged in his daily life. If that were not so it wouldn't be in literature's power to fascinate and engage readers of literature. At the end of the present journey of observation the time has come to ask who 'the reading subject' is.

The 'transitional subject'

I suggest the term 'the transitional subject' to describe a unique phenomenon related to the reader of literature. This definition is a paraphrase that merges Thomas Ogden's concept of the 'third subject' (Ogden, T., 1994) with the 'transitional space' described by Winnicott (1971). In the transitional space of the literary reading, 'a third' is created, where 'unconscious experience is generated both individually and as a co-creation of two or more people (which may include reader and author)' (Ogden, B.H. and Ogden, T., 2012, p. 271). This enables a unique use of the literary object by the reader's 'transitional subject', as I will now try to explain.

The 'transitional subject' characterizes the reader's special state of mind, which offers him psychic freedom to use the literary object in ways that he cannot in his daily life and in certain senses is not even consciously available to him internally. Winnicott's term 'the use of an object' (Winnicott, D.W., 1969) came to be commonly used in the psychoanalysis of object relations. It describes the positive sense of freely 'using' the (m)other, as an opportunity to come into a live and meaningful relation with a significant other.

Through his identification with the literary characters, the reader allows himself 'to share' their experiences and 'use' them in an extraordinarily free and uninhibited way. The freedom of the reading 'transitional subject' is well beyond the subject's freedom in his daily life because he is, at one and the same time, the reader, the characters and the author all rolled into one. On the one hand, he is the subject of the reader and as such he is neither the author nor the characters. On the other hand, on the basis of his identifications with the characters, he is also not just the reader's subject. In the unique situation of reading literature, the reader performs as both 'the subject' and 'the object' and he experiences a transferential encounter between the two.

According to Winnicott the capacity to use an object undergoes a developmental process that includes an attempt by the infant to 'destroy' the object. If the object survives the attack, the infant learns that he can use the object and be less concerned about destroying it (ibid.). The 'transitional subject' who is active at the time of reading 'allows himself to destroy' the literary object – both the characters and the author – in a more impulsive and projective way than readers dare to do in their actual lives. The justified anxiety about destruction in day-to-day relations narrow an individual's authentic movements both in his real relations with others as well as in his inner relations with them and with himself. The reader, on the other hand, can project on to the literary characters and introject from them the darkest of urges and the most infantile needs, secure in the knowledge that when he has finished the book the literary object remains intact, saved from the reader's destructive urges. This process of projection and introjection of drives, phantasies and emotions of the most profound kind enables the reader to engage in processes of reflection and transformation that are not possible in other spaces.

The book's physical form also remains unimpaired and so does the continuity of its plot and the characteristics of its heroes. When the reader next opens the book, its form will be exactly the same as it was the last time he handled it. So too it will be when he has finished reading the book and his stormy encounters with its heroes have run their course. Were he to turn a few pages back he would find the text and its heroes complete and undestroyed. As he reads, the reader feels that he is creating the text. He also senses that he stands outside of the text's omnipotent control. He alters the text in his mind, yet the plot remains unchanged. He discovers that after everything he has projected, identified, destroyed, protested, opposed and influenced, the literary hero and the text itself have survived his use of them and remain whole. As Freud pointed out (1915), even the death of the hero is comfortingly revealed as fictive when he returns to life in a repeat reading and dies again in an aesthetic and identical way next time, and so on and so forth.

The 'literary third' is the unique way in which the text is experienced in every reading, a way that is not only identical to the written creation or exclusive to the reader's experience. Rather, it is a third space that is created by a unique intermingling between the reader's mind and the literary text.

Contrary to the constant written characters, the 'literary third' is created in every reading in a way that differs from its predecessor and thus becomes a new creation with a new meaning, a phenomenon that is of crucial importance. After all, the text and its meanings 'change' from one reading to the next in line with the different encounter the reader establishes with every reading. Thus, the 'literary third' constitutes a part of the developmental processes of the reader's 'self' through the various reading experiences.

For the reader, the use by the 'transitional subject' of the literary object leads to two kinds of understandings. First, there is a developed and new understanding of his individuality, when he returns to it after his visits to the realms of the text. The second understanding is that of the other (the literary character); who is encountered and explored freely in the special circumstances of reading, which also progresses a deep recognition of his otherness.

The widespread psychoanalytic view is that, on the one hand, primitive processes of projection and identification, which include an impulsive outburst, loss of reality testing and the blurring of the borders of the 'self', are the result of developmental regression. On the other hand, processes of mourning, recognition of limitations, separateness and reflectivity result from psychological development and also lead to further psychological growth. This assumption is indeed relevant to relations in actual life. However, in the context of psychoanalytic therapy, regression to primary states constitutes part of what is termed 'regression in the service of the ego' (Winnicott, D.W., 1963), which is to say a regression that the mind 'allows itself' to go through in the presence of a protective framework – the analysis – and a containing and transformational object – the analyst. Nonetheless, even the most tolerant and skilled psychoanalyst cannot allow for an impulsive outburst that includes the possibility of causing real harm nor can he allow his analysand to regress from reality testing in a way that puts his life at risk.

I wish to illuminate the unique way in which 'regression in the service of the ego' becomes possible in the context of reading. The special features of the 'transitional subject' of reading, together with the resilience of the literary object, enables some release of the constant restraint that the ego imposes on everything that fails to meet the demands of reality and of the superego. Thus, the reader can visit in realms of the mind that otherwise would remain excluded and hidden even from him throughout life. The reader uses his literary experiences in order to learn more about his unconscious infantile needs, his latent rage, the death drive that he struggles against, his dependency, his sexual drives and his envy.

In addition to their capacity to release the infantile and tempestuous parts of the psyche, reading experiences enable the reader to be in the company of literary characters to work through together with them existential and spiritual questions and transcend beyond the opportunities that real life – even his dreams – offer him. Alongside this, the reader feeds on reading experiences in order to learn about the 'other' – he learns to recognize the measure of resilience of the other and gets the chance to glimpse into the psychic realms of others that are based on similar and yet different dynamics. Through the literary characters he encounters the overwhelming fact that, like him, the other is also complex, vulnerable and human.

The transitional subject is in constant inter-being and inter-change: between the reading-self and the literary objects; between the paranoid-schizoid position and the depressive position; between the non-reflexive and the self-observing subject; and between the objectifying versus the acknowledging attitude toward the (literary) 'other'.

This rich and multifaceted structure creates a potential for an experience followed by an experience of contemplation and self-reflection. The literary examples showed how the reading experiences served and sometimes saved the readers in the face of radical challenges such as states of blocked thinking, death anxiety, mental freeze, the loss of the capacity for empathy and ethical stand, moral confusion, exile and solitude. The reader gets the chance to examine aspects of his internalized object relations that are concealed in the depths of his unconscious, a process that contributes significantly to his psychic development. This complex process is the source of literature's great transformative power.

An important revelation that arises from working through the literary illustrations is that the power of the transitional subject of reading derives from the fact that these processes are not distinguishable from one another, occurring neither sequentially or in isolation. These psychic processes permeate, nurture and enrich each other and the reader's forms of identification also permeate each other like the multicoloured forms of a kaleidoscope.

Reading's art of mourning

As we reach the end of this book, I suggest using Ogden's term 'the art of mourning' (Ogden, T., 2000) and point to a unique phenomenon that takes place in the course of reading, which I have chosen to term 'reading's art of mourning'. This phenomenon appears in all the psychic processes involved in the reading of literature and is a litmus test as to whether or not the reading becomes transformative. The transformative reading undermines the reader's long-established psychic equilibrium and transforms it *de novo*. It frees the reader of a variation of one kind or another of repetitive compulsion and psychic defences towards mobilization and the discovery of new creative pathways that will lead to reparation and renewal. This transformation involves the question as to whether the reader will use the reading in order to mourn the limitations of psychic and actual existence. We saw an example of such a reading experience in Kulka's deep mourning and inner development that followed his reading of Kafka's 'Before the Law' (Kulka, O.D., 2013, pp. 115–116). Mourning of this kind is a necessary condition for negotiating one's way in life (internally and externally) despite the limitations of existence and even in light of those limitations. The psychoanalyst Thomas Ogden writes about the creative process of the writer Jorge Luis Borges following his father's death:

> Mourning is not simply a form of psychological work; it is a process centrally involving the experience of making something, creating something adequate to the experience of loss. What is 'made' and the experience of making it – which together might be thought of as 'the art of mourning' represent the individual's effort to meet, to be equal to, to do justice to, the fullness and complexity of his or her relationship to what has been lost and to the experience of loss itself (Ogden, T., 2000, p. 66).

The literary examples appearing throughout this book provide evidence that the process of reading can also be regarded as a practice in the art of mourning, which is an active and creative process. As the reader dares to survive his bold entry into the realms of imagination he is able to reflect upon his profound identifications and relations with the literary heroes; to face the literary life situations that harbour catastrophic threats; and to encounter the limitations of existence that are expressed in the texts he reads – he gains the opportunity to mourn in the arms of literature. In other words, in the reader's art of mourning he is involved (consciously and unconsciously) in creating his own story in light of the impossible, ultimate and chaotic, alongside the aesthetic, the good and the beautiful in life and in his mind. He becomes creative in the way he recollects the good internal objects and encounters life out of a position of meaning, reconciliation and resolution and fulfilment. The reader's art of mourning makes good use of literature's transcendental quality, which enables the transitional subject of the reader to transcend the confines of his being through the literary text and reach other perspectives and by this repeated forward and backward repeated movement between the reader and the text to gradually change and develop. When the reader is less anxious to meet life's threats and limitations, he no longer uses massive psychic weapons/artillery to defend himself, thus releasing mental energy to be more creative and more 'alive'. The reader's 'art of mourning' – leads to a new integration between the dialectic tensions he is confronting – between the absent and the present in life, between the homely and the uncanny, between the symbolic order and insanity and between the emergent being and continuous doing. The reader's 'art of mourning' thus leads to the creation of a new equilibrium in the multidialectic space of his mind.

A journey in time: a bidirectional reparation

Reading and the work of mourning that it involves enables the reader to create a reparatory bidirectional movement between present and past.

Retrospective reparation

The first direction of movement in time in the course of reading is 'retrospective', i.e. looking backwards. It entails viewing the past from the perspective of the present, which enables us to see the past in a new light. The reader uses literature's transitional space in order to look again at his past and gain a new perspective of his life and his memories. Thus, looking back is likely to alter the view that had been the basis upon which his 'life story' had so far been written.

'Afterwardness' reparation

The second direction of movement in time mobilized in the reading of literature is that of 'afterwardness' (Freud, S., 1918).[1] This is a special kind of psychic occurrence that Freud associates with psychic time and psychic causality, which he differentiates from linear time and logical causality. Events, impressions and traces of memory that in the past couldn't be merged in a meaningful context are worked through *de novo* at a later stage as a result of the penetration of a different developmental stage and new experiences. It is as if the latter invade an impression formed in the past and alter its original nature and any leftover traces of it. It is in the power of this unique psychic phenomenon not only to establish a new meaning, but to also grant past experiences a psychic momentum, which is to say the experiences of the past 'change afterwards'.

The literary illustrations have shown that the reading experience can also permeate experiences of the past, influence and alter their memory traces in the reader's mind. Moreover, it is not only the impressions of the past that change in the course of reading. Reading literature introduces the reader to momentariness of being, an encounter that is characterized by the dissolution of the linear dimension of time. By dint of this dissolution one can also see in the work of mourning associated with reading a paradoxical opportunity to 'an afterwards change of the future', a course that is difficult to comprehend in terms of linear time but is revealed in literary illustrations. For example in the way in which Sartre in his book *The Words* describes his future readers reading the works of the dead Sartre and so that his future is changed 'afterwards'.

These movements of retrospection and change 'afterwards' turns the reading of literature into a unique space for transformation and reparation of inner experiences that had so far dwelt in an isolated and dissociated way among the reader's past impressions. Reparation is impossible so long as the reader's past experiences remain encapsulated with no bridge between them and the reader's continuous time. As the literary examples illustrated, 'literary time' provides the reader with such a bridge. The linkage between the different periods of time in life and in the mind creates an opportunity for a creative working through and reparation. This can be achieved via a compassionate and reconciled retrospective view over the self and his internal objects, which was not possible previously. It can also come about through a transformation of the memory traces themselves, which change their form 'afterwardly' and find a new place in the mind's total mosaic.

The position of the 'self surveying his past anew' and the position of the 'self altered afterwardly' are not solely temporal versions, nor additional versions living side by side with the previous self. Rather they form a new, more integrated edition of the same self, including the dialectic tensions and inner struggles that will continue to reverberate within him throughout his life.

Reading as a source of inspiration

I am here using the concept of 'inspiration' to describe a receptive connection with the text on the part of the reader, who approaches the reading without any presumptions. In a state of inspiration, the subject matter discards its one form and breaks away from the common language, lending the reader a renewed freedom to view things in their virginal state and variability. For this what is required is a readiness to sacrifice what is certain and dream about what has not yet been and may never be. What has already been written is stored away in favour of what has yet to be named. The organizing word is replaced by a creating one.

At peak moments in the literary examples, which were also the heights of the readers' works of mourning, one could see how inspiration opens up. To reach inspiration a reader has to pass two complementary moments: an erasure of his regular view of things and the freedom to see them as if for the very first time.

The depressive, i.e. developed reading experience, enables the reader to abandon the position of an individual tossed into a world of forced, empty meanings. He can then open himself up to a world beyond the signifiers with which he is familiar and become receptive to a new experience of being. Part of the process of mourning involves a transition from the narrow confines of reality and of the world of signifiers to the discovery of a renewed meaning that breathes life into the spaces between the signifiers. A reading that breathes life in a text escapes the restriction of the world of signifiers and enters the world of vivid meaning, which enables mourning and rejuvenation. In particular moments of inspiration, the reading soul opens its wings and reaches even beyond the world of meaning.

The reading self needs to let go for a moment of knowledge and control, even to suspend recognition of his identity and individuality, in order to devote himself to what is being revealed beyond him. This transcendence beyond the familiar, to which the inspired individual devotes himself, gains him the opportunity to feel that every moment is 'one of a kind', that constantly emerges into being. This is a very private experience because the self is for a moment in touch with existence's blink of an eye. And yet, at the same time, this is the most non-private experience since what is beyond the self belongs both to the world and to nothing at all. The text's narrative and its grammar are the building blocks of the syntax with which the reader paves his way along inspiration's transparent pathways, walking beyond his boundaries and back. For the reader, his moments of inspiration are a source of contemplation, change and creativity.

Conclusion

Man's psyche has no past. The past is in the present. It is harboured in our conscious and repressed memories. It has an unceasing influence on us. In the psychoanalytic encounter the patient forms transference relations with the analyst; he endows the analyst with the characteristics of significant figures from his past such as his father and mother, and also projects into the analyst aspects of his own self-representations. These object- and self-representations, which come to life again in the transference relations, give the patient another opportunity – this time within a therapeutic context – to experience aspects of his past. Those aspects that demand further working though, which influenced and shaped the person's psychic structure and that he unconsciously carries with him into every situation and relationship in his life – are the ones to be revived in the transference relations. The analyst interprets the patient's story and so facilitates a process of understanding, mourning, lending meaning and discovering creative and novel ways of coping with its demands.

On the long voyage covered by this book it became apparent that literature also offers the reader a further opportunity for a revived encounter with himself and with the significant others in his internal world, who inhabit his mind as permanent occupants. The distancing paradox described at the beginning of the book, enables the reader to unravel the existing crystallized psyche, shed his identity for a time and liberate himself from his limitations on the assumption that he has distanced himself sufficiently from himself and entered the other world of the textual space. As we have seen, identification with literary characters creates rich and varied transference relations with them. The reader removes the barriers, releases the tough defences, disrupts internal equilibriums and through relations with the story's heroes he plunges into familiar and highly charged psychic situations from his life and mind. He revisits partings and losses, desires and taboos, conflicts and loss of purpose, ethical and moral challenges. In the course of his life, through the mechanisms of splitting, projection and other primitive defences, the self and the others became internally represented in extreme, distorted ways. Literature unravels these primitive internal representations of self and objects and introduces the reader to some more complex and integrated internalized figures. The reader's connection to literature's elaborated characters arouses understanding, at times even empathy and compassion, towards characters and parts of the 'self' that had been superficially and one-dimensionally established in his psyche. This gap between the internalized objects and the internal relations with them and the literary characters and the relations between the reader and them has a central role. It has the power to create movement in the reader's mind from primitive splits to a more complex and compassionate world view of the 'other's' psyche and the self as one. Consequently, the characters in his psyche also become more integrated as does his own 'self' that gained the opportunity of broadening and deepening his ways of relating. The stories create a richer and more complex perspective and are educative in relation to the drives behind anxiety, pain and guilt, which are at the core of all human manifestations. They remind the reader that everyone has a history that has left its mark and that he defends himself against to the best of his ability, and that alongside the limitations that arouse pain and mourning there is the option at any given moment to lend a new meaning, which always includes the possibility to make a creative choice and the open gate for reparation. The reader 'practices' other ways for psychic existence. In this literature awards him a further opportunity for reflection and growth.

The psychic and existential development that becomes possible by virtue of the human invention that we call 'literature' does not occur as a result of a single reading but rather as an outcome of many different readings. The movement between them contributes to the multilayered nature of reading. Fortunately, we have the privilege to work through the riddles of our mind and existence embraced in the safe arms of literature throughout our entire life.

Note

1 In Germen *nachtraglichkeit*; also translated by Strachey as *deferred action*.

References

Buber-Neumann, M. [1976] (1997). *Milena: The Tragic Story of Kafka's Great Love*. New York: Arcade Publishing.
Freud, S. (1915). Thoughts for the Times of War and Death. In: J. Strachey (Ed.) *The Standard Edition of the Complete Psychological Works of Sigmund Freud, Vol. XIV*. London: Hogarth Press, pp. 273–302.

Freud, S. (1918). From the History of an Infantile Neurosis. In: J. Strachey (Ed.) *The Standard Edition of the Complete Psychological Works of Sigmund Freud, Vol. XVII.* London: Hogarth Press, pp. 1–124.
Kulka, O.D. (2013). *Landscapes of the Metropolis of Death: Reflections on Memory and Imagination.* London: Penguin.
Ogden, B.H. and Ogden, T.H. (2012). How the Analyst Thinks as Clinician and as Literary Reader. *Psychoanalytic Perspectives,* 9(2), pp. 243–273.
Ogden, T.H. (1994). The Analytic Third: Working with Intersubjective Clinical Facts. *International Journal of Psychoanalysis,* 75, pp. 3–19.
Ogden, T.H. (2000). Borges and the Art of Mourning. *Psychoanalytic Dialogues,* 10(1), pp. 65–88.
Pessoa, F. [1982] (2017). *The Book of Disquiet.* London and New York: Penguin books.
Semprún, J. (1994). *Literature or Life.* London and New York: Penguin Books.
Winnicott, D.W. (1963). Dependence in Infant Care, in Child Care, and in the Psycho-Analytic Setting. *International Journal of Psychoanalysis,* 44, pp. 339–344.
Winnicott, D.W. (1969). The Use of an Object. *International Journal of Psychoanalysis,* 50, pp. 711–716.
Winnicott, D.W. (1971). *Playing and Reality.* London: Tavistock.
Woolf, V. (1932). How Should One Read a Book. In: *The Second Common Reader.* London: The Hogarth Press.

Further reading

Ogden, T.H. (2004). The Analytic Third: Implications for Psychoanalytic Theory and Technique. *Psychoanalytic Quarterly,* 73(1), pp. 167–195.
Sartre, J. [1964] (1981). *The Words.* New York: Vintage Books.
Winnicott, D.W. (1953). Transitional Objects and Transitional Phenomena: A Study of the First Not-Me Possession. *International Journal of Psychoanalysis,* 34, pp. 89–97.

Index

Abraham 266, 268–276
absence (the absent) 16, 187–188, 246–247; *The Aspern Papers* 200–208; authors 195–197, 211–216; dual track conflict 210; irony 191–192; mirroring 198–199; motives 189; permanence vs change 199–200; *The Purloined Letter* 189–191; readers 192–195; repetition compulsion 208–209; stealing text 197–198
acceptance 117, 123, 282
adhesive identification 69–71, 82
aesthetics (aesthetic conflict) 208, 219, 263
afterwards: reparation 305–306; repetition 243–245
Agnon, Shai Y. 85–89, 219; *see also* Friendship
Aharon, Edwin 260, 263–266
alienation 72, 111, 162, 274, 287
All the Milk and Honey 64
aloneness 252; *see also* isolation; solitude; solitude (solitary confinement)
alpha function 211–213
ambivalence 91, 197, 226
Amichai, Yehuda 96–97, 100
Amir, Dana 43, 95, 106, 253, 273, 287
amnesia 226, 284
analysts 7, 17, 137; dialectic forces 188, 194, 200, 229, 271; transference relations 26, 88, 91, 99
annihilation 59, 67, 70, 117, 166, 281
anxiety 25, 80, 117, 157, 286; authors 92–93, 99; distancing paradox 34, 37; familiar and uncanny 222, 226–227, 229, 232; *Fear and Trembling*; *Dialectical Lyric* 273, 276;
identification 55, 59, 65–67, 69–70, 72–74; meaning 43–44; self-identity 123, 127
Appelfeld, Aharon 40, 112, 260–266
appropriation 83–84, 148, 210–211
arrogance 102, 194
art 84–85, 241, 243, 258–259, 266, 289
art, works of 97–98, 129, 221
Aspern Papers, The 200–208, 214
assimilation 61, 71
atrocities 40–41, 46
attentiveness 69, 88–89
Auschwitz 35, 37–38, 44, 68, 104–105, 280, 286–287
authors 4–5, 7, 17, 299–300; power of seduction 211–216; present and absent 188, 195–199, 200; *The Purloined Letter* 189–191; transcendence 148, 170–171; transference relations 38, 72, 87–88
authors, idealization of 91–92; depressive 95–98; paranoid-schizoid 92–95; poets as container 99–100; writers as sublime 100–102
avoidance 65, 87, 158, 215
awareness 7, 9, 15, 23, 115, 299; distancing paradox 33; familiar and uncanny 124–126; *Landscapes of the Metropolis of Death* 287; *The Man Who Never Slept* 264–265; meaning 43, 47; mortality 166, 170, 177; order and disorder 242; self-identity 133, 146

Balint, Michael 104–105
barriers 123, 193, 307
Barthes, Roland 4–5, 7, 239
beauty 213–214, 216, 233, 263

Before the Law 287–292
being, emergent *see* emergent being
Bejerano, Maya 96–98, 99–100
beliefs 38, 56, 230; dialectic forces 268, 270, 276, 289–290
belonging 66, 176, 233, 274
Ben-Naftali, Michael 214–215
Berman, Emmanuel 27, 29–30, 72, 149
betrayal 28, 94–95
Beyond the Pleasure Principle 116, 155, 209, 220
Bialik, Nahman (H.N.) 99–100, 101
Bion, Wilfred 13; *Fear and Trembling; Dialectical Lyric* 276; identification 67; meaning 44–45, 52; present and absent 212; resistance to reading 88; self-identity 132, 136; witnessing 105
Blanchot, Maurice 80, 97, 100, 257–259, 266, 277
Bollas, Christopher 14, 68, 97, 127, 148, 176, 258
Book of Disquiet, The 24, 124–125, 146
books 72, 109–110, 129, 167, 169–170, 175, 178
borders 137, 221, 247
boundaries 99, 115, 126, 195, 238, 253; identification 55, 76; mortality 155, 163–165, 170–171, 173, 175; self-identity 135–136, 138, 140–141, 143, 146
Buber-Neumann, Margarete 76, 298
Buchenwald 33–35, 105, 109–110, 160, 164

camps, concentration 298; distancing paradox 33, 36; ethics 110, 112; identification 76–77; *Landscapes of the Metropolis of Death* 279, 281, 283, 285; meaning 42, 45; mortality 160, 164; witnessing 105–106
caretakers (care) 73, 91, 176
Celan, Paul 93–95
certainty (uncertainty) 44, 51, 157, 272–273
chambers, gas 35, 105
change 8, 83, 134, 296, 307; identification 57, 62; *The Man Who Never Slept* 266; order and disorder 239; present and absent 199–200
chaos 9, 16, 246
characters 7, 13, 18–19, 296, 299–301, 303, 307–308; authors 93; distancing paradox 34; *Fear and Trembling; Dialectical Lyric* 271, 273, 275; identification 55, 57, 72, 75; meaning 42–43; mortality 159, 172, 179; order and disorder 237, 245; present and absent 191, 196; resistance to reading 83, 86; self-identity 126, 141–144, 146–150; transference relations 26–30
childhood 25, 83, 200, 241, 269; identification 62, 73–74; *Landscapes of the Metropolis of Death* 286, 288–289; meaning 49–50; mortality 160, 162; self-identity 145, 147
children 14, 71, 87, 106, 245; mortality 166–167, 169–170, 179; present and absent 198–199; self-identity 127, 131
communication 5, 9, 13, 148, 188, 273; transference 26–27, 47, 65, 89
compasses, internal 58, 93
compassion 86, 108, 123, 299, 308; identification 62, 69; present and absent 195, 213, 215
concealment 190, 196
conflicts 25, 129
confusion 227, 228, 231
conscience 58, 116
consciousness (conscious) 125, 126, 143, 240, 247
consideration 108, 111
containers 96, 133, 146, 210, 299; poets as 99–100
containment 65–68, 96, 105, 151
contemplation 303, 307
contents 239, 246
contexts 3, 10–12, 123, 240, 263, 270; intertextual 16
continuity 165, 167, 301
continuous doing 251–253, 300; *Fear and Trembling; Dialectical Lyric* 270, 275–277; *Landscapes of the Metropolis of Death* 280, 282, 284, 286–287, 290–291; *The Man Who Never Slept* 260–261, 263–265; philosophical perspective 253–259
control 177, 298, 301, 307; familiar and uncanny 225–226; identification 59, 71–72, 75; order and disorder 248; present and absent 210, 215
convenant, ethical 108–114
conversations 83–84, 135, 190, 203, 259, 261, 284

coping 25, 29, 299; distancing paradox 33, 36; familiar and uncanny 222; *Fear and Trembling*; *Dialectical Lyric* 269, 273; identification 62, 66; *Landscapes of the Metropolis of Death* 280; *The Man Who Never Slept* 263; meaning 40–41; mortality 156, 159, 164, 177; order and disorder 243; present and absent 210; self-identity 147; transcendence 117–118; witnessing 105
corpses 35, 74, 104, 105, 164
couches 9–11, 188
countertransference 12–13
creativity 7, 299–300, 304, 307; continuous doing and emergent being 251, 253, 257; distancing paradox 38; ethics 108; identification 62, 64; *The Man Who Never Slept* 266; meaning 43; mortality 174; order and disorder 239–240, 242–243; present and absent 200, 209, 212, 214–215; resistance to reading 83–84, 87; self-identity 126–127, 129–130; transcendence 117–118; *see also* movements, creative
crises 47, 62, 231, 260
criticism 1–3, 49–50, 68
cultures 4, 11, 166, 176
curiosity 45–46, 167, 190, 200, 215

Dasein 98, 157–158, 222, 254
deadness 37, 261
death: authors 95; continuous doing and emergent being 256–258; distancing paradox 33–34; ethics 110; familiar and uncanny 223; *Fear and Trembling*; *Dialectical Lyric* 276; identification 74; *Landscapes of the Metropolis of Death* 280–281, 283–285, 290; *The Man Who Never Slept* 265; meaning 41–42; present and absent 211; transcendence 118, 155, 159; witnessing 105
death anxiety 157–158
death drive 68, 108, 116, 156, 157, 209, 220
death object 166–167
Death of the Author 4–5
defences 307; familiar and uncanny 229; *Fear and Trembling*; *Dialectical Lyric* 276; identification 71, 73; *Landscapes of the Metropolis of Death* 284, 291; meaning 44; mortality 156–157, 167, 172; present and absent 209; resistance to reading 80; self-identity 151; transference 25; witnessing 105
denial 92, 210, 244
dependency (dependence) 71, 92, 95, 188, 209, 226
depressive idealization 95–98; poet as container 99–100
depressive position 111, 167, 233, 303; identification 61–64; present and absent 188, 208, 210, 212; self-identity 123, 145, 149
Derrida, Jacques 16, 192, 214
desires 3, 28, 123, 136, 138, 190, 229
destructiveness (destruction) 93, 117, 130, 156–157, 211, 301
detachment 37, 68, 70, 87, 106
development 105, 223, 273, 297, 303; continuous doing and emergent being 253, 257; ethics 108, 111; mortality 158, 172; resistance to reading 82, 85; self-identity 131–132, 145–146
devotion 95, 269
dilemmas 269, 280
discourses 16–17, 75, 122, 146, 160, 263
diseases 241; *see also* sickness (illness)
disintegration 35–38, 70, 71, 158, 252, 253
disorder 236–238, 240–249
distancing paradox 67, 307; disintegration and transition 35–38; Semprún 33–35
distress 37, 227
divinity (divine) 100, 102, 269
doing, continuous *see* continuous doing
domination 53, 89
doubles 220, 282
dreams 298; continuous doing and emergent being 258; *Landscapes of the Metropolis of Death* 280, 291; *The Man Who Never Slept* 262–263, 266; mortality 166; self-identity 123, 126–134, 138, 143, 149; transcendence 115, 118; transference 24, 47–48, 95
drives 14, 25, 99, 123, 145
dual track conflict 210
Dupin 189–196, 199
Durban, Joshua 75, 159, 166

Eating Poetry 60
ego 14, 58, 116, 302

Eifermann, Rivka 14, 147
Éluard, Paul 93–94
emergent being 251–253, 300; *Fear and Trembling*; *Dialectical Lyric* 275–277; *Landscapes of the Metropolis of Death* 280–282, 284, 286, 290–291, 292; *The Man Who Never Slept* 260–261, 263–265; philosophical perspective 253–259
emotions 9, 55, 65–66, 242–243, 284; transcendence 138, 149, 163
empathy 62, 108, 123, 150, 197, 303, 308
encounters 6–7, 160
envelopes 230–231
envy 59, 92, 93, 102, 188, 201, 244
equations, symbolic 132
equilibriums 300, 303, 307; familiar and uncanny 233; *Fear and Trembling*; *Dialectical Lyric* 268, 270, 277; *Landscapes of the Metropolis of Death* 284, 287, 290; *The Man Who Never Slept* 266; present and absent 208
Erlich, Shmuel 253
Essays in the First Person 40–41
ethical convenant 108–114
ethics 93, 94, 95, 111, 277, 303
exclusivity 210, 231
existence: authors 95–96, 102; continuous doing and emergent being 258; ethics 112; familiar and uncanny 222; *The Man Who Never Slept* 260–261; mortality 162; order and disorder 237; present and absent 214; self-identity 124, 137, 140, 142
expectations 3, 28, 91
experiences 5–6, 8, 300, 305; authors 99; ethics 114; familiar and uncanny 231; identification 57; *Landscapes of the Metropolis of Death* 290, 292; *The Man Who Never Slept* 264; meaning 42–43; order and disorder 244; resistance to reading 87; self-identity 122, 140; transference 23, 28; witnessing 105, 107
experiential transcendence 139, 158
eyes 94, 98, 102, 205

Face and the Voice, The 96–97
Facing Others and Otherness 110, 256
facts 42, 133
faith 231, 268, 269, 271, 274, 275, 277
false self 129–130

familiarity (familiar) 129, 219–223, 241; *see also* Friendship
fantasy (fantasize) 12, 118
fathers 74, 167, 168, 174, 245, 269, 272
faults 104–105
Fear and Trembling: Dialectical Lyric 268–277
fears 7, 11, 28, 87, 118, 226
feelings 25, 27, 105, 114, 141
Felman, Shoshana 10, 12; authors 92; *Fear and Trembling*; *Dialectical Lyric* 271–272; *Landscapes of the Metropolis of Death* 280; order and disorder 241–242, 245–247; present and absent 192; transference 27; witnessing 104, 106
finality 95, 166, 172, 173, 233
finiteness 256, 299; *see also* mortality
finitude 209, 243, 258
Frankel, Victor 51, 117
free associations 89, 124, 163
freedom 7, 14, 299–300, 306; self-identity 123, 129–130, 134–136, 138, 140; transcendence 117
Freud, Sigmund 2, 10–12, 126, 301; continuous doing and emergent being 254; distancing paradox 26; familiar and uncanny 219, 231, 233; identification 58, 66; mortality 155–156, 164–165; order and disorder 243–244; present and absent 208–209; resistance to reading 80, 88–89; self-identity 131, 135, 138; transcendence 116, 118
Friendship 223–225; home 228–229; Job 231–233; language 227–228; letters 229–231; readers 225–227

Gadamer, Hans-Georg 4, 6, 165, 177
gas chambers 35, 105
gender 16, 135
grammar 134–136, 137–138
gratification 64, 116, 188
gratitude 60, 61, 62, 102, 108, 244
greed 187, 194, 201, 208
Green, Andre 16, 168, 188
Green, Julien 144–145
growth 116, 172, 200, 215, 302
guilt 61, 73

hallucinations 123, 168
harm 105, 117, 302

hatred (hate) 108, 209
healing 106, 112, 264, 296
health, mental 23, 59, 131
Heidegger, Martin 97–100, 111, 157, 222–223, 233, 254–256, 276
helplessness 162, 167, 171, 212, 241
heroes (heroines) 11, 18, 115, 299, 307; authors 91, 93; ethics 113; familiar and uncanny 225; *Fear and Trembling*; *Dialectical Lyric* 270–271, 274–275, 277; identification 56, 62, 66, 69, 76–77; *Landscapes of the Metropolis of Death* 282; *The Man Who Never Slept* 260, 262–264, 266; meaning 52; mortality 171; order and disorder 244; present and absent 189, 201, 205, 210–214; self-identity 143, 145, 149
history (historicity) 11, 64
Hoffman, E.T.A. 221
Hoffman, Eva 47–49, 51–53
Holland, Norman N. 13, 29
Holocaust 40, 105; *see also* gas chambers
homes (house) 220, 224–229, 231, 233
Horowitz, Yair 236–240, 242–243, 245–248
How to Sweeten the Days 63–64
Husserl, Edmund 2, 111, 256
hybrids 135, 149

identification 55–58, 297–298, 302; bidirectional 299–300; chimeric 75–77; continuous doing and emergent being 255; extractive 68–69; internalized 59–64; intrusive 75; meaning 51–52; present and absent 193, 197; primitive edge 69–73; projective 65–68; psychoanalysis 58–59; raw 73–74; resistance to reading 86; transference 26
identification, readers 143–144
identity 6, 8, 16, 307; continuous doing and emergent being 255; familiar and uncanny 231; *Fear and Trembling*; *Dialectical Lyric* 277; language 130–131, 132–134; *Landscapes of the Metropolis of Death* 285; *The Man Who Never Slept* 263–264; Pessoa 124–126; reader's 150; readers 126–130; symbols 131–132
If I Were You 144–145
illusion, retrospective 171–173

illusions 28, 36, 200, 221, 229, 238; retrospective 171–173
images 24, 143, 164
imagination 116, 127, 128, 150, 166, 280
immortality 115, 156, 164, 169, 170–171, 173
immortality, symbolic 158–159, 163, 164
impermeable reading 262–266
In Search of Lost Time 56–57, 83
In the Penal Colony 283–286
individuation 143–144, 157
infants 15, 301; authors 91; continuous doing and emergent being 251–252; distancing paradox 36; *Fear and Trembling*; *Dialectical Lyric* 272; identification 71, 75; *The Man Who Never Slept* 263; mortality 157, 166, 176; present and absent 200, 202, 210–213; resistance to reading 81–82; self-identity 127–128, 132–133; witnessing 108
inferiority 92, 176, 188
inspiration 215, 257, 258, 306–307
integration 209, 252, 287, 290, 292
interpretation 3, 5, 11–12, 19; continuous doing and emergent being 254–255; *Fear and Trembling*; *Dialectical Lyric* 270, 275; transcendence 122, 175, 178; transference 27, 34
introjections 58, 68, 301
irony 102, 147, 191–192
Iser, Wolfgang 8, 18
isolation 232; *see also* aloneness; solitude (solitary confinement)

James, Henry 210; *see also* Aspern Papers, The
Joseph, Betty 25, 58–59

Kafka, Franz 2, 29, 34, 76
Kalandra, Zavis 94–95
Kierkegaard, Søren 8, 255, 266, 268–277, 287
Klein, Melanie 13, 23, 37, 105, 232, 257; authors 91–92; ethics 108, 111; identification 58–59, 62, 68; meaning 43, 45; mortality 156–157, 167, 169, 173; present and absent 187–188, 200, 209; self-identity 121–123, 131, 144–145; transcendence 116–118
knowledge 16, 307; continuous doing and emergent being 252, 254; *Fear and*

Trembling; *Dialectical Lyric* 273–274; *The Man Who Never Slept* 264; order and disorder 237, 246–247; present and absent 194, 210, 212, 214; transcendence 115, 136–138, 177–178; transference 60, 102
Kohut, Heinz 29, 91, 100, 198
Kulka, Otto Dov 279–282; *Before the Law* 286–292; *In the Penal Colony* 283–286; transformative reading 282–283
Kundera, Milan 8, 28
Kurzweil, Baruch 223–224, 231

Lacan, Jacques 7, 16, 92, 192, 198–200, 227, 233
lacking (lack) 197, 200
Landscapes of the Metropolis of Death 279–282; *see also* Kulka, Otto Dov
language 2, 11, 15–16, 200; authors 95, 100–101; dreams 132–134; ethics 112; familiar and uncanny 227–229, 231–232; *Fear and Trembling*; *Dialectical Lyric* 272–275; grammar 134–136; knowledge 136–138; *Landscapes of the Metropolis of Death* 284, 286–287, 290; *The Man Who Never Slept* 260, 262–264, 266; meaning 43, 47–50; mortality 160; order and disorder 248; present and absent 188, 191, 225; self-identity 126–127, 130–131, 140–141, 147; symbols 131–132; *see also* transcendence; *Language* ; *Closing and Disclosing* 99–100
Laub, Dori 104, 105, 109, 280
laws 134, 273, 282–283
learning 45, 59, 105, 214, 215
Lesser, Simon O. 13–14
letters 229–231, 233, 261, 285
Levi, Primo 45–46
Levinas, Emmanuel 110, 223, 256
liberation 34, 130–131, 215
life drive 68, 108, 116
Lifton, Robert J. 139, 158, 164
limitations 64, 128, 135
literary research 10–12
literary third 301–302
literature 1–4, 9, 192, 221, 289; continuous doing and emergent being 258–259; mortality 160, 175–179;

order and disorder 240–249; symbolic timelessness 164–167
Literature or Life 33–35, 41, 104–107, 160–164
loneliness 232, 274, 292
longings 72, 99, 266
loss 72, 117, 156, 167, 244
Lost in Translation 47, 51–53
love 123, 203, 233, 244, 274; transference 60, 108, 111, 113
loyalty 95, 269, 274
Lubin, Orly 8, 42, 50, 146–147

madness 16, 253
Malraux, Andre 298; distancing paradox 35–36, 38; identification 62, 67, 69; meaning 41–42, 46–47; witnessing 105–106
Man Who Never Stopped Sleeping, The 260–266
Marion, Jean-Luc 111, 256
maturity (mature capacity) 111, 145, 277
meaning 4–5, 7–8, 11–13, 40–41, 285, 302, 304–305; active reading 50–53; continuous doing and emergent being 253; distancing paradox 27, 30, 38; ethics 113; *Fear and Trembling*; *Dialectical Lyric* 268–270, 275–277; identification 59, 66–67; language as objects 47–50; literary characters 42–43; mortality 175, 178; order and disorder 239, 243–244, 246–247; present and absent 192, 198, 211; self-identity 129, 133, 140, 147; symbol formation 43–47; transcendence 116–117; witnessing 105–106
Meltzer, Donald 75, 210, 213–214, 263, 286
memories 10; familiar and uncanny 229; *Landscapes of the Metropolis of Death* 281, 284–285, 287; *The Man Who Never Slept* 262–263; transcendence 136, 143, 145, 147; transference 24, 33, 40, 64
Metamorphosis 29–30
metaphors 9, 60, 130, 133, 139–140, 258, 262
Milena: The Tragic Story of Kafka's Great Love 76, 298
miracles 269, 281

mirrors (mirroring) 299; authors 91; ethics 113; familiar and uncanny 221; *Landscapes of the Metropolis of Death* 284–285, 290; meaning 44, 51; mortality 178; order and disorder 245; present and absent 190, 197–199, 204–205; resistance to reading 86–87; self-identity 135, 146
Morales, Diego 109–110, 112–113
morality 93, 94, 303
mothers 91, 106, 108, 176, 252; *Fear and Trembling*; *Dialectical Lyric* 272–273; identification 66, 75; *The Man Who Never Slept* 262–264, 266; present and absent 198–199, 201, 210, 212–214; resistance to reading 81–82; self-identity 127, 133
motives 189, 273
mourning 302–304, 306; familiar and uncanny 232; *Fear and Trembling*; *Dialectical Lyric* 273–274; *Landscapes of the Metropolis of Death* 290, 292; *The Man Who Never Slept* 266; present and absent 195, 212, 215; transcendence 132, 156, 159, 172; transference 71, 95, 114
movements, creative 97, 200

narcissism 184, 199
narratives 140, 229, 242, 244, 248, 266
narrators: distancing paradox 36, 38; familiar and uncanny 225, 230; *Fear and Trembling*; *Dialectical Lyric* 268, 271, 273–275; identification 55–57, 70; *Landscapes of the Metropolis of Death* 282; *The Man Who Never Slept* 265; mortality 160, 171–172; order and disorder 237, 242, 245; present and absent 191, 193, 196, 202, 204–205, 211, 213; resistance to reading 83–84; self-identity 149; witnessing 107
neediness 72, 167, 226
needs 28, 108, 145
negations 200, 230–231

obedience 268, 274
objectifying identification 71–73
objects 36, 91; internal 23–24; significant 73; transformational 127, 176, 302
Oedipus 11, 58

Ogden, Thomas 69, 169, 300, 303–304; meaning 46–47, 53; self-identity 132–133, 137, 148–150
omnipotence 123, 127, 273
omniscience 178, 214
On Reading 26, 61, 83
openness 88, 108, 195, 215, 251, 297–298; authors 95, 98; self-identity 131, 134
oral drive 59–61, 64
order, symbolic: creativity 239–240; *Fluttering Corridors* 236–238; literature 240–249
orientation 67, 77, 228, 240
otherness (other) 6, 15, 256, 263, 274
ethics 111, 114
present and absent 198, 200, 214 256, 263, 274
others, significant *see* significant others

pain 37, 44, 94, 113, 167, 243; identification 64, 73
paranoid-schizoid 303; authors 91–95; continuous doing and emergent being 257; familiar and uncanny 233; identification 59; mortality 173; present and absent 188, 201, 209–210, 215; self-identity 145, 149
parents 58, 87, 94, 116, 200, 202, 263
partiality 201, 205, 209, 213, 215
partialness 95, 171, 200
participation 7, 82, 241, 243, 248
partners 4–5
patients 9, 17; authors 91, 99; familiar and uncanny 229; *Fear and Trembling*; *Dialectical Lyric* 271; order and disorder 243; present and absent 188, 194; resistance to reading 89; self-identity 137, 140
Pearl, Joel 157, 254, 256
penetration 75, 262
permanence 199–200
permeable reading 262–266
personification 71–72, 74, 166, 169, 225
Pessoa, Fernando 298; *The Man Who Never Slept* 263; mortality 155–156, 179; self-identity 124–125, 134–136, 139, 146, 148–149; transcendence 117; transference 24, 26
phantasies: present and absent 201, 211–212; transcendence 123, 136, 159; transference 36, 59–60, 77

phantasm 200–201, 221–222
phenomena, transitional 14, 35–38
Pirandello, Luigi 27, 121, 133, 141–143, 148–149, 246
placenessness, symbolic 171, 173
places 38, 164, 170, 223
playfulness 5, 14, 198; transcendence 115, 123, 127, 150; transference 28, 36, 86
pleasure 59–60
Poe, Edgar Alan 189; *see also* Purloined Letters, The
poetry 26, 48, 99–101, 130, 237–242, 286; ethics 110, 113; identification 60–61, 63–64; mortality 163–164, 176, 179
poets 94, 95, 98, 99–100
portraits 206, 207
possibilities 116, 140
postmodernism 15–17, 135, 199, 239
potential spaces 14, 126, 149, 252, 265
potentiality 28, 116
Poulet, George 6, 140
power 8, 233, 248, 258, 299; present and absent 212, 221; transcendence 117, 164, 177; transference 51, 65, 92
prayers 286, 292
prejudices 4, 6, 89, 178
presence (the present) 187–188; *The Aspern Papers* 200–208; authors 195–197; author's power 211–216; dual track conflict 210; irony 191–192; mirroring 198–199; motives 189; permanence vs change 199–200; *The Purloined Letter* 189–191; readers 192–195; repetition compulsion 208–209; stealing text 197–198; writers 188–189
projections 11, 15–16, 299, 301–302, 308; authors 92; identification 55, 58, 66, 71; mortality 156, 159, 176; order and disorder 242, 244; present and absent 213
projective identification 13, 144–147, 148–151, 157, 210, 214
prologues 240–241
protection 70–71, 77, 108
Proust, Marcel 2, 8, 26, 56–57, 61, 83–89

psychoanalysis 1–4, 9
Purloined Letters, The 214

Ravensbrück 76, 298
readers 1–4, 16, 299–302, 304, 308; authors 4–5, 92, 95, 98–100, 102; familiar and uncanny 225–227, 231, 233; *Fear and Trembling; Dialectical Lyric* 270–271, 273, 276–277; identification 52, 72, 75–76; *The Man Who Never Slept* 263; meaning 5; methodologies 17; mortality 170–171, 174, 177–178; order and disorder 240, 242, 245–246, 247; present and absent 188–189, 191–192, 196–199, 201, 214; psychoanalytic research 12–15; resistance to reading 80–89; self-identity 128, 131–132, 137, 139–141, 143–147, 149–150; transcendence 115; witnessing 105, 107; *see also* Aspern Papers, The
reading 2, 18–19, 302; continuous doing and emergent being 259; couches 9–10; distancing paradox 34; encounters 6–7; familiar and uncanny 228–229; *The Man Who Never Slept* 260, 262–266; meaning 50–53; mortality 160, 165–166, 170, 172, 177–178; order and disorder 237, 242–244, 248; Pessoa 127–130; present and absent 194, 199–200, 215–216; resistance to 83–89; self-identity 125–126, 133, 140, 149–150; as therapy 8
reading, transformative: Kleist 281–283; *Before the Law* 286–292; *In the Penal Colony* 283–286
reality 86, 99, 106, 252, 298, 302; distancing paradox 34, 36–37; familiar and uncanny 221, 228; identification 75–76; meaning 42, 44–45; transcendence 115–116, 123, 127–129, 150
recognition 112, 302
reconciliation 123, 232, 243, 304
recreation 136–138
reflection 7–8, 297, 302; familiar and uncanny 221, 227; identification 55; *Landscapes of the Metropolis of Death* 289; meaning 42, 44; mortality 173; present and absent 197–200; resistance to reading 82, 85; self-identity 123,

135, 146; transcendence 116;
  witnessing 105
reflections 15, 35, 42, 230–231, 279;
  present and absent 190, 200, 210
reflexivity 8, 287, 299
reformulation, psychoanalytic
  147–151
regression 9, 302
relationships 25, 132, 296, 302;
  continuous doing and emergent being
  251; familiar and uncanny 228; *Fear
  and Trembling*; *Dialectical Lyric* 273,
  276–277; order and disorder 237;
  present and absent 203
religion 175, 203
Remedy and the Meaning, The 112
reparation 299, 303; authors 93, 95, 101;
  bidirectional 305–306; ethics 108–114;
  familiar and uncanny 228, 233;
  identification 61, 73; *The Man Who
  Never Slept* 266; order and
  disorder 243
reparation, retrospective 173–175
repetition compulsion (repetition) 80,
  241–245, 303; familiar and uncanny
  220; *Fear and Trembling*; *Dialectical
  Lyric* 270–271, 276; *Landscapes of the
  Metropolis of Death* 281–283, 291;
  present and absent 200, 208–209, 213
representations 28, 36, 58, 138
repression 80, 175
research, psychoanalytic 12–15
resistance 106, 283
resistance to reading 80–81; detached
  reading 85–89; false reading 83–85;
  false self 81–82; surrender 81
resolutions 239, 304
responses 26, 35
responsibilities 117, 223, 269, 299;
  transference 61, 94, 108, 110
reverie 88, 95, 133
rules 4, 134

sacrifice 269, 274
Sagi, Avi 222–223, 237, 255–256, 286;
  transcendence 116, 122; transference
  40, 110–111
salvation 176, 248
Sartre, Jean Paul 5–6, 15; identification
  55, 65, 70, 73–74; meaning 42, 50;
  mortality 165–166, 167–175, 178–179;
  order and disorder 242, 248;

self-identity 128, 147–149;
  transference 26, 28
satisfaction 61, 123
Schafer, Roy 16, 29
scribbles 168, 174
searching 195, 199
secrets 258, 263, 270, 276
security 60, 70, 129
Segal, Hanna 43, 116, 132
self 298, 302, 306–307; authors 91;
  continuous doing and emergent being
  252–253; ethics 110–111, 114; *Fear
  and Trembling*; *Dialectical Lyric* 277;
  identification 61–62, 68; identity
  131–132, 136, 143, 146–147, 150;
  identity and transcendence 121,
  128–129; *Landscapes of the Metropolis
  of Death* 280, 286, 289, 292; *The Man
  Who Never Slept* 260, 266; mortality
  157, 167; order and disorder 238;
  present and absent 198–199, 200–201,
  209–210; resistance to reading 81–82,
  86–89; transference 24, 27;
  witnessing 105
self-analysis 13–14, 17, 29, 147
self-definition 118, 138
self-identity 115, 141; *see also*
  transcendence
self-individuation 254, 256
self-object 91, 100, 198
self-reflection 116, 141, 303
selfhood 64, 125
Semprún, Jorge 298; distancing paradox
  33–35; ethics 109–110, 112–113;
  identification 62, 67, 69; meaning
  41–42, 46–47; mortality 160–164;
  witnessing 104–107
separateness 15, 75, 205, 214, 215,
  252, 302
separation 71, 77, 132, 158, 167,
  210, 273
sickness (illness) 237; *see also* diseases
significant others 25, 27, 72
signified 44, 131, 241, 273
signifiers 44, 131, 273, 306; order and
  disorder 241, 247; present and absent
  200, 208, 214
silence 272–275
singing 162, 163
Six Characters in Search of an Author
  141–143, 246
sleep 167, 260, 266

solitude (solitary confinement) 70, 76–77, 162, 176, 276, 289–290, 303
sovereignty 111, 204, 223–224, 239, 242, 248, 299
Space of Literature, The 97
spacelessness 115, 167–175
spaces 14, 306; continuous doing and emergent being 252; familiar and uncanny 233; *Landscapes of the Metropolis of Death* 280, 291–292; *The Man Who Never Slept* 265; mortality 164, 171; order and disorder 244; resistance to reading 87; self-identity 135, 149; transitional 126, 148, 150, 232, 298, 300
splitting 287, 308; present and absent 192–195, 204; transcendence 157, 176; transference 55, 92, 105, 108
spontaneity 68–69
stories 9, 106
Fear and Trembling
Dialectical Lyric 271
Landscapes of the Metropolis of Death 282, 290
Thw Man Who Never Slept 265
order and disorder 241
transcendence 124, 172
Strand, Mark 60
structures 105, 240
subjects, transitional 300–303
sublimation (sublimity) 61, 101, 102, 176, 270
suffering 40, 65, 97, 100, 232
superego 93, 116, 302
survival 46, 91, 105, 251, 284
survivors 35, 41, 67, 68–69, 105
symbiosis 214, 252, 272
symbolic immortality 158–159, 163, 164, 167–175; *Literature or Life* 160–164
symbolic placenessness 171, 173
symbolic timelessness 165, 169, 173–175
symbolization 158, 227
symbols 43–47, 131–134, 159, 208, 213, 273

tearing (torn) 69, 230
tensions 99, 188, 231, 248; mortality 166, 172; self-identity 122, 129; transcendence 116–117
terrors 37, 41
testimonies 38, 106, 280

texts 3–4, 6, 14, 17–18, 301–302, 304; continuous doing and emergent being 256–257, 259; distancing paradox 33; *Fear and Trembling*; *Dialectical Lyric* 270, 273–274, 276; *Landscapes of the Metropolis of Death* 289; *The Man Who Never Slept* 263, 266; mortality 159–161, 163, 177–178; order and disorder 239, 243, 247–249; religious 203
therapy 8, 159, 296, 298, 302; transference 29, 38, 40, 91
thinking 44, 59, 105, 196; magical 211; self-identity 132, 138, 141
third subject 53, 148–150, 300
thou 94, 108, 109
time 2, 305–306; continuous doing and emergent being 254–255, 257; familiar and uncanny 223; *Landscapes of the Metropolis of Death* 280; *The Man Who Never Slept* 264; mortality 157, 164–165, 168–170, 172; order and disorder 243; self-identity 126; transcendence 115; transference 35, 38, 88
timelessness 167–168 170–172; symbolic 115, 165, 169, 173–175
traditions 4, 165, 177–178
transcendence 115–118, 304, 307; authors 96, 100–102; death anxiety 155–158; *Fear and Trembling*; *Dialectical Lyric* 276; grammar 134–136; identification 140–141; identity 121–123; *Landscapes of the Metropolis of Death* 286, 292; literary 123–124; *The Man Who Never Slept* 266; meaning 49, 53; mortality 158, 160, 176; order and disorder 243; Pirandello 141–143; projective identification 144–147; reader's identification 143–144; reading literature 159; realistic 177–178; recreation 136–138; reformulation 147–151; symbolic immortality 158–159; symbolic timelessness 164–167; transposition 138–140; *see also* identity
transfer, idealizing 101
transference 9, 12, 307; identification 58; *Landscapes of the Metropolis of Death* 270; meaning 41; order and disorder 237, 243, 245–246; present and absent

188–190, 197–199, 203, 208; resistance to reading 80
transference relations 3, 25–30, 34; object relations 23–24
transformations 14, 296, 305; authors 96; *Fear and Trembling*; *Dialectical Lyric* 268, 274, 277; identification 65; *Landscapes of the Metropolis of Death* 287, 290–291; *The Man Who Never Slept* 266; meaning 48–49; mortality 159, 176; order and disorder 243–244; present and absent 195, 207; resistance to reading 82–83, 87; self-identity 127, 132, 145, 147, 150
transience 95, 166
translation 6, 275
transposition 138–140
trauma: distancing paradox 34, 37; ethics 109; identification 62, 68, 73; *Landscapes of the Metropolis of Death* 280, 284, 286, 291–292; *The Man Who Never Slept* 260, 264; meaning 41, 44; witnessing 104–105
trust 143, 273
truth 16, 57, 111, 124, 129, 178, 276
Tustin, Frances 71, 210
twinship (twins) 66–67, 91, 197, 204; literary 51–53, 113

uncanny 241, 248; Freud 219–221; Heidegger 222–223; Lacan 221–222; *see also* Friendship
unconscious 137, 139, 192, 200, 240, 247
understanding 302, 308; continuous doing and emergent being 254–255; *Fear and Trembling*; *Dialectical Lyric* 270, 273, 276–277; *The Man Who Never Slept* 264; transcendence 147; transference 47, 102, 106
unreadable 246–247
unthought known 99, 258

Vallejo, Cesar 34, 110, 113, 114, 164

value (worth) 110–113
values (value judgements) 93, 113, 194, 248, 253, 284
vantage points 247–249
violations 108, 112
visibility 111, 113, 114
voices 101–102, 168, 237, 284, 287, 292
voices, poets' 98, 99
vulnerability 53, 93, 95, 167

What Is Literature? 50, 65, 128, 248
Wind in the Trees 73–74
Winnicott, Donald W. 14, 301; continuous doing and emergent being 251–253; distancing paradox 36; *Fear and Trembling*; *Dialectical Lyric* 269; identification 81–82, 85, 89; meaning 41; present and absent 198; self-identity 126, 128–130, 148–149; transcendence 118
wisdom 60, 92, 177, 178
witnesses 36, 38, 126, 164, 292
witnessing, mutual 104–107
Woolf, Virginia 7, 50, 297
words 48, 127, 228, 243; *Fear and Trembling*; *Dialectical Lyric* 272; *The Man Who Never Slept* 262, 264; present and absent 188, 205, 211–212
Words, The 15, 42, 55, 70; mortality 165, 167–175; self-identity 147, 149
worth (value) 110–113
writers 139, 170, 188–190, 212; transference 34, 72, 89, 105; *see also* authors
writing 138, 166

yearnings 25, 81, 93, 123, 229; mortality 164, 167; present and absent 190–191
Yehoshua, A.B. 29

Zach, Nathan 63–64
Zoran, Rachel 6, 14, 66, 77, 86

For Product Safety Concerns and Information please contact our EU representative GPSR@taylorandfrancis.com
Taylor & Francis Verlag GmbH, Kaufingerstraße 24, 80331 München, Germany